EXPERT WITNESSES FOR JINGLE JANGLE

Jingle Jangle: The Perfect Crime Turned Inside Out is a remarkable book, a page-turner that asks all the right questions, shocking us out of our complacency by exposing the deep flaws in our criminal justice system. It should be required reading for every college student in America.

– Gary T. Lowenthal, Arizona State University
law professor and author of Down and Dirty Justice

A must for readers of true crime and anyone wondering why so many innocent people are convicted in America. The book satisfies from start to finish, from the opening of Ray Krone's horror story, through the compelling analysis of what went wrong and on to the startling conclusion...

– Sister Helen Prejean, author of Dead Man Walking
and The Death of Innocents

Jim Rix takes us on a remarkable journey inside an American tragedy. He helped win his cousin's freedom from Death Row and now he documents the chain of errors that put him there. The story will chill your belief in the American justice system. With gripping details that can only come from one who has lived the horror, Rix makes us realize that one wrongful conviction is a tragedy for us all.

– Bill Kurtis, producer of the A&E programs
"Investigative Reports" and "Cold Case Files"

An amazing story of the uphill battle required in the fight for truth. For those readers with no experience in the criminal justice system, the measures taken in the name of "justice" will be shocking. The story of Ray Krone offers all readers important lessons—never give up hope, never stop believing in yourself and never stop fighting for what is right. Jim Rix paints a powerful picture of hope, frustration and perseverance. *Jingle Jangle* shows why we must never stop fighting for those whom the legal system has failed.

– Caroline M. Elliot, law school student and 2006-07
President of the UNC Law Innocence Project
and the UNC Law Death Penalty Project

Jim Rix has written an astonishing memoir about his cousin Ray Krone's wrongful conviction for a 1991 Arizona murder. Rix meticulously details every aspect of police corruption, prosecutorial misconduct, defense incompetence, expert witness tampering and jury shenanigans that led to Ray's decade-long nightmare. But Rix doesn't stop there. He dissects each problem, then with careful research explains how it is not an isolated incident but part of a larger pattern of problems in the criminal justice system. Rix's wry humor and occasional sarcasm reveal the depths of his despair at realizing that the justice system, which he once trusted, is so deeply flawed. Scariest about this true story is that if Ray Krone, an honest, law-abiding person, could end up on Death Row, it could happen to anyone.

> – *Rachel King, author of* Don't Kill in Our Names *and*
> Capital Consequences, *teaches legal writing*
> *at Howard University School of Law*

Ray Krone's plight reflects a state justice system that has lost sight of justice in favor of winning convictions at all costs, even at the cost of innocence. These pages present a distressing view not only of the near-loss of innocent life but also of the abuses paving the way—power, political ambition, timid judges, prosecutors' use of the justice system for self-aggrandizement, devotion to junk science by prosecutors and dishonest forensic analysts, all leading to indifference to the very claim of justice that now animates this system in name only. Krone's case is a call for reform from the bottom up, beginning with removing politics from prosecutorial decisions.

> – *Rudy Gerber, retired justice, Arizona Court of Appeals*

Ray Krone's story has so many of the elements we see over and over again in innocence cases—unreliable forensic conclusions, incomplete investigations and overvalued testimony resulting from "confirmatory bias" that occurs because everyone thinks they have the right perpetrator and they ignore evidence to the contrary. Once the conviction occurs, it typically takes extraordinary luck and the work of an individual or the media to get to the truth because the justice system prefers finality. There are more Ray Krones out there—there just aren't many who are lucky enough to have a cousin like Ray's.

> – *Chris Mumma, Executive Director,*
> *North Carolina Center on Actual Innocence*

Jingle Jangle

The Perfect Crime
Turned Inside Out

Jim Rix

ZEPHYR COVE, NEVADA
BROKENBENCHPRESS.COM

Published in the United States by
Broken Bench Press, P.O. Box 920, Zephyr Cove, NV 89448

Grateful acknowledgment is made to the following
for permission to reprint previously published material:
Ram's Horn Music for Bob Dylan lyrics "Hurricane" and "Idiot Wind."
Special Rider Music for Bob Dylan lyrics "Desolation Row,"
"It's All Over Now, Baby Blue," "Love Minus Zero/No Limit,"
"Mr. Tambourine Man," "My Back Pages," "No Time to Think" and
"Tight Connection to My Heart (Has Anybody Seen My Love)."

Grateful acknowledgment is also made to the memory of
Arthur Conan Doyle, William Ernest Henley and Mark Twain for the
use of quotations from their work.

Thanks to Matthew Moss for his dust jacket art, to Rob Esmay for his
mordant illustrations of the justice game and especially to Morris Dean for
designing and typesetting the book and for editing and indexing it.

Manufactured in the United States of America.

First Edition: July 2007

2 3 4 5 6 7 8 9

Rix, James Leland, 1943-
Jingle jangle: the perfect crime turned inside out.

1. True crime. 2. True detective. 3. Criminal justice system.

Summary: "*Jingle Jangle* is two stories: the monumental effort by family and
friends to free Ray Krone and a penetrating indictment of a criminal justice
system so broken that Ray Krone was not once but twice convicted for a
murder he didn't commit. These stories merge into a no-holes-barred tale—a
murder mystery, a courtroom drama, a strange verdict, a quest to make sense
of it all and a righteous battle against assholiness." – The Publisher.

Includes illustrations, glossary, appendices, bibliographical references and index.

ISBN-13: 978-0-9788067-0-5
ISBN-10: 0-9788067-0-0

For my mother, Dorothy May Diller Rix, the sunshine of my life

CONTENTS

Jingle Jangle

The Perfect Crime
Turned Inside Out

PART ONE
THE BITE

Innocence isn't always the best defense.
– *Gary T. Lowenthal, Professor of Law, Arizona State University*

CHAPTER 1
COUSIN RAY

I first learned of his predicament during a phone conversation with my mother. In her eighties, my mother was still one of the brightest people I knew and we often talked about current events. In this particular conversation I asked her if she had watched the TV program the night before about an innocent man released from Death Row. I don't remember now which network magazine show it was or who was profiled. My mother replied that she hadn't seen the show, then added casually, "You have a cousin on Death Row, and he's innocent."

"What?" I thought I'd misheard.

She went on to say that Ray Krone, the son of her niece, Carolyn, had been convicted of a murder in Phoenix. Carolyn had told her that a bite mark found on the victim supposedly matched Ray's teeth. The crime was dubbed "the snaggletooth murder."

I had never met Ray Krone. Mom grew up in southeastern Pennsylvania near Harrisburg. After attending high school in York, twenty-five miles south of Harrisburg, she began to move west. She received a bachelor's degree from Ohio State University in 1937, then moved the same year to Pueblo, Colorado to accept a nursing position. There she met and married the man who would be my father. In 1945, when I was two years old, we moved to San Francisco. When I remember family, it's my father's side I recall, because four of dad's siblings resided in the San Francisco Bay area. Mom's relatives remained in the east, where Ray grew up. I visited there only once, when I was seven, and that was seven years before Ray Krone was born.

Since I knew absolutely nothing about Ray's life, I was skeptical of his innocence. Mom was only telling me what Ray's mother had told her. What mother would believe that her son is guilty of murder? I thought. After all, Ray was convicted by a jury. It's not impossible to have a murderer in the family. So, more out of curiosity than anything else, I wrote Ray a letter introducing myself.

In June 1993 I received Ray's response. First, he talked about his recollection of "Aunt Dorothy," my mother, and her son, who "came one year and helped Grandpa tear down an old chicken coop in front of the house. I was very young then and can barely remember." He thought it might have been me, but in reality it was my younger brother. I was away at college at the time.

Then he outlined his predicament:

The victim was a bartender at a neighborhood bar where I went to practice darts. Her name was Kim. Sometimes, when she wasn't busy, she would join in and shoot darts. To even the teams she was usually on my side because she wasn't a very good player. Dart leagues are very popular in Phoenix. I competed regularly and often in local tournaments.

She was attractive and friendly and showed a real interest in me.

On Christmas, three days before her murder, I was in the lounge playing darts with some friends when Trish, the manager, decided to close early and go drinking and dancing at another bar. My roommate Steve and I drove together in his car and met the group there. When that bar closed Trish invited everyone to continue the party at her apartment. I didn't have to work the next day but Steve did so it was necessary for him to take me home to get my car. Kim rode along. She said she liked convertibles and asked to ride in my Corvette. I think she really wanted to make sure I would go to the party. She rode with us to my house where I switched my truck for the Corvette.

At the party we sat on the floor near Trish's caged iguana and talked. We only stayed an hour or so because Trish and her girlfriend Lu began to engage in some activity that made us uncomfortable.

On the way back to her car Kim told me that she was planning to move out of her boyfriend's house. Trish's husband had left her and she invited Kim to move in with her and Lu. Kim told me that she'd changed her mind now that she'd found out at this party that they were lesbians. Anyway, I dropped Kim off at her car and went home.

On Friday, two nights later, six of us went to the lounge to celebrate a friend's birthday. Kim wasn't working but came in later in the evening and sat at the bar with some friends. At one point she joined us for a game or two of darts. Then she returned to her friends at the bar. That was the last time I saw her. She was murdered the next night.

The birthday party continued at my house until three in the morning. At 6:30 I got up and went to work. I'm a mail carrier. On my way home after work I stopped into the bar to wait for the pizza I'd ordered from a nearby pizzeria. It was late afternoon. The bartender on duty served me a beer without conversation. When the pizza was ready I took it home and shared it with my friends who remained after the previous night's party. We ate the pizza and watched a football game together.

After working all day with just three hours of sleep the night before, I was dead tired. When my friends left I went to bed. It was about 9:30. My roommate, Steve, stayed up until nearly midnight watching TV.

I learned the details of the murder from my attorney and at trial. Kim was killed in the early morning hours after the bar closed. She was found by the bar's owner that Sunday morning in the men's restroom. She had been knifed in the back. There were cuts and bites on her neck. There was also a bite mark on one of her breasts. She was naked and appeared to have been raped, but no semen was found.

The police came to my house that Sunday afternoon. It was one o'clock. I remember because I was heading out to the Black Bull for an awards banquet where I was to receive a trophy.

When I identified myself, one of them said, "Your girlfriend's dead."

"What?" I said more than a bit startled. "What are you talking about? I don't have a girlfriend."

"Kim Ancona," he continued.

Steve had gone to the supermarket near the bar early that morning for a Sunday newspaper. He told me that the bar had been taped off and that there was much police activity. Something obviously had happened there.

"You mean Kim from the bar?" I deduced. I didn't even know her last name then.

The detective nodded.

I told this detective that she wasn't my girlfriend, that I only knew her casually from the bar where we shot darts a few times together. Then he asked me where my dark-rimmed glasses were. I told him I didn't wear glasses. He looked above one of my eyes for a cut that wasn't there. All through the questioning he couldn't take his eyes off my teeth. He checked Steve's teeth, then he took a close look at mine.

Eventually, he asked me to go downtown with him. On the way he stopped into a convenience store and returned with some Styrofoam plates. He asked me to bite into them several times. I did.

At the police station he proceeded to grill me incessantly about being Kim's boyfriend, even though I had already told him many times I was not. He took my picture, my fingerprints and impressions of my shoes.

I cooperated fully and answered everything truthfully. I had nothing to hide. After examining my body for scratches that weren't there, the detective let me go.

The next day this same detective showed up at my house waving a search warrant. He made a big deal of some condoms found in my top drawer. They weren't even mine. My friend Bob tossed them into my room one day as a joke, saying that I should start using them. The detective took some underwear from my dryer, suggesting that they were stained with blood. They appeared at trial, but no blood was found on them. Next, a pair of my socks was found to have some beads on them. These beads were used to lubricate the bar's shuffleboard. The socks also appeared at trial, along with Kim's socks, which also contained some shuffleboard beads.

The police attempted to have Amy, my previous girlfriend, testify that I was a violent person who used knives and had bitten her in the past. She refused, saying it wasn't true.

After the search, the detective took me downtown again. He produced a court order for hair, blood, saliva and teeth impressions. Again I cooperated. Afterwards, he interrogated me over and over about being Kim's boyfriend. The more I denied it the more he accused me of lying to him. When he said he had a witness who told him that I had been dating her and that I had taken her to a party, I told him what happened Christmas night but he acted as if I had something to hide.

He brought out a tape recorder and turned it on. After two hours of being grilled, poked, pulled, jabbed and called a liar, I was seriously stressed. When he put a mic in front of me, I demanded to see an attorney and stopped talking. He slammed off the recorder and said, "There are other ways to go about this."

As I was being released, I told him what I thought of his attitude and suggested he check out whoever was saying I was Kim's boyfriend.

After work the next day the detective arrested me. It was the last day of 1991. He claimed that my bite mark had been found on Kim's body.

He would not question me again. The booking procedure put me into a state of shock.

I remember yelling, "What about DNA?"

"It will be awhile for those results," were his final words to me.

I sat in jail for weeks expecting to be released as soon as the DNA results were known. But it never happened.

At trial, Kate, the bartender who served me the beer as I waited for the pizza, testified that Kim had told her she wouldn't need help closing the bar because she expected me to help her.

When Kim talked to me Friday night, she had mentioned that Trish was no longer the manager and she would be working the next night. Kim wanted to do a good job, hoping she would be named the new manager.

She said, "If you're not doing anything, why don't you stop in tomorrow night?"

I didn't want to be impolite, so I said, "Okay."

When Kim returned to her friend at the bar, Steve said, "You know, she's got a thing for you?"

"Yeah," I answered, "but she's living with some guy. I don't need that!"

Kate ended her testimony by adding that Kim was looking forward to spending the night with me.

I don't know where "helping Kim" or "spending the night" came from. If I were going to help her close the bar, I would have been there at closing time, but I wasn't. No witnesses saw me there that night. Several testified that Kim was alone in the bar when it closed.

My friends verified that I was up all Friday night and with little sleep went to work early the next morning. Steve testified that I went to bed dead tired the night of the murder. He's a light sleeper and said that he didn't hear me leave that night. But the police claimed that I sneaked out and returned without waking Steve. No proof was established to support this theory except for a next-door neighbor who testified that my Corvette was not covered that night or the next morning. He claimed that I always covered it at night—real convincing, huh?

More shuffleboard beads were found in my car. The prosecutor made a big deal about them. But the shuffleboard was right next to the dart board.

None of my fingerprints were found. The footprints found in the kitchen near where the knife was taken were not mine. But this evidence was passed over quickly. DNA from my hair, blood and saliva was not linked to the crime—also quickly passed over.

The main case against me was the bite mark. The prosecutor hired an expert from Las Vegas who testified that my teeth pattern matched the bite found on the victim. This expert showed the jury a videotape which demonstrated how my teeth fit the injury.

While the prosecutor called many experts, my attorney did not call a single one. The local bite mark expert he lined up was somehow on vacation. The judge would not delay the trial until this expert was available.

My attorney kept telling me that the case against me was very weak. I didn't have the $25,000 necessary to retain a good one, so this one was appointed for me.

I didn't think there was any way I would be convicted since I was innocent. I learned a very hard lesson there!

I was the main defense witness and was on the stand for a long and brutal cross-examination. I think I did well—telling the truth is easy. Obviously, it didn't help.

For closing argument, the prosecutor argued that by denying I was Kim's boyfriend, I was covering up my involvement. His idea of a motive was that I raped her because I was denied sex and then killed her to silence her. He held up the bag of condoms for the jury to see while painting me as a cold-blooded killer with the presence of mind to don a condom before committing the rape. That's how he explained the absence of semen.

The jury deliberated only two hours. They asked to see the videotape just before returning with their verdict. They must have believed the bite mark expert, because they convicted me of murder and kidnapping. They acquitted me of sexual assault—figure that out!

My attorney made a motion for a new trial based upon the affidavit of another bite mark expert from Albuquerque. This expert had reviewed the videotape and contested the findings of the Las Vegas expert, but the judge denied this motion.

A few weeks later, the judge allowed the death penalty and after a hearing sentenced me to death.

Ray ended his letter with a quote from the Bible, "Luke 8:17 says, 'For nothing is hidden that shall not become evident, nor anything secret that shall not come to light.'"

π

After reading Ray's letter several times I called a friend, Gene Burdick, who lived in the Phoenix area.

I had known Gene for some thirty years. We met as computer programmers for Lockheed Missiles and Space Company, located in California's Santa Clara Valley, a.k.a. Silicon Valley. In the mid 'sixties the race was on for the moon and there were numerous opportunities for young college grads with degrees in math and science. I had recently been graduated from San Jose State University and he from the University of Santa Clara. Both of us found work at another computer company that eventually transferred us to Seattle.

After reaching the moon, the space program suffered drastic cutbacks. The Pacific Northwest, then primarily dependent upon the Boeing Company, experienced numerous layoffs. It was so bad that some joker put a picture of a light bulb on a billboard with the caption, "Would the last person leaving Seattle please turn off the lights." We both found ourselves unemployed.

Gene moved his family to his wife's hometown, Phoenix.

To make ends meet, I worked briefly as a furniture salesman, then found employment at the University of Washington in the oceanography department. There I honed my programming skills by developing database software for statistical analysis of data gathered by research oceanographers. In 1977 I was transferred to San Francisco State University. Eventually, I returned to Silicon Valley and spent the eighties as a contract programmer for several aerospace and computer microchip companies. On the side I developed a management software product for medical and dental practices. In 1991 I moved to the Nevada side of Lake Tahoe, from where I supported this product, then being used by five hundred or so physicians and dentists.

In Arizona, Gene enrolled in law school at Arizona State University in Tempe, just east of Phoenix. He would eventually settle in Mesa, just east of Tempe, to practice law. There he and his wife Carolyn would raise three boys. Adam, Alex and Chris were away at college at the time of my call.

Gene had a vague recollection of the snaggletooth murder, remembering that the "boyfriend" had been convicted.

"Are you ready for this?" I asked. "The 'boyfriend' is a cousin of mine."

I summarized Ray's letter. Gene had never heard of anyone being convicted on bite mark evidence, let alone *solely* by this type of evidence. When I mentioned that I would like to look further into the case, he cautioned me not to give too much credence to Ray's claims.

"Convicts can be very creative in claiming their innocence," Gene advised from experience. "The real answer as to why your cousin was convicted can be found in the trial record." He volunteered to locate a copy of it for me. It would take several weeks for the transcripts to arrive. In the meantime I found out what I could about cousin Ray.

π

Ray Dennis was born on January 19, 1957. He barely remembers his name being changed to Krone in his first year of school. Dale Krone adopted Ray shortly after his marriage to Ray's mother, Carolyn. They settled into a house on Grandma and Grandpa Diller's property in Dover, just west of York. Harrison and Nellie Diller, my grandparents, were Ray's great-grandparents, as Carolyn's mother, Hazel, is my mother's sister. There on Grandpa and Grandma's farm Ray would grow up with his sister Amy and brother Dale junior. Ray often tagged along while Grandpa did his chores around the farm.

The Krones would move only once, when Dale and Carolyn bought their own home just a half-mile down the road from Grandpa's house.

There's nothing to indicate that Ray's childhood was anything but normal, stable and happy. He played baseball in Little League and was active in sports throughout high school. He was both a Cub Scout and a Boy Scout. He attended Sunday school and church regularly, sang in the choir and belonged to youth groups.

With the same family foundation as me, it's not surprising that Ray's upbringing was very similar to that of myself and my two brothers. Because my father passed away when I was seven, we did not attend church as regularly as did Ray. It was just too much for my mother—who worked as a nurse to support the family—to get three boys off to church every Sunday. Nevertheless, we, like Ray, were brought up with solid Christian values.

Ray was a better than average student and was graduated from Dover High School in the top ten percent of his class. Although he scored well on college entrance exams, Ray chose to enlist in the United States Air Force. There he completed radar repair school and received advanced training in communications. He would serve his country for seven years, repairing computers at Air Force radar installations.

The fateful event that would to lead to Ray's becoming the prime suspect of the murder of Kimberly Ancona occurred shortly after he was stationed near Savannah, Georgia. Traveling as a passenger, Ray was involved in an auto accident that threw him face-first through the windshield. He endured months of reconstructive surgery. Part of his lower jaw was removed so his bottom teeth would align with his upper teeth. Over the next fifteen years Ray's left front tooth would drop noticeably lower than his right one. It would be these uneven teeth that would link him to the bite mark found on Kimberly Ancona.

Ray was next stationed in Maine, seven miles from Canada. For recreation Ray would cross the border and compete at darts. An English game, darts is very popular with Canadians. Dart leagues were numerous and tournaments frequent. Each player in a tournament would donate an entry fee. The pot would be distributed among the players on the winning team. In time, Ray became a very good player.

When Ray's request to be stationed on the West Coast came through, Luke Air Force Base near Phoenix was the farthest west that Ray was offered. He took it. Nine months later, his seven-year hitch was up. He was honorably discharged and remained in Phoenix. With time on his hands, Ray shot darts often. An inside sport, darts is just as popular in Phoenix during the hot summers as it is in Canada during the cold winters. Ray's game improved greatly and he became one of the best players in the area.

In March 1985, with his severance funds dwindling, Ray was considering moving away from Phoenix when a friend he'd met playing darts suggested that he apply at the post office. With an excellent service record as his recommendation, Ray was hired immediately as a mail carrier. He settled into Phoenix, buying a home and acquiring several "bachelor toys": a dune buggy, a boat, a four-wheel drive truck, a Volkswagen bus, a stock car and a Corvette.

Ray received high praise from his supervisor at the post office as a very responsible worker. He'd never had any altercations with the police—not even a traffic citation. Ray was socially outgoing, had many friends and was well-liked. His home was always open to friends who needed a place to stay. Steve Junkin, his roommate at the time, had moved in after separating from his wife. Steve remembers Ray as a "lady's man," never long without a girlfriend.

I discovered nothing from my inquires that would indicate that Ray Krone had a dark side capable of a violent crime. Yet, on the last day of 1991, just nineteen days before his thirty-fifth birthday, Ray Krone was arrested for the kidnapping, rape and murder of Kimberly Ancona. Eight months later he was convicted of kidnapping and murder and sentenced to death.

I anxiously awaited the trial transcripts.

CHAPTER 2
THE SNAGGLETOOTH MURDER

The murder trial of Ray Krone lasted eight days, generated fourteen hundred and twenty-five pages of testimony and took a week to digest.

The first witness to testify was the owner of the CBS Lounge, the crime scene. A week before the murder, Henry Arredondo had purchased the lounge, a neighborhood bar and grill. It was situated within an L-shaped shopping mall located on the southeast corner of West Camelback Road and 16th Avenue, some three miles north of downtown Phoenix. A Fry's super market occupied the south side of the mall. The longer east side comprised several smaller establishments, including the CBS Lounge. It was located at the north end, second only to a shoe store. A twelve-foot-wide sidewalk separated the storefronts from the parking lot.

On Friday, the night before the murder, the door to the men's restroom had been broken off its hinges. That was the same night that Ray and some friends were in the lounge celebrating a friend's birthday. Since the carpenter wasn't available until Sunday, Arredondo temporarily propped the door open using redwood shims. The partially open door was no problem for the male patrons on Saturday night, because the men's restroom was at the end of a hall that emptied into a back alley.

Arredondo arrived at 8:15 on Sunday morning, fifteen minutes late for his appointment with the carpenter. He immediately noticed that something was amiss. The front door, though closed, was unlocked. He passed through an enclosed entry area and turned right through a second door, which opened facing a pool table. Beyond the table against the south wall were three high bar tables, which accommodated the players' drinks when it was their turn to shoot. Another pool table was situated at a right angle to the first and positioned midway between the first pool table and a shuffle board which ran parallel and next to the north wall. Beyond the pool tables was an L-shaped bar, with its long dimension running two-thirds the length of the room and parallel to the south wall. A dozen bar stools with backrests lined the bar. In the center of the lounge were nine more bar tables, each accommodating four backless bar stools. The bar stools had been placed up-side-down on the tables, consistent with the closing procedure. The short end of the bar was nearest the entrance and connected to the south wall. The lounge area was fully carpeted except for the tiled floor in the southeast corner, which served as the entryway to the kitchen. The kitchen was separated from the lounge by a swinging door.

Arredondo noticed that the bar lights, always the last to be switched off, were still on. He next moved east between the pool tables and passed alongside the bar. At the end of the bar he noticed a glass containing a small amount of liquid. Had he continued straight he would have entered the kitchen through its swinging door. Instead, he circled around the end of the bar and paused in front of the cash register, which sat on the counter next to the wall. It was locked. Arredondo opened it and found the night's receipts intact. Turning around he noticed on the ice chest behind the bar an opened but nearly full bottle of Bud Light sitting next to Kimberly Ancona's purse. Then he moved north past the kitchen door and the hallway to the restrooms and entered his office. There he found the day's receipts in the safe also intact.

Arredondo exited his office and proceeded east down the hallway, first checking the women's restroom. It appeared normal. As he approached the door to the men's room, he noticed that the steel bar that secures the back door to the alley was in place.

Peering into the men's restroom, he discovered the body of Kimberly Ancona and immediately retreated to his office and dialed 9-1-1.

Completing his testimony, Arredondo confirmed that most of the closing procedures had been completed—the bar glasses were clean and put away, the sinks were drained, the trash had been emptied, the high tables that filled the lounge area had been wiped clean, the stools had been placed up-side-down on top of them and the restroom floors and entry way to the kitchen had been mopped. All that remained was for the lights to be turned off, the alarm to be set and the front door to be locked.

"They were ready to walk out," Arredondo concluded.

Detective Dennis Olson's testimony enhanced the portrait of the murder scene. Ancona's body was lying face up in a pool of blood with her head in the southwest corner of the small (seven and a half feet by ten feet) restroom, directly under the broken door hinge. She was sprawled diagonally across the room with her legs spread apart. Only her socks remained on her otherwise naked body. A redwood shim, with its tip broken and stained with blood, was on the floor near her left shoulder. Her blouse and tank top had been cut up the front and were found, blood-soaked, under her torso. Her blood-stained bra, cut between the cups, was located under her right leg. Her panties had been cut up the side but had no apparent blood on them. They were visible from the hall, along with her pants and left shoe, lying on the floor under the urinal on the north wall. The other shoe was found resting on the floor near Ancona's right foot. Knife wounds and bite marks on her neck were visible above a gold necklace. Another bite mark was prominently visible on her left breast.

The murder weapon was found under the plastic bag that lined the wastebasket, next to the sink. The Chicago Cutlery brand boning knife appeared to have been taken from the knife rack in the kitchen.

Dr. Larry Shaw, the pathologist who performed the autopsy, detailed the injuries to Ancona. Abrasions were found on her right knee, right elbow, right index and middle fingers. The laceration on her lower lip and contusion on her upper lip were caused by her own teeth, possibly as a result of being hit in the face. Shaw acknowledged that an erect penis could have caused the laceration type tears found in her vagina but felt that they were probably made by something else. (The shim, I thought.)

Shaw determined that the bite injuries occurred at or near the time of death. The five stab wounds to the neck proved to be superficial—not sufficient to cause death. The fatal injury was a single six and one-half inch deep stab wound entering the left side of her back in an upward angle penetrating and collapsing her lung, causing massive hemorrhaging. Small slits in the blouse and tank top at the point of knife entry confirmed that Ancona was wearing them at the time of the knife attack. Within three minutes of sustaining this injury Ancona was dead.

As I finished reading Dr. Shaw's testimony, I shuddered at the horror that Kimberly Ancona must have experienced in her last moments. While I am not a staunch proponent of the death penalty, it would be difficult for me to argue against that punishment for the perpetrator of this crime.

But was it Ray Krone who deserved this fate?

As I read on, I paid particular attention to the physical evidence presented to the jury. How would it link Ray Krone to the crime? I wondered. I looked hard for anything of importance Ray had misrepresented or left out of his letter.

Detective Olson directed the collection of the physical evidence. Lubricating beads similar to those found in both Ray's and Ancona's socks were gathered from the shuffleboard that was situated against the north wall of the lounge. In the small corner created by a wall of Arredondo's office and the north wall of the lounge area, just beyond one end of the shuffleboard, were two electronic dart boards. I could imagine Ray and Ancona leaning up against the shuffleboard chatting as they awaited their turn to shoot darts.

In the brief cross-examination Olson confirmed that the footprints found on the kitchen floor near where the murder weapon was taken did not belong to Ray. But in redirect questioning, Olson stated that it was determined that the footprints were made before the bar closed and hence unrelated to the crime. David Torres, the cook, had mopped the kitchen floor at 9:00 p.m., after the kitchen closed. Torres testified that it was not possible to leave footprints on a dry floor.

Olson submitted fingerprints taken from the scene, pubic hairs found on Ancona's abdomen, hairs found under her body and swabs taken from her wounds to the Phoenix police department's crime lab for analysis.

Fingerprint expert Karen Jones identified most of the prints as belonging to employees of the lounge. She could not match any of the unknown fingerprints to Ray Krone.

As I began reading criminologist Scott Piette's testimony, I thought, Here comes the crux of the case. If there's a bite, there's saliva. Since I have a modest background in science, a bachelor's degree in mathematics with minors in chemistry and physics, I enthusiastically read on, paying particular attention to Piette's analysis and conclusions.

Piette had a bachelor's degree in chemistry and biology from Grand Canyon University, a small Baptist school located in west Phoenix. He'd been employed for three and one-half years at the police crime lab, in the serology section, when he was given the Krone evidence to analyze. Except for a spot found on Ancona's pants, all the blood samples he analyzed belonged to Ancona. While both victim and suspect were blood type O, they differed in a blood subtype called PGM. Piette testified that he did a test for PGM on the pants sample but did not find this subtype present. The best he could do was determine that this sample was human blood of unknown origin. He found no bodily fluids belonging to Ray Krone.

Piette testified that the pubic hair taken from the abdomen was similar to a known sample taken post mortem from Ancona. He further testified that the pubic hairs of both suspect and victim "are similar," and therefore neither could be "excluded" as the donor of this hair. He eliminated the hairs found under Ancona as belonging to either victim or suspect, because they were "dark and black." Later in the transcripts they were argued to be random hairs from the restroom floor.

Among the numerous samples submitted to Piette, none contained semen.

Finally, Piette got to Exhibit 45, Sample 14-A, the swab from the area of the bite injury. But he would merely report that he detected the presence of amylase—"spit," as he called it—which came from a "type-O secretor, and both Ancona and Krone are type-O secretors."

I was disappointed. DNA technology has advanced to the point where such a sample, when properly analyzed, could either exclude the suspect with absolute certainty or match the suspect with near certainty. Yet Piette not once mentioned "DNA" in his testimony. His analysis was from the dark ages of forensic science. According to Piette, half the population have blood antigen type O and eighty percent secrete their antigens into their saliva. Therefore, neither victim nor suspect [nor forty percent (one-half of eighty percent) of the general population] could be excluded as the source of the salivary amylase found on Ancona's left breast. Attempting to explain his analysis to the jury, Piette stated, "It's kind of a weird science thing."

I couldn't help but recall Ray's letter in which he contended that the DNA evidence had been passed over too quickly. Except for the bite mark, most of the remaining testimony was innocuous.

Trish was the bar manager at the time Arredondo purchased the CBS Lounge and was let go the day after Christmas. She testified about Ray's "date" with Ancona on Christmas night. Many of Ray's friends testified about the Friday night birthday party. According to her boyfriend, Paul Clark, he and Ancona had had sex several times before she left for work. Then they showered together and Clark observed no bite marks. Several individuals who were last to leave the bar confirmed that Ancona was alone at closing time. No one saw Ray at the bar the night of the murder. Roommate Steve Junkin confirmed Ray's alibi, that he was home sleeping. Neighbor Roscoe Redden stated that Ray "always" covered his corvette but didn't on the night of the murder.

The most damaging eyewitness testimony came from Kate Koester. She was the bartender at the CBS Lounge who had served Ray a beer while he waited for the pizza he'd ordered the afternoon before the murder. Ancona relieved Koester at 6:00 p.m. Koester remained at the bar socializing until about 8:00 p.m. She stated that before leaving Ancona had told her that she expected "Ray" to come in later and help close the bar. The defense objected to this testimony as hearsay, but was overruled by the court.

There were no surprises in the trial record. Ray Krone had indeed been convicted on the strength of a single bite mark. But the testimony of the state's two bite mark experts was difficult to follow. It repeatedly referred to photo exhibits and a videotape. Without the trial exhibits, the substance of their analysis eluded me. I did, however, pay attention to their credentials and conclusions.

The first expert odontologist to testify was Dr. John Piakas, a local dentist. With a bachelor's degree in chemistry, Piakas entered Georgetown University Dental School. After graduation in 1968, he enlisted in the US Army, spending one year at Fort Hood, Texas and the next year in Vietnam. After being discharged, Dr. Piakas entered private practice as a general dentist. In 1984 he moved from New York to Phoenix, where he soon became Maricopa County's forensic dentist. Piakas assisted the county medical examiner in identifying human remains through dental records. He belongs to the American, the New York and the Arizona Dental Associations. Piakas testified that he was certified by the American Board of Forensic Odontologists (ABFO).

Piakas was called to the crime scene, where he initially evaluated and photographed the bite injury on Ancona's left breast. The next day at the police station, he took impressions for a cast of Ray Krone's teeth. At the autopsy he took more photographs and then made a videotape showing a correspondence between the cast of Ray's teeth and the bite mark. Most, if not all, of the bite photos entered into evidence were taken by Piakas. His experience with bite mark analysis was limited to just one prior case, which never went to trial. Nevertheless, Dr. Piakas rendered the opinion that, "The bite mark on Kim Ancona matches the dentition of Ray Krone."

Dr. Raymond Rawson was eminently more qualified. In 1964 he received a bachelor's degree in zoology and chemistry from the University of Nevada at Las Vegas. Two years later he received a doctoral degree in dentistry from Loma Linda University. A decade later he received a master's degree in physical anthropology while maintaining a dental practice in Las Vegas. Additionally, Rawson held professorships at UNLV, Northwestern and Community College of Southern Nevada. He was a deputy coroner for Clark County. Active in community and church, Rawson was a member of the United Way and the Boy Scouts of America and was a stake president of the Church of Jesus Christ of Latter-Day Saints. Rawson had been a

Nevada state senator since 1984 and served as the assistant majority floor leader and chairman of the human resources and facilities committee. For fifteen years, Dr. Rawson had been board-certified by the ABFO and at one time served as its president. Over the years he received numerous honors and awards, published many articles, presented many lectures and testified in a number of bite mark cases.

As the state's star witness, Dr. Rawson stated that bite marks are better evidence than fingerprints and concluded that the bite mark evidence exhibits "an excellent match and would be held in high regard by forensic odontologists."

CHAPTER 3
THE VIDEOTAPE

From what I'd learned so far, the theory that Ray Krone had murdered Kim Ancona made little sense. If he were planning to help Ancona close the bar, why did no one see him there at closing time? The prosecutor argued that the crime was committed in a fit of violent passion. Why then would Ray think to go into the kitchen, a place unfamiliar to him, for the murder weapon? I suppose if he were looking for a knife, the kitchen would be a logical place to find one. But why, then, did his footprints not obscure the footprints already on the kitchen floor near the knife rack? Why was the DNA evidence so flimsy? How could Ray have committed such a crime without taking some of Ancona's blood with him or leaving some of his bodily fluids with her? How could he bite her and not leave some of his saliva?

But there was no denying the bite mark. I could not see how Ray could be innocent of the murder if his teeth had made the mark, as three experts said. In addition to Dr. Piakas and Dr. Rawson, Dr. Bruce Etkin had evaluated the evidence. Etkin had been retained as a defense expert. He and the defense attorney, Geoffrey Jones, traveled to Las Vegas to meet with Dr. Rawson. Both were duly impressed by this expert odontologist and his analysis. Dr. Etkin could not disagree with Rawson. Jones wisely did not ask Etkin for a written report or call him to testify.

In a meeting set up by Gene Burdick, Jones outlined the strategy he had used for the trial. He said he had planned not to call an expert but would challenge the validity of bite mark analysis and Rawson's scientific methodology. As the trial approached, the prosecutor hinted that some additional evidence was coming. The afternoon before the trial was to begin, Jones received a second videotape. He had previously received the videotape made at the autopsy by Dr. Piakas and was prepared for it. But this tape, produced by Dr. Rawson, caught Jones completely by surprise. Before jury selection, Jones vigorously objected to its admission and asked the court to either disallow the tape or continue the trial at a later date to give his expert time to evaluate this new evidence. The judge, however, denied both requests, agreeing with the prosecutor that the videotape was merely another representation of the bite mark evidence already disclosed.

"The videotape hurt," said Jones.

Blindsided by the videotape and with Dr. Etkin on vacation, Jones sought the help of Dr. Homer Campbell, the bite mark expert from Albuquerque. In desperation, Jones sent the tape to Dr. Campbell. But it was too late. Before Campbell could respond, the trial was over and Ray Krone was convicted.

It didn't look good for Ray with three experts affirming that it was his bite mark on victim Ancona. Nevertheless, I was curious what Dr. Campbell might have to say. I located him at his office at the University of New Mexico. By now, more than a year had passed since the conviction. While Campbell recalled the videotape, he was unable to locate it and believed he'd returned it to Jones. After a brief discussion, Campbell agreed to evaluate the Krone evidence. He would need transcripts of the bite mark testimony, photographs of the bite injury, the videotape and a cast of Ray's dentition.

I already had the transcripts. The rest of the material was housed in the evidence room in the basement of the superior court building in Phoenix. I was able to view the material there, but there was no easy way to have evidence temporarily removed. Copies would have to be made.

Gene introduced me to a friend of his, Mike Pain, a private investigator. Mike sent a photographer into the evidence room to copy the photos.

The videotape was a little more difficult. The evidence room merely warehouses evidence. To view the videotape, one would have to provide one's own TV monitor and tape player. To make a copy would require two recorders. While this procedure, however cumbersome, was doable, it would require permission. I learned early on that any request out of the ordinary was met with extreme reluctance from the evidence custodian.

To solve this problem, Mike contacted John Antieau. At the time, Ray's case was in the automatic appeal process afforded all individuals facing capital punishment. Antieau was Ray's court-appointed appellate attorney. Of course, he had access to the evidence. Antieau was allowed to check out the videotape. At Mike's request, Antieau did just that and a copy was made.

The cast of Ray's teeth was more difficult. It could be viewed in the evidence room, but was not allowed to be removed. Mike pursued other avenues, which would take some time.

π

In early 1994, with no cast of Ray's dentition on the horizon and not wanting to wait any longer, I contacted Dr. Campbell and asked if he would evaluate the material I did have. He would be happy to. However, it would have to wait a few weeks, until he returned from the annual meeting of the American Academy of Forensic Sciences, held that year in San Antonio. Thinking this meeting might be informative, I suggested we meet there. Campbell agreed.

As my route to San Antonio on Southwest Airlines passed through Phoenix, I took this opportunity to once again visit Gene and Carolyn. Carolyn loved to cook, and I certainly enjoyed her meals and their company. I'd been to Phoenix several times by then and had begun to refer to Alex's room as "my room." But I had not yet made the hour's drive south to Arizona State Prison to meet Ray Krone. If he were indeed a killer, I had no desire to do so. Should Dr. Campbell confirm Rawson's findings, I would report the results to Ray's family, offer my condolences and be done with the case.

After dinner, Gene and I viewed the videotape. Mike had already reported that he and Antieau thought it to be very powerful evidence of guilt. As we watched, Gene plowed through the associated transcripts of Rawson's testimony as best he could.

As the tape ended, Gene said, "Well, I'm not convinced."

I wondered whether Gene's skepticism derived from his experience as an attorney or from his desire to avoid the endless dialogue ("What about this? What about that?") that would ensue if he were to agree with Mike and Antieau's assessment? Gene needed to be rested for his court appearance the next day.

π

I met Dr. Campbell in the lobby of his hotel. After exchanging introductions, I handed him the stack of bite mark photos. He quickly got down to business, slowly moving from one photo to the next.

First, he looked at the color photographs of the bite injury, slowly rotating each photo, sometimes closing one eye. Occasionally he placed what appeared to be a small version of a carpenter's square on the photos. Sensing my interest, he explained, "This is an ABFO ruler." It was really two rulers connected at a right angle, each about four inches long but calibrated in millimeters. It had been designed by the American Board of Forensic Odontologists.

"In this business, it's metric analysis, pure and simple," Campbell continued. "If this ruler does not appear next to the bite mark, the photo has no analytic value. Look at this photo. The distance between these two marks measures forty-one millimeters on my ruler. But on the scale in the photo, forty-one translates to twenty-seven millimeters—about right for the distance between the upper canine teeth. Attention to scale is extremely important."

I watched patiently as Dr. Campbell continued through the stack of photos. I surmised that he was determining the corresponding tooth (incisor, canine, bicuspid, molar) responsible for each mark of the bite. A logical first step, I thought.

The long silence was broken as Campbell picked up the first black-and-white photo. "Who marked this?" he asked abruptly, handing the photo to me.

"I don't know for sure—either Piakas or Rawson," I suggested.

Dr. Campbell went on to explain that in dentistry each tooth is numbered. For dental examinations as well as bite mark analysis, it is much easier to reference teeth by number than by name. The upper right and left central incisors, the two front teeth, are numbered 8 and 9, respectively. Campbell believed that the marks annotated 8 and 9 in the photo were not made by the assailant's two front teeth, but by teeth 8 and 7, the right front tooth and the smaller lateral incisor to its right. This discrepancy was one of several pointed out to me. A quite obvious one was the mark annotated "11." It was not a bite mark at all, but a mole on the victim's breast. Another one indicated that two lower teeth, the left central and lateral incisors, were responsible for making one and the same mark.

From the tone of the remainder of our discussion that morning, it was clear that Dr. Campbell had taken an acute interest in the Krone case—particularly the bite mark evidence. He wanted to show the photos to some of his colleagues. We agreed to finish our meeting in the afternoon.

Since I had discovered an expert odontologist who evidently did not hold the evidence in the same regard as did Dr. Rawson—at least as far as the interpretation of the raw data, the bite mark, was concerned—I had now taken a much keener interest in the science of forensic odontology. I attended a few lectures on the subject while waiting to talk with Dr. Campbell again.

At our afternoon meeting, he reaffirmed his opinion that the photo was erroneously marked. He couldn't render an opinion as to whether or not it was Ray's bite on the victim until he could evaluate the cast of Ray's teeth. He would need time to read the bite mark testimony and view the videotape before he could critique it. We agreed to a future meeting in Albuquerque. Before parting, Dr. Campbell left a copy of his curriculum vitae with me.

Homer Richardson Campbell was born in 1931 in Tulsa. He entered Baylor University in 1948, where he received his undergraduate and then his dental degree. After three years in the US Navy, he opened a private practice in Albuquerque. He remained active with the Naval Reserve until 1987, when he retired with the rank of captain. He received his first training in forensic odontology in 1974 and had been active in the forensic science community ever since. Like Dr. Rawson, he had given many lectures, presented numerous scientific papers and written many articles on the subject of forensic odontology. Dr. Campbell had served as both vice president and president of the American Academy of Forensic Science. He was the forensic odontologist for the State of New Mexico in the medical examiner's office at the University of New Mexico School of Medicine. All unattended deaths in New Mexico passed through the medical examiner's office, where Dr. Campbell not only analyzed bite mark evidence but evaluated all types of pattern injuries. In 1976 he, with several colleagues, founded the ABFO and was among the first group of expert odontologists to be certified.

ABFO membership now numbers approximately one hundred throughout the United States and Canada. Dr. Campbell was one of fewer than five individuals who were full-time odontologists. For most ABFO members, forensic odontology is an avocation augmenting their dental practice.

π

A month later Dr. Campbell was enjoying a cup of coffee in my Albuquerque hotel room while I set up the videotape player.

"I know what he's doing," said Campbell referring to Rawson's testimony. "He's claiming to see multiple bites. He calls this the twelve o'clock bite." Campbell was pointing to the marks at the top of the photograph he was holding. "Over here's the ten o'clock bite."

"They're not even the same shape," I observed. "The twelve o'clock mark appears longer and thicker." Campbell nodded his head and smiled.

The tape began at the autopsy, showing the cast—the model of Ray's teeth—being rotated about the actual bite injury. It did appear as if Ray's teeth matched the bite. But Dr. Campbell pointed out that the position of the cast was continually being adjusted.

The cast was then positioned with the two front teeth behind the most prominent marks of the injury. In this position Dr. Campbell acknowledged that the twelve o'clock bite did appear to match Ray's two front teeth, but then emphasized, "It's not laid out correctly. Those marks were not made by central incisors."

Next came the overlay demonstration. With two cameras plugged into a single tape recorder and TV monitor, Rawson could fade in and out between two separate images. One camera was focused on a photograph of the bite injury, the other on the Styrofoam impression of Ray's teeth. Using this "double exposure" technique, Rawson demonstrated how he believed Ray's teeth fit the twelve o'clock bite.

"It's very impressive, isn't it? But look here," Campbell directed my attention to the left side of Ray's arch. "It's devoid of bite marks." Indeed, while the front and right side of Ray's teeth pattern did cover some of the bite marks, the left side did not.

The tape ran some forty-five minutes. Most of it concentrated on Rawson's twelve o'clock bite. Briefly, at the end of tape, the demonstration was repeated for his ten o'clock bite. Several times during its viewing, Campbell would shake his head saying, "It's laid out all wrong."

Concluding our meeting, Dr. Campbell emphasized, "It's a single bite," then reiterated that the bite mark had been initially misinterpreted. The bite injury had erroneously been marked one tooth clockwise from actuality.

"But is it Ray Krone's bite mark?" I asked.

"I can't say until I see his dental model."

π

When Mike Pain's attempt to have the prison dentist make a cast of Ray's teeth stalled, I invited Dr. Campbell to Phoenix. After breakfast at Sky Harbor Airport, we drove directly to Maricopa County's superior court building. I had been in its basement the day before cataloging the exhibits Dr. Campbell wished to view. In addition to Ray's dental model, he would evaluate Styrofoam bite impressions of six other suspects.

First, Dr. Campbell applied his ABFO ruler several times to the cast of Ray's teeth, each time making notes on his yellow note pad. Next, he did the same with each of the other suspects' teeth patterns recorded in Styrofoam. He was finished in less than an hour.

Afterwards, in the courthouse cafeteria, we discussed his findings. "Ray Krone is excluded," he affirmed.

Dr. Campbell could not exclude three of the other suspects. He seemed to like one suspect in particular. Without their dental models, "not excluded" was the best opinion he would render. He did assure me, however, that the bite mark contained sufficient information, that with the dental model of the actual biter in hand, he could render the strongest possible opinion, "The suspect made the mark to a reasonable degree of medical certainty."

"The way the analysis should have been done," he concluded, "was for dental models of all suspects to be taken and then compared to the bite mark."

π

Two weeks later, mid-June 1994, I received Dr. Campbell's written report. In it he formally excluded Ray Krone as the donor of the bite mark, then stated, "It is a single bite injury, not a multiple injury as assumed, [and therefore] it is not possible for an adult dentition to produce the injury as marked in the black and white photos."

As for the videotape, "It is of no evidentiary value and obscures rather that enhances any analysis."

CHAPTER 4
A SHADY PERSON

My first visit with Ray Krone was not too long after my trip to Albuquerque, where serious doubts had been raised about Ray's guilt. Because the bite mark was the only substantial evidence against him, I was all but convinced that his conviction had been a mistake. Since no experts had testified in his defense, the jury had only the state's version of the forensic evidence to consider. Their verdict was understandable. Had Dr. Homer Campbell testified, I believed, the results would have been the same as in another quite similar case tried in Flagstaff, *Arizona v. Abney*. Defendant Abney was charged with murder based upon a mark on the victim's breast that Dr. Raymond Rawson believed was made by Abney's teeth. Campbell demonstrated that it was not a bite mark at all by showing the jury that he was able to duplicate the mark on a cadaver using a pen knife. Abney was acquitted.

Arizona's Death Row inmates reside at the state prison in Florence, a small town halfway between Phoenix and Tucson. When not in their cells or a secure exercise yard, these inmates always have their hands cuffed and shackled to a leather belt secured around their waist. Once an inmate is spirited and locked into the visitation cage, his handcuffs and belt are removed and collected by the guard through a small window in the door to the cage.

Ray kept his smile during this process. We were separated by thick glass. Communication was via telephone.

We became acquainted by reminiscing about family. But Ray was more interested in my visits with Dr. Campbell. He listened intently, asking few questions, mostly shaking his head as I detailed what I'd learned from Campbell.

I assured Ray, "I expect Dr. Campbell to exclude you as the source of the bite as soon as he is able to get a look at the cast of your teeth."

"You know," said Ray a bit naïvely, "I couldn't understand how it was possible for the murderer and me to have the same teeth pattern."

He, too, had been impressed with Dr. Raymond Rawson and his videotape. Until my visit, it never dawned on him that Rawson might have made a mistake. Ray really believed that it was just his bad luck that his dentition also fit the bite mark.

Ray listened as I speculated on whose bite mark it might be. The police reports contained several references that named Trish, the former bar manager, and her girlfriend Lu as suspects. Arredondo, the bar's owner, reported that the talk around the bar was that it was a homosexual homicide and that Trish and Lu possibly killed Ancona. Lu was described as "Indian female, former military." She was also on the list of suspects whom Dr. Campbell could not exclude and the one Campbell liked the best.

"What do you know about Trish and Lu?" I asked.

"Not much—just from the bar," Ray answered. "Trish is very good looking. I asked her for a date one time. It was after Amy and I broke up. I was having a lasagna party at my house. I called Trish at the bar and asked if she wanted to come over. She wasn't interested, but said Kim might be. But I wasn't interested in Kim.

"I shot darts against Lu a few times at the bar and in tournaments. At first, I thought she was a man and worked at the bar, because she was always there and seemed to do whatever Trish asked.

"It was disappointing to find out they were gay."

I could attest to the fact that Trish was attractive. I'd had a chance encounter with her on one of my early visits to Phoenix. While waiting for my return flight, I had ordered a beer from a waitress whose name tag read TRISH. When she returned with the beer, I attempted to find out if she were *the* Trish. Removing my half-height reading glasses and flexing my abdominal muscles in an attempt to elevate the mass that over the years had succumbed to gravity, I gave her my best move—but to no avail. My ego wanted to conclude that the reason this attractive waitress wasn't interested in having a conversation with me was that she was gay. Reality suggested other reasons. Trish is a reasonably common name, this waitress was too busy and it was probably not her anyway, I rationalized.

Mike Pain, at my request, was making inquiries into the case. He'd located Trish. She was a bartender at Sky Harbor Airport. A copy of her driver's license picture confirmed that I had indeed been served a beer by one of my suspects. Mike saved Trish for last to be questioned. Before the intended meeting, Trish left town.

"When you shot darts with Lu, did you notice whether she shot left-handed?" I asked Ray, continuing my "investigation."

Ancona was killed by a single well-placed stab in the back. Since there were also knife injuries to the neck, I theorized that the victim had been held from behind at knifepoint to the neck before being fatally stabbed in the back—not unlike a combat soldier taking out a sentry. If so, I reasoned, the assailant was most likely left-handed, because the knife had entered the left side of the back and penetrated the left lung. Ray was right-handed. But what about Lu?

Ray thought for a bit. "I don't remember. But I do remember," he volunteered, "that she wore Converse shoes."

The murder weapon was determined to have been taken from the knife rack in the kitchen. The kitchen floor had been mopped around 9:00 p.m. by cook David Torres. A single set of footprints was found on the kitchen floor leading to the knife rack. These footprints were easily determined to have been made by Converse brand tennis shoes. The trademark CONS is clearly visible in the photographs taken of the footprints.

Why, I wondered, would Ray, some two years later, be able to remember Lu's shoes and not be able to remember with which hand she shot darts? I asked him.

"I always watched for foot faults" was the simple explanation.

When shooting darts, a player is required to stand behind a line some nine feet from the dart board. Should the player's foot cross this line, the player's shot is foul and doesn't count. Early in his dart playing career, Ray had gotten into the habit of watching his opponents feet when they were shooting. This fact was confirmed by one of Ray's friends, who described Ray's dart playing as "intense." Ray never hesitated to call foot faults, especially when there was a prize riding on the outcome of a game.

It would have been easy for Ray, in his situation, to encourage his cousin who was "investigating" his case. Knowing that his cousin had developed the theory that the murderer was left-handed, he could easily have speculated, "I think so," regarding Lu's suspected left-handedness. I learned from this visit and many others that Ray and I have very similar values, which is not surprising, as the source of our formative training was the same, Grandma and Grandpa. For me it was passed on through one of their children, my mother. Ray had the additional benefit of being able to learn directly from Grandma and Grandpa, having grown up on their farm.

If Ray didn't know something, he would say so, which added to his credibility when he did say something. Ray confirmed that Lu wore Converse tennis shoes. It would be some time before I would find out whether Lu was left-handed or not.

Lastly, we discussed his options. As everyone knows, there is a lengthy legal process between conviction and execution. Ray was at the first step, his appeal to the Arizona Supreme Court. An appeal focuses on errors that occur at trial. That's one reason why good defense attorneys frequently object during trial. Each time the judge overrules an objection the possibility for error under the law is introduced. The appeal process is essentially a check by a higher court on the performance of the trial judge. Factual innocence supported by new evidence is not an issue at the appellate level. Should an appeal fail, as most do, the next step is post conviction relief, known in Arizona as a "Rule 32," whereby any and all new evidence is presented to a superior court judge, usually the same one that presided over the trial. The judge, at his discretion, may then order a new trial.

Since it would be at least a year for Ray's appeal to be decided, I suggested that he consider proceeding with a Rule 32 right away. The appellate issues, the late discovery (or release of evidence) of the videotape and the hearsay testimony of Kate Koester, did not seem as promising as did the new bite mark evidence. By proceeding with a Rule 32, Ray might win a new trial sooner. But there was a risk—should both fail, his execution would occur sooner. It was his call.

"Let's do it!" he said without hesitation.

I left this first visit liking him. My friends tend to be honest, intelligent people. Ray Krone was in that category. But a Maricopa County prosecutor had successfully convinced twelve people that he was a shady person and had murdered Kimberly Ancona. This prosecutor would soon discover another shady person poking his nose into the Krone case to try to change this perception of Ray Krone.

John Antieau would continue with Ray's appeal. A different attorney would be retained for the post conviction relief. I volunteered to find one. Ray accepted. To be safe, we would wait for Dr. Campbell's report to be issued.

At the time Ray was going through his trial, I was also having an unpleasant experience involving attorneys, although of minor consequence compared to Ray's ordeal.

Shortly after moving to the Lake Tahoe area, I acquired a boat. I traded a car for it, a Camaro IROC-Z, which I had repossessed from my younger son. Marlon had been allowed to use it while going to college, but he had decided to do something else and would have to make do with a lesser vehicle.

The boat was a well-constructed aluminum craft designed to pull parasailers, but it needed some refurbishing and repair. Before the trade, I contacted its manufacturer in Tacoma and was assured that four thousand dollars would make it shipshape. The boat originally sold for thirty-five thousand and in good shape would be worth thirteen thousand. A good deal, I thought. I delivered the old boat to the manufacturer, visited some friends I'd made during my Seattle days, then returned to Tahoe and impatiently waited.

The invoice I eventually received was a shocker. Not only had the hourly labor charge escalated from the quoted forty dollars an hour to sixty dollars, the total bill was within one hour's labor of thirteen thousand dollars.

I retained a Tacoma attorney, who arranged for me to take possession of the boat provided I deposit thirteen thousand dollars with the court. The money would be distributed at a later date pending arbitration to settle the matter. At the arbitration hearing, attorneys outnumbered litigants. In addition to my attorney there were two attorneys for the defendants (one for each defendant present) and a fourth attorney acting as the arbitrator. Somehow I, the plaintiff, became the defendant and was subjected to a barrage of questions. My attorney responded by asking the real defendants only one question, "What's a hose barb?" The invoice had noted numerous "hose barbs," each requiring an hour's labor to install. Hose barbs, it turned out, were simply hollow bolts screwed into the bulkhead and the engine to which a water hose is attached for the purpose of cooling the engine.

The arbitrator awarded the defendants seven thousand dollars then announced the zinger, "I'm inclined not to award attorney fees." I was coincidentally facing six thousand dollars in attorney fees. Seven plus six equals thirteen. Hmm...I left the arbitration feeling as if I'd just been examined by an army of proctologists.

All was not lost, however. Under Gene's tutelage, I instructed my attorney not to accept the results of arbitration and to request a jury trial. When this was done, I discharged him and, acting as my own attorney, settled with the defendants. The court returned six thousand dollars directly to me. Yes, I stiffed my attorney. I had the strong suspicion that this guy was subtly in cahoots with the other attorneys for the purpose of divvying up my money among them.

In the well-crafted [with Gene's help] letter that relieved my attorney of his duties, I strongly suggested that he was incompetent. When a collection agency contacted me about this matter, I forwarded a copy of this letter to them. They were never heard from again.

I am living proof that the two happiest days in a boat owner's life are the day he gets the boat and the day he gets rid of the boat. Gene's assistance between these two happy days proved to be invaluable. When it came time to locate an attorney for Ray, I recalled how, after hearing my version of the arbitration, Gene had appropriately verbed a noun, "They really hometowned you!"

Gene advised that Ray should have an attorney experienced with death penalty cases and recommended three Phoenix attorneys for consideration. All three were highly qualified. However, recalling the "hometowning" and having learned that Jones, the prosecutor and the trial judge had at one and the same time all been Maricopa County prosecutors, I was reluctant to consider a Phoenix attorney. I looked elsewhere.

During my meeting in San Antonio with Homer Campbell he had said, "There's someone I want you to meet." We strolled about the convention center until he spied an individual loitering outside a meeting room smoking a cigarette. He was wearing faded blue jeans and a wrinkled blue shirt. I wouldn't have guessed him to be a member of the forensic science community, but his badge read "Christopher J. Plourd, Jurisprudence." Campbell introduced us and left us to get acquainted. I learned that Plourd was a criminal defense attorney from San Diego and he specialized in DNA cases. Asked about my area of interest, I introduced him to the Krone case and told him that Dr. Campbell had expressed serious reservations about the bite mark evidence.

I asked him how he knew Campbell.

"Homer? We've worked on a few cases together. Good man. When he renders an opinion, you can pretty much take it to the bank."

Before Chris Plourd left to attend a lecture on serology, I got his business card. Then I caught up with Dr. Campbell at a seminar on odontology.

On the first Sunday after receiving Dr. Campbell's written report I met with Chris Plourd at his office, which was located a mile or so from San Diego's Pacific Beach. Obviously unshaven since Friday, he was even more casual than in San Antonio, this time wearing tennis shoes, shorts and a Chargers T-shirt. We moved to an outside patio so that he could enjoy a cigar while we talked.

I'd already done some homework on him. He grew up in El Centro, the seat of California's Imperial County. After school he spent many hours at the county courthouse observing his father, a respected and accomplished criminal defense attorney, try cases. In 1978, while Plourd was attending law school, his father passed away. With a bachelor's degree from Indiana's Butler University and a jurisprudence degree from San Diego's Thomas Jefferson School of Law, Plourd followed in his father's footsteps by going to work for his father's former law firm. Soon he was recruited by the Imperial County Public Defender's Office, rapidly rising to the position of assistant public defender. In 1986 he accepted a position with Defenders, Incorporated, a private San Diego law firm specializing in criminal cases. By then he was accepting only the most complex death penalty cases. For a death penalty attorney, success is measured by the number of clients saved from execution. None of Chris Plourd's clients had received the death penalty. Several had been set free. A notable case was that of Jim Wade, a San Diego man accused of raping his eight-year-old daughter. The Wade case gained national attention in 1993 when it was profiled on PBS television's NOVA program. Plourd's expertise with DNA evidence lead to the dismissal of all charges by the district attorney and to the factual finding of innocence by the court, as well as to the arrest and conviction of the actual rapist.

Self-taught on the intricacies of DNA analysis, Plourd was a nationally recognized expert on forensic serology. A long-time member of the American Academy of Forensic Sciences, he frequently gave seminars to instruct colleagues on the techniques of presenting and cross-examining expert witnesses as well as to instruct expert witnesses on what to expect when they venture into court to testify. Plourd was also experienced with cross-examining bite mark experts. In one case, without calling an expert witness, he successfully challenged the scientific validity of the bite mark evidence and won freedom for his client.

The interview went well. I was most impressed by Plourd's unpretentious air. Before our meeting ended, Ray Krone had counsel for his Rule 32. Should Ray win a new trial, Plourd was more than qualified to try the case.

Plourd went to work immediately. Quickly he became familiar with *Arizona v. Krone*, especially with the evidence collected in the case. Soon he traveled to Florence to have his "heart to heart" talk with Ray. It's a talk he has with every new client. After explaining the benefits and drawbacks of DNA testing, he itemizes each piece of evidence that could produce results. He then asks which items should be tested. Most clients are selective. However, Ray's instructions were simple and unequivocal, "Test it all!"

An out-of-state attorney must first have permission of the state's supreme court to represent a client within the state. On the application to appear pro hac vice a member of the state bar must be named as local contact. Gene Burdick volunteered for this duty.

Without the usual hello, Gene said anxiously, "I just learned that someone has been furtively viewing the Krone evidence."

"Why are attorneys being used for laboratory experiments instead of rats?" I asked, attempting to change the subject, knowing that Gene always enjoyed a good attorney joke.

"Aha! Why did I know it was you?"

I confessed it was me and asked, "Don't you want to know why?"

"Okay. Okay. Why?"

"Like rats, there's an abundance of attorneys, lab technicians don't become attached to them and there are some things a rat won't do."

After a brief chuckle, Gene went on to say that he'd just finished a conversation with an official from the county attorney's office who said that someone was observed possibly tampering with Krone evidence.

I had viewed the Krone evidence on several occasions, but the event in question occurred the day before Dr. Campbell's visit to the evidence room. In previous meetings with Campbell he had taken time to offer instruction in the art of bite mark analysis. If Ray Krone were innocent, someone else was guilty. Maybe the real biter was one of the other suspects whose Styrofoam impressions Campbell would soon evaluate? Maybe Campbell would be able to identify the real killer? I would help. I selected the plastic bag containing the Styrofoam bite impression of my suspect. Then I removed a staple from the plastic bag and slid out the impression. Using a ruler, I compared it with several bite mark photos before putting it back into the plastic bag.

"You unsealed an exhibit!?" I could almost hear Gene's hand hitting his forehead.

"You can't do that?" I asked naïvely.

Gene then expressed his concern that his friend might soon become his client. I whimsically assured him that nothing could be pinned on me because I'd been careful to remove my fingerprints from the telltale staple before discarding it. As calm returned to the conversation, I further assured Gene that I would make it easy for him by pleading "guilty by reason of insanity."

He chuckled again. "That would work."

π

The renewed interest in the Krone case that summer of 1994 obviously had not gone unnoticed.

Chris Plourd filed the notice of post conviction relief with the superior court. The law calls for post conviction relief to be automatically provided to every Death Row resident once his appeal is decided. However, no Arizona convict had ever asked for post conviction relief from a death sentence while his appeal was pending.

The county prosecutor argued that since no one had, no one could, and filed a motion to dismiss notice of post conviction relief.

Plourd had also filed a motion for release of evidence for independent analysis. The state responded with a motion to seal the trial exhibits, arguing in part that the evidence should be under the control of the court to prevent "potential exhibit tampering by a 'Mr. Rix,' an apparently shady person, who cannot be located."

These issues would be decided by the same judge, the Honorable Jeffrey A. Hotham, who presided at Ray's trial. I was present for the oral arguments in case there was a need for me to be "located" to explain the "tampering."

The hearing was held in the judge's chambers. After listening to the arguments, Judge Hotham dismissed the notice of post conviction relief as "premature," denied discovery and sealed the evidence.

In short order the Rule 32 was thwarted, the evidence was off-limits and Ray Krone would have to wait for another summer to arrive for the outcome of his appeal.

π

Gene was relieved to know that being branded "a shady person" was all that was going to happen to his friend for the alleged tampering, but he said of the prosecutor, "He's pretty smart. He figured out right away what it's taken me thirty years to figure out."

CHAPTER 5
SUGAR AND HOT LIPS

I n the fall of 1994 I heard of a bounty hunter who had co-authored two books about his exploits. Under the guise of a truck driver, Tex Brown (his pseudonym) roamed the Mexican borders of Texas and New Mexico as an undercover agent for the US Drug Enforcement Agency. I wondered if he were the real deal and acquired both of his books. I read and studied first *18 Wheels of Justice* then *a.k.a. NARC*, "the TRUE STORY of the renegade trucker who became a dangerous secret weapon in the war against drugs." The books detailed many instances in which Tex helped bring criminals, mostly drug smugglers, to justice. As an undercover agent, Tex was not hampered by the border. Several episodes took place in Mexico.

I contacted Tex using a New Mexico area code. I reached him in Moriarity, a small town in the mountains east of Albuquerque. After listening to my rendition of the snaggletooth murder, Tex assured me that he could be of help—on the street level. For a fee, he would go undercover, solve the crime and "walk Ray right out of jail."

The fee was less than would be required for Ray's defense. Tex required an up-front retainer and the rest when "Ray walks." While this solution seemed to be a long shot, a gamble, I thought it would be worth a try. If Tex were successful, Ray would be a free man. If not, a few dollars would be lost...

Tex was retained.

As the appointed time for my meeting with Tex approached, I became apprehensive. While his books purported to be nonfiction, I wondered if they really were? On the morning I was to catch the flight to Albuquerque I woke up with the inclination to call it off. While sipping a cup of coffee, I studied the cover of *a.k.a. NARC*. It depicted a stocky Tex in a red shirt and blue jeans, wearing a Stetson hat and dark glasses, sporting a full beard. A bowie knife and revolver were tucked into his belt, secured by a rodeo-size buckle. He was standing in cowboy boots, leaning against a Mack truck with arms folded and legs crossed. It was not a photograph but an artist's rendition.

In previous conversations Tex had mentioned that he was no longer on good terms with his co-author of *a.k.a. NARC*, Raymond Angus. Remembering that Mr. Angus lived in Phoenix, I opened my Phoenix phone book and found his name in the white pages. He answered on the first ring. After I introduced myself, Mr. Angus verified that indeed there had been an altercation with Tex over royalties and movie rights to the book. Some years later a TV series appeared entitled "18 Wheels of Justice" and loosely based on Tex's escapades.

Could he verify that Tex was genuine? Mr. Angus stated that he had composed the manuscript using cassette tapes that Tex had sent him. He had no personal knowledge of the dictated episodes, but did mention that before publication Tex had been required to supply written documentation to the publisher's attorney verifying the authenticity of his exploits.

With this bit of assurance, I made the plane and was in Albuquerque that afternoon. I could still bail out, I thought, if the meeting didn't go well.

Tex met me at the arrivals curb. He appeared as on the cover of *a.k.a. NARC*, except without the beard and, to my relief, without the knife or gun. The Mack truck had been replaced with a beat-up pickup. However, as I jumped into the truck's cab, I noticed a .38-special resting on the seat.

Now, I'm not comfortable around guns. This uneasiness stems from an incident that occurred when I was a preteen and my older brother and I were playing cops and robbers. We were at a friend's house, each armed with a BB gun trying to shoot each other. I positioned myself behind a tree in the back yard. My brother appeared out of a second story window and fired several times, missing his mark. After his volley, I took aim and fired. My eye followed the BB on its upward trajectory. It passed over my brother's gun barrel into his aiming eye. Fortunately, gravity had worked its magic, sufficiently reducing the BB's energy to where no real damage was done. However, later that day at home, where guns were outlawed, the law being Mom, word arrived before I did that I had almost put out my brother's eye. I was disciplined many times in my formative years, like having my mouth washed out with soap when I said something I shouldn't have. Whippings were saved for special occasions. This special occasion was one of my two most memorable shellackings. The other occurred when I lost my brand new baseball—it was also accompanied by a soaping. Although dad had passed away when I was seven, his belt remained. Its presence during a lecture guaranteed an attentive audience. Although the lecture was repetitive, short and to the point—"You are never to play with guns!"—Mom's delivery was one of her best, and I listened well.

I kept the peacemaker that rested near Tex's hip in the corner of my eye the entire time the truck was moving. Before we could sit down to talk, Tex needed to check in with one of his local operatives, Mississippi Mike.

We pulled into a huge vacant lot surrounded by trees adjacent to a freeway. It appeared to have been at one time a shopping center, now demolished. Observing that there was no way out other than the way in and that there were no buildings of any kind visible, I wondered what was going on. Holding tightly to the package that contained more cash than I'd ever assembled at one time, I thought to myself, I do believe Tex is going to get paid!

As we rambled across the lot, the gun grew in stature, now looking to be .44 in caliber. To my relief, a campsite became visible through the trees at the far end of the lot. Mississippi wasn't in. Tex explained that he had sent Mike undercover as a homeless person to get some information on a case he was working on in Albuquerque.

At a truck stop, over a lunch of cheeseburger for Tex and tuna sandwich for me, we discussed the case. Rather than have Tex start from scratch, I would set him in the "right" direction. By now I'd learned more about Trish and Lu. Chris Plourd had discovered that DNA testing suggested that the pubic hairs found on Ancona belonged to an American Indian. Lu was Navajo.

Tex agreed to center his investigation on them. He would immediately go undercover and, over the weekend, would locate Trish and Lu. He wanted to meet with me again the following Monday in Phoenix. Tex moves quickly, I assured myself. I parted with the package containing the cash and assorted pictures and material pertaining to my suspects.

Arriving Monday morning for the appointed rendezvous, I noticed that the license plate was missing from Tex's pickup truck, replaced by what appeared to be a registration sticker in the rear window. Tex mentioned that he always operated this way while undercover so that he and his truck could not be traced. The .38 special was no longer visibly present as we began traveling the streets of Phoenix.

Tex had arrived Friday afternoon and immediately gone into action. When Tex goes undercover he really goes undercover. For the next three days and nights he checked out several massage parlors in the vicinity of the crime scene. He had learned that there was a large prostitution ring operating out of massage parlors throughout the Southwest, from Louisiana to Arizona. The trademark of these parlors was that they were all painted the same color. Tex verified this fact by giving me a tour past three or four of them. At the last one, he backed into a parking space, left the motor running and said, "Wait here." He'd met someone inside the night before whom he'd recruited to find the whereabouts of Trish and Lu.

After a time that seemed much longer than necessary, Tex emerged in the company of a young woman. She pointed down the street and said something. Tex tipped his hat and jumped behind the wheel. "We're looking for a red Ford pickup," he said anxiously as we hurriedly exited the parking lot and headed in the indicated direction.

Tex changed lanes and streets a few times before abruptly turning into the parking lot of some dive bar pointing out a red pickup parked in back and saying, "There it is!"

"But it's a Toyota," I observed, to which Tex instantly responded, "Look out! We're being follered," oblivious to my comment.

We continued down an alleyway at increasing speed before returning to the streets of Phoenix. After zigzagging through traffic for awhile, Tex found an on-ramp to Interstate 10. After ten miles or so, it was apparently "safe" because Tex slowed to seventy-five miles per hour.

We left the freeway and pulled into a roadside diner. It was lunch time. "Going undercover is rough," Tex commented as he perused the menu. "I've had nothing but fast food hamburgers for three days. Today I'm going to have something different." He ordered a chicken fried steak.

Tex looked the part of a bounty hunter. He had scars on the back of his neck and on one side of his face. His nose had clearly been broken a few times. A noticeable limp, possibly in both legs, kept him from moving very fast—at least in boots.

Tex did not appear to be in the best of health. His plate was devoid of anything green. I consumed a bowl of soup and a plate of salad. Tex's colon began speaking, its loose translation being, "How about a vegetable? I'm dying down here!" In the past I had been mildly "lectured" a few times on the benefits of vegetables.

After the steak disappeared, Tex outlined what he'd uncovered so far. Trish was not involved in the crime and had moved to Bullhead City, an Arizona town across the Colorado River from Laughlin, Nevada. Both Lu and Ancona had been part of the prostitution ring, and Lu still was. The ring periodically and routinely moved its "girls" between parlors. Lu had been ordered by a ring leader to kill Ancona. She had committed several other ring-related murders. Tex had the name of a cab driver who had been at the bar the night of the murder and knew what happened. He would send one of his agents in Florida to New Jersey to find this cabbie. The cab driver's name would not be revealed until he'd been located.

π

I was relieved to be back in my rental car. Doubts were rising about Tex. The red pickup truck or who might be following us was never explained. I feared I had made a hasty decision, no doubt influenced by the presence of his partner, the .38 special, which I was thankful had remained his silent partner. But the bet was irretrievably on the crap table. The dice were in the air. I hoped for a seven. Snake eyes would not surprise me. If it proved to be the latter, I would chalk this adventure up to experience, rationalize that I'd been taken for an amusement ride and try not to dwell on the price of the ticket.

Snake eyes it would be. Over the next several weeks Tex and I were in touch by phone. Stories changed and did not jive with each other or with the facts of the case as I understood them. The cab driver was never mentioned again. Try as I might, however, I was not able to confirm or refute any of Tex's claims. Then, surprise of surprises, he would need more money—"to relocate two families"—"children were involved." The appointed time for the next installment came and went. I received an anxious call from Tex.

"It went priority mail yesterday," I fibbed.

Relieved, Tex assured me that the case was progressing on schedule and would be completed within two months. He would need the final payment at that time.

"So you'll walk Ray out then?" I said, reminding Tex of the original deal.

He'd forgotten. "I never said I'd walk Ray out."

"What will I get, then?"

"Righteous affidavits from non-felons," he answered.

"Ooookay," I said, ending the conversation. The "Dear Tex" letter was posted later that day.

Earlier in the week I'd received a call from Mike Pain. "I just got off the phone with Trish. She's moved to Lexington [Kentucky] to be close to family. She apparently has breast cancer." I had kept Gene appraised throughout my adventure. Hearing of it from Gene, Mike had taken it upon himself to locate Trish.

Tex made several attempts to be reinstated. But Lexington's a long way from Bullhead City. His last report was taken by my answering machine, "Trish and Lu are not involved. I know where the clothes are buried. You should be looking for Sugar and Hot Lips."

In the meantime Chris Plourd had been continuing his limited investigation and had discovered some interesting facts about another Mike—Tennessee, presumably no relation to Mississippi. Tennessee Mike was a neighbor of Ancona who had been seen at the bar the night of the murder. His name was mentioned only once in the police reports. I did not consider Tennessee Mike to be a viable suspect because I assumed from his Hispanic surname that he was Caucasian and therefore could not have donated the pubic hairs. But Plourd had in his hand a copy of an employment application filled out by Tennessee Mike with the American Indian box checked. Since he had not been named as a suspect, his Styrofoam bite impression had not been taken. Further investigation would discover much more about Tennessee Mike. I wondered if he was left-handed?

When I enthusiastically asked Chris Plourd if I could help investigate Tennessee Mike, he replied, "I've saved a much more important task for you. I want you to find Sugar and Hot Lips."

π

It would be some time before I would be allowed to forget the Tex episode. Like Ray Krone, I would patiently have to wait on the Arizona Supreme Court.

CHAPTER 6
BRADY MATERIAL

"The core issue here is the admission of the bite mark evidence. Some evidence has been presented—at least a suggestion—that this Dr. Rawson is a quack, a charlatan, a *guérisseur*."

I glanced over at Chris Plourd with a look of, "What woke up John Antieau?"

It was two weeks before Christmas 1994. Chris and I were seated in the front row facing the Arizona Supreme Court to hear the oral arguments for and against the appeal of Ray Krone.

I had had just one conversation with Ray's appellate attorney, John Antieau. After several attempts, my phone call had, at last, been returned. I introduced myself as his client's cousin who had taken an interest in his case. I attempted to update him on what had been learned from Dr. Campbell, but he abruptly interrupted, saying he wasn't interested in new evidence.

Factual innocence is irrelevant to an appeal. His focus was on errors that occurred at trial. Nevertheless, I informed Mr. Antieau that I was interested in obtaining a copy of the videotape for Dr. Campbell to review. Since he had access to it, could he help? He responded by mentioning that he had recently viewed the tape and strongly suggested that I was wasting my time. For an appellate attorney, a relative suggesting that his client is innocent can be somewhat of a nuisance. Sensing that Antieau had placed me in that category, I left it up to Mike Pain to obtain a copy of the tape.

John Antieau had initially been impressed with the bite mark evidence presented by its proponent, Dr. Raymond Rawson. What had changed his mind now? Where had the suggestion of evidence questioning Rawson's credibility come from? It wasn't in the trial record.

Chris Plourd returned my glance with a wry smile, then returned his attention to the yellow note pad resting in his lap.

Plourd had not gone away quietly when Judge Hotham created a catch-22 that sealed the Krone evidence. In *Brady v. Maryland* the United States Supreme Court held that the suppression of material evidence favorable to the accused violates the due process clause of the Fourteenth Amendment of Constitution. *Brady* requires that exculpatory evidence be made available to the accused, even after conviction. In response to Hotham's ruling that post conviction relief was premature, Plourd filed a petition for special action asking the Arizona Supreme Court to sort out the catch-22 of the Rule 32—that is, to allow Ray Krone to proceed with post conviction relief while his appeal was pending.

In the petition, Plourd detailed the Brady material—exculpatory evidence—to which he wanted access. He wanted Ray Krone's dental model, the Styrofoam bite impressions of the other suspects, along with their transparent overlays, and all bite mark photos, so that qualified forensic odontologists other than Dr. Campbell could independently evaluate them.

Not only would it cost prohibitively to bring bite mark experts into Phoenix, it was no longer feasible. Shortly after Dr. Campbell's visit to the evidence room, all the bite mark photos had been transferred to the state supreme court, where the appeal was pending, while the dental model, the Styrofoam bite impressions and the transparent overlays remained with the county superior court. With the bite mark evidence stored in two separate locations, it was impossible for any comparison analysis to be done on-site.

Included in the petition was Dr. Campbell's report excluding Ray Krone as the biter and questioning the validity of Dr. Rawson's videotape.

John Antieau was obviously familiar with the petition. He finished his opening statement with, "The question is: Does the defendant have the right to call into question the evidence presented against him?"

"Did anybody ask for a *Frye* hearing?" asked a justice of the supreme court.

Courts make no judgment upon the reliability of expert scientific testimony unless it is challenged. Hocus pocus is routinely allowed into courts. One such instance was a dog whose owner claimed that it would bark if it recognized a particular scent. Several months after a crime the dog took a good whiff of the victim's clothing then stuck its nose into the suspect's vehicle and barked. The suspect was convicted. Years later, it was determined that the dog's bark was in response to subtle signals from its master and unrelated to olfactory sensation. (Incidentally, it was prosecutor Hotham, later to become Judge Hotham, who retained the dog.)

The mechanism for challenging scientific evidence is the *Frye* hearing. In the 1923 case, *United States v. Frye*, Frye challenged the validity of the test that purportedly indicated that he was lying. The court ruling set the standard that determines the admissibility of scientific evidence. The proponent of a new type of forensic evidence has the burden of proof to show that the techniques and procedures used are commonly accepted within the scientific community. As it turns out, the polygraph test, also known as the lie detector test, is only as good as the objectivity or subjectivity of the administrator of the test. *Frye* prevailed. That's why lie detector tests are not admissible in courts today. However, they are still used as investigative tools, usually by the side benefiting from the result.

Incidentally, Ray Krone asked for but never received a polygraph test.

"No *Frye* hearing was held," Antieau informed the court.

Still interested, the justice continued, "Do you have any founded reason based upon some authority that such evidence is not recognized within the scientific community as based upon presently recognized scientific principles?"

John Antieau had indeed read and absorbed the petition for special action. He used this opportunity to remind the justices facing him, "There is now before this court a petition asking this court to review the summary dismissal of the Rule 32 petition. Appended to this petition is an affidavit from a forensic dentist stating that Dr. Rawson's methodology is not accepted within the scientific community."

Because defense attorney Geoffrey Jones did not request a *Frye* hearing, the admissibility of bite mark evidence itself could not be raised as an appellate issue. However, the admissibility of the videotape was raised as an issue because Jones objected to the fact that his copy had been delivered to him just before the trial was to start. Although the validity of bite mark evidence was not an issue in itself, the court seemed very interested in it.

Other than the bite mark, the only evidence that tended to place Ray Krone at the scene of the crime was the testimony of Kate Koester that Kimberly Ancona had told her that "Ray is going to help me close [the bar]." Jones's objection to Koester's statement was overruled. Antieau raised the admission of this "hearsay" testimony as another issue worthy of consideration. "But for Koester's testimony," was his argument, "there's nothing to show that Ray Krone was other than an occasional dart player at the bar."

John Antieau finished with, "This is probably the most anomalous murder case in my experience. The defendant was advancing into middle age with never any problem with the law. He was a veteran gainfully employed for years and years. If in fact Ray Krone did murder Kimberly Ancona, it was the most aberrational murder I've ever seen. It was a hundred and eighty degrees away from the rest of his life."

π

Assistant Attorney General Jon Anderson, representing the people of Arizona, began his statement by defending the state's experts. "Dr. Piakas is the Maricopa forensic odontologist and testified that there was a match...The record will suggest, if this court reads Dr. Rawson's qualifications, that he is indeed a very qualified expert."

Answering the concern that Ray Krone did not have a bite mark expert testify on his behalf, Anderson informed the court, "They [the defense] did have an expert appointed for them. The trial court spent two thousand dollars paying for Dr. Etkin, an odontologist, a dentist, who for whatever reason chose not to testify. I guess the inference being that he would not have offered any helpful evidence."

Mr. Anderson must not have been thoroughly familiar with the petition for special action, because appended to it was the affidavit of Dr. Bruce Etkin, secured by Chris Plourd. Etkin himself had stated that, although a practicing prosthodontist, he had no experience with bite mark cases nor did he have any training in forensic odontology. He did not believe he could qualify as a bite mark expert and viewed his roll as that of a "consultant." Dr. Etkin's and Geoffrey Jones's wives had been friends for many years. Despite this affidavit it would be some time before the advocates against Ray Krone would cease referring to Dr. Etkin as "Krone's expert."

"That may be a Rule 32 problem," noted the court. "But what about this tardy videotape? Why in the world would the state try to get into evidence the videotape that had been disclosed but two days before the trial?"

"Dr. Rawson wasn't going to testify for ten days," Anderson responded.

"But counsel's in trial now. You're asking him to—at night I guess—sit down with his expert and go over a professionally prepared videotape...and just have a few days to prepare a videotape of his own?"

Anderson countered, "All the videotape showed, except for the last few minutes, was Dr. Piakas's videotape, photographs, the appellant's teeth and so forth. Ninety percent of this videotape had already come in through other evidence. That's one reason why he [Judge Hotham] did not exclude it. It was basically a rematch."

Apparently Anderson had not had the opportunity to view the videotape. The first five minutes can be attributed to Dr. Piakas, but the remaining forty minutes were devoted to Dr. Rawson's impressive overlay techniques and CAT scanning, a computer aided X-ray technique not previously disclosed.

Then, in a slow crotchety voice coming from the justice seated on the far left, the question and answer session regarding the videotape was interrupted. "Obviously the bite mark evidence looms very large in this case, but let me ask you. Am I correct? Didn't I find somewhere in the briefs that on the victim's body there were found pubic hairs that matched neither the victim nor the defendant?"

Chris Plourd again smiled.

The bite mark evidence was not the only Brady material of interest to Plourd. He also wanted access to all physical evidence, including the hair samples and the swabbed samples of bodily fluids collected at the crime scene. To justify his request, Plourd had included in the petition for special action a copy of the report prepared by Thomas Wahl of the Analytical Genetic Testing Center in Denver. Tom Wahl was a senior forensic geneticist for the AGTC. He had received from the Phoenix police department pubic hair and serologic swabs collected at the crime scene for analysis. Tom Wahl reported that none of these samples matched known samples from Ray Krone. Plourd noted that these findings were contrary to the testimony of criminologist Scott Piette. Piette had testified that Ray Krone could not be excluded as the source of amylase—which he called "spit"—swabbed from the area or the bite injury.

Plourd asked Wahl to review Piette's testimony. Wahl called into question Piette's overall knowledge of DNA. Amylase, for example, is not "spit" but a component of all bodily fluids. Two other highly qualified serologists reviewed Piette's testimony. Both agreed with Tom Wahl.

In the petition, Plourd emphasized that the prosecution, either through neglect, mistake or intentional act, had ignored the exculpatory results contained in the report. Using the fact that both Ray Krone and Kimberly Ancona had blood type O, the prosecutor had elicited testimony from criminologist Scott Piette that incorrectly included Ray Krone as a source of saliva found on Kimberly Ancona. Tom Wahl's report had stated that no DNA foreign to Kim Ancona was detected. That is, the source of the type-O antigen was Ancona's own blood or perspiration. Using this improper and incorrect foundation, the prosecutor had argued to the jury:

[Piette] found salivary amylase on Kim Ancona's left breast and nipple, right breast and nipple and left cheek. Saliva samples were taken from Ray Krone. They were compared to the saliva samples taken from Ancona's body. They were type O and they were from spit. I suggest to you that Kim Ancona, also a type O, is not going to kiss her left cheek or her breasts, but Ray Krone did.

The questionable uses of the forensic data available to the prosecution were not limited to the serologic evidence. The same situation applied to the hair samples recovered from Ancona's body. Piette had also incorrectly stated under oath that the suspect's and victim's hairs were similar and, therefore, Ray Krone could not be excluded as their source. Yet Wahl's report clearly indicated that the DQα ("D-Q-Alpha") genetic marker detected in the hair samples did not match that of Ray Krone.

Wahl's report had not gone unnoticed by the justice on the left. Jon Anderson now found himself answering questions about pubic hairs, saliva and blood secretions before returning to the issues on appeal. Not wanting to revisit the late discovery of the videotape, Anderson turned to the "hearsay" issue.

The Sixth Amendment of the United States Constitution grants the accused the right to confront his accuser. Sometimes the accuser is understandably unavailable. The hearsay statement of a murdered victim is allowed if it is used to support the victim's state of mind, such as what the victim intended to do.

"Here we have the victim stating not what she intends to do, but what she expects someone else [Ray Krone] to do," a justice pointed out to Mr. Anderson.

Whether Ancona's statement to Koester was based upon something Ray Krone said or upon something else was the issue.

"We don't really know what Ray Krone said to Ancona," Anderson replied, "so it's not a statement of his intent, it's her statement."

"It's sheer speculation if it's not based upon what he said to her."

"No, it's not sheer speculation because it's the victim's statement of intent—" came Anderson's frustrated reply before being interrupted.

"I'm expecting justice Martone in my chambers at five. Now that's based upon what justice Martone says or it's based upon some fond hope of some kind. That is sheer speculation."

Objections to the admission of hearsay testimony are perhaps the most hotly debated issues in appellate courts. In the absence of other evidence prosecutors frequently need the murdered victim's hearsay to establish that their suspect was at the scene of the crime. The Krone case was no exception. Absent the bite mark and the hearsay, there was nothing in the record to establish that Ray Krone was in the CBS Lounge the night of the murder. No eyewitnesses. No forensic evidence.

The Arizona Supreme Court has consistently ruled that hearsay cannot be used for the purpose of placing the defendant at the crime scene. However, sometimes the court lets this type of hearsay slide as "harmless error" if the other evidence presented at trial is overwhelming.

At least one justice, the one questioning Anderson, seemed concerned. "This [hearsay] wasn't evidence to prove Ancona's state of mind because her state of mind had some independent significance. This was evidence directly offered to prove that the defendant was there. That was a critical point in the case," concluded chief justice Stanley Feldman.

I was very optimistic. Of the five supreme court justices, one was absent but would be provided an audiotape of the proceedings and would participate in the decision. Only two justices had spoken and both seemed favorable to Ray Krone. "We need just one more," Plourd said, cautiously optimistic as we descended the steps into the parking lot.

Phoenix is both the capital of Arizona and the seat of Maricopa County. The supreme court, county superior courts and federal district courts are all within a few blocks of each other. On the way to Tom's Tavern, a popular lunch spot and watering hole for this judicial community, we discussed politics. Arizona courts, like their constituents, are by and large conservative. A public servant perceived to be soft on crime can at the next election pretty much kiss his job good-bye. Chris Plourd felt that the court would not be able to agree on the hearsay issue. Defendants almost always object to hearsay, the trial court almost always overrules the objection, appellate attorneys almost always raise it as an issue, the attorney general almost always argues that it is "harmless error" and the supreme court almost always agrees. Hearsay, although technically a violation of one's right to confront his accuser, is commonly viewed as a technicality favorable to criminals. Plourd liked the late-discovery issue.

As for the petition for special action, there is little doubt that Chris Plourd had an ulterior motive for "peppering the record," as he put it, with the abundance of exculpatory evidence, correctly interpreted, that he had been able to assemble before Judge Hotham catch-22'd the Rule 32. The supreme court now had not only Ray Krone's appeal to consider, but also Plourd's petition raising serious questions as to Ray Krone's guilt. Regardless of one's politics, "no honest person likes to see an innocent man convicted," Plourd observed.

π

Four months later, in March 1995, the Arizona Supreme Court unanimously ruled:

> We hold that Rule 32.4(a), Arizona Rules of Criminal Procedure, does not preclude a defendant under sentence of death from filing a notice of post conviction relief before his direct appeal is concluded. We point out, however, that rarely will it be advantageous to do so if the only purpose is to present all issues that are ultimately routinely presented in capital cases. We do not close the door, however, on the occasional case in which an early proceeding will likely lead to early relief. We vacate the order of the trial court...

Chris Plourd was back in business.

Present at the discovery hearing that followed the ruling, I observed firsthand the Honorable Hotham dismiss the feeble objection of the prosecutor and then render the only decision he ever made favorable to Ray Krone. Plourd was given complete access to the Brady material.

CHAPTER 7
DECISION

I t was just after eight a.m. on the longest day of 1995 when my phone rang in Nevada. Arizona is one of two states that doesn't participate in Daylight Savings Time, residents preferring not to save hot summer daylight. So it was the same time there for the reporter who was calling me from *The Arizona Republic.* I'd introduced her to the Krone case. She had just arrived at work and seen the story.

"No kidding?" I said attentively. After listening to the details, I immediately called Chris Plourd.

"Guess what?" I asked.

"You've found Sugar and Hot Lips."

I ignored his little jest. "No, no, they've reversed Ray's conviction!"

"No kidding!"

Indeed they had. The Arizona Supreme Court unanimously agreed:

> The bite marks...were critical...Without them, there likely would be no jury-submissible case against Krone...We reverse the conviction and remand for a new trial where Krone will have the opportunity to meet the full force of the videotape.

The conviction was overturned on the late-discovery issue. As predicted, the court could not agree on the hearsay issue:

> The resolution of one [issue] disposes of this appeal [and] makes it unnecessary for us to address the admissibility of Ancona's statement that "Ray" was going to help her close the bar.

However, chief justice Feldman, in a concurring opinion, offered guidance to the trial court:

> We cannot make any final decision on the admissibility of the statement at retrial. For instance, we do not know whether the statement will be needed and really be offered for its undoubtedly permissible use—to prove Ancona's state of mind—or for its potentially impermissible use—to prove Ancona's expectation of Ray's conduct. We raise the question

and leave it to the trial judge to decide on the complete record available at retrial.

Upon hearing the news, Chris Plourd offered some hearsay of his own. Apparently the attorney general's office was furious with the county attorney's office for challenging the Rule 32 and with Judge Jeffrey Hotham for dismissing it. At the time the supreme court was considering Ray Krone's appeal, Plourd's special action was also placed before the court. It detailed the Krone case evidence, which, except for the bite mark and hearsay, favored Ray Krone. One never knows what judges consider in rendering their opinion, but chances are that the special action had some influence. The AG's office didn't like to lose appeals.

Maricopa County Attorney Rick Romley didn't like to lose either. Acquittals of individuals prosecuted by his office were not good for his political career. The same was true of convictions overturned on appeal. It was reported that Romley was equally furious.

π

Ray Krone once again was innocent until proven guilty. He was anxious for a speedy trial.

For the three prior months, Plourd had been working fast and furiously on the Krone evidence, preparing for the Rule 32 hearing. The supreme court's decision rendered it moot. Plourd could be ready for trial in short order. However, it would be eight months before Ray Krone's second trial would begin. DNA proved to be the bottleneck. The experts chosen to analyze and report on the serologic evidence were busy working on another case of some notoriety, *California v. OJ Simpson*.

CHAPTER 8
DISCOVERY

Chris Plourd was anxious. We were in Tom's Tavern again, after a morning hearing before the Honorable James E. McDougall, who had been assigned to the Krone case. Before trial, numerous motions are presented to the court by both sides. The judge then determines which evidence, experts and witnesses the jury will see and hear. But at lunch this mid-summer day, Plourd had something else on his mind. His pager was on the table. A criminologist from Ed Blake's lab would have the results of the Krone serologic evidence they had received sometime in May. Today Chris Plourd would know just where his client fit into the crime scene DNA.

His pager went off, his lunch unfinished. The next moment he was in the phone booth with a yellow note pad.

Deoxyribonucleic acid, DNA, is the stuff of life, the genetic blueprint for all organisms on this planet that reproduce. Bacteria and everything on up the evolutionary ladder have it. It's a huge molecule as molecules go, structured like a spiral ladder. The side rails are made up of nucleotides—compounds of a phosphate and deoxyribose, a substance similar to table sugar. The rungs are made up of pairs of four nitrogen-based compounds called adenine, cytosine, guanine and thymine. Because adenine always pairs with guanine, and cytosine with thymine, DNA makes exact copies of itself. It reproduces. First it splits apart down the middle of each rung. Then, with the help of enzymes, each side grabs free-floating nucleotides and associated nitrogen bases and rebuilds itself rung by rung into two identical DNA molecules. Those two become four, then eight and so on.

Imbedded in the DNA molecule are pairs of chromosomes, one from mom and one from dad. Human DNA contains twenty-three chromosomes, of which twenty-two are identical pairs called autosomes. The twenty-third pair contains the sex chromosomes X and Y—two Xs for females and an X and a Y for males. Paired chromosomes are further divided into genes. Each gene is the paired combination of traits, called alleles, inherited from the parents. The combination of allele pairs of a particular gene determines a specific trait, such as eye color. Some alleles dominate their pair. A dominant brown-eye allele paired with a recessive blue-eye allele yields brown eyes. It takes two pared blue-eye alleles to yield blue eyes. That's why blue-eyed people are rarer that brown-eyed people.

It's possible for two brown-eyed parents to yield blue-eyed offspring, provided that each parent has a recessive blue-eyed allele. Since one must have only blue-eyed alleles to be blue-eyed, it is not possible for two blue-eyed parents to have brown-eyed children. If this does happen, momma's in trouble! A common use of DNA technology is to determine paternity.

The relative number of people with a particular eye color in a particular group is known as its population frequency. For example, the population frequency of blue-eyed people among Scandinavians is greater than among Italians; that is, there are more blue-eyed Scandinavians than blue-eyed Italians. DNA analysis goes a little deeper. Brown-eyed people can have two brown alleles or one brown and one blue, with frequencies for each. And, of course, more than two eye colors are possible.

The essence of DNA analysis is this—the number of people with specific traits diminishes as the number of traits increases. Traits with low population frequencies further reduce the number of possible candidates. That's why there are so few blond, blue-eyed, left-handed persons with a pair of X chromosomes.

Scientists are able to chemically look inside some specific genes and determine the specific allele pair (trait) for each. For example, hanging out on the short end of chromosome six is the genetic marker DQα. There are six possible alleles for this genetic marker—1.1, 1.2, 1.3, 2, 3, 4. (Why they're not numbered 1 through 6, I don't know.) Kimberly Ancona inherited a 3 and a 4 allele. So she had DQα type [3,4]. Ray Krone is DQα[3,3]. There are twenty-one possible DQα types, each with its own population frequency—[1.1,1.1], [1.1,1.2], [1.1,1.3], etc. For a genetic marker with n alleles, the formula for the number of possible types is $n(n+1)/2$.

For the first trial, only this marker, DQα, was typed. The swab from the area of the bite mark was determined to be consistent with Ancona. But it was argued that Ray Krone could not be excluded if the sample were a mixture from Ancona and Krone. A mixture of DQα[3,3] and DQα[3,4], when tested, would yield type DQα[3,4], since only alleles 3 and 4 would be in the soup. The argument was that Ancona's DNA was masking Krone's DNA.

Ed Blake's lab typed DQα and five other markers by a method called polymerase chain reaction (PCR). Polymerase is an enzyme. For some samples, a seventh marker, D1S80, was typed by another method called electrophoresis.

An explanation of how PCR and electrophoresis work would take far longer than it took Plourd to return from the phone booth and is a known cure for insomnia. Let's stay awake for the rest of this story.

While it's mathematically possible that your DNA and mine are the same, suffice it to say that, to an extremely, extremely high probability, they are different. That's why I'm ruggedly good looking with hazel eyes and brown hair and you're...Well, I don't know what you are, but I do know that a scientist can take a sample of your DNA and of mine and compare them with samples taken from the Ancona murder crime scene and tell with certainty that you and I were not there—unless, of course, you are the actual...

Anyway, determining exclusion is straightforward enough. If just one marker type of a particular person is not present in a sample, that person is positively excluded as a contributing donor to that sample.

Plourd returned wearing a jubilant smile. "He's excluded!"

There were fifteen results from the crime scene samples to check against Ray Krone's DNA typings. Most were swabs taken from the victim's body—rectum, vagina, mouth, cheek and the area of the throat that had bite marks. There were also results from Ancona's sanitary pad, tank top and bra.

Plourd had made a few preliminary determinations while on the phone. While eating his lunch he continued down the sample typings listed on his yellow pad. He stopped on the next to last sample.

"Hmm...I can't get an exclusion on this one," he said, a bit perplexed. "I'll have to talk to Blake. Levy's going to be all over this!" Noel Levy was the prosecutor on the case.

Receipt of DNA results is always an anxious time for defense attorneys. While most clients profess innocence, DNA results say otherwise for many. This is the time the defense strategy takes shape for a case with DNA. Exclusion is simple, the client was not at the crime scene—end of story. But for non-exclusion, the defense attorney is challenged to come up with a plausible explanation favorable to his client. If the defendant is innocent, the task is not too difficult. If not...

I recalled the far-fetched explanation concocted by the OJ Simpson defense team to explain the abundance of their client's blood at the crime scene. "The police planted it." This had worked for OJ.

Plourd's client was innocent and, no doubt, he would be able to come up with a much better—and most likely accurate—explanation.

He didn't seem too concerned as we traversed Pioneer Plaza on our way back to the court building. He was less concerned about what Dr. Blake would say of the bra DNA results than about what Levy would do with it.

CHAPTER 9
BLOODY TOOTH MARKS AND THE SCRATCH

Kim Ancona's bra was found under her body soaked with blood, along with the tank top and blouse she had been wearing before her death. All three garments were cut up the middle in the front. They were most certainly removed as Ancona lay dead or dying on the men's restroom floor, because the tank top and blouse each had a slit in the back that corresponded to the single stab wound that had killed her.

Now that Ray Krone could not be eliminated as a possible donor of a DNA sample taken from the bra, the bra ended up in Dr. Raymond Rawson's hands. At prosecutor Levy's suggestion, Dr. Rawson looked at the bloody bra to see if he could find any evidence of Ray Krone's presence. Indeed he could.

"[T]he [blood] stains," he said, "are clear examples of tooth marks…[that] can be correlated to the bite injuries on the left breast of Kimberly Ancona, which were caused by Ray Krone…It is likely that one of [the outer garments] was covering the brassiere at the time of the bite…the bloody tooth marks should be tested to determine if the blood is Kim Ancona's."

It seemed that Rawson was now claiming that Ray Krone had a mouth full of Kim Ancona's blood before biting her. He never did explain how such a detailed bite mark as the one found on Kim Ancona's left breast could have been inflicted through not one, but two articles of clothing.

At the taped interview that followed this latest revelation, Plourd hammered away at Rawson's latest opinion. During the interview, Rawson went so far as to annotate a photo noting which particular Krone tooth was responsible for each of several of the bloody marks on the bra. Interestingly, the photo did not even contain an ABFO ruler. A photo taken without a ruler next to the bite mark is, by ABFO standards, of no evidentiary value because the scale is unknown. Apparently, a bite mark on a garment is held to a standard different from that of a bite mark on flesh—at least for Dr. Raymond Rawson.

Plourd enlisted the services of Bart Epstein, a nationally renowned blood spatter expert. Epstein wet his teeth with his own blood and bit an identical bra. The resulting pattern looked nothing like any of the patterns on Ancona's bra. Then he demonstrated how similar patterns could be created by dropping a similar bra into a pool of blood and then subsequently folding it and placing it in a plastic bag, much like what happened to Ancona's bra.

The patterns on Ancona's bra were not unlike patterns found on tie-dyed shirts. One marvels at what the ramifications might have been—inspired by Dr. Rawson's unique vision—had Kim Ancona been wearing a tie-dyed blouse.

π

Rawson seemed to be at the forefront of technology. Several months before the trial he had issued a quite impressive thirty-five page forensic report of his analysis of the bite marks. It was prepared using state of the art software that included the ability to insert color photographs, charts and diagrams into the text. Many of the ninety plus figures were annotated with tooth numbers. These figures were of three types: those of the bite marks found on Kim Ancona's left breast and neck, those of Ray Krone's dentition and those comparing dentition with bite mark.

The photos containing bite marks were taken at autopsy. A cast of the left breast made at autopsy was also pictured. Dentition photos included an actual photo of Ray's upper teeth, many photos of his dental model, his bite impression in Styrofoam and clay and outline diagrams of his teeth pattern. Some comparison photos showed the teeth pattern overlaid upon photos of the bite mark, others linked several photos together with impressive computer generated lines and arrows explained by the accompanying text. Three photos taken at autopsy showed the dental model resting upon then being rotated about the actual bite mark.

In the introduction to his report Dr Rawson stated, "There is sufficient detail in the marks to identify…Ray Krone as…causing the marks…to a high degree of confidence that no other individual caused the bite marks." His conclusion reiterated the same. In between he supported his analysis using several technical methods: split screen verification, scanning electron microscopy and computer axial tomography (CAT) scanning.

Commenting on the report, Rawson stated that he reached his opinion according to the guidelines recommended by the ABFO and then used these technical methods, presented on videotape, merely "to demonstrate the match."

Plourd focused on CAT scanning technique. In medicine this procedure is used to take a series of radiographs through successive planes. It produces a three-dimensional view of a tumor, for example, giving the physician an accurate view of its size and position. Rawson took CAT scans of the dental model producing transparent overlays that represented teeth patterns at various bite depths.

Plourd used the fact that Rawson was the only bite mark expert to use the technique to file a motion for a *Frye* hearing. He asked the court to preclude Rawson from presenting his unique CAT scanning technique at trial because it was not a commonly used method of evaluating bite marks.

Dr. Rawson appeared first at the hearing, scheduled to last a full day. On the stand all morning he was grilled by Plourd in detail about his CAT scanning method. Rawson had developed a device to hold the dental model while it was being scanned. Plourd asked if there were any standards for its construction? Any protocols for its use?

"No. That is my method," was the answer.

The holder had a set of adjustment screws. Rawson acknowledged that mounting a dental model in the holder was "subjective in the sense that [the models] can be moved in different directions."

Hence, Plourd argued, the resulting images would vary depending upon the person doing the CAT scan.

Dr. Campbell had flown in that morning from Albuquerque to testify in the afternoon session in opposition to the validity of CAT scanning used for bite mark analysis. Plourd discussed the morning's testimony with Dr. Campbell over lunch.

"It's really hokey, what Rawson's doing," he concluded. "I want the jury to see this. But I think McDougall just might grant the *Frye* motion."

Plourd surprised both Judge McDougall and prosecutor Levy by beginning—and ending—the afternoon session by withdrawing his *Frye* motion. Dr. Campbell was able to catch an early afternoon flight back to Albuquerque.

The truth is, Chris Plourd was not concerned at all about Rawson's CAT scanning. The *Frye* hearing was a ruse to pin Rawson down on "the scratch" without spilling the beans to Levy. In his forensic report Rawson still claimed to see two bite marks on Kim Ancona's left breast, one in the twelve o'clock position, the other in the ten o'clock. In the arch of the ten o'clock bite Rawson noted a "scratch that is typical of a cusp tip drag mark with the class characteristics of a cuspid [a canine tooth]." On Ray Krone's dental model he further noted that "tooth number eleven [the upper left canine] has a tiny facet that sharpens the cusp tip" and then concluded that "the scratch has individual characteristics of Ray Krone's tooth number eleven."

Looking at photographs of the bite mark, Plourd had noticed early on that in some photos "the scratch" was clearly evident, while in others "the scratch" was not there. He scrutinized each and every bite mark photo. There were more than a hundred of them. Only photos taken at autopsy contained "the scratch." Those taken at the crime scene did not. Plourd had the smoking gun he needed to challenge credibility. The state's star witness, bite mark expert Dr. Raymond Rawson, had identified a scratch made at autopsy as having been made by suspect Ray Krone.

During the *Frye* hearing, Plourd subtly maneuvered Rawson, under oath and on the record, into circling "the scratch" and annotating it "11." Prosecutor Levy didn't have a clue. Plourd was ready for Rawson. He would wait for an opportune time during trial to spring "the scratch" on Levy.

CHAPTER 10
THE PERFECT WITNESS

"**N**inety per cent of trial work is investigation and preparation," said Chris Plourd. It wasn't only the DNA and the bite mark for which he prepared. Plourd was very thorough about every aspect of the case. He spent hours poring over forensic reports, pretrial motions, witness interviews and trial transcripts. He put page numbers and a table of contents on the nearly four hundred pages of police reports for quick and easy reference. He lived in the evidence room until he had scrutinized each and every piece of evidence. He made copies of every photo in evidence and obtained a copy of those photos in police custody that didn't make it into evidence.

One tool of the trade is a portable photo stand. Lights and a camera are mounted on a poll attached to the base. With the lights lighting an item of evidence placed on the base, the camera, adjusted vertically, takes its picture. One such item was Ancona's phone book, opened to the "R" page. She alphabetized by first names. On this page was Ray Krone's name and phone number. On the opposite page was another "Ray," listed with no last name and no phone number but with an address, though not Ray Krone's.

The Friday night before the murder, Ray Krone was in the bar celebrating a friend's birthday. Kim Ancona was also there as a patron. She did not work that night but was scheduled for the next night. Hank Arredondo, the bar owner, and Denise Newman, an employee waiting tables that Friday night, saw Ancona sitting with an individual they both described as a dark-haired white male, five feet, eleven inches, one hundred and sixty pounds, with a noticeable cut above his right eye and wearing dark-rimmed glasses with thick lenses. Arredondo did not know this person's name, but Denise Newman did. It was "Ray." This "Ray" had no facial hair. Ray Krone was sporting a full beard at the time.

How did the notion arise that Ray Krone and Kim Ancona were "dating"? They were both in the CBS Lounge that Friday night and, except for a polite hello, Ray spent the evening with his friends, while Ancona spent her time at a separate table drinking and conversing with this other "Ray." Was this the "Ray" Kim Ancona was heard to say might come by to help her close up? According to Kate Koester, Ancona did not use a last name when she talked about "Ray." Koester indicated that she had no knowledge of this other "Ray." But Koester did know Ray Krone. Perhaps she assumed...?

Why was Ray Krone's number in Ancona's phone book anyway? He hadn't given it to her. It was possible that Ancona wrote Ray's number in her book when Trish called to tell her about Ray's lasagna party and suggested that she give Ray a call. Ray had invited Trish, but she declined, telling Ray that Kim might be interested in coming to his party. Ray did not call and invite Ancona.

Armed with "Ray" from Newman and "Krone" from Koester, the detective began his investigation with the "Ray Krone" found in Ancona's phone book. Even though the description did not match, the detective ended his investigation with Ray Krone, whom he found at home about to leave for a darts award luncheon at the Black Bull Bar & Grill. One look at Ray's teeth most likely convinced the detective that he had found the murderer of Kim Ancona. Other detectives investigated other suspects, but the lead detective seemed to ignore them.

"Are you going to investigate this other 'Ray'?" I asked Chris Plourd.

"Absolutely." But he never got around to it. He needed just one viable candidate to present to the jury as the actual murderer of Kim Ancona, and one was emerging with close ties to the murder scene.

In investigating Tennessee Mike, Plourd had found several items of evidence that were either misrepresented or not presented at the first trial. These items were destined for the second trial, because they favored his client.

At the first trial, Phoenix police criminologist Scott Piette had testified that the pubic hairs found on Ancona's abdomen were "similar" to those of Ray Krone. Soon after the supreme court reversed Ray Krone's conviction, prosecutor Levy sent the pubic hairs to the FBI crime lab for a more complete analysis, perhaps hoping that "similar" would become "match." The hair samples didn't have enough hair follicles, which are necessary for DNA typing. But the FBI lab was able to determine that the pubic hairs were "Mongoloid," consistent with having come from an American Indian. Tennessee Mike was one. Ray Krone wasn't.

At the first trial, testimony involving the footprints found at the crime scene had limited them to the kitchen area. They were presented to have been made earlier in the evening and were argued to have been unrelated to the crime. But in reality these footprints were all over the crime scene. Photographs verified that they were found not only in the kitchen near the knife rack that was missing the murder weapon, but also in the bar area on the tiled entryway to the kitchen. And, most importantly, these same footprints were found on the restroom floor surrounding the victim.

It was difficult to dispute that these footprints were in fact related to the crime. One of the last closing procedures was to mop the floors in the bar area and the restrooms. The cook, David Torres, left a bucket of clean soapy water just inside the kitchen door for this purpose. Ancona had done her job. The bucket was found the next morning filled with dirty water. If the restroom floor had not been mopped, one would expect a high traffic area like a restroom to be loaded with footprints. Yet the only prints found were made by a single pair of Converse brand tennis shoes. Tennessee Mike wore Converse shoes. Ray Krone wore MacGregors.

The pair of Levi pants worn by Kim Ancona the night of the murder was one of the items in evidence. In the back pocket Plourd found a business card along with two one-dollar bills. This evidence was overlooked by the investigating detectives. Robbery had not been considered to be an element of the crime. But what happened to Ancona's money? Presumably she would at least have had some tip money on her—hopefully more than two bucks for a night's work.

The business card belonged to a woman named Kathy. She had not been contacted for the first trial. When contacted this time, Kathy stated that she was Ancona's next-door neighbor and had come into the bar near closing time to buy cigarettes. Kathy gave her business card to Ancona, with her home phone number written on the back. She expected Ancona to call her later that night. This fact contradicted Koester's "understanding" that Ancona expected to spend the night with "Ray," whom she assumed to be "Krone." Ancona did not mention to Kathy that she planned to have a date with anyone, let alone Ray Krone. Others testified that Ancona had party plans for that night. One was her best friend Beth. Beth waited with Tennessee Mike at Mike's place for Ancona's call. Tennessee Mike was also a neighbor. He lived directly across the street from Ancona and Clark. Beth and Tennessee Mike had been at the CBS Lounge most of the evening and were the last to leave the bar. They proceeded to Tennessee Mike's house to wait for Ancona. There they drank some and finished the methamphetamine (speed) that they'd acquired earlier that night at the bar, possibly from Ancona. At the autopsy it was determined that Ancona was on speed at the time of her death.

Before long Tennessee Mike became a bit randy and attempted to forcibly spirit Beth into the bedroom. Beth became extremely upset and demanded to be taken home. Mike took her. The quickest route was down West Camelback Road, passing the CBS Lounge. Tennessee Mike—then a loaded pistol high on speed—would have been returning from Beth's place about the time Kim Ancona was murdered. As he passed by the CBS Lounge, did he observe that Ancona's car was still in the parking lot and decide to check up on her? Was he the one Dale Henson had seen enter the CBS Lounge early that morning and then exit a short time later?

Dale Henson worked for Techniques Hydro System. This company had the contract to clean the sidewalks of the strip mall where the CBS Lounge was located. The sidewalks were cleaned once a month with a high-pressure water system. This system generated four thousand pounds of nozzle pressure of hot water. Because of the associated danger to the public, sidewalk cleaning was done at night. First, a garden hose was connected between a water source and special equipment on a truck. This equipment heated the water and increased the water pressure. A high-pressure hose was then unreeled from the truck and laid out along the section of sidewalk to be cleaned. When the water was hot enough, cleaning could begin. Hosing down the sidewalk required two passes. The first was made along the inner half of the twelve-foot-wide sidewalk. Then whoever was operating the equipment would return to the starting point and make a second pass along the outer half, hosing the debris into the parking lot. Because the length of the hose was limited, the process was repeated in sections.

Henson was on the job the night of the murder. At 11:00 p.m., he began cleaning the corner of the sidewalk furthest from the CBS Lounge. By 2:30 a.m., Henson was halfway through the first pass of the last section to be done. He was directly in front of the CBS Lounge and facing the parking lot. He observed a vehicle described as a foreign-made compact sedan, medium-green in color, enter the lot and park about sixty feet away from where he was standing. A person exited the vehicle and headed directly toward Henson. Walking across the freshly cleaned sidewalk, this person passed within eight feet of Henson—so close, in fact, that it was necessary for Henson to divert the stream of water from hitting him. The person then disappeared into the CBS Lounge with shoes wet from the freshly cleaned sidewalk—ready to leave prints on the freshly mopped floor inside. A half-hour or so later, Henson was making his second pass in front of the CBS Lounge when the same individual reappeared from behind him and returned to the car. Henson watched as the car exited the parking lot and turned onto Camelback.

Dale Henson gave a good description to the investigating detective—a male of medium build, approximately five feet, ten inches tall with shoulder-length hair and no facial hair. At a photo lineup presented two days after the murder, Henson failed to single out any of the six photos with certainty. He could not tell that the person pictured in photo number four was of slender build and six feet, two inches tall. He did notice the shoulder-length hair tied in a pony tail. But it was the full beard that made Henson absolutely sure that this person was *not* the individual whom he saw enter the CBS Lounge. Number four was Ray Krone. Tennessee Mike was five feet, nine inches.

Dale Henson was sure of one other thing. The man who entered the CBS Lounge was wearing a "fatigue green military-style field jacket, an Army coat." When shown the jacket found in Ray Krone's closet, Henson was sure that it was not the same one. He described Krone's coat as "a lime green ski parka." How could Henson be so sure about the jacket he'd seen? Because he owned one just like it, a gift from his older brother, who was in the Army. Tennessee Mike owned one too, but his picture was not in the photo lineup.

All this discovery cast great suspicion upon Tennessee Mike. But there was more. Another acquaintance of Kim Ancona, a woman named Teri, was also a patron of the CBS Lounge the night of the murder. She too had made plans with Ancona to party later that night. But more interestingly, she dated Tennessee Mike a few times around the time of the murder. She stopped seeing him because she said he liked to bite.

Dale Henson had not been called to testify at the first trial.

Plourd enlisted Mike Pain to locate prospective witnesses and to do the preliminary interviews. The last name on Plourd's list was "Dale Henson." His mention in the police reports was innocuous at best. Since he hadn't appeared at the first trial, it seemed unlikely that he would have much to offer.

Mike Pain located Henson just two weeks before the second trial was to start.

Chris Plourd grinned noticeably as he read through the typed transcription of Mike Pain's taped interview. Then he looked at his calendar.

"Tell Henson he'll be subpoenaed to testify," he told Mike Pain.

"See that Levy gets a copy of these," he added, putting his copies of the Henson tape and transcript into his briefcase.

Discovery works both ways, with one difference. Defense attorneys must disclose only evidence they intend to introduce at trial. There is no legal obligation for the defense to disclose incriminating evidence. Prosecutors, on the other hand, are obligated by law to disclose *all* known evidence to the defense, including and especially exculpatory evidence. Burying the Henson interview deep within the stack of police reports given to Ray Krone's attorney qualified as disclosure. But defense attorney Geoffrey Jones must not have made it to the bottom of the stack, because he did not contact Henson for the first trial.

I asked Chris, "Aren't you going to talk with Henson?"

As the trial approached, I spent more and more time tagging along with Chris as he prepared his case. I observed him spend many hours with his forensic experts and lay witnesses. At formal depositions, taped interviews, court hearings, he would pin down his witnesses as well as the state's witnesses on key points. "I want to know what to expect from each witness. I don't want them going sideways on me at trial," he would say. I'd observed Chris meet with every prospective witness at least once. But Pain's interview was enough. Chris did not meet Henson until the day he testified.

Levy didn't interview Henson either. But the Phoenix police department did. Henson was called in to take a Polygraph Test— several times.

"It's not necessary," Chris answered. "Henson doesn't know any of the players—not Ray, not Ancona, nor anyone else from the CBS [Lounge]. He lives in another part of town far from the CBS—never been inside. He's just an average guy who happened to be there late that night doing his job when he saw something. And he's sure about what he saw. He's the perfect witness."

One element of Henson's story remained a mystery, however. Tennessee Mike drove a blue Toyota pickup. The color of the vehicle used by the murderer appeared green to Henson. Blue could be mistaken for green, as the vehicle was some distance away and illuminated by a yellowish light. Yellow mixed with blue yields green. But there is a substantial difference between a pickup and "a foreign-made compact sedan." Efforts were made to discover who drove such a vehicle. But it was neither Ray Krone's nor his roommate's nor Tennessee Mike's nor his roommate's nor Beth's nor Paul Clark's nor Kim Ancona's nor Trish's nor Lu's.

Such a car and whoever owned it could not be found. Was Henson mistaken about the vehicle the murderer drove to the CBS Lounge?

CHAPTER 11
RELATIVE TRUTH

"The verdict's in," said Chris Plourd after my "Hello."

"That was quick," I said, noting that the jury had deliberated an unusually short time after a very long trial.

"It's got to be an acquittal."

"How can it be? OJ's blood was all over the crime scene."

π

Richmond is one of many cities that surround the San Francisco Bay. On several occasions I drove from my home at Lake Tahoe to Oakland to pick up Chris and accompany him to Ed Blake's lab in Richmond, some thirty minutes north of the airport.

Dr. Blake had been provided with forty-three items of evidence from the Krone case. While it was fairly straightforward to do the laboratory analysis, it was time-consuming to correlate the results in a detailed report. At the time, Blake and his entire staff were tied up with another case, *California v. OJ Simpson*. No doubt, they had a few more than forty-three items of evidence to analyze and the Simpson case commanded a bit more attention than did the Krone case. For strategy planning purposes, however, Chris did not want to wait for Dr. Blake's report, which, as it turned out, would take five months to complete. He especially wanted to know Blake's position on the bra sample, the results of which included Ray Krone as a possible donor.

The start of Ray's trial was twice delayed awaiting the report. On one occasion, attempting to speed up the process, I asked a serologist working at Blake's lab what was taking so long. "Can't you find any of OJ's blood?" His response was a wry smile.

While waiting for Dr. Blake's report, Chris became quite familiar with the Simpson case. He appeared several times on "Court TV" as an expert commentator, clarifying the DNA testimony for its audience.

Being somewhat privy to the inside scoop on the Simpson DNA evidence, I reminded Chris that the crime scene reeked with OJ's blood. Understanding the dynamics of the case and drawing from experience, he dismissed this fact as inconsequential in relation to the verdict. He predicted that a short deliberation favored acquittal. He was right and, unlike myself and most Americans who followed the case on TV, was not surprised by the verdict.

"In this business the truth is relative," he said. It took me a while to understand how that explained the acquittal of OJ Simpson...and other verdicts that went against the evidence.

π

"The verdict's in!" This time Chris Plourd made no prediction.

It was Friday, April 12, 1996. The jury had heard the final arguments of the eight-week trial three days before.

Chris waited for the verdict in a room he'd taken near the courthouse. For the trial, he had camped in an RV borrowed from his brother, parked in the driveway of Bob Lewis's house. I stayed at Bob's. Bob was and still is a good friend of Ray's. He had been at the birthday party with Ray and other friends the night before the murder. Bob stayed in touch with Ray, visiting him frequently at the county jail in Phoenix and then at the state prison in Florence.

"I'm on my way." I hung up the phone in Bob's guest room.

Once again and for the last time I was in my car driving the three miles to the county courthouse. On the way Bob Dylan—courtesy of the cassette in the tape player—began singing:

> *Here comes the story of the Hurricane,*
> *The man the authorities came to blame*
> *For somethin' that he never done.*
> *Put in a prison cell, but one time he could-a been*
> *The champion of the World.*

π

Some twenty years earlier, Dylan's ballad "Hurricane" introduced me to the story of Rubin Carter. Before being convicted of a triple murder that occurred in Paterson, New Jersey, "Hurricane" Carter had been the number-one contender for the middleweight boxing crown.

One night in 1966, two black men entered the Lafayette Café and began shooting up the place. Two men were dead at the scene. A third, badly wounded, said he could identify his assailant.

Alfred Bello and Arthur Dexter Bradley, both white, were apprehended at the scene. They told the police that they had entered the café after the shooting and were "just robbing the register." They described the getaway car.

Shortly after the shootings, Carter's car was stopped on another side of town by policemen who thought it resembled the getaway car. Driving Carter's car was John Artis, whom Carter had just met. They lived near each other, so Carter had offered to give Artis a ride home.

Both were taken to the crime scene to see if anyone could identify them as the gunmen. No one could, including Bello and Bradley. Then they were taken to the wounded man's hospital room. The dying man told the detectives that it was neither Carter nor Artis who shot him. Both were released.

Several months later, Carter was arrested and charged with the triple murder. Artis, also arrested and charged, was offered a plea bargain—a lesser sentence—if he would finger Carter as the gunman. He refused. Both were subsequently convicted upon the eyewitness testimony of Bello and Bradley. Each received life imprisonment.

Sometime after the trial, Bello, now a felon serving time for robbery, recanted his story. So did Bradley. Carter was granted a second trial. But Bello and Bradley went back to their original story. Carter and Artis were convicted a second time, again upon the testimony of these two drunkards from the slums.

In 1981 John Artis was released, after serving fifteen years. Rubin Carter remained in prison.

Some years later, based upon new evidence that suggested the time of the 9-1-1 call reporting the crime had been altered, Carter was finally released. This new evidence supported the fact that the actual time of the shooting occurred while Carter was verifiably with friends.

Rubin Carter spent twenty years in prison.

π

As I drove to the courthouse, I thought how lucky Ray was compared to Rubin Carter. Forensics had been no help to Carter. The murder weapon was never found, so there was no ballistic or fingerprint evidence to consider. DNA testing was nonexistent at the time, but the gunmen were in and out of the café so quickly that they didn't leave any. The victim who exonerated Carter had died.

Ray Krone had Dale Henson and much more going for him. I went over everything in my mind.

π

Trish testified that she had managed the CBS Lounge for two years. In that time she never closed the bar alone and stated that it would be unusual for someone to do so. She remembered that Ray and his friends began frequenting the CBS Lounge about six weeks before the murder. Mostly they played and practiced darts, preparing for matches in the dart league. Kim Ancona managed the CBS Lounge dart team. Because Ray was a very good dart player, perhaps the best in the league, Kim asked him to substitute on her team whenever there was a cancellation. Trish stated that Kim seemed to have an interest in Ray.

Ray called Trish at the bar one time to invite her to a lasagna dinner party. She declined but called Kim, mentioned the party, gave her Ray's phone number and suggested that she "give him a call."

Trish detailed the Wednesday night party that had started at the CBS Lounge and ended up at her apartment by way of the Library Lounge. It was Christmas night. Ray, with some friends, came into the CBS Lounge to play darts. Kim was bartending. Except for Ray's group and two or three others, the bar was dead that night. Trish decided to close early and invited everyone to meet at another bar, the Library Lounge. Ray showed up with his friends. Kim, Trish and Lu arrived in Lu's pickup truck. When that bar closed, Trish invited everyone to continue the party at her apartment. That's when Ray was casually paired with Kim. Because it was after 1:00 a.m. and liquor sales were prohibited, Ray made a quick stop at his house for some beer before he and Kim arrived at Trish's place. There they sat on the floor next to a caged iguana drinking a beer or two while conversing. Trish said that she observed them "kissing and hugging" a few times. After an hour or so they left together.

Trish told how she had been fired after her shift the next night. Furious with the owner, Hank Arredondo, she stayed up most of those early morning hours phoning employees, including Ancona, asking them to quit in support of her. No one did. Perhaps in frustration, she and Lu decided to get out of town for the weekend. She said they left the next day, the Friday of the weekend Ancona died, and headed for Indian Wells, a small outpost on the Navajo Indian reservation in the northeast corner of Arizona. There, she said, they visited Lu's relatives. A police report noted that Lu's mother, Minnie, had confirmed the one night visit from her daughter, who was traveling with "an Anglo female."

Upon returning to Phoenix on Sunday and learning of Kim's murder from a note left by a neighbor, Trish went to the CBS Lounge. There she gave her statement to a detective, including her account of the Christmas party.

Except for the impromptu Christmas party, no other testimony was offered to establish that Ray Krone was ever out or alone with Kim Ancona. But the detective construed this encounter—Ray driving Kim to and from a party—as a "date." In his testimony the detective stated that he believed Ray to be lying when Ray denied having ever dated Kim. The detective also testified that, from the preliminary evaluation of the bite mark made at the crime scene, it was determined that the biter had "uneven" teeth. He stated that when talking to Ray he observed uneven teeth and felt that Ray was "distancing" himself from the crime by "lying" that he ever dated the victim.

The detective seemed to have made the mistake of relying on the initial misinterpretation of the bite mark (to be clarified by upcoming defense experts) and reading too much into Trish's statement.

Kate Koester testified that she had worked the afternoon shift the Saturday of the murder. Kim relieved her at 6:00 p.m. Kate stayed at the CBS until about 8:00 p.m., chatting with Kim. Kim was the only one working after 9:00 p.m., when the cook, David Torres, left. According to Koester, she asked Kim if she needed help closing. She said that Kim said she didn't because she expected "Ray to help her close" and expected "to spend the night with Ray."

Koester's testimony was neutralized when she acknowledged under cross-examination that Kim mentioned only a "Ray" and not specifically "Ray Krone." Further, a number of witnesses who were in the bar at closing time stated that they expected to see Kim after she closed the bar. A few said they offered to help close, but Kim insisted she didn't need help and ushered them out.

The state offered no eyewitnesses who saw Ray Krone in the bar that night. Other than Koester, no one heard Kim say anything about "Ray" helping her close or about spending the night with anyone.

Kim's next-door neighbor, Kathy, testified that she came into the bar near closing time to buy cigarettes. She said that she talked with Kim briefly about getting together later, at home after work. She wrote her home phone number on the back of a business card for Kim. Then she returned home and waited for Kim's call. The business card, along with two one-dollar bills—still in the back pocket of Kim's pants— were shown to the jury when the pants were entered into evidence.

Also waiting for Kim that night, in the house directly across the street from Kathy's place, were Beth and Tennessee Mike.

π

With Dale Henson waiting in the wings to testify for the defense about the person he saw enter the CBS Lounge and with several items of evidence pointing to Tennessee Mike, Levy, perhaps to lessen their effect, called Tennessee to the stand as a witness for the prosecution.

Mike remembered the night of December 28, 1991. He had a date with Beth. She had been out with Kim most of the afternoon. The two women returned to Kim's house about 5:00 p.m. Kim got ready for work. Beth walked across the street to Mike's house. They first went to the Caravan for a few drinks, then to the CBS Lounge, arriving about 8:00 p.m. Mike preferred the Caravan, but Beth wanted to go to the CBS because Kim was working that night.

Most of the evening Mike drank and shot darts with his friends, while Beth kept Kim company. He said he did not socialize with Kim at all that night other than when she served him twenty or so Bud Lights—by his count. At 1:15 a.m. bar time, somewhat ahead of actual time, Kim dimmed then turned up the house lights, the usual signal that the bar was closing. Mike, Beth and a few others were the last group to be ushered out. The two drove back to Mike's place. He did not remember the vehicle he was driving that night but said it was either his blue Toyota pickup or a vehicle from work he described as a white Ford van.

He admitted that after drinking a few more beers he carried Beth into his bedroom with the intention of having sex. He said that Beth wasn't in the mood and asked to be taken home. Mike obliged, denying that there had been any serious altercation. Coincidentally, they both lived on West Oregon Avenue, he on the corner of North 21st Avenue, she two miles east. Since Oregon is not a through street, Mike said he first drove south and turned onto Colter Avenue, which runs parallel to Oregon, then drove east on Colter and turned north onto 7th Street toward Beth's place.

Tennessee Mike said he returned by the same route. He denied returning on Camelback, four blocks south of and parallel to Colter.

Mike said he couldn't sleep the rest of the night. He said he was wired, admitted he had taken speed while at the CBS Lounge and again at home. He watched TV until his roommate awoke. They heard Paul Clark's revving engine as he left in a big hurry that morning. A little while later the roommate took Clark's phone call. "Some asshole just killed Kimmie!" was the message. Mike stayed home while his roommate went to the CBS Lounge to investigate. After the roommate returned, Mike went over to Beth's place and told her the news. Later in the day, they were both interviewed there by a Phoenix detective.

Mike's favorite tennis shoe since he was a kid was Converse, but he denied that he ever wore the style of shoe that had the logo "CONS" on its sole. He did not remember whether he still owned a pair of Converse tennis shoes at the time of the murder, but said he would have been wearing either tennis shoes or hiking boots that night. He denied throwing away any tennis shoes after the murder. He acknowledged that he never wore a beard because he was not able to grow one. He insisted that he'd had his moustache since leaving the service in 1981. In the service his duties had been those of a security guard. He admitted having combat training, but denied having any training with a knife. He still had his green military field jacket, but testified that he rarely wore it. He did remember that that night he had worn a blue baseball jacket with "Leisure Club" embroidered on the back. It was a prize for winning a dart tournament.

Paul Clark remembered Mike's green military jacket. Under cross-examination he stated that he saw Mike wear it "many times, particularly in the winter months."

The first time Mike gave an impression of his teeth was a few weeks before he testified—some four years after the murder. Now he had false teeth. He took his denture out and showed it to the jury. It replaced three of his upper front teeth. While Mike claimed to have had the denture prior to the murder, one might wonder how his teeth were patterned before he had them fixed.

A month or so before the trial, Chris was in San Diego preparing the case when out of the blue he received a phone call from Teri, another friend of Ancona's who was in the bar the night of the murder. She confirmed her expectation, shared by several other friends of Ancona, that Ancona would meet up with them and continue to party after Ancona closed the bar. She volunteered one additional important tidbit. She had had a run-in with Mike's teeth. Chris called her to testify. She stated that she and Mike had dated twice prior to Kim's death and that during sex Mike had bitten her about the neck and left breast. "It was painful and left marks," she affirmed.

Previously, under Levy's direct examination, Mike had denied ever having had sex with Teri. But under Plourd's strong cross-examination he admitted to the opposite.

Before leaving the witness stand Tennessee Mike revealed his ethnic background. "I'm part Mexican, part Apache Indian, part Sioux, part Cherokee and a little white boy."

π

Following Tennessee Mike, Levy called Beth to the stand.

Beth and Kim had been best friends. They supported and confided in one another. Beth would frequently come into the CBS Lounge to keep Kim company while she was bartending.

Beth had met Ray Krone the first time at the Black Bull, another Phoenix bar, where Ray was playing darts in a league match. Ray was well known and respected in the dart world of Phoenix. It was commonly understood that to win a tournament one would have to beat Ray Krone. Kim was at the Black Bull to watch Ray shoot darts. She had the schedule and knew when and where Ray's team played. Beth met her there. Beth testified that Kim told her she had a "crush" on Ray, that he was "the real deal." Beth related how she and an infatuated Kim had driven around late one night trying to find Ray's house. They never found it.

Neither Beth nor any other witnesses testified that Ray had a reciprocal interest in Kim.

Beth told the court that she had planned to be with Tennessee Mike the night of Kim's death. She showed up early at Kim's place that afternoon, interrupting her and Paul Clark during the last of the day's several love-making sessions—four according to Kim, Beth said. Clark testified to three. Beth and Kim spent the rest of the day together, out and about, before Kim had to get ready for work.

Beth said that Kim was in high spirits. Arredondo was considering her as replacement for Trish, who, two days before, had been relieved of her duties as manager of the CBS Lounge. Kim felt she had a good chance of getting the job. It would be quite a step up from part-time bartending. It would give her the financial freedom to get her own place. According to Beth, Kim's relationship with Paul was more for convenience than for love.

Under direct examination, Beth related the same set of events for that night as had Tennessee Mike. But, under cross-examination, discrepancies arose. Plourd interrogated her about her altercation with Mike that led to Mike's taking her home. She seemed to downplay the incident. Plourd also wanted to know why, in pre-trial interviews, Beth first remembered the time she was taken home to be close to 2:30 a.m. and then revised it to 3:30 for her trial testimony. The earlier time was closer to the time Kim would have been finishing her closing chores and about the time Dale Henson saw someone enter the bar.

Initially Beth seemed to have suspected Mike. In a previous statement she had said that she asked Mike if he had stopped at CBS Lounge after dropping her off. But under oath she denied ever asking Mike about his trip home.

Beth and Mike admitted that they had been in telephone contact at the time of their pre-trial interviews. Mike also admitted that he had told Beth she was wrong about the time. Plourd questioned Beth long and hard about the discrepancies between prior statements and her testimony. While Beth under cross-examination admitted to talking with Mike shortly before her testimony, she denied that it had influenced her in any way.

One could not mistake the implication of Plourd's cross-examination—that Beth was covering for Mike.

For Beth the cross-examination was tense and traumatic. Plourd kept her on the stand longer than expected that Friday afternoon. He was not finished with her when time ran out. Beth did not reappear Monday morning. Over the weekend she had checked into a mental hospital because of a "nervous breakdown." Nine days later, with her therapist waiting outside the courtroom, Beth finished her testimony.

Initially she had denied ever having had sex with Mike. Now she admitted it but affirmed it hadn't happened the night of the murder

From the witness box Beth said, "We're still friends. We're not intimate or close now, but I always loved him."

π

The state's lay witnesses had been cross-examined quite effectively, I thought. And Ray Krone had forensic evidence in his favor.

Karen Jones, the fingerprint specialist who testified at the first trial, took it upon herself to reevaluate all of the latent prints found at the crime scene. This time, a fingerprint found on the paper towel holder was identified as belonging to an individual by the name of David DeGroff.

DeGroff now lived in Flagstaff and was called to testify. He had been the opening cook the day of the murder, arriving at the CBS Lounge about ten o'clock in the morning and leaving about three o'clock. He stated that he had recently scrubbed down the walls in the restroom and used the towel holder to prop himself up as he cleaned the adjacent wall.

And Jones found another print of interest in the restroom—a palm print on the lever of the sink faucet. Clearly some cleanup had occurred after the murder, as evidenced by the bloodstained paper towels found in the recently emptied plastic-lined wastebasket. Everyone accepted that the assailant used these towels to wipe fingerprints from the knife found under the basket's plastic lining.

Jones was not able to determine who had left the palm print. But she was certain that neither it nor any of the numerous other unidentified latent prints taken from all corners of the crime scene belonged to Ray Krone.

The Converse tennis shoe prints found at the end of the bar, going into the kitchen to and from the knife rack and moving all around the body, could not be linked to Ray Krone. The best that prosecutor Levy could do was to emphasize that Ray Krone's shoe size, 11½, fit within the alleged shoe size range of the footprint, 9½ to 11½. But 11½ is not an uncommon shoe size.

Phoenix police criminologist Scott Piette appeared again for the prosecution. He had nothing of substance to offer in support of the state's case. Under cross-examination he appeared confused about his own notes. At one point he confirmed his opinion, offered at the first trial, that there was no blood on the victim's panties. That opinion had been based upon a visual inspection. He acknowledged that there is a simple presumptive test for blood, which he had used on other items of evidence. Would he, with the court's permission, demonstrate the test to the jury? Sure.

In court the next day he performed the Kastle-Meyer Test on Ancona's panties. To his surprise and bewilderment he found blood on them. Whose blood it was went undetermined, because additional tests would take weeks to complete and the trial would be over before then.

The overall impression Piette left with the jury was that his work on the Krone evidence had been imprecise at best.

Moses Schanfield appeared for the state. Dr. Schanfield was a well-qualified expert who brought into court more than fifteen years of experience doing DNA analysis. He had earned his Ph.D. in human genetics from the University of Michigan. He was a member of the American Academy of Forensic Scientists and of the American Society of Crime Laboratory Directors. Over the years he had worked in several related fields, from research genetics in San Francisco to paternity testing in Atlanta, before becoming the laboratory director for the Analytic Genetic Testing Center in Denver.

The AGTC had done the initial DNA testing at the request of prosecutor Levy. But for the second trial, Levy called Schanfield into court to interpret Dr. Blake's findings regarding DNA Sample 4B, taken from the bra cup.

Chris Plourd knew Dr. Schanfield well. Like the jurors, he listened quietly to his testimony. "The Sample 4B appears to be a mixture...and Mr. Krone cannot be excluded as contributing to that mixture."

Other than Sample 4B, Dr. Blake had favorable things to say about the DNA. But, perhaps not wanting to have the 4B results unduly emphasized under cross-examination by Levy, Plourd dropped Ed Blake from his witness list. Besides, Plourd knew he could get the results he wanted under his own cross-examination of Dr. Schanfield. For this testimony, Plourd concentrated on the DNA sample taken from the area of the bite.

The swab of the victim's left breast—the area of the bite—received by Dr. Blake's lab for analysis was useless. It was basically a stick with fuzz where the cotton tip used to be. Try as they might, the lab could obtain no results. Plourd would have to use the DQα results produced in Dr. Schanfield's lab at AGTC for the first trial.

Probes sensitive to each of the six possible DQα alleles are imbedded on "typing strips," along with a dye. This dye produces a blue dot whenever the probe is stimulated by a DNA source. The probes are numbered corresponding to the allele they are programmed to detect. The typing strip for Ray Krone's DNA shows only one blue dot, number 3, verifying DQα type [3,3]. On the typing strip for victim Ancona—DQα type [3,4]—both probes 3 and 4 have a blue dot.

The 3 and 4 probes on the typing strip of the DNA found on the bite mark also turned blue. One possibility was that this sample contained only Ancona's DNA. Another possibility that had been argued—and not challenged—at the first trial was that Ray Krone could not be excluded as a donor of this sample because Ancona's 3 allele could be "masking" both of Krone's 3 alleles. Plourd noticed a subtle difference between the blue spots, which suggested a third possibility.

Responding to Plourd's questioning, Dr. Schanfield confirmed that typing strips are designed so that equal amounts of two different alleles will illuminate corresponding dots with equal intensity. Then Plourd asked Schanfield to look closely at the typing strip for the DNA swabbed from the bite mark.

"The 4 dot is darker than the 3 dot," observed Dr. Schanfield.

Plourd then asked, "Because the 4 is darker, it suggests that there is a mixture of a [3,4] person and another person. What type would the other person be?"

"If it is a mixture of a [3,4] person and somebody else, then the other person would have to be [4,4]," Dr. Schanfield confirmed.

"Mr. Krone would be positively excluded because he is a [3,3]?" Plourd continued, with emphasis.

Dr. Schanfield agreed. "That's correct."

Plourd seemed to have won the day. Levy had established that Ray Krone could not be excluded from the DNA mixture of many sources found on the bra, but Plourd established that Ray Krone is excluded if the bite mark sample is a mixture of Ancona and her assailant's DNA.

Moses Schanfield seemed surprised and impressed with the result. Apparently, he had not been asked to revisit the typing strips prepared by his lab for the first trial. Passing Plourd on his way out of the courtroom, Schanfield smiled and whispered, "Very good!"

The next day it was Levy's turn for the redirect examination. He returned to the bra sample and asked Schanfield what percentage of the population could be included as possible donors of that sample.

"One in one hundred and seventy," said Dr. Schanfield.

This caused quite a stir in the courtroom because this fraction of the population, which included Ray Krone, amounted to less than one percent, and it could be argued that there was a ninety-nine point four percent chance that it was Ray Krone's DNA on the bra—very compelling for a jury to consider.

But statistics can be viewed in many different ways. In a city the size of Phoenix, with more than a million people, the zero point six percent of Phoenix's residents who could also be included as possible DNA donors to Ancona's bra amounted to more than six thousand individuals. Nevertheless, Plourd objected, citing an Arizona law that prohibits the use of the "product rule" in determining probabilities.

The product rule works like this: if it is known that one-half of the population are female, one-fifth have blue eyes and one-tenth are blond, then the proportion of the population that is blond blue-eyed female is one in one hundred (1/2 times 1/5 times 1/10 = 1/100), or one percent.

The product rule is a valid tool in statistics, provided accurate population frequencies are known. The problem is—just as I guessed at the above frequencies to arrive at one percent in the above example—the population frequencies of DNA genetic markers are pretty much guesswork. It is not know with any reliability what percentage of the population have a particular genetic trait. Even Schanfield's testimony illustrated this dilemma. Before arriving at his guess of one in one hundred and seventy, Schanfield stated that "[Ray Krone] is within the population of less than one in one hundred...actually probably closer to one in two hundred."

Because of this damaging misuse of the product rule, Judge McDougall not only sustained Plourd's objection, but also offered to grant a mistrial.

It was decided instead to have Schanfield's inappropriate remarks stricken from the record. The jury was instructed to ignore Schanfield's statistical conclusions.

π

The trial had proceeded. Slowly but surely, the state's case against Ray Krone had boiled down to Dr. Raymond Rawson and the bite mark.

Chris Plourd did not wait long to unveil "the scratch." Cross-examining Levy's first forensic expert witness, Dr. Larry Shaw, the pathologist who did the autopsy, Plourd asked the witness to compare bite mark photographs taken at the crime scene with those taken at autopsy. Dr. Shaw confirmed that the scratch appeared only in the autopsy photos and felt that somebody had inadvertently scratched the breast during the autopsy. He was sure that the scratch did not exist at the time of death. Plourd would call other expert witnesses who independently affirmed that the scratch was a postmortem artifact, an abrasion made at the time of autopsy.

Levy grasped the ramifications of this revelation immediately. He realized that Rawson's boner in identifying the scratch as having been made by one of Ray Krone's teeth created a major credibility problem. With Dr. Shaw still on the stand, Levy suggested that someone tampered with the crime scene photos. But soon he dropped this strategy because these photos were taken, developed and printed by the Phoenix police department.

Kevin Denomine worked for the PPD in their crime lab as a fingerprint specialist. He also had expertise in photographing crime scenes and was the one who took most of the photographs of the Ancona murder scene. He did not photograph the bite injury, but was present when Dr. John Piakas did.

With Denomine on the stand, Levy suggested that the scratch was really in the crime scene bite mark photos but that not everyone was capable of seeing it. Denomine agreed. Levy referred to this phenomenon as "eye-brain coordination."

Chris Plourd seemed to be having fun cross-examining Officer Denomine.

"What is the science of eye-brain coordination?" Plourd asked. "What is it all about?"

Denomine struggled for an explanation. "Basically that your brain needs to...if you are looking at something it cannot...you can either see fine details or sometimes eyes can be tricked as far as individuals seeing specific details. Not everybody's capable of seeing the same amount of detail."

"That's eye-brain coordination?" Plourd continued.

"I'm not a medical doctor. I'm just assuming that if I'm using common sense that I do think it would have something to do with it. I could be incorrect on that."

"Is there a science you learned in your photography courses on eye-brain coordination?"

"No. I remember something from my psychology classes. That's quite awhile ago." Then perhaps hoping to end this line of questioning he added, "I'm not an expert in that area."

But, Plourd continued to test Denomine's eye-brain coordination. He showed him a photograph of the bite mark with autopsy stitches visible in one corner and asked, "Do you see this mark here that's called a scratch?"

"Yes."

"Does eye-brain coordination affect that at all?"

"I think everyone in the room can see that."

Plourd then handed Denomine another photograph, "Now, using your best eye-brain coordination, do you see the mark in Exhibit 162?"

For a long moment, Denomine intently studied the exhibit. Then slowly he looked up from the photo. "It's not recognizable to me. Not in this photograph."

Throughout the trial, Plourd continued having fun with "eye-brain coordination." Several times after an expert witness rendered his opinion, Plourd would ask in jest, "Now that didn't take eye-brain coordination, did it?" The witness would appear dumbfounded. Some jurors would chuckle. The judge would shake his head. Levy would remain motionless. After pausing a bit, Plourd would withdraw the question.

Dr. Ray Rawson's appearance began with some eye-brain coordination of his own. Over Plourd's objection to relevance, Rawson placed on an easel one at a time three drawings for the jury to see. The first depicted an old hag or a young woman, depending upon how one looked at it. The second appeared to be a vase or the silhouette of two people looking at one another. The last contained just straight lines, but the parallel lines appeared to be curved. When asked which way he saw these optical illusions, Rawson responded, "I see them both ways."

Throughout his testimony, seer Rawson claimed to see "the scratch" in all photos of the bite mark. He did not back away from his opinion that "the mark was made by Ray Krone's tooth number eleven."

Overall, Rawson's testimony remained the same as in the first trial. The injury to the victim's left breast consisted of multiple bites, two of which he matched to Ray Krone's dentition. "The scratch" was part of the ten o'clock bite.

He demonstrated his findings with a newly prepared videotape. The same sliding overlay and fade-in/fade-out techniques were used to demonstrate the matches between each bite mark and Ray Krone's dentition. In addition, the actual excised breast tissue made an appearance on this tape.

When Plourd had asked to see the breast tissue during the discovery process, he was informed that it had been misplaced. No one knew what happened to it. He was provided instead with a plaster cast, a model, of the excised breast. Rawson used this model to show how Ray Krone's lower teeth corresponded to the lower arch of one of the bites. To get the lower teeth to match the model, Rawson tilted it awkwardly and claimed that "the bite came in at a high angle."

"To a reasonable degree of medical certainty," Dr. Rawson concluded, "Ray Krone inflicted the bite injuries to Kim Ancona."

Dr. John Piakas, the forensic dentist working for the Phoenix police department, had testified prior to Dr. Rawson and supported Rawson's conclusion.

Forensic dentists primarily are asked to identify human remains through dental records. Piakas aspired to becoming a member of the American Board of Forensic Odontology. To do so he would also need to master bite mark analysis. Although he listed in his curriculum vitae that he had been involved in nine bite mark cases, he had testified in only one of them, and that was the first Krone trial. Prior to the first trial he had met with Dr. Rawson. After the meeting he too saw two bite marks. But he did not see "the scratch" back then. Just a few days earlier, Levy had pointed it out to him. Then he saw it in both the crime scene and the autopsy photos he'd taken. However, the bite mark trainee's eye-brain coordination was not yet fully developed.

"What made this mark?" Plourd asked.

"I don't know," he told the jury.

Dr. Piakas would have to work on his eye-brain coordination if he wanted to become a full-fledged bite mark expert. He rendered the second strongest opinion (Rawson's being the strongest) permitted under the guidelines set by the ABFO.

"It is very probable that Ray Krone did cause the bite injuries," opined Dr. Piakas. He explained that "very probable" equates to "more likely than not."

Throughout his cross-examination, Plourd tested Rawson's eye-brain coordination. At one point he read from the transcripts of the first trial, "It was obvious to me that the scratch mark on the ten o'clock bite was not a tooth mark but was made by some kind of sharp pointed instrument. It is superfluous to the bite mark. It was made after the bite mark."

"Was that your testimony, Dr. Rawson?"

"Yes, that was," replied the bite mark expert.

"And is it your testimony now that that mark was made entirely by a tooth belonging to Ray Krone."

"That's correct."

Then, with Rawson positioned between the jury and an enlargement of a bite mark photo placed on the easel, Plourd, armed with a laser pointer, maneuvered Rawson counterclockwise around the ten o'clock bite tooth by tooth. When he arrived at tooth number eleven, he asked, "Do you see the scratch?"

"Yes," Rawson affirmed.

"Doctor, I would like you to measure straight down from the mole until you hit the scratch and tell us the distance," Plourd directed.

A pause, then equivocation, "I wouldn't do it that way. Normally I would work in my lab with several photographs and I would verify back and forth..."

"Your honor," Plourd interrupted, "I would ask you to order the doctor to do as—"

"Doctor," the judge directed, "the question is fairly simple. Can you measure it? If you can, please do it. If you can't, just say 'no.'"

Rawson went to work. "Nine millimeters," came the belabored response.

In an autopsy photo "the scratch" measured only six millimeters below the mole. Oops! Rawson saw "the scratch" three millimeters below where it actually was. A measurement error of fifty percent. Not very good. Apparently, eye-brain coordination worked only in his lab.

Dr. Raymond Rawson shuffled out of the courtroom and was overheard to mutter, "I've never been cross-examined like that." Indeed, the bite mark expert seemed to agree that Plourd had effectively challenged his credibility.

To testify for the defense, Plourd had called three eminently qualified expert forensic odontologists, Dr. Norman "Skip" Sperber from San Diego, Dr. Jerry Vale from Los Angeles and Dr. Homer Campbell from Albuquerque. All three were highly respected founding members of the American Board of Forensic Odontology. All three had agreed that "the scratch" was just a scratch, that there was just one bite inflicted on the left breast and that Ray Krone was excluded as its source.

π

Other than these three expert odontologists and the perfect witness, most of Plourd's case had been made during cross-examination of the state's witnesses.

Meeting for the first time with his perfect witness, Dale Henson, Plourd had become concerned. Henson was to testify early in the morning. He was tired and nervous. He had been up the previous night cleaning sidewalks and came to court directly from his last job. But he

was nervous for another reason. Plourd had just learned from Mike
Pain that Henson and been given five polygraph tests by the Phoenix
police department.

Before the jury entered the courtroom, Plourd told the judge,
"He's very nervous because of this situation. It's extremely unusual.
He's no different from any other witness. I think he has really been
harassed. It's unbelievable what he's been put through in the nature of
questioning. I've never seen this happen before."

Levy wanted to offer evidence that Henson had lied about the time
he'd seen the individual enter and exit the CBS Lounge. The lead
detective reported that Henson had told him it was approximately 6:00
a.m. But Henson insisted that he had told the detective 2:30.

"He did tell the examiner that he lied to the detective in December
'ninety-one with regard to the time," Levy offered.

"I never heard that before!" Plourd responded. "It would be nice to
get some discovery, your Honor."

After a brief consultation with Mike Pain, who had done the
Henson interview for the defense, Plourd continued, "After five tests
the polygrapher said, 'Well, it looks like on the polygraph you may not
have told the detective the truth about what happened at 2:30.' Henson
responded 'Well, whatever.'" It was this innocuous response by a
badgered Henson that Levy offered as "proof" that Henson had lied
about the time he witnessed the individual enter then leave the CBS
Lounge.

Henson's polygraph results were favorable overall. Plourd wanted
to get them in front of the jury. But Judge McDougall ruled,
"Polygraph results aren't admissible." He did, however, allow Levy to
ask Henson about the time discrepancy so long as he referred to the
"polygraph examiner" as a "police technician."

Levy must have been concerned about Henson's expected
testimony, because behind him—seated in chairs in front of the fence
that separates spectators from defendant, attorneys, witnesses, jurors
and judge—were several police polygraph examiner technician types
watching Henson's every move and ostensibly taking notes.

Levy asked Ray Krone to don his lime green ski parka and stand
approximately eight feet from the witness. Then, adjusting the lights to
try to simulate the night lighting in the CBS parking lot, Levy asked,
"Under these conditions, would you look at Mr. Krone? Does he
resemble the person that you saw that evening?"

"No, sir, not at all," Henson answered firmly.

Levy's gallery filed out.

π

As I pulled into the court parking lot, still reflecting upon the trial that I had watched religiously for the past eight weeks, I felt confident and optimistic. Interrupting Dylan, I parked the car, hurried into the courthouse and awaited the verdict.

That evening I was back in my car heading north out of Arizona. Ray Krone wasn't. His trial had gone south. He was once again the convicted murderer of Kimberly Ancona.

Perhaps the skeptical reader is thinking, No way! Or is wondering what significant fact I've omitted. Perhaps you've heard that sheets soaked with Ancona's blood were found in the trunk of Ray Krone's car. That's what detective Dennis Olson told the television audience watching the syndicated show "Arrest and Trial." In the episode titled "Biting Postal Worker," a scene depicted a pair of bloody sheets being removed from Ray Krone's Corvette with Olson stating, "We later found out through the crime lab investigation that the blood came from Kim Ancona, the victim."

Why did detective Olson lie about the sheets found in Ray Krone's car? Perhaps, desiring to be on TV, he was just responding to the producer's head-scratching question, "You mean, all you've got on this guy is a bite mark?"

Doesn't common sense want to know why bite mark evidence would be needed if sheets stained with the victim's blood were found in the suspect's possession?

Whatever the stains on the sheets were, they were not Ancona's blood. Although misrepresented on the TV show as being material to the case, these sheets, useless as evidence, were not presented at either of Ray Krone's trials.

Prosecutor Levy, also appearing on the show, didn't mention the sheets either. He said, "The bite mark was crucial because the rest of the forensic evidence was not strong enough."

So, that's it. Ray Krone stood convicted a second time solely upon bite mark evidence disputed by three respected board-certified forensic odontologists and supported only by an expert wannabe and one who fancies himself blessed with a supernatural power of eye-brain coordination that allows him and only him to see a phantom mark that he is certain was made by one of Ray Krone's teeth.

π

As the lights of Phoenix faded in the rearview mirror, my thoughts were testing my own eye-brain coordination to the max. What was the explanation for the verdict I'd just witnessed? The relative truths of the

Rubin Carter and OJ Simpson verdicts, though the opposite of one another, were easily explained as racial prejudice. The federal judge, when granting Carter habeas corpus, cited that "racism rather than reason" contributed to the verdict. One OJ attorney said of another, "He played the race card from the bottom of the deck." But what could explain the Krone verdict? Suspect, victim, judge, jurors, attorneys and witnesses were, one and all, Caucasians.

Haunting me on my long journey home was a comment made some time before, of which I took little notice at the time but which now loomed large. Present when I first introduced the Krone case to Chris Plourd in the patio behind his San Diego office was Don Levine, an attorney who shared office space. Levine listened silently as I outlined the case. At the end of the meeting—with Chris formally retained as Ray's counsel—Levine congratulated his colleague with a pat on the back and a simultaneous "Good luck!"

Then, as an afterthought, he added, "Arizona juries do strange things."

Indeed they do, I thought, now surrounded by darkness except for headlights guiding me out of Arizona. I wondered *why* Arizona juries do strange things. But I could come up with no sensible explanation for the strange verdict. Maybe Dylan knew? I turned on the cassette player. A cymbal cracked like a bullwhip, keeping the wailing violin in pace with his hard rocking guitar. Before his harmonica joined the violin, Dylan finished singing his lyric:

> *Now all the criminals in their coats and their ties*
> *Are free to drink martinis and watch the sun rise*
> *While Rubin sits like Buddha in a ten-foot cell*
> *An innocent man in a living hell.*

> *How can the life of such a man*
> *Be in the palm of some fool's hand?*
> *To see him obviously framed*
> *Couldn't help but make me feel ashamed to live in a land*
> *Where justice is a game.*

PART TWO
THE GAME

The jury system puts a ban upon intelligence and honesty, and a premium upon ignorance, stupidity and perjury.

– Mark Twain, circa 1871

CHAPTER 12
DOING TIME

South Central Arizona's Valley of the Sun was settled in the late eighteen sixties on the banks of the Salt River around a network of irrigation ditches abandoned by the Hohokam Indians five hundred years earlier. The intense summer's heat was no doubt a challenge for the early pioneers, who after ten years in the valley, named their settlement after the a mythological Arabian bird that immolates itself every five centuries on a pyre and then rises again from its ashes. Egypt adopted the bird as their sun god, dying every evening to be reborn the next morning. Early Christians adopted this bird as their symbol for immortality and resurrection.

Phoenix was incorporated in 1881 and became the capital of Arizona Territory in 1889 and in 1912 the capital of the forty-eighth state, the last of the continental states to enter the union.

The city must have begun near present day Patriot's Park because the park's northeast corner, the intersection of Washington and Central, is the mathematical origin of the city, address numbers increasing in all directions from this point. Numbered streets and avenues run parallel to Central, streets to the east and avenues to the west. Roads parallel to Washington are named after other presidents in the downtown area. Camelback Road and the scene of the crime are five miles to the north. You learn early on to pay attention to north versus south, east versus west and streets versus avenues when getting around Phoenix. You're a long way from the CBS Lounge, located at West Camelback Road and 16th Avenue, if you're looking for it near East Camelback Road and 16th Street.

Patriot's Park occupies one square block of mostly brick walkways winding through patches of grassy knolls. Facing north at its south end is an outdoor amphitheater protected from the valley's sun by a huge canvas tarp. It's not unusual for street vendors to line the walkways or for a free noontime concert to happen. Under the park is a parking garage accommodating the area. North and east of Patriot's Park one finds predominately businesses, banks, hotels, restaurants, shops and office buildings. Government buildings are located in the opposite direction. Within a mile and a half of the park are the governor's office, the state capitol, the state supreme court, the county attorney's office, the public defender's office, the superior court, the sheriff's office, city hall, the county jail and the Phoenix police department, with its crime lab.

The courthouse where Ray Krone was tried and convicted is the government building closest to Patriot's Park. It stands kitty-corner to its southwest corner. The park was traversed many, many times in the course of the trial. The favorite lunch spot was Tom's Tavern on Washington Street, facing the park.

Occupying the square block south of the courthouse is the Madison Street Jail, a monolith of ten stories. It was here that Ray began doing time and here he returned from Death Row to await and endure his second trial. It is one of eight jails administered by the sheriff's office under its colorful boss, Joe Arpaio. It houses primarily those individuals awaiting their day in court. Once convicted, if jail is their fate, the convicted are usually moved to another Maricopa County facility. Tent City, for example, accommodates non-violent individuals such as DUI offenders. Those going to prison are moved to a department of correction facility in—to name a few—Yuma, Tucson or Florence.

The sheriff of Maricopa County for three years, Joe Arpaio had become quite the celebrity. He fancied himself, as the title of his book modestly suggested, *The Toughest Sheriff in America*. Frequently in the press and occasionally on TV, the sheriff promoted his own brand of toughness. One such promotion involved pink underwear. Significant numbers of monogrammed jail underwear were being smuggled out of the Madison Street Jail. Apparently it was prized as a status symbol on the outside…of the jail, of course, not the pants. As a deterrent, Arpaio ordered that all county issued underwear be dyed pink. But this plan backfired big time. The street value for the now pink underwear skyrocketed. Enter entrepreneur Arpaio. I guess part of being tough is recognizing that when you can't beat 'em, join 'em. In three months Arpaio sold $420,000 worth of pink underwear. This money was used to finance other toughness programs, such as the neon VACANCY sign set atop Tent City and full page newspaper ads appearing while the Super Bowl was in town to warn revelers what would be in store for them if they didn't behave.

Arpaio seemed to relish his notoriety in an article illustrated with a picture that was captioned "Ray Krone is wearing pink underwear in the jail of the 'Toughest Sheriff in America'" and showed Arpaio proudly displaying a pair.

But pink underwear was the least of the toughest sheriff's toughness. To keep costs down, Arpaio located some baloney at a rock bottom price. No matter that it had turned green and was unfit for human consumption. While it lasted this baloney was lunch day in and day out for the jail population. It made good press when Arpaio boasted that each inmate could be feed for thirty-five cents per meal. At one time or another coffee and cigarettes were banned.

"I'm tired of hearing about rehabilitation and education. Jail," said Joe Arpaio, "should be punishment."

Indeed, Arpaio had found a way to use education as punishment. He limited TV to only three channels: the Disney Channel, C-SPAN and an educational channel broadcasting a college course given by Newt Gingrich. This cruel and unusual punishment caught the attention of Washington. There was also concern about rumors of beatings within Arpaio's jails. But the sheriff's department survived the justice department investigation.

Sheriff Joe was not without local critics as well. An article in *The Arizona Republic*, "Innocence No Obstacle for Sheriff," reported Arpaio's desire to have the names of the approximately two thousand people arrested and booked into his jails each week published in the newspaper as a deterrent. Arpaio expressed little concern that most of these arrests were for misdemeanors that were usually resolved with a fine or that many were released without ever being charged with a crime, leaving only a handful that would ultimately plead to or be convicted of a felony. When someone suggested that "probable cause" does not equal "probable guilt," the sheriff replied, "Maybe?"

The newspaper declined Arpaio's offer, perhaps concerned about the huge awards Maricopa County had already paid to citizens who had been brutalized while in jail. One settlement in the millions went to the family of an individual who died while in the custody of Arpaio's deputies. The settlement could have been much higher, but death was determined to have been the result of a beating and unrelated to any adverse reaction to the teachings of Newt Gingrich.

The public, however, seemed enamored of its sheriff. "Presumption of innocence" is one of those bantered about, lofty phrases that, if practiced by a politician, adversely affects public opinion. The reality seems to be that the public presumes that anyone who presumes innocence is weak. Tough sheriff Joe Arpaio enjoyed an eighty-four percent approval rating.

For Ray Krone, pink underwear and baloney in sandwiches and on TV were the least of his concerns while doing time in the Madison Street Jail:

I was confined to a four-man cell about the size of my bathroom at home, 7' x 10'. It had two bunks. There was no privacy at all. The commode was out in the open at the base of the sink. Showers were in a dayroom—rusted, moldy, smelly, with peeling paint...I was in the cell more than twenty-two hours a day. A group of cells called a "pod" shared a "dayroom." At each mealtime the cell door would open and I and my cellmates would walk twenty feet down a hallway to the dayroom and take seats at one of two four-man tables. We had fifteen minutes to gobble down the food waiting for us on trays before having to return to our cramped cell. Each day each cell received one hour more in the dayroom for "recreation." There we could make phone calls and shower. I would always wear my slip on shoes when showering. I didn't want to be barefoot in case something went down. The rubber soles kept me from slipping on the wet cement floor. It was the worse days of my life—worse than being on Death Row! There I at least had some privacy.

Cellmates changed frequently. There were drunks and druggies moaning and vomiting. They'd stink up the whole cell and wouldn't get up to take a shower during rec hour. Junkies would have fits and go wild ranting and raving. They'd be incoherent and disrespectful of what little space and dignity a man had in that hole. After causing much trouble they'd get bailed out or released after a few days only to be replaced by another one.

Time was spent by and large playing cards and sleeping. Mostly I read and kept to myself. I had little or nothing in common with these people. They'd talk about all the trouble they'd been in as if it were their resume. I wasn't going to tell them I was in the choir and boy scouts.

Unless bleeding badly, medical treatment was almost non-existent. Grubby guys would come in with lice or scabies only to be discovered at the end of the week when a staff member would exchange the dirty laundry for a clean set of clothes and bedding. One such individual came into the pod with a form of meningitis. He passed out in line waiting for medications— Thorazine was dispensed freely to keep us all mellow. The whole pod was quarantined. Each of us was issued one plastic cup for the duration. There we were about eighty of us sitting around all over the place for a whole week keeping track of our own little Dixie cup while waiting to take three daily pills that produced orange urine to fight a highly contagious disease. Incredible! It was nerve racking. I couldn't sleep. To cope, I claimed stress. The psych doc prescribed a stronger antidepressant to help me stay calm and be able to sleep. I took it for months on end.

Incidents and confrontations were a daily occurrence within the pod. I witnesses one podmate take a backward swan dive from the top tier onto a table below in an attempt to commit suicide. Word through the grape vine was that his attempt failed and he ended up permanently paralyzed.

The reality of that place is scary and overpowering. I was out of my element but got through it with only a few confrontations.

π

His first few days in jail after his arrest, Ray remembers being not too worried. The click on the loud speaker signaling that an announcement was imminent would bring silence to the entire pod. He thought that it was just a matter of time before he would hear, "Ray Krone, roll it up. You're going home." The click became his only friend.

His optimism ended after about two weeks, however, with a visit from his assigned public defender. The first thing he remembers her saying to him was, "You've been charged with capital murder. You can be expected to be found guilty. We'll fight it on appeal."

This presumption of guilt by this court appointed attorney, who apparently had already thrown in the towel even before talking to her client, naturally agitated Ray. His vehement demands for an explanation and protestations of innocence were met with, "I'm not going to be yelled at like that," and she left.

At that point real fear set in. One can imagine that fear is common within institutions of incarceration. There's the continual fear of confrontations. Ray was not in Tent City, he was in with the big boys, those charged with violent crimes. But Ray could deal with this fear. He was tough enough to handle confrontations, smart enough to adopt lowlife lingo and jail jive and savvy enough to stay neutral when possible. If forced to take a side, it would be that of the inmates. They were more dangerous than the guards. At one point on Death Row in Florence, he was given a cushy job in the library. It allowed him to be out of his cell for a significant part of the day. But it didn't last long. As he quickly learned, the price to have this job was to become a snitch. He politely declined.

The real fear for Ray was not knowing what was happening with his case on the outside. He naïvely believed that the justice system actually looks out for the innocent. So he was somewhat relieved to learn that the public defender's office, because of a conflict of interest, could not take his case. Kim Ancona's ex-husband was also a suspect in her death. He was at the time also being represented by the public defender's office, having been charged with molesting one of his daughter's girlfriends. Maricopa County routinely contracts with private defense attorneys to handle cases when there is a conflict of interest. Ray was assigned a contract attorney, Geoffrey Jones.

Jones seemed to take an interest in Ray's case. He told Ray that the evidence against him was not very strong. He interviewed Ray's friends and called several to testify. An investigator assigned to the case to work with Jones came into the jail and listened to Ray's story. Ray was encouraged when Jones hired an expert to look at the bite mark but confused when that expert did not testify. He did not know at the time that the "expert" was no expert at all, but merely a dentist who was a friend of Jones. Nor did he know that the real reason this non-expert didn't testify was that he agreed with the state's bite mark expert.

Jones was granted a motion declaring Ray's case "complex." This ruling meant that Jones could charge hourly in addition to the fixed contract amount. What he did in those extra hours is still a mystery.

Ray did not learn until long after his first conviction that "zealous attorneys don't get contracts," according to a caption in *The Arizona Republic* introducing an article critical of the selection process for contract attorneys. It mentioned an attorney who lost his contract after winning an acquittal in a first-degree murder case. Apparently the lucrative contracts (eighty thousand dollars per year) are reserved for defense attorneys who don't rock the boat. It seems that the way for an attorney to prosper on taxpayer money in Maricopa County is to be a prosecutor or a bad defense attorney. You wouldn't even have to be a good prosecutor to face one of these contract attorneys. Perhaps this reality explains the attitude of Ray's initial public defender?

On court days Ray would wake at 4:00 a.m. His shower was quick. Others needed one too. After a 5:00 a.m. breakfast he was moved to the basement into a fifteen by fifteen holding cell. There he camped cramped in with forty or so others for the next few hours. One open stall and a couple of bunks attached to a wall serviced the lot. After 8:00 a.m. groups of four or five were removed from the cell. When his group was called, Ray would proceed outside the cell where his hands would be cuffed to his waist and his ankles shackled together with a chain just long enough to take small steps. Another chain shackled him to the rest of the group. Then he and his shackled mates would cross under Madison Street through a tunnel into the court building and up an elevator into another smaller holding cell outside the courtroom. There they would wait for a bailiff to take them into court.

For pretrial hearings Ray and the group would usually be taken into court still shackled together and made to sit in the jury box. He would stand up when his case was before the court. On trial days he would remain behind in the holding tank. There he would change clothes and wait for court to begin, which rarely happened before 10:00 a.m.

Ray learned early on how to pace himself in this waiting game. He would eat and especially drink very little for breakfast. Facilities were few and far between. Frequently he would not be able to relieve himself until he was returned to his cell.

For the second trial, Ray waited in a small conference room outside the courtroom. There he could change clothes in private and relax on a folding chair. He had access, with George's supervision, to a restroom down the hall leading to the judge's chamber. George was his bailiff.

George Schuester and his wife Dottie came to Phoenix some fifteen years earlier from Canton, Ohio. Steelworkers there had been laid off in droves. In his forties, George found his opportunities limited. To get a job in law enforcement it was necessary for him to challenge via lawsuit the county's age discrimination policy prohibiting anyone over forty years of age from being hired by the sheriff's department. In the suit George noted that the application for employment as a correction officer stated, "The applicant must be under forty years of age," but also stated, "We do not discriminate based upon race, sex, age..." George won the suit and at age forty-five, with no prior law enforcement experience, went to work for sheriff Joe as a guard in the county jail. It was dangerous work. It was not unusual for George to be in with a hundred or so prisoners with only a radio as his weapon, which more than once failed to work. George welcomed a new assignment as transportation officer moving prisoners between Arizona's jails and prisons. When a vacancy for court bailiff became available, George jumped at the opportunity. He was selected because he had studied and understood the rules a bailiff must enforce in the courtroom.

George mastered the nuances of his new job very quickly. To be a good bailiff, you had to strike a medium between everyone in the courtroom, the judge, the attorneys, the jury, the spectators and the families of the victim as well as the defendant. You had to protect the court from an unruly defendant as well as protect the defendant from those who may wish him harm. A bailiff's duty is to enforce order in the court.

George took charge from the beginning. In his very first assignment, the defense attorney wanted his client uncuffed during a pretrial hearing. Recognizing the defendant to be "a bad dude," George signaled the judge that this was not a good idea. The attorney insisted and the judge again asked for the handcuffs to be removed.

"Judge," said George, "if you want those cuffs removed, order me to do so on the record."

After a moment's pause, the judge said, for the record, "The cuffs stay on!"

Later, Judge Ron Reinstein took George aside and complimented him, "Smooth, George, smooth." The judge was impressed with how George had shifted the responsibility for the consequences of removing the handcuffs from a potentially unruly defendant away from himself onto the court.

George had no problem taking control when it became necessary. Years later he was again in Judge Reinstein's court for a bail hearing. The defendant, a kid, George remembered, in for something stupid like not paying child support, jumps up and goes off at the judge. George immediately calls for backup, which arrives soon but not soon enough for the whole courtroom to hear the kid suggest that the judge wouldn't be so "up tight" if he would get a date with one of the streetwalkers who loitered on Van Buren Street. George takes it upon himself to have the kid forcibly removed from the courtroom. Reinstein isn't finished with the defendant and orders him back into court. The courtroom is cleared and the kid is returned kicking and screaming.

"Before you say another word," the judge says, quite agitated, "sixty days for contempt of court."

The kid continues his outburst. George approaches the bench. "This kid's totally out of control," he informs the judge. "He's not going to shut up."

The kid is again forcibly removed to the holding tank.

When George returns he approaches the bench and says, "I know you're the presiding judge but, your honor, you can't sentence this guy for contempt."

Now agitated with George, Judge Reinstein asks, "Who in the hell do you think you're talking too?"

"I'm talking to you, your honor, and you can't sentence him."

"Are you telling me I can't sentence some guy who went off like that?"

"That's what I'm telling you."

"And just what makes you think I can't do that?"

"Six years ago I was in your court and you made a ruling that a judge in anger cannot sentence someone for contempt of court. It has to go to another judge. The other judge can sentence him but you can't because you've lost it."

"Oh really?" comes a surprised response, followed by a pregnant pause. And then, "I want to talk to you in chambers."

While waiting, George thought, Why did I open my big mouth? I'm going to be reprimanded. My captain is going to chew me up one side and down the other.

"Send George in," was soon heard from inside Judge Reinstein's chambers.

"Have a seat, George."

"I'll stand if you don't mind"

"Why did you take the kid out like that?" the judge asked.

"Well, Judge, I was watching you this morning. You were red as a beet. You were mad. Twelve other inmates are watching. All their families are watching. You're getting angry. This kid is getting to you. I don't blame you for that. But the longer that situation keeps going the more it's going to escalate. The boy was not going to back off. He doesn't have any brains. He's burnt out from drugs or something. He's screaming the whole time we're taking him out. I'm telling him, 'you're going to do ninety days because of your mouth.' 'I don't care,' he tells me."

After listening, Judge Reinstein picked up a law book with its pages already opened, "I looked it up, George. Six years ago I made a ruling...I can't believe you remembered it."

"Well, I was very impressed when you made that ruling, your honor," George responded tactfully.

George had a knack for his job. In another instance George was assigned to a new judge, a lady who had for a short time previously been a prosecutor—all white collar cases. Obvious to George, she had spent her career thus far in an ivory tower. She thought herself well equipped to be a judge. She had little respect for anybody—attorneys, police officers—let alone bailiffs. She had gone through five bailiffs in her short time on the bench.

George told one defendant before court started not to play silly games, that it would only make things worse. The defendant, a young woman, didn't care.

While being sentenced on a drug offense, the young woman began looking up at the ceiling, pointing with her finger, apparently counting light bulbs.

"Excuse me, young lady I'm talking to you," said the judge sternly.

"And who are you?" the young woman asked, still looking up and counting.

"I'm the judge."

"Big deal! You sit up there in a robe. I'm down here in stripes, big deal." She turned her back on the judge and continued counting light bulbs.

The judge angrily demanded, "What do you think caused you to be here?"

She had to ask the question several times. Finally the girl said, "Crack. Crack, man. You know what crack is, don't you, Judge? Crack!"

In front of a full courtroom, the judge then said, "I'm going to help you to become a better person. I'm going to put you in a place with a drug free environment," and sentenced her to three years in the state pen. The whole courtroom burst out laughing. George shook his head and leaned his forehead into a hand.

When the court recessed, the judge took George aside.

"You know, George, I've gotten rid of every bailiff who's come into my court. What's this?" she asked, mimicking George's head in hand.

"Your honor, did you hear everybody laugh?"

"Yes, I did."

"Do you know why they laughed?"

"No, but it made me very angry. I almost found everyone in contempt. And when my bailiff puts his head in his hand like that I am really ticked."

"Well, Judge, that girl can get more drugs in prison than she can on the street."

"You're kidding," replied the judge naïvely.

"Think about it—built-in clientele."

"I'll remember that," the judge responded, somewhat enlightened.

George was excused.

The next day in court the judge told another defendant that she was revoking his parole. George shook his head once again into his hand. Seeing the signal again, the judge recessed the court and took George into her chambers.

"Now what?" she asked.

"Well, Judge, you can't revoke his parole. That's done by the state and you're only a county judge. You can revoke his probation upon the recommendation of the probation officer, but you can't revoke his parole."

"No bailiff is going to tell me what I can and cannot do," she told George. Then she called a colleague to report the situation.

George heard, "Yes, sir. Yes. Yes, sir. Yes, I understand."

Being as nice as possible, Judge Reinstein had advised her, "If George says you can't do something, listen to him. He's been doing this for fourteen years. You just got on the bench."

George was aware of everything going on inside the courtroom. He could quickly interpret a person's demeanor. Defendants were easy. He dealt with them everyday. He knew or quickly found out who everyone was who entered the courtroom. He watched the spectators for potential trouble. For example, with members of the Arian Brotherhood sitting in the gallery while one of their bothers was on the stand describing how he, without remorse, had killed a prison guard, George noticed two burly police officers stand up in the back row with fists clenched. George made the signal to the judge, his flat hand passing back and forth at his neck. The judge, who wanted to be finished with the defendant's testimony, ignored the signal. George could sense tension building in the courtroom even though the judge could not. "Excuse me, your honor," was all George needed to say for the judge to take notice and call recess.

George was preferred and requested by many judges to handle high profile cases. By the time he was assigned to guard Ray Krone, he was in his late fifties, approaching retirement age. He had done close to one hundred murder-one trials.

George had been advised by his superiors, "Ray Krone is a vicious, vicious killer. You treat him like it!" The bailiff for Ray's first trial had told George, "He's guilty. Don't you forget it!"

This type of advice is not unusual. But George quickly saw that things were different with this trial. First there was the accused.

George did not see in Ray what he saw in other defendants. Ray looked rough and tough but didn't act it. Residing for any length of time in prison or jail, you have to become rough and tough to survive. Ray, however, could, in court, once again be himself. He politely obeyed George's rules.

George did not treat Ray any differently or give him special favors. He did, however, talk with Ray. When asked, Ray affirmed his innocence but unlike most other defendants did not elaborate. There were no claims that it was a bad rap or that he'd been railroaded. As George watched the evidence unfold, he would draw his own conclusions.

Then there was Noel Levy. George had watched him prosecute some two dozen cases. For other murder trials, Levy was full of fire and brimstone. Not this time. He'd never seen Levy employ so many delaying tactics trying to figure out how to counter the endless roadblocks defense attorney Plourd effortlessly placed in his path: exposing the police criminologist's shoddy analysis of the pubic hairs, having Levy's own DNA expert exclude Ray as the source of the saliva taken from the bite mark, tongue-tying Levy's star witness by asking this expert odontologist to find in a crime scene photo the nonexistent scratch he'd identified as having been made by Ray Krone, on and on.

Whatever wind was left in Levy's sail disappeared during his cross-examination of Dale Henson when Henson confirmed that Ray Krone was not the one he had seen entering and leaving the murder scene about the time the murder occurred. From that point, as if caught in the Sargasso Sea, Levy floundered through his cross-examinations of the remaining defense witnesses.

George had never seen Levy give such a subdued closing argument. Yet it was polished and precise. As he had throughout the trial, Levy emphasized that the exculpatory evidence didn't mean anything and that the only evidence of importance was the bite mark.

To George, however, the most unusual thing about this trial was the defense attorney. He had never seen anyone like Chris Plourd. He was very impressed to see the gallery fill up with crime lab technicians and public defenders taking notes whenever a DNA expert was on the stand. DNA was new to Maricopa County justice. Plourd was giving lessons not only on DNA technology but also on how to question DNA experts.

Most surprisingly, George had never seen a defense attorney so insistent on his client's innocence. Most defense attorneys in Maricopa

County simply went ahead and did the trial. It was a shock to George to see Plourd continually in Levy's face. "On Levy's best day," George remembered several years later, "Plourd chewed him up and spit him out."

From its beginning the trial seemed bizarre to George. On its second day George confided in Dottie, "Something's wrong with this trial," unknowingly prophesying the verdict. He had to restrain himself from giving her any details. As are jurors, he was prohibited from discussing court proceedings with anyone, including his spouse. But this case disturbed him. George recorded in a diary notes on each day's proceedings. He'd never done that before at any other trial.

George couldn't sleep the night before the verdict was read. He had a bad feeling about it. It had arrived in the afternoon. Judge McDougall decided to wait until morning to announce it. He admonished the jurors to keep it secret over night.

Chris got word less than an hour before the verdict was to be read and called me from his hotel room. I arrived some thirty minutes later, hurried down the sidewalk past TV cameras sprouting tripods near Ray's Corvette, which was conspicuously parked in front of the courthouse, climbed steps while dodging members of the press milling about, entered the foyer, where I waited impatiently for my turn at the metal detector—this day patrolled by twice the usual number of deputy sheriffs—then rode in a packed elevator, passed between more deputies stationed outside the courtroom and finally squeezed through the crowd blocking the double set of double doors leading into the ceremonial chamber.

Entering the courtroom was not unlike entering church. The center aisle separated three rows of backed wooden benches differing from pews only in that there were no padded rails for kneeling. Padded rails were not needed because prayers in this room were silent, private and personal. Like a wedding in which the center aisle separated the bride's family and friends from the groom's, this aisle separated the accused's family and friends from the victim's. Unlike a wedding, however, it separated adversarial prayers. The fence facing the congregation was divided in the middle by a pair of swinging gates, which allowed participants to enter the ceremonial area. Beyond it to the right, like a choir stall, was a box accommodating twenty chairs facing a small pulpit, empty now but on previous days occupied by witnesses. Instead of being mounted on the far wall, the symbol of this ceremony rested on a larger pulpit furthermost from and facing the congregation. The gavel conspicuously awaited the appearance of the individual clad in a robe who would preside over this ceremony. When he did appear, seemingly out of nowhere, he took the symbol in hand to signal the beginning of this, the final phase of the proceedings. Until now the choir had been silent observers. Today was their day to sing.

Because I'd arrived late, the benches on the left, behind the table at which the defendant and counsel waited, were packed. Ray's mother and Jim Leming were in their usual spot, the front row directly behind the defendant's table. Sister Amy sat next to her mother near the door where Ray entered and exited the courtroom. Behind them were most of Ray's Phoenix friends, who had supported him from the beginning, Bob Lewis, his lady Selina, Nick and Bonnie Meyer, Robert Cooper and Steve Junkin.

The other side of the aisle was equally packed. When everyone stood as the jury filed in, I was able to squeeze into the last row behind the prosecutor's table. Except for today, I preferred this side, sitting against the right wall adjacent to the jury box, because it was the most advantageous spot for a spectator to observe the drama. For some testimony, especially the complicated DNA testimony, Judge McDougall would leave his bench and join me there—although he would take one of the vacant chairs inside the jury box.

As soon as the jury walked past the defendant, who was facing them, George knew what the verdict was going to be. Experience had taught him that a jury carrying its verdict into the courtroom will make eye contact with the defendant when it has acquitted. This jury looked straight ahead as it passed Ray Krone. George inconspicuously leaned over and whispered something into Ray's ear. Then he returned to his normal position behind the defense table, glancing in the direction of Ray's mother Carolyn, who was standing between her daughter Amy and her husband Jim Leming. George thought, This is going to be the worst day of their lives. Amy's really going to hate me today.

Amy and her brother had always been close. Though Ray had left home some fifteen years earlier, they continued to support each other during their ups and downs. Amy remained in Pennsylvania. A few years before, she had come out west and stayed with Ray for some months to avoid an unpleasant situation with a former boyfriend back home. No one was more in touch or supportive of Ray during his ordeal than Amy. She had come to Arizona for the first days of Ray's trial but had to return to her job back home. She'd returned for the verdict fully expecting to walk out of the courtroom with her brother. She looked daggers at George every time he cuffed Ray and led him the other way.

As the moment of relative truth approached, only Chris Plourd's head was bowed. His left arm was around his client. His right hand grasped his client's right arm above the elbow. Had Chris Plourd too sensed the devastating outcome about to befall? He seemed ready to restrain his client. It would not be necessary, for George's whisper had been, "Whatever happens, don't lose it."

All other eyes were focused on the judge.

The wailing began as soon as the word "guilty" was heard. It came from the right side of the aisle. Understandably, the victim's mother, Patricia Gasman, began sobbing amid the rustling of the spectators who surrounded her. More crying was to come not from the left side of the aisle but from an unexpected direction. Those sitting behind Ray Krone bowed there heads in unison, silently holding onto their emotions. Ray remained stoically still as Chris Plourd rose seemingly unaffected by the verdict. Before the gavel's final fall, which would release the jurors from their duty, Chris, a warrior to the end, wanted to interrogate them, a custom usually allowed the losing attorney after the verdict.

Chris first asked the court to poll the jury. When it did, nearly all of the ten female jurors joined Mrs. Gasman's sobbing as each in turn repeated the word "guilty." Then, wanting to know what facts the jurors considered in reaching their verdict, he questioned them briefly in open court. As he did, the events of the last three years raced through my mind, especially those of the last eight weeks. I had sat religiously through the trial. I'd witnessed the witnesses the jurors had witnessed and now I witnessed this strange verdict. What happened? How had the jurors missed the obvious—at the very least—the abundance of "reasonable doubt"? What jurors, I wondered, cry almost in unison when affirming their verdict?

"Ever see that happen before?" I would ask before leaving Phoenix that evening.

"Never," said Chris.

The court adjourned, George allowed Ray some extra time to say good-bye to those who had begun the day expecting to escort Ray to his waiting Corvette. The group was by and large a dejected lot. An independent person, Ray was always a bit embarrassed by the attention and help he was getting from others—some who barely knew him. He thanked everyone. I believe he felt sorrier for these others at that moment than he did for himself. He was the only one who attempted cheer.

"Take care of yourselves. Don't worry about me. I'll be fine," he said with a big smile. Then as George ushered him out of the courtroom, he added, "I know how to do time."

Ray's smile was one of two I remember that day. The other one came from prosecutor Noel Levy as he faced the news media and expressed his delight at the verdict. He never smiled much. As I passed him speaking into a TV camera, I could remember only two other occasions in which I'd noticed him smiling.

π

Ray Krone had more time to do. But he wasn't the only one doing time for the murder of Kim Ancona. One cannot know the extent of the suffering a victim's family goes through. The conviction of someone—anyone—for the crime perhaps alleviates their suffering somewhat by offering closure.

But Ray's family would continue doing time. It had begun at almost the same time as the suffering of the victim's family, when they first learned of his arrest more than four years earlier. Amy was the first in Dover to hear about it from Ray. At Ray's insistence, she kept it to herself initially. But after the visit from the public defender, when Ray began to grasp the seriousness of his situation, he reluctantly allowed Amy to tell their mother.

There is no good time to hear that your son has been arrested and charged with murder. But that particular time of life was especially difficult for Carolyn. She was three years into a divorce from Dale, which would take another year to settle. Although Ray assured her that he would be all right, she would have helped him if she could but her assets were tied up in divorce court. For the second trial she and her new husband, Jim, would spare no expense to help Ray. While it's one thing for a distant cousin with a moderately successful and not too encumbering computer business to gallivant about the countryside pursuing Ray's cause, it was quite another to pay for the defense of one charged with murder. This burden rested on Jim and Carolyn's shoulders.

Jim Leming moved from Colorado to York in the fall of 1989, the same year Carolyn initiated her divorce. He joined his son Scott, who was already there working in construction. Jim rented a house with Scott and went to work as a heavy equipment operator for the same construction company. Jim worked his way into a position supervising the excavation of land being prepared for construction. Jim met Carolyn at church the next year. They were in similar situations—both were going through a divorce after more than twenty-five years of marriage. Eventually they moved in together and were married soon after Carolyn's divorce became final.

Although he would meet Ray for the first time on Death Row, Jim had no doubt about Ray's innocence and shared Carolyn's distress. After Ray's conviction was reversed by the Arizona Supreme Court and granted a new trial, the Lemings began to raise the money they knew would be necessary. They literally mortgaged the farm. Jim sold his house in Colorado and donated the proceeds. Gifts from family and friends who heard of Ray's plight helped. From her divorce Carolyn had received just forty percent of the assets, which included what was left of Grandpa's original property, a farm. Carolyn mortgaged it and borrowed against everything else she owned, including two retirement plans.

Jim and Carolyn had left home some weeks earlier, leaving behind no viable collateral unencumbered but with high hopes that it would be well worth it. With these hopes and their prayers, they religiously attended the eight-week murder trial of their son. Now they were returning without Ray, hopes shattered, prayers unanswered, to face enormous debt. Both were approaching sixty. The prospect for retirement in the foreseeable future was gone. Jim would return to his job, Carolyn to her's as assistant billing director for York Hospital. They would spend their time doing what was necessary to recover from their disappointment and to pray that somehow someway it would work out for them and Ray. Others would be praying for Ray too.

George fully expected Ray to be acquitted. If he had been convicted of a crime he didn't commit he would have gone ballistic upon hearing the verdict. The last surprise of this strange trial for George was that Ray did not. As George led him from the courtroom, all that Ray said was, "I'll change my clothes and get back into my stripes."

"I don't claim to be a good Christian but I will pray for you every day," George confided as they rode together down the elevator to the tunnel. "This bothers me badly. Keep you eyes and ears open. Someone did this murder. You know how inmates talk. There's a network in there that will blow your mind."

Ray already knew about the "network" and he well understood the truth of George's last words to him: "The only way you're going to get out is to find the real killer."

George expected never to see Ray again. He had done something he was cautioned against. He'd gotten involved. George openly criticized the police for their rush to judgment and the prosecutor for ignoring solid evidence in favor of a hokey bite mark. Word spread that George was defending someone accused and convicted of murder. To his colleagues, George had become an "inmate lover" who was "getting soft." It wasn't long before he was transferred away from the courts. He retired soon thereafter.

Ray's "only way" was obvious to everyone else as well. Perhaps Ray would hear something through the grapevine while doing time? Perhaps the blood on the victim's panties, which had been overlooked by the Phoenix police crime lab only to be discovered during the trial, harbored the identity of the killer? Perhaps finding the car that Henson saw transport the killer to and from the crime scene would be the key that would unlock Ray's cell door?

To Maricopa County, Ray Krone was the "official" murderer of Kim Ancona. But we who were rocked by the enormity of this injustice would keep looking for the real killer.

CHAPTER 13
HOMETOWNED

Fueled by emotions rising from defeat, you sometimes blame the one who fought the battle. On my long drive home, starting the evening following the verdict, such thoughts crossed my mind.

Since my introduction to Chris Plourd in early 1994, I had gotten to know him well. In the early stages, whenever possible, I would travel to Phoenix when Chris was there working on the case. I met him in the evidence room and helped him take pictures of every item in evidence, attended the hearing at which Judge Hotham denied the petition for post conviction relief, accompanied him to the state supreme court to hear oral arguments for the appeal, watched him fry Rawson at the *Frye* hearing—to name a few occasions.

As he prepared the case, Chris would call frequently with updates. He was totally accessible. And I wasn't special in having his home phone number. He routinely gives it out to his clients—something few attorneys do, requiring their clients to make contact only at their office. Having clients call all hours of the day and night, frequently from the county jail, contributed to his divorce, which happened a few months after his return from Phoenix. "She doesn't like what I do for a living," was his only comment to me about it

I acted as liaison between Chris and Ray's family. The first order of business was Chris's requested fee, a reasonable amount. It did not include monies needed for investigation or to retain experts, a sizable additional amount. When I reported to Chris that the amount the Lemings were able to raise was thirty percent less than what he'd requested, he said, "Send it on," and not once did he ever mention the balance due. While most attorneys require a written contract to bind assets, there was none such with Chris. He took on Ray's case with a simple handshake, accepting whatever funds were available. When the money earmarked for experts ran out, Chris personally guaranteed payment.

Though working on a shoestring budget, Chris nevertheless did a thorough investigation. To conserve expenses he did most of it himself. He used the talents of Mike Pain as needed. Mike had done the early investigation for me, donating his time. He asked only that his expenses be paid. Mike continued the same arrangement with Chris. For Chris, Mike would locate the lay witnesses and do initial interviews.

Chris checked the police blotter for anyone arrested near the time of the murder for similar offenses. One individual piqued his interest. An American Indian had been arrested for a sexual offence in the vicinity of the CBS Lounge four weeks after Ancona's murder but he didn't pan out. Chris scrutinized the evidence and orchestrated the necessary forensic testing. He analyzed the crime scene photos in minute detail. He was the one who discovered "the scratch" in the autopsy bite mark photos. He had to point it out to the bite mark experts he retained, causing one of them to comment approvingly, "We should have found it! That's our job."

On one occasion Chris and I spent two days driving around Maricopa County trying to locate the getaway car Henson saw. Chris settled on Tennessee Mike to present to the jury as "the other dude." Neither Tennessee's car nor any of his friend's cars fit the bill. Chris even checked the vehicles Tennessee had access to at work. He had to let it lie. I believe it would have been found if resources and time hadn't been so limited.

As the trial approached, another vehicle unrelated to the crime entered the picture. Instead of flying, one of my trips to Phoenix had been in my other car, an 'eighty-nine Mercury Cougar. I left it at Bob Lewis's place so it could serve as our local transportation. The "Kronemobile," as Chris dubbed it, was waiting for us there when we rolled into town in a motorized camper for the trial. For this trip to Phoenix, I had flown to San Diego and accompanied Chris and his assistant, Ron Serna, to the small California town where Chris and his four brothers and sister grew up. El Centro is located very close to the Mexican border, about fifty-five miles from Arizona. There Chris and I switched to the RV one of his brothers used for camping and continued on to Phoenix. Ron returned to San Diego.

In San Diego Ron served as Chris's legal assistant during trials. He had finished his course work and was waiting to take the bar exam to become a licensed attorney. Because of limited accommodations and budget, Ron was not used for the Krone trial. Since I was in town for the trial anyway, Chris, without formally saying so, enlisted me. Taking advantage of Bob and Selena's gracious hospitality, I'd already moved into their guest bedroom and set up shop. I was able to take care of business back home by way of telephone modem communication between computers. Chris set up camp in the driveway outside my window.

Ron was more equipped than I to help Chris with the trial, even though I'd learned a lot about the justice system after hearing of my cousin's dilemma. So far it bore little resemblance to my Hollywood perception of the innocent's righteously winning and the guilty's dramatically losing. I looked forward to this new duty and the continuing education. For eight weeks I made daily trips to the cleaners to see that Chris had a clean shirt and tie for court. I made early runs to Kinko's to have enlargements made of some of the many, many visual aids Chris used to make his case. I chauffeured him between camp and court. One time, with explicit instructions from San Diego, I detoured him to a bank so he could transfer funds to pay his staff. While he was taking his morning shower I would fetch his favorite Starbuck's blend. Running late one morning I tried to substitute a convenience store blend. It was duly snubbed and we suffered a minor delay in going by Starbuck's on the way to court. Each day, Chris loaded his dolly with boxes of transcripts, exhibits and other materials and wheeled it into court. I lugged the excess until a trip to the chiropractor—the first of my life—persuaded me to get a dolly of my own.

Nevertheless, the education was well worth it. Not only did I observe the action in court, I was able to observe the pregame preparation of one of the combatants. I found prepping witnesses the most interesting. Prior to trial Chris deposed (questioned under oath with Levy and a court recorder present) most of the lay witnesses, especially the potentially hostiles ones, to pin down each witness's statements prior to trial. Should a witness go astray in front of the jury Chris would whip out the deposition and correct the situation.

Chris thoroughly deposed Levy's experts—some several times. It was in one of many depositions of Ray Rawson that Chris locked the expert onto "the scratch" by having him circle it and annotate it as having been made by the defendant's tooth number eleven.

Chris had worked extensively for many weeks with each of the friendly experts—those he would call to the stand. When it came time for their testimony, it was my duty to see that they had air transportation in and out of Phoenix and hotel accommodations while in town. Ground transportation was provided courtesy of the Kronemobile and its chauffeur. The chauffeur would usually join Chris and the expert for dinner. Then, chauffeurless, they would disappear to the expert's hotel room, where Chris would smooth out the witness. This preparing of the witness was occasionally referred to as "sandpapering his ass." I was never privy to sandpapering sessions but could imagine what had transpired by observing next day's testimony.

Sometime before the trial, Chris had remarked, "To be a good trial attorney you must be a good actor."

Indeed, I thought, watching each day's performance.

For pretrial appearances Chris was his jovial self, joking when appropriate. I particularly liked his comment, in Levy's presence, to the lead detective who arrested Ray, "After the trial we're going to put you in charge of finding the real murderer." Neither Levy nor the detective found it funny.

But when the jury appeared, Chris's demeanor changed. Dinners no longer dragged on. When an expert witness was in town Chris would drop me off at Bob's house and disappear in the Kronemobile. When not, he would retire early to his camper. Its light, visible from my window, was always on when I retired and always on when I arose the next morning. It was impossible to visit him in his lair. It was littered throughout with crime scene photos, trial exhibits and assorted paperwork (depositions, transcripts and notepads) necessary to prepare for the day's skirmish. Breakfast changed from the more robust variety to a lean and mean coffee and scone. Conversation was limited to what had happened in court the day before and what was going to happen with today's witnesses. His approach to each one was different, depending upon what he wanted to achieve. In the case of Tennessee Mike's date the night of the murder, for example, poor Beth seemed to be doing her best to tell the truth on the stand. But Chris, in a politely aggressive manner, twisted her to the point where she appeared to be (even if she actually wasn't) covering for Mike. She was so traumatized by Chris's interrogation that she checked into a mental hospital rather than face more of the same the next day. I felt sorry for Beth watching what she was going through but understood that Chris's loyalty was to his client, not to a vulnerable witness.

Then there was Chris's handling of Dr. Raymond Rawson. At the *Frye* hearing Chris grilled him hard, perhaps crossing a line and offending Judge McDougall. In his opening statement to the jury Chris aggravated McDougall's affront:

> The defense will contend that Doctor Rawson is a maverick who promotes unscientific theories that no other forensic expert accepts. His unique and controversial methods are not recognized by the American Board of Forensic Odontology and he does not adhere to their guidelines. He overstates the validity of bite mark analysis in claiming that it is better evidence than fingerprints. He believes that he can see things nobody else can see. Doctor Rawson does not look at the

evidence and come to an objective opinion. He assumes that the suspect matches the bite mark even before he sees the evidence. He presumes the teeth fit and that the police's suspect must be identified. Originally in this case, Dr. Rawson sees one bite mark and is unable to match it to Mr. Krone's teeth. Then he cooks up the two-bite theory. Now it fits. He's been paid twenty thousand dollars, is owed an additional ten thousand dollars and will be paid even more to testify before you. Unlike his peers, who agree that no bite mark can be matched with certainty to a suspect, Dr. Rawson sees a one hundred percent match. As he puts it, "Absent aliens from outer space coming in and doing something or the intentional manipulation of evidence, Mr. Krone's teeth made the bite marks."

Perturbed, Judge McDougall took Chris aside prior to cross-examination and admonished him. "I know you're gunning for Dr. Rawson. Take it easy. Cross the line and I'll stop the proceedings."

Before Rawson was called to the witness stand Chris noticed that the doctor was studying a copy of the transcript of the opening remarks. Apparently Levy thought it would prepare his star witness for cross-examination.

Chris began by asking, "You've read some statements I made that were in the form of allegations, is that correct?"

"That's correct."

"In your direct examination, have you corrected anything that was improperly or incorrectly alleged?" was the follow-up question.

"I don't believe so."

"Do you feel that my statements were not accurate?"

"Yes, they were preposterous!"

"You were personally offended?"

"Yes, I was!"

Then Chris shifted gears and for the rest of his cross-examination adopted a condescendingly respectful manner of questioning the witness. First he proved his allegations by having Dr. Rawson read transcripts of statements made while under oath at previous trials and depositions. Next he exposed Rawson's bogus bite mark analysis. Finally he trapped Rawson by asking him to find the non-existent scratch he claimed to see in the crime scene bite mark photos. Chris had effectively metamorphosed the expert into a buffoon.

As the jury filed out, Chris inconspicuously approached the bench and asked just loud enough for only the judge to hear, "How was that, your honor?" Judge McDougall simply smiled, shook his head and disappeared into his chambers.

π

Lost in hypotheses on the long drive home, I could easily imagine that he should have done this, or he should not have done that, or he should have done this instead of that. Should Chris, for example, have accepted the offer for a mistrial when Levy's expert misused science to include Ray as a possible source of DNA found on the victim's bra? In hindsight, of course, he should have. But at the time the jurors seemed confused by this expert's testimony and relieved when the judge ordered it stricken from the record. Any imagined fault with Chris's performance diminished into a triviality as the miles increased.

Like George, I had been there each day of the trial and saw what he and the jury saw. "He proved his case way beyond a reasonable doubt," George remembered some years later.

As I neared home, I recalled Chris's difficulty and frustration in confronting Phoenix's police department and crime lab and Maricopa County's courts and attorney's office. Particularly, I recalled Noel Levy's shenanigans (with the help of Judge Jeffrey Hotham) in stifling Chris's efforts to gain access to the evidence and how Levy repeatedly referred to Chris not by name but as "the California attorney." I remembered the inspirational letter Chris in frustration wrote to Ray a year after he took the case, in which he detailed the difficulties he was having dealing with the Valley of the Sun's judicial club. In recalling it I could not escape its portent for Ray, now facing more hard time, if not death, its message particularly appropriate now.

I wondered if Chris had had a premonition of the hometowning when he wrote:

Dear Ray:

It hardly seems possible that a year has passed since I agreed to represent you in your effort to win a new trial and demonstrate your innocence. I decided to write you on this anniversary to express my thoughts about how I have grown to feel an overwhelming commitment to your cause and express my regret for the difficult situation you still find yourself in. Although I'm telling you these things, this letter is equally pertinent to my thoughts for your lovely mother Carolyn, stepfather Jim Leming and cousin Jim Rix. Not only have I come to know you as a person, I've had the privilege to become acquainted with your supportive family, whom I find to be some of the finest people on the face of God's good earth.

Reflecting back now, I recall waiting several hours on a sweltering late June morning outside the gates of Florence State Prison, where we met for the first time. I've traveled many miles, talked to many people and written a ream or two of legal paperwork on your case since that hot June morning. Much has happened and is happening with your case. However, nothing has altered my initial opinion of you and your manifestly unjust circumstances. I knew, like I have known with only a handful of other clients I have represented in the past, that you are truly innocent. I guess I've developed a sixth sense about knowing when a client is truly innocent, which, by the way, is not so often in my business.

I sincerely wish I could have secured your freedom by now, an entire year's effort now behind me. You must realize that the forces that are keeping you on Death Row in the State of Arizona, I've learned, stretch far beyond the circumstances of your individual prosecution. The attitude of the criminal justice system in Phoenix, Arizona is frightening. I've traveled to many states, tried numerous cases, talked to many judges and juries about the responsibility they have to be fair with my clients. I've never seen such a pervasive attitude bent on denying people accused of serious crimes a fair and just trial as I have witnessed in Maricopa County. As an attorney learned in the law who has always trusted in our great constitution, I am ashamed of the criminal justice system that put you on Death Row. I believed in and love the criminal justice system in this country. The saddest thing I could ever tell you, a person who has suffered and continues to be imprisoned for a crime you didn't commit, is that your case is not an isolated incident of injustice from Maricopa County. My first viewpoint that your case was a unique unfortunate case, an anomaly, which slipped through the cracks of an otherwise fair justice system vanished with the heat of last summer's Arizona sun. There are many cases where people are not justly treated in your former community. Particularly disturbing is the evil attitude that the so-called "providers of justice" in Maricopa County have where people of color are concerned; African Americans, Hispanics and Native Americans. You might say that white people are served a plate of injustice that is not quite as plentiful as the ones served to our brothers and sisters whose skin happens to be a different color.

A colleague who read the recently published favorable newspaper account of your case commented to me that I must be extremely satisfied with the "great results" I've thus far accomplished on your behalf. Without a second thought I replied to him that I most certainly was not satisfied with anything about your case. How can I be satisfied when a client of mine who, after three years, still sits on Death Row for a crime in which he has no responsibility? No, I am not satisfied.

As you well know, it was only a matter of weeks from our first meeting that I was able to demonstrate to the trial judge who sentenced you to die that the evidence presented against you at trial was fundamentally flawed, and in a significant part actually false. Almost a year later, nothing has been done by this judge to remedy the injustice in which he was such an active participant. How can I be satisfied with Judge Hotham's novel decision that dismissed your request for a new trial hearing last August on an arbitrary hyper-technical interpretation of the law where he concluded, in effect, that an innocent person facing a death sentence does not have the basic opportunity to come to his court and present factual evidence demonstrating that a man was wrongfully condemned to die. It took nine months and a unanimous decision of the Arizona Supreme Court simply to secure the simple right to be able to walk into court with your case.

This same judge, whom I now have appeared before on several occasions and have literally begged to look at the factual and legal errors committed before and during your trial, would not even direct the prosecuting attorney to share with me copies of police reports, allow me the opportunity to see evidence being held by the court or police, view photographs of the crime scene, allow our dental experts to borrow a duplicate copy of your dental models. Should I be satisfied with your trial judge who went so far as to ban me, personally, from seeing the exhibits introduced at your trial (trial exhibits which are typically opened to the general public) without having to petition him for a special court order, giving the prosecuting attorney the opportunity to object to what should be a basic right of any attorney representing a condemned man. I will never be satisfied with this judge, who continues to delay and deny the day when the truth will be permitted to rise in his courtroom, a courtroom that belongs to the citizens of the State of Arizona. No, I am not satisfied.

I am not satisfied with Noel J. R. Levy, the county prosecutor in your case, for his continued and deliberate efforts, *to this day and minute*, to conceal evidence that demonstrates your factual innocence. How can any diligent defense attorney be satisfied with a government prosecutor who, instead of dealing with the objective truth of a case, directs his efforts at hiding evidence and investigating my background simply because I happened to be an attorney working on your case? This prosecutor viciously attacks my integrity in and out of court with false assertions, innuendo and character assassination tactics. This prosecuting attorney still delays his fundamental obligation to provide me with discovery materials vital to your fair and full defense. I will never be satisfied by the Maricopa County Attorney's Office or its prosecutor's morally reprehensible treatment of you through the only attorney who has thus far made any effort to adequately represent you and determine the truth of who brutally murdered Kimberly Ancona.

I will not be satisfied by the Maricopa County justice system, which continues to be indifferent to the needs of a poor person to be adequately defended against serious criminal charges. A system where appointed attorneys are unable—or paid too little to be able—to present a proper defense on behalf of an innocent man. How can one ever be satisfied with a system of justice in a country like the United States, which prides itself as the finest democracy in the history of human civilization, that hires whorish experts to the tune of tens of thousands of dollars who have but one agenda?

I will never be satisfied until you are free and the individuals who are responsible to administer justice in Maricopa County treat people fairly, with the presumption of innocence that our constitution demands. Nor will I ever be satisfied until the Maricopa County Attorney begins serving the citizens who empower him with the moral principle that truth is the only legitimate lifeblood of a judicial process, when each deputy prosecuting attorney assigned to prosecute a case is dedicated to nothing less than *punishing the guilty and protecting the innocent.*

In my heart I have not become a cynic because of my unfortunate experiences in defending you in the courts of Arizona. I will say that I have faith in the jurists who sit on the Arizona Supreme Court. The presiding justice and associate justices seem to be correctly concerned that no innocent person be executed by the State of Arizona, a refreshing attitude, unlike their brethren who don the black robes in the trial courts. When your cousin Jim Rix and I visited the supreme court in May to view part of the trial exhibits that had been transferred to the court, we were treated fairly and respectfully by a helpful court staff. Upon finishing our work we thanked one of the courts clerks who assisted us and joked with her that the Arizona Supreme Court was our favorite court in the entire State of Arizona because it was the only court that had ever made a ruling in support of Ray Krone.

Many well-meaning Maricopa County defense attorneys have told me not to push the system too hard, that to make effective change in the court system takes time. Ray, as you all too well understand, WAIT means NEVER. Waiting for a change is what put you on Death Row. I'm saying that we have waited long enough. We are left with no alternative but to press the justice system with every ounce of energy God may give us. Your mother, stepfather, cousin and I are standing shoulder to shoulder with you against the judicial powers in Arizona that brought about your unjust captivity. We have come a long way. Some people have said and continue to say we will never secure the release and vindication of a condemned man. I reject this and tell you we are not turning back. I for one, no matter how difficult the situation, am more motivated than ever to keep the drive moving ahead to secure your well-deserved freedom. No matter how difficult a case may look for a client I have always been a believer that justice always prevails in the end, that when I walk out of court for the last time, with or without my client, justice was served. I know that in the end your conviction will be erased. How long it will take I can't say. You must believe that no lie can live forever; that truth no matter how suppressed will eventually rise and become evident. You must also accept the fact that your unmerited suffering in prison is redemptive, Ray Krone's cross to bear in this life.

As I prepare the final thrust to finalize your petition to obtain a new trial I believe our basic defense strategy we agreed upon last year continues to be appropriate. Let's continue to do everything to find out what truly happened to Kimberly Ancona—who caused her brutal death. Even though the prosecutor of your case has been uncooperative and defiant we should continue to provide him with the new evidence we uncover. It is my hope that this evidence will eventually break down Mr. Levy's moral defenses, work on his conscience, appeal to his sense of justice. If it does not, fine, so be it, then we will have to wait and present our case to a judge then a jury.

You would think that, given the fact that you had no qualified expert testify at your first trial and that four superbly qualified dental experts have come forth with opinions one hundred percent opposed to the state's expert, that would give some concern to the prosecutor that his evidence is incorrect.

I want to leave this letter on the anniversary of our first meeting with a few words, a favorite poem that has been inspirational to me over the years in my work:

INVICTUS
By William Ernest Henley

Out of the night that covers me,
Black as the pit from pole to pole,
I thank whatever gods may be
For my unconquerable soul.

In the fell clutch of circumstance
I have not winced nor cried aloud.
Under the bludgeoning of chance
My head is bloody, but unbowed.

Beyond this place of wrath and tears
Looms but horror of the shade,
And yet the menace of the years
Finds, and shall find me, unafraid.

It matters not how straight the gate,
How charged with punishments the scroll,
I am master of my fate,
I am captain of my soul.

I hope this poem gives you comfort in the difficult hours and days to come.

Christopher J. Plourd

π

Though stoic on the surface, Ray Krone surely suffered inner anguish in the days that followed the conviction. His first trial had been a farce. But for the second, in the final analysis, everything that could have been done seemingly was done. In the days to come Ray would confide to his sister Amy, "This is it. I'll die in prison." But he would have to languish several more months in the county jail before sentencing would determine his ultimate destination and fate.

No doubt it was a long trip home for Carolyn, Jim and Amy. Ray's friends sadly returned the Corvette to storage. It is an understatement to say that everyone close to Ray was affected deeply by the grotesque verdict. No one more so than Chris Plourd.

After the verdict, George had observed a private moment in the hall leading to the judge's office. "I've never seen an attorney that upset. I was looking at him closely, saying to myself, This man is really devastated. I've seen many attorneys in my time. This one was totally different."

Chris continued to represent Ray through the aggravation and mitigation hearings preceding sentencing. It would be six long months before Chris made his final appearance in court as Ray's attorney.

Much like a professional soldier, Chris experienced melancholy at the end of each war regardless of whether he'd won or lost. The next one would bring him out of the doldrums. But to lose a case that in his heart he knew should have been won pushed melancholy into depression. In the months that followed he became reclusive, avoiding his office whenever possible. He screened his phone calls, particularly avoiding Krone case creditors. The case had not, to say the least, been a profit making venture. It was obvious from the beginning that Chris was not in it for the money. He was distressed when he was compelled to pass some outstanding obligations on to the Lemings. The Lemings would in time make good on all debts incurred defending their son.

A failing marriage only contributed to Chris's angst. To his credit, and evidence of being a quality father, the only area of his life that didn't suffer was his commitment to his three children. His dedication to them continued uninterrupted.

At one point, Chris may have considered getting out of the business. "I thought we were going to lose him," remarked a troubled colleague who knew him well and who was close to him in those dark days.

I, however, was oblivious at the time to the depth of Chris's melancholy. I did not see him again until the following February in New York, at the annual meeting of the American Academy of Forensic Sciences. He continued to take my calls without interruption or any indication of anxiety. We frequently chatted philosophically and at length about the trial and its outcome. We also compared notes about another legal matter we independently had in common. I found this skilled defense attorney no more equipped to handle divorce without legal counsel than I. Compared, however, with what had happened to Ray Krone, it was a minor nuisance

In time Chris recovered and continued to practice law. In the years to come we kept in close touch. He even represented me in two civil matters.

For one, someone at the IRS had gotten the notion that I had assumed a second identity for the purpose of hiding income and put me under criminal investigation. Opting for my right to remain silent, I quietly watched for two years as the ladies and gentlemen of the Treasury Department's Criminal Investigation Division floundered in making a case against me. Sharing this experience with my friend while in New York, I suggested that perhaps I should end the episode by sitting down with the good people at the CID and politely explain the situation. Chris strongly intimated that these people were not my friends and volunteered for the duty. The IRS is less than sympathetic with someone whose memory is failing. In short order the CID was able to grasp Chris's contention that it's not a felony to lose your mind. The misunderstanding was resolved with a straightforward though somewhat costly audit.

The second matter concerned an egregious sales rep who after being relieved of duty believed that he owned part of my company. He sued for an unbelievable amount of money—just short of googol dollars. After several months Chris whittled him down to the point where he made a demand for one hundred thousand dollars.

"Offer him fifty thousand," Chris advised.

"I don't want to pay that idiot a dime," I said.

"Don't worry, he won't take it. Before I'm done with him he'll take ten thousand and be happy to get that much."

Reluctantly, I made the offer. As predicted it was refused. Then, after deposing several key witnesses, Chris put the plaintiff on the hot seat. I had informed Chris that his target believed UFOs were extraterrestrial. He saved the best for last. At the end of a full day's contradictory testimony in which it was established that the plaintiff had altered his employment contract and forged another legal document, Chris asked, "You know what truth is, don't you?"

"Yes, I do."

"So if I were to claim to you that aliens from outer space walk among us, you would say that that's not true?" was the next question.

"Not necessarily," was the answer.

It was great fun watching the plaintiff's attorney squirm as Chris elicited elaboration from the witness, a bona fide space case. This attorney seemed bewildered from the outset that Chris would not simply negotiate an amount that everyone would get paid—by Chris's client, of course. Perhaps he'd never been up against an attorney who was not part of the club but really meant it when he said, "My client comes first."

The offer went out the next day at noon by fax. It was accepted two hours later, also by fax. As predicted, ten thousand dollars disposed of this nuisance and nonsense. Chris had taught a lesson to the younger attorney. Never take a space case on a contingency. Always require a sizable retainer up front.

π

For me, the only positive aspect of Ray's continued predicament was that, whenever something negative entered my life, I would remember Ray Krone then say to myself, "Stop complaining! You think you've got it bad?" By comparison, the nuisances in my life amounted to nothing, a mere few dollars. Ray had lost everything. His bank accounts were gone. His house went back to the bank after its contents had been pilfered and its inside trashed from neglect. Only his Corvette and dune buggy had been rescued. Gone were his boat, his truck, his Volkswagen bus and his stock car. But these things were the least of his loss. Gone was his freedom. For the better part of five years his world amounted to sixty square feet. How long, if not forever, it would remain this way was anybody's guess.

I can think of nothing more difficult in this world than to correct a jury's erroneous verdict. I'd entered the scene about halfway through the process. Now it was back to square one. Fantasies of a quick solution were just that. Ray's case would once again have to move through the court system at the usual snail's pace. Though Ray would be represented by two other attorneys during the process, Chris stayed involved. Throughout the journey he remained able, available and willing to advise...

CHAPTER 14
WHAT TO DO?

The ball was in the court's court. Until Ray was sentenced, nothing could be done. If sentenced to death, Ray would get an automatic appeal to the state supreme court. A life sentence would mean Ray would have to initiate the process himself in the court of appeals.

Another Rule 32 to present new evidence was possible. But everything that could have been known about the murder of Kim Ancona was to date known. Considering Plourd's thoroughness, it seemed bleak that any significant undiscovered evidence existed. He was, however, curious about the unanalyzed bloodstains on Ancona's panties, whose existence he first discovered during trial with the help of the Phoenix police department's criminologist. Possibly it belonged to victim, but there was also the speck of blood on the inside of Ancona's pants, which was known not to be Ray Krone's. The jurors must have bought Levy's "logic" that Ancona wore "borrowed" bloody pants to work on her last night. Nevertheless, finding someone else's blood on the panties or identifying the source of the blood on the pants would be of great interest. Too get at these items, though, would require a court order because the pants and panties were in the custody of Maricopa County. And the county attorney was not about to release them for "frivolous" testing. It would not be prudent to go into court right away and ask that just the pants and the panties be tested because the law allows the convicted only one chance to present *all* new evidence. Other unknown evidence might be out there waiting to be discovered. Also, advances in DNA technology that could make test results more definitive were believed to be on the horizon. We agreed that the most reasonable course of action was to let the lengthy appeals process run its course and at the same time pursue all avenues of discovery.

One such path was through the forensic science community. An exposé of the exploits of a bite mark expert from Hattiesburg, Mississippi had helped Tony Keko. Perhaps a similar exposé of his Las Vegas colleague would help Ray Krone?

Doctor Michael H. West had become active in the forensic community upon receiving his Doctor of Dental Surgery degree from Louisiana State University in 1977. Entering the Air Force, he served as a forensic dental officer for four of his five years of enlistment.

After being discharged with the rank of captain, West went into private practice. He remained active in death investigations, spending fifteen years in the Forrest County Coroner's Office, five of which were as coroner/chief medical examiner. For eleven years he was a professor at LSU's School of Dentistry. In the years since becoming a dentist West had investigated more than four thousand deaths, attended more than twenty-two hundred autopsies, performed more than six hundred dental identifications, analyzed more than three hundred bite marks, given more than one hundred forensic lectures, made more than seventy appearances in the courts of nine states as well as in federal court, given more than sixty forensic presentations, published more than fifty-five articles, exhumed more that thirty-five corpses, received four research grants and worked one mass disaster.

Some cases of interest in which Dr. West's forensic talents were used were:

Louisiana v. Patricia Van Winkle. West matched a bruise on a murdered boy's stomach to a hiking boot belonging to the boy's mother. Van Winkle was convicted of manslaughter and sentenced to twenty-one years in prison. The Louisiana Supreme Court subsequently *overturned the conviction* due in part to "the equivocal nature…of the forensic evidence."

Mississippi v. Henry Lee Harrison. West identified more that forty-one bite marks found on a raped and murdered seven-year-old girl as having been inflicted by Harrison—sometime after the child was dead. No experts appeared for the defense. Harrison was convicted and sentenced to death. After the conviction, another expert odontologist, Dr. Richard Souviron, examined the marks and scoffed at West's findings. He believed the marks to be ant bites. The Mississippi Supreme Court *overturned the conviction* because the trial judge had refused to authorize funds for a defense expert.

State v. Johnny Bourn. West positively identified the bite mark on an elderly rape and robbery victim as having been inflicted by Bourn. However, DNA from hair found at the crime scene did not match. Neither did any of the crime scene fingerprints. Undaunted, West first claimed that the DNA results were faulty then claimed that Bourn had an accomplice, presumably the one who did the raping while Bourn did the biting. *The charges were eventually dropped*, but not until after Bourn had spent two years in jail.

Mississippi v. Calvin Banks. West matched the bite pattern on a half-eaten baloney sandwich found in a murdered woman's apartment to a plaster model of Calvin Banks's teeth. After his analysis, West tossed out the baloney sandwich because "it would have changed shape as it spoiled." Banks was convicted. The Mississippi Supreme Court *reversed the conviction*, stating, "The admission of the baloney sandwich rendered the trial fundamentally unfair. Dr. West's destruction of the sandwich was unnecessary and inexcusable."

Mississippi v. Larry Maxwell. First, West identified a knife with exposed rivets as the murder weapon used in the stabbing deaths of three elderly people. Then, while wearing orange colored glasses, he examined Maxwell's hand under a blue light. To his amazement the pattern of the rivets invisible under normal light became visible on the suspect's palm. Excited, he called this new "scientific" breakthrough "the West Phenomenon." To document his findings, West photographed Maxwell's hand illuminated by the blue light. But the film was "accidentally overexposed" so he drew from memory the rivet pattern on a photocopy of Maxwell's hand where he "remembered" the marks to be. Maxwell spent more than two years in jail awaiting trial before being *freed* after West's orange glasses/blue light testimony was ruled to be inadmissible. "It may well be," wrote Judge Larry Roberts, "that Dr. West is a pioneer in the field of alternative light imaging for the purpose of detecting trace wound patterns on human skin, and it may well be that the future will prove that his techniques are sound evidentiary tools that result in the presentation of inherently reliable expert opinions. But at this time I am not so convinced."

Louisiana v. Anthony Keko. In his next application of the phenomenon bearing his name West exhumed the body of Louise Keko, fourteen months after her death. Using the blue light and orange glasses to examine the remains, West found a mark on the right shoulder that he matched "indeed and without a doubt" to the dental model of Louise's estranged husband Tony. This time West was able to photograph the mark. He also preserved the tissue, but "accidentally" placed it in embalming fluid. The mark forever disappeared. Two highly qualified bite mark experts disputed West's findings before the jury. They believed the mark to be anything but a bite mark. West, however, demonstrated his phenomenon by providing orange glasses to each member of the jury and, with the judge's permission, paraded them into a basement room in the courthouse where previously prepared marks on the floor magically appeared under the blue light. It took just four hours for the jury to convict Keko. He was sentenced to life imprisonment.

This list could go on and on, but I will stop here because it was these last two cases that might prove helpful to cousin Ray.

At the time of the Keko trail, Dr. West was in trouble with his colleagues. The forensic community was even less impressed with "the West Phenomenon" than was Judge Roberts in the Maxwell case. The main complaint was that West used an untested scientific technique not generally accepted within the scientific community. His use of orange glasses and blue lighting allowed him to see things that only he could see and for which he could offer no documentation. Also, West presented his undocumented findings with an unheard of degree of scientific certainty. "Indeed and without a doubt," was his standard opinion.

The American Board of Forensic Odontologists, upon the recommendation of their ethics committee, suspended Dr. West. Facing other similar ethics charges, West resigned before being expelled from the International Association of Identification and the American Academy of Forensic Sciences.

Upon learning of the sanctions imposed upon Dr. West by his peers, the trial judge *reversed the conviction* of Tony Keko.

If Dr. Rawson could be similarly sanctioned, Ray might also win a new trial. After all, Rawson had used a scientific technique—CAT scanning—not generally accepted or used by other odontologists. He saw things that only he could see—the "scratch." He rendered an opinion of ambiguous scientific certainty—"It's a match." And, as an added bonus, he misrepresented the validity of bite mark analysis—"Bite marks are better than fingerprints."

In the fall of 1996, while we were waiting for Judge McDougall to sentence Ray, an ethics complaint was prepared against Dr. Raymond Rawson and presented to the American Board of Forensic Odontology. For good measure a similar complaint was filed with the American Academy of Forensic Sciences against Dr. John Piakas for "misspeaking" his credentials while under oath.

CHAPTER 15
ETHICS

In 1955, at age twelve, I lived with my mother and two brothers—one older, one younger—in Daly City, a small town bordering San Francisco. Dad had passed away five years earlier, at age fifty. The cause of death was listed as heart failure, but years later Mom suspected it was lung cancer. Dad had been a smoker since age twelve.

Mom did her best to support the family as a public health nurse. It was tough then, as it is any time, for a single parent to support a family. To help, I took a paper route delivering the now defunct *San Francisco News* to some thirty homes after school. The subscription fee was one dollar and fifty cents per month. It was my responsibility to collect from each subscriber at the end of the month. I would give a dollar to the newspaper company and keep fifty cents for myself. The fifteen or so dollars I earned was all the money I had to spend for the month. Mom couldn't really afford to give allowances. If I were unable to collect from someone, I would lose my fifty cents and be out the dollar—a sizable sum back then.

One time I had trouble collecting. I went to this one subscriber's house three times. The first two times he didn't have the money. The third time, a bit annoyed, he told me that he'd already paid and not to come back.

Mom asked me, "Are you sure he didn't pay you?"

I said I was and showed her his stub, the last one still in the receipt booklet given to me each month by the newspaper company. The stubs had the names and addresses of each subscriber on my route. Upon paying, each subscriber was given his stub as receipt.

"Are you sure you didn't give him the wrong one?" Mom always assumed the best in people.

"Pretty sure."

"Well, let's find out," she said.

We went to the man's house. I stood next to Mom holding the receipt as she rang the doorbell. The man opened the door and upon seeing me became agitated.

"We're here to collect for the newspaper," Mom said politely.

"I told your son I'd already paid him," was the curt response.

"May I see your receipt?" Mom asked, again politely.

The man's eyes darted from Mom to me. He no sooner spied the receipt than he grabbed it out of my hand and waved it in Mom's face. "Here it is!"

Mom moved swiftly—like a cat after a rat. In an instant the man released the stub in favor of his gonads before hitting the floor. Quickly picking up the receipt and handing it back to me, she said, "Wait here!" Then, leaving me on the porch, she stepped inside and closed the door behind her. I could hear the man moaning still.

A moment later, after a few garbled sounds from within—the only recognizable word being "horseshit"—Mom reappeared and exchanged the receipt for six quarters. She tossed the stub toward the man, who had managed to make it to one knee while cradling his now aching stub. Quickly Mom ushered me down the porch steps into the safety of her car.

The 'fifty-three Chevy was still in first gear when Mom, obviously quite agitated herself, said, "That asshole is lucky all he got was a knee in the balls!"

Well, that was the first time I can recall hearing a human being referred to as that particular part of the anatomy. Mom had at one time been an emergency room nurse. In the ER, when situations were tense, expletives were not uncommon. Mom could keep up with the best— when appropriate. I remembered her saying one time about another such individual, "That man has his head stuck where the sun don't shine," and me wondering what she meant. Now I knew. Most of the time she referred to these types of individuals as "nincompoops." Her rare use of this stronger term was reserved for extra special nincompoops—like this man who refused to pay his debt to her son.

π

I was reflecting upon this particular lesson in ethics while waiting for another to begin. My thoughts were interrupted by none other than Dr. John Piakas.

It was February 1997, two months less than a year after Ray Krone's second conviction. Jim Leming, Amy and I had come to New York City where the annual meeting of the American Academy of Forensic Sciences was being held. Their main mission was to meet that evening with the incoming and outgoing presidents of the American Board of Forensic Odontologists and register an ethics complaint against Dr. Ray Rawson. In the afternoon a lecture on ethics was being given by an odontologist and member of both the AAFS and the ABFO. Jim and Amy took two seats together close to the podium. I took a seat in the last row near the center aisle.

As the lights began to dim, signaling the start of the lecture, Dr. Piakas sauntered up and took the vacant seat next to me.

This is going to be interesting, I thought. Dr. Perjury just might learn something. Piakas was on notice that a claim against him had been lodged charging that he had violated the forensic scientist's code of ethics by lying about his credentials while testifying at the first Krone trial. He'd already earned an appropriate nickname for this transgression.

π

The American Academy of Forensic Sciences was established in 1948 by a few visionaries led by Dr. Rutherford B. Hayes Gradwohl, a medical doctor and the Director of Research for the St. Louis police department. He and a few of his fellow scientists were concerned about the significant amount of misinformation that was entering the courtroom under the guise of forensic science. These founding fathers envisioned an organization that would promote objective science as the lifeblood of truth and justice. The preamble to their document proposing the formation of a permanent forensic science organization reads:

> There can be no justice without truth, whether that truth be attested by lay or expert witnesses. That truth of which we speak is something more than the mere willingness of witnesses to relate what they saw, heard or know. Individual fidelity to this moral standard, which we term honesty, is only one aspect of truth and is not always sufficient to serve the ends of ultimate justice...The witnesses at witchcraft trials many years ago were honest enough in the testimony they gave. Yet they were imperfect gatherers of knowledge and their testimony was not truthful in the larger sense that it corresponded with reality...it is commonly known that all knowledge is either consciously or unconsciously encumbered not only with the imperfections of the observer, but mostly by preconceived notions, prejudices and inadequate mechanisms for differentiating between appearances and reality.
>
> Science, as an empirical method of discovering eternal truths in nature, is the one important handmaiden by which truth and then justice may be unfolded.

The newly formed AAFS began publishing the *Academy Newsletter* and the *Journal of Forensic Science*. Meetings comprising numerous seminars and lectures on forensic sciences began in 1950 and have been held annually ever since. Membership grew from less than one hundred individuals to more than four thousand today.

The organization is divided into sections such as criminalistics, pathology, psychiatry, toxicology and physical anthropology. Odontology appeared as a section in 1970. Within each section there is a group of members, called a board, who have met certification criteria consisting of a college degree, advanced course study, casework, comprehensive examinations and presentation of scientific papers. A board-certified diplomate is recognized by his peers as a forensic expert.

The founding members recognized that the solution to the problem of eliminating pseudo science—formally known as "witchcraft" and today referred to as "junk science"—from the courtroom required more than merely increasing knowledge, improving techniques, standardizing testing, setting guidelines and awarding accreditation. The ethical behavior of their colleagues was also a concern.

At the first AAFS meeting a committee was formed to create a "code of ethics for the forensic science professional." This initial committee, however, did not produce. A second committee, ten years later, presented a code of ethics for approval. It was tabled after three years of discussion because "it was felt that it was not feasible to legislate morality and integrity."

In 1977, seven years after odontology became a part of the AAFS, a code of ethics entered the bylaws and a four-member ethics committee became a permanent part of the organization. Interestingly, members of the odontology section felt that the AAFS code of ethics was not adequate for their needs and the year after Ray Krone's first conviction instituted one of their own.

By telling the jury that he was a member of the American Broad of Forensic Odontologists, Dr. Piakas had violated the very first canon of his section's code of ethics, "Every member shall refrain from any material misrepresentation of education, training, experience or expertise."

π

No sooner had the lecture begun than the speaker asked if someone would man the slide projector situated on a table set up in the center aisle. It was only a few feet away from where Dr. Piakas and I were seated. He volunteered. So instead of taking notes, Dr. Piakas putzed with the projector throughout the ethics lesson.

Rather than relate to you the details of this dry lecture, which ended with the obvious conclusion, "above all else, do no harm," let me relate to you the most memorable ethics lesson ever given to me.

About the time I had the paper route, Mom gave me a baseball, a bat and a glove for my birthday. After school, I would play baseball with some neighborhood friends. One day I was playing catch with a friend when an errant throw sent the baseball through someone's living room window. My friend split immediately upon hearing the sound of breaking glass. I followed suit. Upon arriving home, Mom, always observant, knew something had happened.

"Where's your baseball?" she asked.

"I lost it," I answered, without conviction.

It wasn't long before she was able to determine that I'd fibbed and broken a neighbor's window.

"What are you going to do about it?" she continued, more than a bit perturbed.

"I don't know." I was hoping it could be forgotten.

"Don't you think you should have the neighbor's window fixed?" she suggested.

"How?"

"Why, with your paper route money, of course."

"Why?" I answered without thinking. "No one saw me break the window and, beside, it's cheaper to buy a new baseball."

With that Mom went into high gear, directing me to retrieve dad's belt. After the "lecture" she took me into the bathroom and washed my mouth out with soap, emphasizing that she didn't ever want to hear me fib or make such a suggestion again. Finally, she accompanied me to the neighbor's house and stood in the background while I made arrangements to replace the window.

A few weeks later I arrived home without my newly purchased baseball, which had been batted this time, through the window of a different house. Mom wasn't home. I had Dad's belt ready and waiting for her arrival.

"What's the matter?" she asked upon entering my room.

"I broke another window," I said, handing her the belt.

"And...?"

"Well, no one was home so I left a note telling them what happened to their window. I left our phone number on it so they could call me to have it fixed."

Mom handed Dad's belt back to me. " "You can put this away. It won't be needed anymore."

π

At their meeting with the president and the president elect of the ABFO, Jim and Amy emphasized in no uncertain terms that Ray Krone was convicted solely upon the bite mark testimony of ABFO member Dr. Ray Rawson—testimony that many other board-certified members disputed. Specifically, their complaint charged that Rawson had violated the ABFO code of ethics by:

Making comments critical of fellow scientists: After Abney's trial at which Rawson testified for the prosecution, Rawson, attempting to explain the acquittal, said of the defense expert, "The fact is [Dr. Homer Campbell] used a cheap trick in the courtroom—and it worked."

Misrepresenting the data: Rawson routinely claimed that as evidence bite marks are better than fingerprints. He claimed that a single tooth mark is as good as a fingerprint—"We could look at one tooth and…that one tooth would allow us to really say that nobody else could have created the mark."

To get Ray's teeth pattern to fit the bite mark, Rawson fudged the scale on his video overlay demonstration. Using the scale on the bite mark photo, the distance between the upper two canine teeth that Rawson matched to Ray's teeth measured thirty-three millimeters. Yet the actual distance between these teeth measured twenty-eight millimeters on the cast of Ray's dentition. It appeared that Rawson enlarged one image to fit the other. Under cross-examination Rawson admitted, "there are some differences in scale."

Testifying beyond area of expertise: Rawson claimed to be a blood spatter expert and testified that the blood spatter on the victim's bra is "a scientific match" with the defendant's dentition.

Exhibiting bias: "You always start with assuming there's a match."

π

In the evening I caught up with Jim Leming at the reception hosted by the American Society of Forensic Odontologists. The ASFO is an informational and social organization open to anyone with an interest in forensic odontology. Jim and I were members at the time. It publishes a quarterly newsletter containing articles of interest to its members. While it meets in conjunction with the annual AAFS meeting, the ASFO has no real affiliation with the AAFS and no real clout within the scientific community.

To establish his qualifications at the second trial, Dr. Piakas this time correctly told the jury that he was a member the ASFO, not the ABFO.

"Who can join the ASFO?" Plourd asked during voir dire.

"Anyone who wants to," Piakas replied.

"You mean attorneys can join?"

"You should know, Mr. Plourd. You're a member."

The chuckles heard in the jury box assured Plourd that his message was clear—membership in the ASFO does not imply expertise.

During cross-examination, Levy asked, "At the first trial, did I inadvertently ask you if you were a member of the American Board of Forensic Odontology?"

"Objection!" Plourd interjected before the answer could be given. He didn't want Levy to take the heat for Piakas's ethical boner.

"Sustained," came the decision from the bench.

π

At the reception, Jim Leming engaged Dr. Piakas in a discussion on ethics. Jim attempted to point out to the doctor that he had exhibited bias during his testimony. According to the speaker on ethics earlier in the day, one should be his own man and not look to the hiring attorney for assurance or assistance during cross-examination. As I strolled up, Jim was emphasizing that after each of Plourd's questions Piakas's eyes would dart back and forth between Plourd and Levy as if he were watching a ping pong tournament.

Dr. Piakas took my arrival as an opportunity to leave immediately. Pointing to me he said, "And you! You're rude to me!"

I was a bit confused as I hadn't said word one to him.

Sometime later I discovered that my notes on the ethics lecture were missing. Could it be that they inadvertently got mixed in with his pile of stuff while he was manning the projector? Oh well, Dr. Piakas had more use for them than I.

π

Over the next few weeks four large boxes, each containing a copy of the complete transcripts of the bite mark testimony along with copies of the videotapes, were assembled. One was sent to each member of the ethics committee. Then we waited, hoping to get an ethics sanction à la Dr. Michael West that could be taken into court to discredit the bite mark experts. Absent the bite mark evidence, as with the Tony Keko case, there would be no case against Ray Krone and he too would have to be released.

But Ray Krone would not be so lucky as Tony Keko. It took one full year for the AASF and ABFO ethics committees to do nothing. Neither Rawson nor Piakas was sanctioned. Ethics committees change membership periodically. The committee that considered "the West Phenomenon" was long gone. The one that considered Dr. Rawson's ethical behavior concluded that Rawson's statements were "not made unequivocally." They justified this finding with ersatz logic, and their argument that Dr. Piakas "inadvertently" misrepresented his credentials was equally unconvincing.

π

While it took some time to legislate a code of ethics, it seems it's going to be a long, long time, if ever, before one will diligently be enforced. Dr. West's suspension was a feeble slap on the wrist. After one year, he was reinstated by the ABFO and continued his career as an expert forensic odontologist.

If the forensic community ever really wants to get serious about holding their members accountable for ethics violations, they might consider bringing in someone like Mom. With such a person in charge, violators would easily be recognized. The blackballed would be seen hobbling around comforting their root with a new appreciation for the root of the word "testimony." In lieu of that solution, perhaps this august community will someday wise up and abandon all pretense of having a code of ethics. Isn't it better to stop talking about it if there's no real intention of doing anything about it or if they're actually trying to send the message that it's okay to misrepresent credentials or mislead juries so long as it's done "inadvertently" or "equivocally"?

The best the AAFS has been able to do in its fifty years in existence is to note the existence of the ethics problem within its ranks by meaningless actions such as creating do-nothing ethics committees or choosing "truth or consequences" as its theme for their year 2000 Reno meeting or giving dull, predictable, repetitive lectures on ethics that seem to proliferate when controversial cases like Ray Krone's are cooking.

Everyone knows what ethics is supposed to be. If given a chance, even Dr. Piakas could pass an ethics exam. Do you think if he were asked if it's all right to lie about his credentials he would say "yes"? So why did he do it? No one but he knows the specific reason for sure. Maybe it's as he told the second Krone jury, "I misspoke." But maybe it's something else.

Ethics, like the truth, is relative. If you haven't had the good fortune to have had it whipped into you in your formative years, you're never going to get it. Might the offspring of the man who attempted to welsh on his newspaper subscription not grow up believing that it's okay to do anything for a buck? And they could very well grow up to be doctors, lawyers, judges or forensic scientists.

There is no excuse for anyone to behave unethically or for any organization to tacitly condone unethical behavior within its ranks. The AAFS and its affiliates have over the years paid valiant lip service to their ethical dilemma without having been able to make any discernable inroad into its solution. Their wishy-washy handling of Ray Krone's complaints against Piakas and Rawson suggest that they have thrown up their hands and realize that the problem is bigger than they are. You see, forensic scientists are merely tools of the trade used by defending or prosecuting attorneys, the adversaries of the justice game, where winning, not truth, is rewarded. As such, no procuring attorneys are going to hire a forensic expert whose testimony will hurt their chances of winning. Even experts testifying on the side of truth not infrequently espouse junk science. To be in business, all a defender or prosecutor needs to do is to find a doctor of something with Ray Rawson's ethical outlook: "If someone is retained by a side, then they have an obligation to that side; I guess I just picked that up from my own ethical system"—a statement he made under oath in a deposition.

Most forensic scientists begin their career bright eyed, but they all soon learn that playing the game pays. One wants to believe that most forensic scientists are ethical, intelligent, competent and strong enough to avoid this moral pitfall. But most isn't good enough. It takes just one venal expert to produce a krone for his employer. (I propose the term "krone" to refer to an innocent person convicted of a crime, particularly by the use of false or misleading scientific testimony and/or by the use of pseudo science. The verb "to krone" would mean to convict an innocent person, particularly in that false or misleading way.)

π

Science is not immune to the economic forces of supply and demand. When the justice game demands junk science, the forensic community supplies it. While this demand infects almost ever branch of forensic science, nothing epitomizes junk science more then the bite mark analysis component of forensic odontology. Bite mark analysis should more aptly be classified as…

CHAPTER 16
OUIJA SCIENCE

For Christmas one year in my teens I received a Ouija board. It was a simple toy consisting of a board and a pendulum—a pointed weight with a string attached. The board resembled a compass. The vertical axis was labeled YES and the horizontal axis NO. Points on the arcs between the axes were labeled with various other possibilities: UNLIKELY, LIKELY, MOST LIKELY, etc. The object of the game was for a player to hold the pendulum still with its point hovering slightly above the intersection of the axes and to ask the Ouija board a question. The pendulum, according to the instructions, would swing in the direction of the correct answer.

With eyes fixed on the motionless pendulum, I tried it.

"Am I fifteen years old?" In a short time the pendulum began swinging toward YES.

"Am I a senior in high school?" This time it pointed toward NO.

To my amazement, the Ouija board seemed to know everything. It answered question after question correctly and unequivocally.

Then I asked the Ouija board a very important question: "Does she like me?" "She" was the girl who sat next to me in French class.

YES, the Ouija board assured and delighted me.

After the holidays, however, much to my disappointment, the girl came to class wearing some senior's class ring on a chain around her neck—the flag for "going steady."

My confidence in the Ouija board was shattered. I tried it again, this time consciously and conscientiously holding the pendulum motionless. But, no matter how hard I tried to keep the pendulum still, in time it would begin swinging—always in the direction of my adolescent wishful thinking. Then my brother asked a question of no interest to me and to which only he knew the answer. The pendulum remained motionless. When he took hold of the string, the pendulum in no time began swinging toward the correct answer.

Well, it didn't take long to figure out that the person holding the string was unconsciously directing the pendulum's pointing. While the direction of the swing did not always correspond with reality, it always favored the holder's predilection.

$$\pi$$

Bite mark analysis is no stranger to biased pendulums. Most of the third to last page of *The Manual of Forensic Odontology* is devoted to bias, defined to be "a process at any stage of inference tending to produce results that depart systematically from true values." Several types of bias are listed:

> *Expectation bias:* The expert expects to find a certain outcome,
> *Influential bias*: The expert believes that the hiring or referring agency is always right,
> *Second opinion bias*: The expert is influenced by opinions of his colleagues,
> *Ego bias:* The expert believes that his opinion is the only acceptable one, and
> *Remuneration bias:* The expert can expect a sizable paycheck for rendering a favorable opinion.

The authors of the section on guidelines and standards caution that this last bias is the worst kind, noting that experts whose opinions are influenced by expected remuneration are "anything but neutral, impartial and objective" and are commonly referred to as "hired guns." Experts are advised in not so many words to keep their pendulums holstered, especially when cash is placed on their Ouija boards.

My introduction to remuneration bias came at the very first seminar on bite mark analysis I attended. It was at the annual AAFS meeting in San Antonio, where I introduced the Krone bite mark evidence to Dr. Homer Campbell and he introduced me to Chris Plourd. Chris and I chatted for awhile about the Krone case in the hall outside the meeting rooms before the lectures began. When Chris left to attend the one on serology, I attended the one on odontology.

The moderator introduced a series of speakers who presented various bite mark cases. Using two slide projectors, one speaker displayed a photo of a bite mark on one screen and a photo of the suspect's dental model on a screen alongside it.

Raising his hand, the speaker asked the audience of seasoned and aspiring bite mark experts to do likewise, "if you think the suspect can be excluded."

No hands appeared.

"Okay," the speaker continued, hand still in the air. "Who thinks the suspect *cannot* be excluded?"

The audience's pendulums remained motionless.

Then an obviously experienced and savvy expert realized that the speaker had left out one vital bit of information. "Who's paying me?"

The sustained laughter from the experienced experts introduced me and the wannabes to the Ouija nature of bite mark analysis.

π

Hmm. They write about it, they joke about it—two suggestive clues. I wondered whether an experiment could be designed to actually demonstrate bias in this branch of forensic science—a *sting*, if you will, to expose what I believed to be odontology's inherently pliable pendulum. A bite, a mark and a cast of someone's teeth were needed.

Photos of the bite from the Krone case were plentiful, and I acquired a cast of the teeth of one of my dentist's patients. But who would be the mark? For the experiment to be meaningful, a bona fide board-certified expert would have to be found.

Using the Krone case bite mark was risky. Prior to and during the second trial, propaganda under the guise of a newsletter entitled *The Ray Krone Story* was disseminated by some shady person to everyone listed on the ABFO membership roster. It was highly likely that a candidate selected from this list would recognize the bite mark, for a picture of it had appeared in one issue of the newsletter. The dilemma was resolved when the shady person noticed that Dr. Michael West's name was not on that ABFO roster. He had been serving his suspension at the time and was thereby spared *The Ray Krone Story*.

In reinstating Dr. West a majority of ABFO members presumably must have felt that he had locked away his Ouija board and would keep his pendulum under control.

In any event, Dr. West was again a board-certified odontologist recognized by his peers as a bona fide bite mark expert. I selected him, hoping that he had not become familiar with the Krone case bite mark through one of his colleagues.

To complete the experiment, Dr. West would have to be given a plausible reason for comparing the dental model with the bite mark. Now, I'm not very good at pretense. The reason has to do primarily with Dad's belt. But also I remember Mom's observation that "the problem with lying is that you must always remember what you said." Indeed, most fabricators are tripped up by inconsistencies in their stories, especially as their stories become more elaborate. The story concocted for the experiment would necessarily have to be somewhat detailed.

Enter ace private investigator Phil Barnes. I asked Phil to investigate the murder of a college coed who had not really been murdered (in fact, she didn't exist), but which fictitious murder involved a bite mark. Phil accepted the challenge with enthusiasm. He made extensive notes on the unsolved crime so as not to be tripped up by unexpected questions from Dr. West.

Phil left the following message on Dr. West's answering machine:

> Hello. This is Phil Barnes. I'm investigating a murder that involved a bite mark. You've been highly recommended. If interested, send your CV to...

He provided a post office box number in Zephyr Cove, Nevada, a fax number and the phone number of an unused phone line in my office that he had borrowed for his business, Phil Barnes, Private Investigator. He was rarely in the office, though. An answering machine took his calls.

The next morning, while enjoying his morning cup of tea, Phil studied Dr. West's twenty-five page curriculum vitae, which had arrived via fax late the previous evening. Phil's fax machine was in his home, where he did most of his work. Phil noted that Dr. West had testified seventy-two times, mostly in the courts of southern states but also in a few to the north and west: Ohio, Michigan, California and Washington. Thirty-three of his seventy-two court appearances involved bite marks.

Phil thought it was good that his mark had yet to have a case in Nevada, where his unsolved murder had occurred. Phil added to his notes that the victim attended the University of Nevada in Reno.

However, one item noted in the CV concerned Phil. In the section "Mississippi Supreme Court Opinions," the case *Mississippi v. Calvin Banks* was described by the single word, "baloney." Phil feared that Dr. West, having that expertise, might detect the same in Phil's ruse.

Dr. West had included an e-mail address with his CV. Phil responded accordingly, detailing Reno's snaggletooth murder, which had some similarities to a Phoenix murder of the same name:

> Dr. West—I was very impressed with your credentials. Thank you. I have bite mark evidence to be evaluated. Briefly, my client's daughter was raped and murdered three years ago. She was a college student who worked nights as a waitress in a bar/grill. She was found stabbed to death in the bar's kitchen early one morning after working the evening shift. The PD botched the investigation and ceased investigating the crime when the lead detective accepted a job in another city. The family wants the murder solved and retained me six months ago.
>
> The PD wasn't able to make a case against their prime

suspect. Another suspect was a bartender. He wasn't working the night of the murder and had an alibi. His fingerprints were found on the condom machine in the restroom. (No semen was found on the victim.) He claimed the fingerprints were there because he was the one responsible for loading the condom machine. This guy left town shortly after the murder.

I've located two witnesses who saw him in the bar the night of the murder. DNA from blood found at the scene matched only the victim. DNA from the left breast, where she was bitten, was contaminated and proved worthless.

Two months ago I located the suspect. When asked for a sample teeth impression so that he could be excluded, he refused. Subsequently, I was able to locate his dentist and "borrow" his dental model. I also have photos of the bite injury. I desire to obtain an expert's opinion. If interested, let me know your fee and where to send the material.

Phil

I thought Phil's e-mail satisfactorily stroked Dr. West's pendulum. Phil started with flattery appealing to possible ego bias. He then included sufficient detail about the suspect to elicit any influential bias that might exist. All scientific evidence other than the bite mark was cleverly excluded so that the level of Dr. West's expectation bias would not be tainted with the thought that he might be up against solid forensic evidence like DNA. Testing second opinion bias was not advisable since having Dr. West contact one of his colleagues might put the kibosh on the entire operation. Last, but not least, Phil opened the door to remuneration bias.

The reply arrived the next day:

Phil, my retainer is $750. If your bartender is NOT your man the dental model and photos of the bite mark should very easily exclude him. Mail to Dr. Michael H. West...

So far so good—the package was on its way—dental model, photos and retainer.

Dr. West opined quickly. The day the package arrived he sent an e-mail asking Phil to call to discuss the opinion. Phil arrived at his computer late that evening after a few beers. Though anxious to hear Dr. West's opinion, he thought it best to wait until morning to call him. So far he had not talked directly with Dr West and he wanted to have a clear head and time to study his notes thoroughly to anticipate any questions Dr. West might ask about the crime.

"Hello."

"Dr. West, Phil Barnes."

"Ah, good to speak with you, Phil," came the affable greeting in a slow Southern drawl. "I got your package. I didn't get a chance to check if those photos were life sized. They appear to be."

Phil knew they were but responded, "I was told they're one-to-one, but you'd have to check that out."

"Well, this is a unique bite. It should be very easy to exclude this man—to say 'no, it's not possible that he did this bite.'"

Indeed it should, Phil thought, listening intently.

"Looking at the injuries on the breast, I note that it would appear that what we would call tooth number ten, the upper lateral incisor, should be rotated...and sure enough it's rotated in his mouth." Then after a short pause, Dr. West said, "I cannot exclude this man."

Phil remained silent, thinking, So much for the experiment if the weak opinion, "not excluded," is as good as it gets.

Dr. West left the bite mark and asked, "Tell me the story. How did the investigation go awry?"

"Uh...I got into it recently." Phil stumbled a bit, thumbing through his notes. "Uh...basically the investigating detective...uh...got onto the wrong track...uh...put all his marbles into the one basket...uh...went after the wrong guy and...uh...that went dry and...uh...then he lost interest in the case and...uh, uh...you know...took another job elsewhere..."

Dr. West interrupted, "How far y'all from Las Vegas? I know an odontologist who works with the Vegas police, Ray Rawson."

"Quite a ways," Phil answered, somewhat taken back.

Getting Dr. West's Las Vegas colleague involved would result in a stinging pendulum for Phil. He immediately realized that a change in jurisdiction was in order. "But the crime took place in Idaho," he said.

Phil scratched out "Reno" and wrote "Idaho." Fortunately, Phil knew that the University of Idaho was in Moscow, if asked.

"Oh...Idaho..." said Dr. West. "We're talking about Idaho..."

"Yeah, I'm representing the family," Phil continued. "They have a place on Lake Tahoe. At Incline Village. The daughter was away at college at the time. I'm just helping them...just wanting to see if I'm on the right track..."

"Oh, you're on the right track," Dr. West assured him.

"Really?" said Phil, trying to hide his surprise.

"You got the right guy!"

Phil listened intently to the rest of the doctor's gobbledygook.

"The breast is conical shaped and it's very flexible. Looking at the bite mark in a two-dimensional photograph, you don't have a rubber stamp effect like taking the teeth and setting them down. One has to take into consideration the folding and flexing of the skin as these teeth bite into the flesh. There's going to be a lot of distortion of the skin. But I can find unique characteristics not only of the upper jaw but also of the lower. He has a space between lower front teeth and when you use that to line it up you'll see the lateral and canine come into play and then the centrals. They all have the right spacing. You've got much more distortion in the uppers. When you think about how the lower jaw swings, it would crush the tissue up above up into the inside of the upper teeth. To me it's very obvious."

Because of "liability" considerations, Dr. West was reluctant to write a report until the suspect was arrested. He ended the conversation by assuring Phil that he would come up with something that would help Phil convince the authorities to arrest the man.

Over the next few weeks, Phil monitored West's progress with the bite mark. At one point Phil was concerned that West was having trouble making it match.

"This bite mark is very complicated," Dr. West e-mailed. "I believe there are two bites, one slight, the other severe. The interplay between the skin and the closing teeth and the wrapping around and the distortion of the skin by the biting teeth will give the best results for comparison." He wanted to know if the breast tissue had been excised or if the body could be exhumed. It hadn't and it couldn't, Phil reported, adding "cremation" to his notes.

Phil was encouraged that Dr. West was leaning toward the multiple bite theory because that was how Rawson had misinterpreted the bite. But in the end the doctor proved just how good he was. Returning to the one-bite interpretation, he produced a videotape with accompanying audio that persuasively demonstrated the match. West rotated the midline a half-tooth counterclockwise from Rawson's bite number one. This view meant that one mark would have to accommodate the "suspect's" two front teeth. West demonstrated this orientation nicely by explaining that the right front tooth was slightly chipped and that the wear pattern on the left front tooth caused only half of it to leave a mark. For the lower arch, West showed how the spacing between the teeth matched the spacing in the photograph. He then demonstrated the flexing of the breast by pushing the life-size photo from behind into the upper and lower teeth casts respectively.

Marks that didn't quite match were the result of "dragging" as the bite was being made. The overall demonstration was quite convincing.

Showing how the three marks that essentially led to the conviction of Ray Krone lined up with three of the "suspect's" teeth, Dr. West stated, "Notice as I flex the photograph across these teeth how it conforms to the outline very nicely. The odds of that happening if these weren't the teeth that created this bite would be almost astronomical."

West's final remark was, "I feel very confident that there are enough points of unique individual characteristics in this study model to say that these teeth inflicted this bite mark."

The bite on the mark, alter ego Phil Barnes went into hiding.

$$\pi$$

During the West sting, Dr. West mentioned that he'd recently been interviewed by *60 Minutes* for a segment they were doing about him. As soon as West's videotape was in hand I contacted a producer at *60 Minutes* and detailed Phil Barnes's caper. The producer was very interested and I immediately forwarded a copy of the videotape to him. He liked it, but it was too late to include it and the show exposing Dr. West's pendulum was aired a month later. The show profiled two of West's triumphs, Tony Keko and Kennedy Brewer.

Brewer was convicted of the rape and murder of a young girl based on West's testimony that numerous marks on the victim's body matched Brewer's upper teeth pattern. The jury ignored the fact that no corresponding lower teeth marks were present. "How can we have 'forty some' bite marks all left by the upper teeth?" asked Dr. Richard Souviron, who testified in Brewer's defense. "It's so outrageous that it's hard for any normal person to comprehend." Souviron believed that the marks were in fact insect bites. "He [West] got a set of teeth from a suspect the police said [did it], and he took that model of the man's mouth and placed them on the ant bites and made it fit!" Subsequent DNA tests proved conclusively that the young victim was raped by two men and that Brewer was not one of them. "I never testified that Mr. Brewer raped or sodomized her," West told Steve Kroft on *60 Minutes*. "I testified that Mr. Brewer bit her." Despite the DNA evidence Kennedy Brewer remained on Death Row.

Eddie Castaing, Tony Keko's defense attorney, told *60 Minutes* about what Castaing believed was Dr. West's blue light magic, the West Phenomenon. "This was the case of the disappearing bite mark. It wasn't there on the day of the death in the autopsy photographs and it wasn't there on the day of exhumation [fourteen months later] until

[West] put the [blue] light on it—then it appeared. Then it disappeared ten days later. That wasn't a bite mark. That was a case of the Emperor's New Clothes." When asked why the jury was unable to see through Dr. West's blue light phenomenon, Castaing added that West is "very persuasive—a dangerous, dangerous witness" for defendants.

π

Dr. West's videotape was at least as convincing as Rawson's, if not more so. Could it be that Dr. West was right and that Ray Rawson was wrong? Maybe the actual murderer was also a patient of my dentist? Well, I don't think so. You see, the model provided to Dr. West was my own. That's right, Dr. Michael H. West, board-certified bite mark expert extraordinaire, recognized by his peers and by the courts as such, matched my dentition to the bite mark found on Kimberly Ancona with the same medical certainty as his equally qualified and recognized Las Vegas colleague had matched cousin Ray's dentition.

"I hope you have an alibi," said Chris, a bit tickled after hearing of Phil's caper and viewing the videotape. It was quite amusing to those in the know. Should Levy get wind of this new videotape, someone conjectured, he might reopen the case and refer to it now as "the case of the biting cousins."

Humor aside, this caper chillingly suggested that *anyone* arrested for Ancona's murder could quite easily have been kroned based on the testimony of some forensic cowboy who rode into town square, whipped out his pendulum and waved it high in the air for the assembled townsfolk to see. This realization sobered me. Had I been the one arrested instead of cousin Ray, I could have been the krone.

π

Bias is such a subtle thing. We're all infected with it to some degree. But some cling on to it with religious fanaticism. My experience with Dr. West leads me to believe that he is in denial. He genuinely believes that what he sees is reality. He has given convincing lectures on many of his cases and techniques, including one on his use of the blue light in the Keko case to show how he exhumed the body, examined it and like magic found a bite mark on the victim's shoulder. He seems to sincerely believe that his skeptical colleagues are either "ignorant" or harbor "personal jealously" and appears to fancy himself an "expert for the truth." I think he truly believes that he is a qualified expert on everything: bite marks, gunshot residue, gunshot reconstruction, bloodstains, bleach spills, use of ultraviolet light in detecting evidence, crime scene investigation and—in the case of a sandwich—baloney. The real West phenomenon is that he apparently believes his own baloney.

π

Some areas of forensic science are less infected with bias than others. Fingerprint analysis and bite mark analysis share similarities in that they both require pattern recognition skills. Yet it is virtually unheard of for one fingerprint expert to reach a conclusion opposite that of another. Why? The answer is: (1) quality—bite marks are commonly found on flesh, a surface subject to distortion, while fingerprints are usually recorded on rigid surfaces, (2) quantity—unlike the average bite mark, which is lucky to have eight individual tooth marks, a single fingerprint contains an abundance of information and, most importantly, (3) reproducibility—a valid scientific procedure exists that virtually guarantees that every competent fingerprint technician examining the same evidence will reach the same conclusion. No such scientific procedure exists for bite mark analysis.

To conclude that there's a match between a suspect's fingerprint and a "latent print" lifted from a crime scene, concordant points must be found. A point can be a distinctive arch, loop, whorl, dot, etc. The number of concordant points required to declare a match varies. Sweden requires seven, Brazil thirty, Scotland Yard twenty-three.

If the probability of finding a single concordant point by chance is the same as flipping a coin, one-half, then the probability of finding, say, twenty concordant points by chance is less than one in a million (1 multiplied by ½ twenty times is 1/1,048,576). That is, if twenty concordant points are found between two fingerprints, then the probability that they were not made by the same individual is more than one in a million.

Furthermore, fingerprint technicians do not sort over points of comparison looking only for concordant ones. Should a non-concordant point be encountered during a fingerprint comparison, a mismatch is declared and the analysis ceases. Bite mark experts are not hindered by this constraint. In Rawson's analysis, for example, just three of the six marks in the upper arch fit Ray Krone's dentition. Two marks that didn't fit he interpreted as part of another bite. He simply ignored the sixth mark.

While bite mark analysis is relatively new, fingerprint analysis has stood the test of time. Although fingerprint identification has had its controversies over the years, it's rare for two fingerprint experts to disagree, whereas, "We are wrong half of the time," Dr. Jerry Vale said to an audience of fellow board-certified odontologists and aspiring wannabes. He supported his conclusion by the observation that in virtually every bite mark case there are experts who testify for the prosecution and say the defendant's dentition matches the bite mark and experts who testify for the defense and say the opposite.

"Either the defendant made the mark or he didn't. There's no other possibility. Therefore, one group of experts is wrong," he concluded.

Truly concerned about these "pissing contests," as he calls them, Dr. Vale proposed that peer review be required for all bite mark cases. But this was soundly rejected by ABFO membership the same year that the ethics complaint filed by Ray Krone's family against Dr. Rawson was dismissed. Most bite mark experts seem to prefer to keep their pendulums private and insulate themselves from peer review. On the other hand, fingerprint technicians routinely verify each other's work. Peer review happens only involuntarily for the bite mark expert—when the defendant hires an opposing expert.

Occasionally, fingerprint analysis produces unjust results. But it's not because of the science. Consider the case of Rick Jackson. When arrested in Upper Darby, Pennsylvania and charged with murdering a friend, he was told that his bloody fingerprints were found at the crime scene. The local police also convinced Rick's father, Richard Jackson, Sr., of this. "Several [police department experts], with their professional experience, had read the prints and they, without a doubt, knew they were my son's."

Mr. Jackson hired a local attorney, Mike Malloy. Instead of throwing up his hands at this foolproof evidence, Malloy called two veteran FBI examiners, Mike Wynn and Vernon McCloud.

"Are you kidding me?" Malloy exclaimed when both experts agreed that Jackson's fingerprints were nowhere close to matching the latent prints.

Whoa! What happened?

"The underlying problem is not the evidence itself," said Malloy, "but who's allowed to be qualified as an expert. The police experts were really just your local police officers, who on any given day might do anything from getting a cat out of a tree to examining fingerprints."

The two police officers who pointed the finger at Jackson were not certified experts. The International Association of Identification (IAI) certifies only professionals actively working in the field. The qualifying exam has fifteen items. A successful candidate may miss no more than three questions. Half of the candidates fail.

"These two police officers are not qualified experts," Malloy informed the court.

The judge's response amounted to little more than "Who cares?"

To be safe, the prosecutor hired a gun, an out-of-state IAI certified examiner willing to dust off his Ouija board and grease his pendulum for the task at hand. The hired gun followed the two police officers into court and pointed his pendulum directly at Jackson.

Despite the fact that the two ex-FBI certified experts, Wynn and McCloud, had told the jury that the fingerprints did not match, Jackson was convicted and sentenced to life in prison.

There was no other evidence against Jackson. The jury's logic might have been, Why would the police lie? Perhaps the real answer for the jury was as simple as black and white. Jackson was black, and the police officers were white.

After the trial the IAI reviewed the prints and concluded that they were not Jackson's. The pressure was on the district attorney, but he didn't believe the IAI. Why would he if he didn't believe FBI experts Wynn and McCloud with their collective seventy-five years of experience reading fingerprints? Was it because they were retired? Or was it because they were hired by the defense? Succumbing to the pressure, the DA hired his own FBI experts. When they too agreed with their retired colleagues, the DA had no alternative but to release Jackson.

Recognizing that a hired gun had infiltrated their ranks, the IAI decertified the out-of-town expert and he lost his job. But what about the cops who initially misread the fingerprints?

"The men who put my son away for over two years are still allowed, and have not been removed from the ability to read prints," laments Richard Jackson, Sr., rightfully incensed.

Rick Jackson sued the cops. He lost, but nevertheless he was lucky to have a family who cared and an attorney willing to dig below the surface. It can take your breath away to imagine how many innocent people have suffered and how many others will suffer because these two cops have been and continue to be allowed to make fingerprint identifications.

π

Jackson was ultimately saved because fingerprinting's professional organization, the IAI, intervened and exposed the venality of one of its members. While the American Board of Forensic Odontology failed to censure Rawson for alleged unethical behavior, perhaps if they looked at the Krone case evidence in a different context they would conclude that one of their own had misinterpreted it?

A few months after Ray's conviction, I sent a letter to every board-certified bite mark expert inviting them to evaluate the bite mark evidence first hand. Eight out of nearly one hundred responded. They received several photographs of the bite injury as well as duplicates of Ray's dental model and were asked to answer some specific questions. The results were disappointing. True to form, as Dr. Vale had noted, one-half said Ray could not be eliminated as the source of the bite. The other half eliminated Ray. None, however, went so far as Dr. Rawson in matching Ray's teeth pattern with the bite injury "to a reasonable medical certainty."

These experts were asked to annotate and return a photograph noting which tooth made which mark. Only two obliged. Both saw two bite marks and marked them accordingly and incorrectly, as did Rawson. One of them, perhaps out of sympathy for Dr. Rawson, attempted to mark the "scratch." This expert wrote "#11?" on the photograph, with an arrow pointing to a dimple. The photograph had been taken at the crime scene and showed no scratch.

One respondent wrote, "[Since] Ray Krone did not inflict the bite mark injury...it is not possible to mark which teeth made which injury."

Does this make any sense? For bite mark analysis to be a valid science, shouldn't all experts independently interpret the injury the same way before attempting to determine who or what inflicted it? But the opposite type of thinking seems to be what bite mark analysis is all about. Start by assuming there's a match, as Rawson admits he does, and then work backwards to make the suspect's teeth fit.

From what I've seen, bite mark identification is devoid of any meaningful scientific guidelines or standards. Odontologists are all over the Ouija board employing all sorts of gimmickry and gadgetry, such as blue light photography, CAT scanning and multiple screen overlays. They routinely disagree among themselves and shun peer review. They do not censure their own for ethical violations or bad science. In fact, they have in some cases rewarded it.

Consider Dr. John Piakas. The sum total of his experience was the Krone case. In doing the Krone case he misrepresented his credentials, misinterpreted the bite mark and rendered an opinion opposite to that of three of his board-certified colleagues. For his fine work in helping krone Ray Krone, Dr. Piakas was rewarded. Unlike the IAI, which decertified the hired gun within its ranks, the ABFO opened its arms to Dr. Piakas and certified him. That's right, Dr. Piakas was voted into the club by its membership at large and is today a board-certified bite mark expert. How could they do otherwise? To expel members for being wrong would mean, according to Dr. Vale, that at least half of the ABFO members would have to go. The most they could do as far as censuring one of their own was to suspend Dr West for a year, and they probably did that only because other professional organizations were actively expelling him.

It seems that the ABFO is engaged in self-preservation, because the fact of the matter is that bite mark analysis has no demonstrable scientific validity. Validation was tried once. It was done in 1999 and called Bitemark Workshop #4. Twenty-five bite mark experts volunteered to match four sets of bite marks to seven sets of dental models. The error rate for positive matches was a whopping sixty-three percent, which means that sixteen of the experts got it wrong. As a result, the ABFO took immediate action. They ceased doing validity tests and, to answer their critics, issued the following statement:

> Bitemark Workshop #4 was neither designed as, nor can be used as, a proficiency test for forensic odontology. Tests of consistency and validity…were neither accomplished nor attempted and, as subsequent reviewers of the data correctly pointed out, the construction of the examination…was not designed to produce an examination that had statistical validity and statistical consistency.

Had Joseph Heller been an ABFO member he might have put this mumbo jumbo more succinctly: "A validity test that demonstrates that bite mark analysis has no validity is not a validity test."

π

Bite mark analysis, like fingerprint identification, could be a science. Both require pattern recognition. But fingerprint identification is supported by the principles of mathematical statistics. Finding twenty concordant points absent a single non-concordant point, verified independently by one's peers, is statistically very powerful. Unless bite mark analysis employs similar scientific principles, supported by blind testing and peer review, it will never rise above junk science and guesswork.

Identification of human remains through dental records is extremely reliable, but unless and until bite mark analysis demonstrates similar reliability, I suggest it be dropped as a scientific discipline or that the ABFO replace the "A" in their acronym with an "O" and become the OBFO, the Ouija Board of Forensic Odontology. Their motto could be, "Your guess is as good as mine."

CHAPTER 17
PUPPET SHOW

T he Ray Krone Did It investigation seems to have begun the moment detective Charles "Chuck" Gregory saw Ray's uneven teeth. While the police reports of other detectives suggested other possible suspects, there is not a hint in any of Gregory's reports that he seriously considered anyone other than Ray Krone.

Gregory was a nineteen-year veteran of the Phoenix police department when he arrived at the CBS Lounge, responding to the 9-1-1 dispatch, "possible homicide." He'd only recently been assigned to homicide after having seen duty as a night patrolman, an undercover cop, a warrant officer and a burglary detective. The murder of Kim Ancona was one of his first homicide cases. When he arrived at the scene it had already been cordoned off and other officers had begun collecting evidence. In what appeared on the surface to be a rape/murder, the bite mark on the victim's left breast loomed ominously. Biting is a relatively rare occurrence during hostile attacks. The victim had been found lying face up, so the bite mark could easily be examined without disturbing the corpse. Gregory did just that. He'd recently attended a lecture given by Dr. John Piakas on bite mark analysis. Piakas was called in and would show up later in the day to examine and photograph the injury.

As lead detective, Gregory directed the investigation. When he was confident that the crime scene was being processed securely, he went outside and began interviewing the bar's owner, Hank Arredondo, and others who had gathered in the parking lot outside the crime scene. Word of Kim Ancona's death had spread like wildfire. By ten a.m. that Sunday the parking lot was abuzz with the bar's employees and with friends of the victim, many of whom had been in the bar on Ancona's last night. Several reported that she was alone when the bar closed and that they expected her to join them later to party. One such witness gave Gregory the name "Ray" and a description of a man who had been sitting at the bar with Ancona Friday night. Another associated "Ray" with "Krone." Someone had seen Ray Krone and Kim Ancona together at a Christmas party. In the address book in the victim's purse were found two phone numbers annotated "Ray." The phone company provided Gregory with the associated street addresses. For starters, the detective selected the one closest to the CBS Lounge. He never got around to the other one.

It was just before one p.m. Ray Krone's dart team had taken first place in league play. He was about to leave for the awards banquet when he heard his dog barking outside. Looking out the window, he saw two men in suits walking up his driveway. Ray went out his side door to quiet his dog as the men approached. The larger, heavyset man merely observed. He did not speak the entire time. The other was detective Gregory.

"Are you Ray Krone?"

"Yeah...can I help you?"

Gregory identified himself and asked, "You know Kim Ancona?"

"No, I don't think so."

The two men glanced back and forth at one another.

"You don't know Kim Ancona from the CBS Lounge?"

Hearing "CBS Lounge," Ray thought for a moment then said, "I know a 'Kim' that works there. She's a bartender."

Gregory again looked at this partner. "Well, you're her boyfriend, aren't you?"

"No."

"You're not dating her?"

"No," Ray emphasized. "What's this all about?"

"She was murdered last night."

Ray knew something had happened at the bar because that morning his roommate Steve had gone to the supermarket at the opposite end of the strip mall from the CBS Lounge. He'd noticed police commotion in front of the bar and had told Ray about it when he returned with the Sunday newspaper.

"Gee, I hope no one got hurt," Ray had said and didn't think much more about it until he heard the bad news from Gregory.

"I need to ask you some more questions," the detective continued.

"Sure," said Ray, "Come on in."

Gregory declined, saying, "This can be better handled downtown."

Not knowing that his final fifty hours of freedom had begun, Ray cooperated. He really wanted to go to the awards banquet, but felt that it was more important to help the detective with his investigation. If he were a suspect, he thought, he wanted to resolve the matter sooner rather than later.

A black and white was called. Until it arrived, Gregory questioned Ray about his vehicles. Ray showed them to him—a sand rail, a pickup truck, a Volkswagen bus and a Corvette. The Corvette parked in the driveway interested Gregory the most.

A patrol car arrived and a uniformed officer got out and approached with handcuffs drawn.

"Hey!" Ray exclaimed. "What's going on?"

"It's okay," said Gregory. "Just give him a ride downtown."

Ray wondered why he couldn't have just ridden with the detectives.

But Gregory had a stop to make. He'd spied Ray's uneven teeth. He'd learned from Dr. Piakas's lecture how to get a bite impression from a suspect. At a convenience store, he picked up a package of Styrofoam plates.

Ray had a short wait in the interrogation room before Gregory arrived. He submitted voluntarily to all of Gregory's requests. He gave his fingerprints. He took off his shirt and allowed Gregory to search for scratches. He loaned his shoes to one of the other investigating officers. He bit into several squares of Styrofoam Gregory had cut from the plates.

Ray answered all questions without hesitation. He told the detective that he'd been frequenting the CBS Lounge for about three months to play and practice darts. The previous place where he shot darts had changed ownership and become a gay bar. Ray wasn't about to switch so he switched bars. The night before the murder Ray had been in the CBS Lounge with a group of friends celebrating a birthday. Kim was also there but not working. They talked briefly in passing. Ray played darts most of the evening with his friends while Kim sat at the bar with someone else [maybe the other man named "Ray"?].

The birthday party moved to Ray's place and continued into the morning hours. With only two hours' sleep he went to work the next day. On his way home he stopped into the CBS Lounge and had a beer while waiting for the pizza he'd ordered. He then went home, drank beer, ate the pizza and watched a football game with the few friends who were hangovers from the birthday party. Shortly after the game ended his friends left. Ray went to bed soon thereafter and explained his early retirement to Gregory by saying that he was "running on empty." Steve, his roommate, remained in the house and watched TV for a few hours before he too retired.

After answering Gregory's questions, Ray was driven back home. Three hours at the police station and he had the uneasy feeling that the detective didn't believe him.

Gregory had repeatedly asked Ray about being Ancona's "boyfriend" and "dating" her. He would not leave it alone. Ray assured the detective many times that he had not associated with her outside the bar. Ray wouldn't understand Gregory's confusion until they met again the next day and Gregory mentioned the Christmas party. To Ray it was simply an extension of the party, which moved from bar to bar and then to a bartender's apartment after closing time.

Ray had gone to the bar with Steve Christmas night. Steve was driving. He had to work the next day but Ray didn't. Not wanting to continue with the party, he took Ray home to get his Corvette and some beer for the party. Kim rode along and she and Ray returned to the party. After the party he drove her back to her car, parked in front of the CBS Lounge. It was an innocent, innocuous event, which Gregory misinterpreted.

After his trip to the station, Ray consoled himself that the bite impressions he'd left with Gregory would resolve the matter.

The detective returned to the crime scene with the Styrofoam squares in hand. Dr. Piakas was busy photographing the injury when Gregory walked in. Together they compared Ray's teeth pattern directly with the bite mark on the victim. Before long their pendulums were swinging in unison.

Prosecutor Noel Levy also visited the crime scene. He was delighted to learn that a suspect had already been identified—one who denied being the victim's "boyfriend." His pendulum too must have been aroused when he was shown the bite mark evidence. Leader Levy congratulated his teammates. Satisfied that the investigation was well underway, he went home and Piakas continued taking pictures of the corpse.

Gregory went outside. There he continued to interview witnesses. He'd already forgotten the description of "Ray" given to him earlier that day. It didn't match Ray Krone. What he wanted to learn more about was his suspect's relationship with the victim. He did. He learned that Ray had invited Kim to his house for lasagna, that he had sent her a Christmas card and that he and Kim had been seen hugging and kissing at the Christmas party at Trish and Lu's place.

The next day after work Ray stopped into the Library Lounge, another neighborhood bar, for a few beers. Before long a waitress who had just finished her shift returned to tell Ray, "Hey, there's a bunch of cops all over your car."

"Great!" Ray exclaimed and then told the small audience about being a murder suspect.

As much as he'd been hassled, Ray didn't want to chance driving home after drinking beer. The bartender who'd just finished his shift offered to give Ray a ride. They left together out the back door to the bartender's car. Ray was home in five minutes. It was just after five p.m.

"That cop's been looking for you," Steve informed Ray, handing him Gregory's phone number.

Ray called immediately and left a message that he was at home. Then he headed for the shower. He didn't make it. Gregory was already knocking at the door. He must have been hiding in the bushes, thought Ray, who again went voluntarily downtown.

This time Gregory was antagonistic. His first order of business was to get hair samples. Gregory had Ray pluck hairs from every imaginable part of his body. Ray soon became annoyed. How many hairs does this guy need? he thought.

Gregory roughly swabbed the inside of Ray's mouth for saliva, causing Ray to wonder, What's this maniac going to do next? He found out.

"Now I'm going to take your blood."

"No, you're not!" said Ray emphatically.

"Oh, yes I am," responded Gregory, handing Ray the court order to do it.

"*You* are not sticking a needle in my arm!" exclaimed Ray even more emphatically.

"No, no, a nurse is here to do it."

"Oh, that's okay," said Ray, relieved.

This little exchange, however, allowed Gregory to claim that Ray was "uncooperative."

Also waiting in the wings was Dr. Piakas. He was there to photograph and make molds of Ray's teeth. After Ray surrendered four vials of blood, Piakas came in and stuck a plastic apparatus in his mouth, spreading his jaw apart and moving it every which way while taking pictures. Then Piakas made two molds each of Ray's upper and lower teeth by inserting a horseshoe-shaped boot filled with a plaster-like substance into his mouth. It took several minutes for each one to dry.

With the biological samples extracted, Gregory continued his interrogation in earnest. Ray again asserted that he had nothing to do with Kim outside of the bar.

"I have information that you had Ancona over to your house for lasagna one evening."

"What!" said Ray, going on to explain that it was Trish, the bar manager, whom he invited for lasagna. Trish couldn't make it so she suggested that Ray ask Kim. Kim called Ray soon thereafter, obviously having heard about the lasagna party from Trish. Ray was not interested in Kim and did not invite her.

"You sent her a Christmas Card."

Ray explained. Kim had left a Christmas card for Ray at the bar. Trish had given it to Ray when he stopped in. Ray didn't want to be impolite so he reciprocated by leaving a card for Kim with Trish the next day.

"You took Kim to a Christmas Party."

"Oh, that," said Ray for the first time understanding Gregory's confusion about "dating." Ray went over it for the detective, concluding that "it was simply a ride from a bar to a party and back, nothing more."

"You were seen hugging and kissing her."

"It was Christmas. There was mistletoe everywhere. I hugged and kissed most every female at the party at one time or another that night."

But Gregory continued to insist that Ray was "dating" Ancona.

In frustration Ray told the detective, "If you call giving someone a ride 'a date' then I've dated half of Phoenix."

Gregory would not relent. "You're lying and I have a witness who will testify to that fact."

"Bring him in," shouted Ray, "and let's find out just who's lying."

But Ray would have to wait until his trial to find out that it was Trish who was filling Gregory's ear with lies and exaggerations about him and Kim. Kim had apparently been infatuated with Ray. Late one night, for example, she and a friend had driven around town trying to find Ray's house. Kim had shared her infatuation with Trish and others. Ray, however, was briefly interested in Trish. "She was hot," he explained to me later. "She always wore short dresses. She had great legs and this Southern accent. I asked her out a time or two until I found out that she was lesbian."

Trish was playing cupid. When Ray asked her to the lasagna party, she suggested Kim. Trish may have been the reason Ray's phone number got into Kim's address book. Trish's twisted facts encouraged Gregory to embellish "the date." The truth according to Ray is that Trish engineered Kim and Ray's being together Christmas night. "Why don't you give Kim a ride to the party?" Trish had suggested to Ray.

For some reason Trish reversed everything. She made Ray out to be the aggressor pursuing Kim, not vice versa. While we don't know exactly what she told Gregory, it is known from her testimony that she represented Ray and Ancona as boyfriend and girlfriend. And Gregory had to get his basis for insisting that Kim and Ray were "dating" from someplace. And Trish knew better. Were her exaggerations motivated by a desire to help Gregory or by something else? In any event, Gregory, with his pendulum dangling over the bite mark, chose to believe Trish.

The interrogation ended abruptly when Gregory pulled out a tape recorder and set a microphone in front of Ray. After introducing himself he returned to the other end of the long conference table. Ray had taken the time to read the court order. It allowed Gregory three hours.

"My name is Ray Krone. I've been here for more than three hours and am now being held against my will…"

Gregory bolted from his chair and stumbled across the room. Before he could hit the "off" button, Ray had more to say for the tape recorder, including the word "lawyer."

π

Nearly thirty years earlier, Ernest Miranda had been in the same pickle as Ray Krone. Perhaps even in the same chair. In 1963 Miranda voluntarily went downtown with a Phoenix police detective. His Packard was "similar" to the "Ford or Chevy" remembered as the instrument of abduction. Before being questioned, he passed through a line-up in front of the rape/robbery victim. The detective lied to Miranda, "You flunked," as he ushered the suspect into the interrogation room. Miranda was not advised of his Fifth Amendment right against self incrimination or his Sixth Amendment right to legal counsel. The detective denied that the confession had been coerced with promises of leniency that included dropping the robbery charge. After the conviction, Miranda's confession was the subject of intense debate all the way to the United States Supreme Court. On June 13, 1966 Miranda's rape conviction was overturned and the well-known "Miranda warning" was created.

If there had been promises of leniency, they'd been broken. Miranda did not go free. He'd also been convicted of robbery and he remained in prison. He was retried and again convicted of the rape by another Maricopa County jury, but without the infamous confession. In 1972, after serving one-third of his sentence, he was paroled. Four years later, at the age of thirty-six, Ernest Miranda was stabbed to death in a Phoenix dive bar over a handful of coins in the pot of the poker game he was playing with fellow down-and-outers. When arrested, his suspected murderer was advised:

You have the right to remain silent. Anything you say can and will be used against you in a court of law. You have the right to speak to an attorney and to have an attorney present during any questioning. If you cannot afford a lawyer, one will be provided for you at government expense.

π

Ray initially had waived his Miranda rights. He had nothing to hide and had cooperated fully with the detective. But it was going nowhere. Gregory didn't believe him. By requesting a lawyer Ray invoked Miranda, thereby ending the interrogation.

The detective was undeterred. Maricopa County cops had learned to deal with the Miranda handicap they'd brought on themselves. "There are other ways to handle this…" were Gregory's last words. He drove Ray home in silence. Ray would not see the detective again until his trial.

The next day, a fleet of patrol cars surrounded Ray as he arrived home after work. "Freeze!" He was tossed to the ground, guns pointing, handcuffed, thrown into the back of a patrol car and taken to the county jail, where he was booked.

Gregory had been busy that day. Around noon, he'd met Dr. Piakas at the morgue. Ancona had been autopsied. He watched Piakas rotate the cast he'd made of Ray's teeth back and forth over the bite mark. A videotape clearly showed the cast being pressed into Ancona's flesh. Then a mold of the breast was made and the breast was excised. The excised tissue subsequently disappeared, having last been known to be in the possession of Dr. Ray Rawson. But the cast made from the breast mold appeared at trial. And it appeared to fit Ray Krone's dentition. One is appalled to consider to what extent this careless procedure of pressing the cast of Ray's teeth into rigor mortis literally produced the apparent match?

In any event, Gregory was convinced. The arrest warrant was issued at four p.m. After the arrest a search warrant was obtained and executed upon Ray's residence. Except for three pairs of underwear confiscated from the dryer, Gregory reported "negative results" from the search. The detective sent the underwear to the crime lab, hoping that the spots on them matched blood from the crime scene.

Gregory may have cut the search short, because he had an important meeting with a significant eyewitness. He'd learned that Dale Henson had been cleaning the sidewalks in front of the CBS Lounge during the early morning hours when the murder occurred. Henson told the detective over the phone that he had seen someone drive up, enter the bar, spend a half-hour or so inside, exit and drive away. He said he could identify the individual. With the bite mark and a positive ID from Henson, Gregory could all but wrap up the case. Anything the crime lab discovered would be gravy.

Gregory arrived at Henson's residence ten minutes early for their ten p.m. appointment. The photo line-up was prepared and ready to go. Henson looked closely at the six photos. The individual in photo number three was "close." Henson told Gregory that the individual in photo one "was most likely the guy." The guy in photo four was definitely *not* the one. He had a beard. He was Ray Krone.

π

Gregory's notes on his meeting with Henson made their first appearance halfway into his rebuttal testimony orchestrated by Levy. It was the last week of Ray's second trial and the final act of The Chuck and Noel Show was on stage. After Plourd rested his case, prosecutor Noel Levy called detective Chuck Gregory to rebut Henson's testimony. The detective whipped out his notes on cue. Chris Plourd became furious, but he didn't let on. The jury was present. He politely stopped the show.

"May we approach with reporter, your Honor?"

"Yes."

At the sidebar (a powwow that occurs behind the judge's bench out of earshot of the jury), Judge McDougall listened to Plourd as he chastised the performers. When an eyewitness to a crime is interviewed, notes are taken. Later the detective transcribes his notes into a police report. By law the defense has the right to see the detective's notes. On the record, Plourd reminded the judge that he had made several requests for Gregory's notes over the past two years. Gregory admitted that he had testified under oath that his notes had been "destroyed." Numerous court orders had failed to resurrect the "destroyed" notes. But when Levy needed them, voilà, they magically appeared.

"Recently," Chuck informed the judge, "I was going over some stuff and found some [notes]."

"When?" the judge wanted to know.

"About a month ago."

The time at which Henson saw someone—not Ray Krone—enter and exit the bar was critical. If it were between 2:00 and 2:30 a.m., as Henson insisted, then that individual was most certainly the murderer. Gregory's police report, however, showed the time to be "6:00 a.m.," well after the time the murder had occurred. Levy wanted to show

Gregory's notes to the jury to "prove" that they agreed with the report and, therefore, that Henson must be mistaken, not Gregory.

The judge interrupted Gregory's rebuttal and ordered him back to the stand the following day, after the defense had had time to look over the new discovery. Plourd was allowed to handle the original notes briefly before he was given a copy. While it appeared that the paper stock of the page noting the Henson interview was different from that of the rest of the pages, this didn't prove that the notes were altered. That would have required a document expert to examine them for authenticity, which would have delayed the trial significantly.

Continuing the cross-examination, Plourd negated the effect of Chuck's cheesy notes. He questioned the detective's veracity by grilling him about a recent backstage argument in which Henson was pressured to remember "correctly."

"If Henson was correct then he saw the murderer of Kimberly Ancona?"

"Yes, but there were two interviews done of him in detail," Gregory informed the jury. "Four years is a long time ago. I think he's having a hard time remembering."

"You confronted Mr. Henson," Plourd continued, "even though you are not working with the police department anymore, and he stuck to his statement. He flat out said right to your face, 'Look, I told you two to two-thirty.' Is that true?"

"Yes, but...," Gregory rebutted.

π

The Ray Krone Did It investigation would have gone unnoticed had Ray Krone actually done the murder. But since he didn't, the evidence naturally didn't fit. The only way to continue with the investigation was to make as much evidence as possible fit Ray and cover up the rest. Gregory could simply have let Ray go and started looking for a clean-shaven American Indian who wore Converse brand shoes—as the evidence suggested. Had he done so he might actually have solved the crime. Was he simply lazy? He certainly was convinced that Ray Krone had lied to him. Was he not bright enough after hearing Ray's explanation to figure out that his initial interpretation of the "dating" scenario was wrong? What did he think five hours after he made the arrest when he learned that a bona fide eyewitness had excluded his suspect? Henson's identification exclusion was the first item of evidence that didn't fit. More would follow—saliva, footprints and fingerprints. Even the bite mark was questionable until the Las Vegas hired gun came on board.

All police reports are time-stamped. If accurate, then within an hour of returning from the interview with Henson, Gregory typed his police report, almost certainly noting incorrectly the time at which Henson saw someone other than Ray Krone enter and exit the murder scene. This report would be buried deep down in the stack of discovery stuff that would eventually end up on Ray's overworked, underpaid, court appointed attorney's desk. This strategy worked because either defense attorney Geoffrey Jones did not read the report or he tossed it aside after concluding that Henson's testimony would be irrelevant. Henson was not contacted again until he was called to testify at Ray's second trial four years later.

The day after Ray's arrest was New Year's Day, a holiday. Gregory and his crew did not work that day. At least, there are no police reports dated 1/1/92. They were back on the job the next day. Gregory was assisted by several other officers, including Joseph Petrosino and Dennis Olson. Olson had been in charge of collecting the evidence at the crime scene and seeing to its delivery to the Phoenix police crime lab. Latent prints were analyzed by fingerprint expert Karen Jones, the biological evidence by criminologist Scott Piette. Olson handled the footprint evidence himself. Officer Petrosino assisted Gregory in interviewing the numerous witnesses. Petrosino returned to the bar the day after the murder at the request of the owner, Hank Arredondo, who reported the "talk on the street" that the murder was lesbian related and that the former bar manager, Trish, and her Indian lover, Lu, were possibly involved. In a police report, he writes: "I told him [Arredondo] I would give the information to detective Gregory. However I did not believe that the homicide was a homosexual related crime."

Trish had been fired by Arredondo the day after the Christmas party. She was very upset. She stayed up all Thursday night trying to enlist the support of the bartenders she had hired. All were sympathetic except for Ancona. Word was that Ancona coveted Trish's job and had bad-mouthed Trish to the owner. If Ancona moved up to manager, she would have the resources to move out of Paul Clark's house. Her relationship with Clark was apparently one of convenience. She had even considered moving in with Trish and Lu, but at the Christmas party she found out that they were gay. She wanted her own place so her kids could live with her.

The next day Trish, reportedly miffed at Ancona, left town with Lu to visit Lu's aunt, who lived on the Navajo reservation at a crossroad called Indian Wells, in northeastern Arizona, some two hundred and fifty road miles from Phoenix. They left just after noon but decided to spend that Friday night in Flagstaff, only two hours north of Phoenix. Saturday morning, according to Trish, she and Lu continued on to Aunt Minnie's. They were seen back in Phoenix the next day, the Sunday of the early-morning murder. That was the afternoon in which Trish embellished Ray and Kim's relationship and the Christmas "date" for the interested detective Gregory. It was also that afternoon that she was observed confronting Arredondo, yelling at him, "If you hadn't fired me this wouldn't have happened!"

I'd learned this little tidbit from Mike Pain. Early on, when I first took and interest in Ray's case, the references to Trish and Lu in the police reports intrigued me. Not only did Mike greatly assist me in acquiring copies of the bite mark evidence for Dr. Homer Campbell to evaluate, but also, at my behest, he investigated Trish and Lu. What he was able to discover further piqued my interest.

Before leaving town, Trish had left the key to her apartment with a neighbor, whose name was also Kim. This Kim left a note on the kitchen sink to inform Trish of the murder when she got home. Trish called her after picking up the note. According to the neighbor, Trish acted as if she were hearing the news for the first time, when in fact she had already been interviewed by Gregory. Upon receiving a phone call, Trish again acted as if she were hearing the news for the first time. Neighbor Kim thought Trish's overreactions suspicious.

Louisa Valdez was a friend of Trish and Lu and had been at the Christmas party. Valdez reported to detective Petrosino that on the Monday after the murder Lu had called and asked if she, Trish and their friend Gloria could stop by her house. Valdez said it was okay so long as they did not bring Gloria. Valdez was uncomfortable around this hardened butch lesbian, who wore leather and rode a motorcycle. Trish and Lu told Valdez that they were going "skiing" near Flagstaff for a few days and asked to borrow several hundred dollars. Valdez did not have the money to lend. Nevertheless, Trish and Lu left town right after their visit with Valdez. Ray was arrested Tuesday. Trish and Lu returned to Phoenix Wednesday with a picture of themselves frolicking in the snow. Valdez told the detective that she was "uncomfortable with Trish and Lu and upset and worried that Kim Ancona could have been killed by them." It's reasonable to believe that lead detective Gregory saw Petrosino's report of his interview of Valdez.

Lu could easily have fit Henson's description. She was obviously clean-shaven. Two individuals stated that when they first met Lu, they thought she was a man. Described in the police reports as "Indian female military type," Lu was one tough individual. She had spent time in the Army, where she learned to wield a knife. She also bragged that while in the Army she had killed someone and that "it wasn't hard to do." She still had her Army-issued green fatigue jacket, consistent with the one Henson saw entering the CBS Lounge. She doted on and was very protective of Trish. It was rare for them not to be seen together. One time Lu broke a beer bottle over the end of the bar and held it threateningly up to the throat of a man she had thrown up against the wall for being too friendly with Trish.

On Saturday, six days after the murder, Gregory again interviewed Trish. He also interviewed Lu. He showed both of them his photo lineup so that they could identify Ray as the one seen with Ancona at the Christmas party. In his police report, Gregory discounted the street talk reported by Petrosino, eliminating Trish and Lu as suspects because he believed their story of their whereabouts at the time of the murder: "They had gone to Indian Wells in northern Arizona to visit some relatives."

It is clear from the police reports that by then Gregory was investigating only Ray Krone. He accepted Trish and Lu's alibi verbatim without bothering to check it out until months later. He did not look at their shoes. I was able to locate a DUI police report of Lu being stopped for driving while intoxicated. The event occurred not long after Ancona's murder. It is usual before administering a sobriety test (since wearing high heel shoes could in court be explained as the reason why one was unable to walk the line) for the officer to note the type of shoes the suspect is wearing. Lu was wearing tennis shoes. I can only wonder what brand of shoe Gregory would have discovered Lu to be wearing had he bothered to look at her feet.

π

The opening act of The Chuck and Noel Show must go on soon after the arrest in order to keep Ray Krone in jail. And the audience, a grand jury, must like it. But rehearsals weren't going very well. By show time, the only skits Chuck was able to contribute were his impression of Ray's date and Ray's denial that it was a date, his narration of bartender Kate's hearsay statement that the victim had said, "Ray is going to show up and help me close," his implicit allegation that he'd investigated many suspects and his bite mark song and dance.

And by show time, the crime lab had nothing to offer. It could find no fingerprints, no footprints, no semen, no blood and no hairs that could be tied to the suspect.

But showman Levy knew what to do.

Noel opened the show by asking Chuck to describe the victim, the crime scene and the murder weapon.

"The victim of the homicide was one Kimberly Ancona, an attractive woman, thirty-six years old. She was an employee of the CBS Lounge at the time of her death. She was found at 8:10 in the morning in the men's restroom, nude, lying on her back, her clothes strewn about the floor. She'd received five stab wounds in the neck and one in the left-side of the back thrust upward. A knife was found in the trash container in the restroom. It had blood on it and the blade was bent. There was a knife missing from the kitchen."

Next Noel introduced the bite mark and established that it was part of the assault.

"Were any bite marks found on the body?"

"Yes, sir—on the throat and on the left breast."

"Was the bite mark on the left breast obvious from your initial view of the body?"

"Yes, sir."

"Did it appear to be pre or postmortem?"

"I believe it was postmortem."

Chuck and Noel would return to the bite mark for the finale, but first they needed to explain the absence of any real evidence.

"The Phoenix police department has a crime lab, is that so?"

"Yes, sir."

"But they can't do everything instantly and they have other cases, is that so?"

"Correct."

"Has everything been analyzed yet?"

"No, sir."

A grand jury proceeding is ex parte. Neither the defendant nor his counsel is allowed to participate. A prosecutor is loosely obligated to mention all known exculpatory evidence. The following dialogue is how Chuck and Noel handled the problem evidence:

"Was there any evidence of semen found in the vaginal vault?"

"No sir, not at this time."

"Have any fingerprints been analyzed?"

"Some of them have. Some of them haven't."

"Any of Krone?"

"Not yet."

"Feet prints? Shoe prints?"

"There were some shoe prints found, but I haven't been able to connect them to him."

"Have you been able to exclude or include anybody?

"No."

"As an experienced homicide investigator, what was your observation of certain clothing obtained with the search warrant?"

"In the dryer at Krone's residence we found three pairs of underwear. One pair had what appeared to me to be bloodstains on them."

"But you can't conclude that because it hasn't been specifically analyzed yet?"

"Right."

"What kind of hairs did the lab say were found on the victim?"

"Some were pubic hairs."

"What did they say about comparing the hairs to Krone and Ancona?"

"They couldn't make any determination because the victim's hairs and Ray's hairs and the hairs found on the victim were all similar."

With the quick disposal of the exculpatory evidence, Chuck and Noel finished with the bite mark song and dance.

"So, the available forensic evidence, then, would be the hair and the bite marks, the bite marks being the most definitive?"

"Yes, sir."

"At the time of the first interview with Ray Krone, was there something about his teeth that drew interest?"

"Yes, I had already seen the bite marks on the victim. When I was talking with him I noticed that his teeth seemed awfully similar to them. I had him bite into some Styrofoam and showed it to Dr. Piakas. Subsequently a court order was issued and teeth impressions were obtained. At the autopsy Dr. Piakas compared the casts directly to the teeth marks on the victim's left breast. I was there and to me they looked perfect."

Noel interrupted Chuck's exuberance. "But you are not an expert?"

"I am not an expert," Chuck agreed, then added, "Dr. Piakas could find no inconsistencies between the bite mark and Ray's teeth."

The show was over. Noel rested.

A curious grand juror, obviously not impressed with the performance, asked Chuck, "I'm assuming there was a lot of blood in the restroom where Kimberly was found?"

"[Yes,] around the head," Chuck answered.

"Was Mr. Krone's car checked for blood?'

"Yes."

"And was any found?"

"No."

π

The grand jury tradition dates back to twelfth-century England, when this secret organization was a tool of the monarchy whereby trusted nobles could fink on less trusted individuals. Secrecy was paramount, as those under inquisition might flee the kingdom or, worse, take up arms against the crown. Relief from royal abuses came the next century when King John came to terms with barons who had united to invade and capture London. On June 15, 1215 John accepted the barons' demands and signed the Magna Charta, or Magna Carta. Among other things, this Grand Charter guaranteed that life, liberty or property could not be taken from any individual without the judgment of his peers. Henceforth juries were to be made up of the people and not the powerful privileged few.

However, the struggle for liberty by the people against the powerful is ongoing and cyclic. In 1487 the King of England argued that it was his ancient right as monarch to establish a judicial council comprised of members of his choosing. Parliament, under Henry VII's intense pressure, created this king's court. It met in the Royal Palace of Westminster, in a secluded chamber that had stars painted on its ceiling. Two centuries later James I and Charles I used this secret Star Chamber to dish out cruel and excessive punishment to those who challenged their authority. In 1641 the people got back on top when parliament abolished this hated court. Today "star chamber" is synonymous with any group that acts in a secret, one-sided, arbitrary, unfair manner.

The Fifth Amendment of the Constitution of the United States established the grand jury as a safeguard against the tyranny of King George III over the American colonists. But that was two and a half centuries ago, when the people had a healthy disdain for unchecked authority. Over the years, grand juries have devolved essentially into what they are today—puppets of prosecutors.

Not only in Arizona but nationwide and at the federal level, criticism of grand juries abounds. Prosecutors by and large run the show. The proceedings remain secret, with only the prosecutor and his selected witnesses having speaking parts. Hearsay is allowed and abundant during the show. Prosecutors also act as the grand jury's legal advisors, explaining the law as it fits their agenda. While rules vary from state to state and at the federal level, prosecutors make the sole determination as to which evidence is relevant. In a state that requires prosecutors to present known exculpatory evidence, they can argue later that they omitted it because *they* determined it to be "irrelevant." (The Henson interview comes to mind. It was not mentioned by Chuck or Noel.)

In a study of thirty-seven hundred and fifty grand jury cases from the State of New York, prosecutors won outright ninety-one percent of the time. Two percent were sent to other jurisdictions. Most of the remaining seven percent ended with a plea bargain or guilty plea. These lopsided results support the wry observation of Sol Wachtler, a former chief judge of New York's highest court: "Even a moderately competent district attorney can get a grand jury to indict a ham sandwich." If the Krone case is any indication, in Arizona it would be a baloney sandwich.

While the president of the National Association of Criminal Defense Lawyers recently urged Congress to adopt a "grand jury bill of rights," it may take a long time for the cycle to reverse itself. At the moment prosecutors are on top. One interim suggestion might be to have stars painted on the ceilings of grand jury chambers to eliminate any pretense of justice as prosecutors spoon-feed grand jurors baloney.

π

By Star Chamber standards, The Chuck and Noel Show wasn't very good. Their performance mustered just nine thumbs up—the exact minimum number required by law to indict a baloney sandwich in Arizona. Thumbs up for Chuck and Noel meant thumbs down for Ray. On January 8, 1992 he was indicted for murder, rape and kidnapping.

Rehearsals for the next act—the trial five months later—could proceed. Dr. Piakas was given the task of finding a bona fide board-certified bite mark expert who would corroborate his finding that the bite fit the accused. Piakas would report back to Levy at the end of the month. While waiting for Piakas and the crime lab to do their work, Gregory and his boys would continue with the one-sided investigation.

Other indications of a blinkered-eyed investigation can be gleaned from police reports, such as the ones pertaining to the footprints found between the victim's outstretched legs. Initially detective Olson took photos of the prints to a local shoe store and acquired the type and size of shoe that fit the prints—a 9½ Converse brand high-top tennis shoe. Olson wrote in his report that the size was between 9½ and 10½.

The fact that no such brand of shoe could be shown to belong to Ray Krone was no problem for Olson. The bloody shoes were thrown away after the murder, he "reasoned." What was a problem was that Ray Krone's shoes were size 11 or 11½. The initial police report noting the "incorrect" size needed to be fixed. Olson had the shoe size reevaluated and a new report was written a week later. "The shoe size from the shoe print...is estimated to be approximately...10 to 11."

That the footprint evidence troubled Gregory is documented by the police report dated January 16. Both Gregory and Olson returned to the CBS Lounge and performed a "test." They mopped the floor and walked on it at various time intervals. They noted that, "Once dried, a shoe print would not adhere to the floor at any location." Since David Torres, the cook, had mopped the kitchen floor at 10:00 p.m., the footprints, they concluded, must have been made shortly thereafter. If the size discrepancy were to surface at trial, the footprints would be "irrelevant," as the murder occurred much later, sometime after the bar closed at 1:00 a.m.

However, their "test" *would* offer Gregory an explanation for the footprints found in the kitchen, though not for the identical footprints found around and about the victim's body. Part of the closing procedure was to mop the restroom floors. The dirty water found in the bucket Torres left for this purpose indicated that Ancona had done her job. And she would have done it after the bar had closed—several hours after the companion footprints found in the kitchen were made, according to Gregory's time line. Ancona had essentially left the restroom floor clean, ripe and ready to record her murderer's footprints, which it did. The restroom floor could not have been mopped at Gregory's time because, had it been, numerous dissimilar footprints due to high traffic would have been evident.

At the first trial, Gregory was not called upon to explain the footprints around the victim. He told defense attorney Jones under cross-examination, "Footprints were found in one part of the bar" [implying the kitchen]. Jones, for whatever reason, neglected to quiz

Gregory about the ones found in the restroom. Consequently, the first jury did not know about those telltale footprints.

π

About the middle of the month, the crime lab must have finished testing Ray's underwear without results because Gregory obtained another search warrant. Netting only clean underwear from the initial search, Gregory and Olson returned to Ray's residence two weeks later, on January 16. Detective Olson confiscated every shoe he could find. All of them were size 11 or larger. Some condoms were found in Ray's room and would surface at trial and be used to explain the absence of semen on the victim. Lint and hair were extracted from the drier. Ray's lime green goose down ski jacket was taken, presumably as the answer to the army fatigue jacket Henson saw enter and exit the bar, should the defense call Henson to testify. Also taken into custody was Ray's Corvette.

Over the next three days, the Corvette was scoured, particularly for crime scene blood. None was found, although Olson hoped that the stains on the sheet found in the trunk came from the victim. They didn't. All that was found in Ray's car of any use to the prosecution was shuffleboard beads, the same kind that were found on Ancona's socks. But no one questioned that Ray had been in the bar frequently playing darts next to the shuffleboard, as had Ancona. Again coming up empty, Olson returned to Ray's place for a third search. This time he confiscated Ray's bed sheets and miscellaneous vacuumed debris. Nothing fruitful there either.

Dennis Olson was the consummate police detective—completely subservient to his superiors. Because Gregory was no longer with homicide at the time of the second trial, Olson had become the case detective. Levy's go-to guy was not the sharpest puppet on the police force. When Levy asked during direct examination, "Did you see anything suspicious in the men's bathroom?" Olson's dumbfounded look required a frustrated Levy to tug one of his strings. "Like a dead body?"

Olson hadn't been rehearsed well for the cross-examination. First, Plourd stroked the detective about the good job he had done in collecting evidence. Then he pinned him down on how thoroughly the murder scene had been cleaned immediately prior to the murder.

"So the hairs you collected could not have been stray hairs from the bathroom floor?" Plourd was of course implying that the hairs must have been the murderer's.

Backed into a corner, the go-to guy had nowhere to go. He agreed. Olson glanced up at Levy with eyes that said, "Oops!" The puppet master was obviously not happy with his puppet's performance in another master's hands.

The hairs were a problem for prosecutor Levy at the second trial. At the first trial, another puppet, Scott Piette from the crime lab, had dutifully determined that the telltale hairs were "similar" to Ray Krone's. But for the second trial, the FBI's crime lab had determined that these hairs were in actuality donated by an American Indian.

But the possibility that an American Indian might have been involved in the crime had been a problem for Levy from day one. Besides the hairs, there was Robert Alan Frederickson. Frederickson lived in an apartment overlooking the alley behind the CBS Lounge. While getting ready for work in the early morning hours after the murder had occurred, he peered out his bathroom window and observed a suspicious loiterer. Later in the day he noticed the commotion in the strip mall and went to investigate. Hearing of the murder from a bystander, Fredrickson scribbled a note and hailed the police officer who was standing in front of the CBS Lounge. As the officer approached, Fredrickson dropped his note for the officer to retrieve and quickly disappeared around the building, down the alley and into his apartment. His note [unedited] read:

> Your looking for an Indian about 5'8" to 6'1"...I seen him about 3:30 and 4:30 hanging around out back of CBS...about 190 to 210...get him please...black hair...fat looking...blue jeans. I was to far away to make him out good his face...I don't want to go to jail or i would come forward...i have a warrent

Frederickson was subsequently located and subpoenaed to appear at the first trial. His note was entered into evidence and he gave his testimony about the loiterer he'd seen. Other witnesses who were inside the CBS Lounge the night of the murder had reported seeing an American Indian sitting quietly at the bar overdoing the booze. That the loiterer and boozer might be one and the same individual who just might have exited through the back door adjacent to the men's restroom and into the alley for Frederickson to see was a problem for Levy.

Levy must have been concerned that the jury might consider the loiterer/boozer viably the actual murderer. He needed a candidate who would dispel any juror's notion that an American Indian might be responsible for the crime. Also, it would be nice to create the illusion for the jury that Phoenix's finest had diligently investigated all suspects. Arnold Lomatawana was selected and presented to the jury as the American Indian in question. Lomatawana was a clean-cut family man who occasionally took his wife to the CBS Lounge for dinner. He fit the bill, obviously having nothing to do with the crime and offering the jury a plausible alibi to excuse it from considering any longer that an American Indian might have killed Ancona.

Frederickson died before the second trial. His testimony at the first trial was read at the second.

Kenneth Phillips was another American Indian who frequented the CBS Lounge. He lived within walking distance. He'd been arrested three weeks after Ray's arrest and charged with an unrelated sexual offense. He was serving time in Florence when his name came up as the possible loiterer/boozer. Olson's questioning of Phillips demonstrated the go-to guy's usual deference to the Maricopa County Attorney's Office. Lasting for less than half an hour, it amounted to little more than "You weren't at the CBS Lounge the night of the murder, were you?" and "You didn't kill Kim Ancona, did you?"

Dennis Olson reserved for show biz, however, his most blatant display of Watergate mentality (in which loyalty rather than intelligence and honesty is rewarded, especially in the Maricopa County criminal justice system). A shortlived syndicated television show, "Arrest and Trial," told stories "through the eyes of police and prosecutors." Chuck Gregory and Noel Levy began one of its shows by giving their unique interpretation of the facts that to them implicated "The Biting Postal Worker," the title of the episode. While hearsay is technically not allowed in court, on TV it makes for effective entertainment. Noel depicted the victim as a sexually promiscuous, attractive woman *with* a romantic interest in Ray. *But* she didn't want to have sex with him, *so* he killed her. Chuck set up Dennis by describing how Ray's Corvette had been confiscated and scoured in the hope of finding something that would tie Ray to the crime. Maybe some "bloody clothing." Then the go-to guy went for it and delivered the punch lie.

π

"Hey, Ray! You're on TV!" yelled an inmate from the other end of the recreation room. Ray was playing cards. He got up and cautiously joined the crowd around the TV. The commentator was saying, "…in the trunk the detectives uncovered a pair of bloody sheets." Then he cut to the detective on the show. "We later found out through crime lab investigation that the blood came back to Kim Ancona, the victim."

Ray unobtrusively backed away from the crowd and returned to his "house"—prison jive for cell. Except for child molesters, no one in The Big House is lower than a rapist/murderer. Ray neither talked about the offense for which he was convicted nor claimed innocence. In prison it's survival alone that counts. Ray had been in his share of obligatory fights. To survive he'd had to show strength and earn respect.

Back in his house, Ray changed into battle gear—a sweatshirt and long pants for some protection against the ground and possible makeshift weapons. He still had a festering sore from the pencil lead imbedded in his back during a recent skirmish.

"Ray, we need to talk!" challenged a voice from the crowd assembling outside his door.

"I'll be right there." Ray finished tying his high-top shoes, cinching them as tight as possible to ensure the best traction.

Though lean, at six feet, two inches he had a height advantage over most of his fellow inmates. But this crowd was larger that any he had previously faced. He didn't know how many of them were potential participants or merely observers. He preferred to avoid confrontation whenever possible. And he knew how to handle a crowd like this one. He could play the odds that some of these guys had also had run-ins with lying cops.

Emerging from his house, he looked intimidatingly into the eyes of the apparent leader but spoke to everyone.

"You know who I am. Did you come to my house to insult me? Look at who was doing the talking. Anyone who wants to believe *them*, step forward!"

After a tense, motionless moment, the apparent leader turned away. "Ahh, Ray's okay. Let's go."

They all returned to what they had been doing. Ray's gambit had worked.

π

About a month after Ray's arrest, Chucky Cheese, Go-To Guy and Dr. Perjury had assembled to report on the status of the Krone case. (In an athletic contest it's not unusual for the players on one team to refer to their opponents by secret nicknames. The same is true of the justice game.)

At the meeting, the two detectives laid out the marginal hearsay and circumstantial evidence against Ray. They noted that no physical evidence yet implicated him. No one mentioned Henson. The hairs had been tucked away deep within the crime lab. The troubling footprint evidence had been resolved with Gregory's "test" and Olson's revision of the shoe size.

With nothing substantial, the detectives looked to Dr. Piakas for encouraging news. They eagerly hoped he had found an expert who would corroborate the bite mark evidence. But he disappointed them. He had sent photos of the injury and a cast of Ray's teeth to his friend and mentor Dr. Norman "Skip" Sperber of San Diego. After carefully evaluating the material, Sperber told his protégé, "I hope there is other evidence because this bite mark evidence is not very good."

That this meeting happened is certain, but exactly who attended and what was discussed is not known for sure. Investigating for the second trial, Plourd got wind of the meeting. Gregory, Olson and Piakas remember it, but say that they can't remember who else was there or what was discussed. Prosecutor Levy claims that he wasn't there. But does it make sense that the puppets would meet without their puppet master? Could Piakas's likely revelation of Sperber's findings at the meeting be the reason why Levy claims he wasn't there? Prosecutors are obliged by law to inform the defense attorney of any and all known exculpatory evidence. Yet, first-trial defense attorney Jones never heard of Dr. Sperber.

It was Chris Plourd who happened to discover Sperber's early opinion. Shortly after being retained as Ray's attorney, Plourd called Dr. Piakas to introduce himself. Hearing that Plourd was from San Diego, Piakas asked whether he knew Sperber. "Sure I know Skip." They chatted awhile about this mutual acquaintance. Later Plourd thought it was odd that Sperber had not been called as an expert, for he knew how it worked within the forensic odontology clique. Rookie bite mark experts are guided by a veteran along the path to certification. Typically, when the rookie gets a case, he works it up under the guidance of his mentor and both testify at trial. Plourd wondered why Rawson had testified in mentor Sperber's stead.

Before the Krone case, Plourd knew Sperber only as a prosecution expert. Six months earlier he had raked Sperber severely over the coals during cross-examination in another bite mark case. They hadn't spoken since then. Leaving court one day, Plourd by chance ran into Sperber in the hallway.

"Hey, Skip, how are you doing? I just talked with your Phoenix buddy John Piakas not a week ago."

"How's John doing?" Sperber asked. "I haven't talked with him for awhile."

"He's okay. I just took on a bite mark case over there. He's one of the experts."

"Really?" Skip was obviously surprised that he hadn't heard from his protégé. "Which case?"

"Ray Krone."

"Really!" Skip was even more surprised. "I know that case...that was two years ago. What happened?"

"He was convicted."

"No kidding! On what evidence?"

"The bite mark."

Now seriously curious, Skip had forgotten the animosity of their previous encounter. He wanted to know more. Plourd outlined the case. They met later that week in Skip's office. Skip detailed what he remembered about the bite mark and in particular what he'd told Piakas. In short order Skip was retained as another bite mark expert in addition to Homer Campbell.

I would like to have seen how the status meeting participants reacted when Piakas reported his mentor's opinion. With absolutely no substantial evidence implicating Ray Krone, it was a perfect moment for someone's pendulum to stand tall and suggest that perhaps they had the wrong man. Instead, all their pendulums must have dangled in bewilderment until one perked up and pointed north toward Nevada. Fortunately for them, Sperber's opinion had been expressed orally and not in writing. They could easily forget it. And they did.

Piakas was a neophyte. He had yet to learn just what role bite mark analysis plays in a justice biz market plan. The most important rookie rule is: When your mentor doesn't deliver, find a new mentor. Chuck, perhaps with Noel's Machiavellian advice, took the matter into his own hands. In no time he was on a plane to Las Vegas to meet with Dr. Ray Rawson. No doubt Chuck prefaced his bite mark presentation with cheesy tidbits calculated to stimulate the doctor's pendulum. Your reputation precedes you...You come highly recommended...We've arrested the guy she was dating but he denies being her boyfriend...A witness said the boyfriend came to the bar to help her close up just before she was murdered...The boyfriend admitted to biting her but we can't use it because he wasn't Mirandized...

Somewhere along the line Rawson got the idea that Ray had taken responsibility for the bite mark. In his letter to the ABFO ethics committee, responding to the charges of ethics violations, Rawson stated, among other things, "I was informed by Mr. Krone's counsel that...Mr. Krone admitted to the biting activity." This incorrect statement, clearly designed to influence the ethics committee, may be the reason why Rawson was not sanctioned. In any event, Jones categorically denied telling Rawson any such thing. And it makes no sense that any defense attorney with attorney/client privilege would divulge such information even if it were true. Therefore, if Rawson didn't make it up, the question is, who led him to believe that Ray had confessed?

Be that as it may, soon after viewing the bite mark evidence, Rawson assured Gregory that they had the right man. Dr. Walksonwater's pendulum was retained and Dr. Piakas had a new mentor. Rawson's written report followed some weeks later. Teacher and pupil met privately before the trial. The veteran showed the rookie a useful Ouija tool known as "garbage in, garbage out." In the study of logic, it's well known that anything can be proved when your premise is false. When the fact that it was a single bite injury doesn't fit your suspect, you concoct a garbage-in theory such as that it was a multiple-bite injury and, voilà, out comes more garbage to the effect that Ray Krone inflicted those injuries.

With the bite mark boys on board, Levy had only to deal with the real evidence, like the crime scene hairs and bodily fluids. This task was the easiest of all because he had the Phoenix police department's crime lab at his disposal. He merely needed to find a pliable cop in a lab coat within its ranks.

Not everyone working in the crime lab liked Levy. He had the reputation of pressuring lab technicians to be less than objective. I personally witnessed one such instance. For the second trial, fingerprint expert Karen Jones had taken it upon herself to reevaluate all latent prints found at the crime scene. Levy suggested in court that she was less than competent, not having found any prints matching Ray Krone. Noticeably offended, she paused to look sternly into Levy's eyes before responding. Nevertheless, Levy had no problem recruiting criminologist Scott Piette.

I guess—unless he comes clean—we'll never know whether Piette was instructed not to analyze but just to file away the pubic hairs found on the victim's abdomen...or simply understood that he was to take it upon himself to do so. In any event, Piette testified at the first trial that the victim's and Ray's pubic hairs were "similar...both Caucasian" and concluded, therefore, that neither could be "excluded" as the source of the evidence hairs. With a similar lack of scientific foundation, Piette also testified that Ray could not be excluded as the donor of the saliva swabbed from the bite injury.

To this day Chris Plourd cannot talk about Scott Piette without getting riled up. "He never actually looked at the evidence. [His testimony] was bogus—a total fraud!"

I had the opportunity to visit Scott Piette and the Phoenix police department's crime lab. I'd already toured the crime lab in Albuquerque as Dr. Homer Campbell's guest. But it wasn't that easy to get in to see Piette. Until the supreme court ruled that new evidence discovery could continue, Plourd's requests to Piette for an audience had been by phone. These requests were invariably denied. After the supreme court ruling, Levy was still uncooperative and Piette would not make a move without Levy's okay.

So Plourd had to go to court. Judge McDougall suggested that Levy and Piette meet with Plourd after lunch. Levy agreed. I jumped at the opportunity to tag along.

We arrived at the downtown police station just before one o'clock, the appointed time. Plourd signed the register and flashed his bar card for the desk sergeant. When I signed in, the desk sergeant wanted to know who I was. Plourd told him that I was his assistant and I was allowed to pass.

Even before this visit, it was fairly obvious that the crime lab operated under the watchful eye of the Phoenix police department. We took an elevator to the basement. When we arrived at the lab's reception desk, Piette was notified. He appeared a short time later. We were not invited into his office. Small talk ensued. Piette was not about to offer anything substantial until Levy arrived. After waiting more than an hour, we concluded that Levy wasn't going to show. We left.

The next time Plourd was scheduled to meet with Piette and Levy, I opted to avoid the rigamarole of getting past the gestapo at the booking desk. I waited on the bench outside the double glass doors leading into the police station and read a local newspaper. After a short while I saw Levy inside talking with the desk sergeant. The sergeant held one of the glass doors open as Levy exited. When he saw me he said capriciouisly to the sergeant, "Whatever you do, don't let him inside."

Levy's broad smile, the first one I noted, seemed calculated to make the desk sergeant think that he was merely joking. It wasn't clear whether he had gotten over the article in an issue of *The Ray Krone Story* in which his name and that of Adolf Hitler appeared together.

Levy's chipper demeanor as he exited the police station revealed his satisfaction over the results of the meeting between Plourd and Piette. Plourd emerged shortly thereafter and told me that he would have to get what he needed from Piette at the deposition.

The difference between the Phoenix crime lab and the one in Albuquerque was like night a day. After sitting down with Dr. Campbell in my hotel room to view and hear his analysis of the videotape, I was offered a ride to the airport. On the way he treated me to a tour of the crime lab where he worked. It was located on the campus of the University of New Mexico. The state medical examiner's office occupied a wing of the School of Medicine. We stopped into his office briefly and talked more about bite mark analysis. He showed me some gruesome photos of one of his cases, known as "the Lake Waco murders." Then we casually toured the rest of the facility. The autopsy labs were across a wide hall from a tier of refrigerated crypts. This tier moved hydraulically up and down the wall. To select a corpse you entered its number into the control panel and the row containing the selected crypt moved to floor level. Dr. Campbell referred to this retrieval system as "dial-a-body."

Unlike the crime lab in Phoenix, this one had a comfortable, relaxed, academic atmosphere. There was no hint of a police presence. I asked if police or prosecutors came into the lab. "Yes, when they're invited." The difference between the crime labs of these two adjacent states was clear. In New Mexico forensic scientists run the crime lab, in Arizona police and prosecutors run the show.

While perceived as impartial by the general public, the reality is that police crime labs throughout the nation operate by and large in an environment of prosecutorial advocacy. It's difficult in this adversarial atmosphere for crime lab technicians and scientists to be objective and at the same time placate their cop prosecutor bosses. Some, all too many, succumb to ever present inquisitional pressures and become nothing more than cops in lab coats—to spin, twist, obscure and fake evidence. Of the copious examples from which to choose, the most egregious perhaps are Fred Salem Zain and Joyce Gilchrist, arguably the reigning king and queen of Ouija cops.

In 2001, after a twenty-one-year career as a chemist in the Oklahoma City police crime lab, Joyce Gilchrist, a.k.a. Black Magic, was fired in disgrace under suspicion that she routinely doctored notes, intentionally destroyed or lost exculpatory evidence and gave capricious testimony not supported by or contrary to bona fide forensic results, all under pressure to do so from Oklahoma County District

Attorney Robert H. Macy. Macy subsequently resigned after Gilchrist's "Okie science," as it was referred to in the press, was exposed. Black Magic touched approximately three thousand cases. Several separate agencies independently investigated her work. One found significant flaws in sixteen percent of her cases. Another concluded that seventy-five percent of Gilchrist's jangle "went beyond the acceptable limits of forensic science." That's anywhere from four hundred and eighty to as many as two thousand, two hundred and fifty tainted cases. A few of her victims have been exonerated by DNA technology. A dozen still linger on Death Row, perhaps to follow the dozen or so souls who have already been executed after being convicted, at least in part, by Black Magic's touch.

In 1979 Fred Zain turned in his state trooper's uniform for a lab coat supplied by the West Virginia police crime lab. Ten years later he resigned to become chief serologist for Bexar County's police crime lab in San Antonio, Texas. His career ended three years later. He was fired when evidence vital to a murder case disappeared. Trooper Zain's forte seemed to be "dry labbing," also referred to as "dry benching"—reporting results of tests that were never done. Always packing a positive pendulum, Zain never ever pointed it away from the prosecutor employer's suspect. If forensic tests were actually performed, negative and inconclusive results were reported as positive and conclusive. When his work was in danger of being subjected to independent analysis, the physical evidence not infrequently went missing. The American Society of Crime Laboratory Directors reported at the request of the West Virginia Supreme Court that Zain "fabricated or falsified evidence in just about every case he touched." The court subsequently ruled, "Any testimony or documentary evidence offered by Zain, at any time, in any criminal prosecution, should be deemed invalid, unreliable and inadmissible." A Texas investigation similarly concluded, "Everything that Fred Zain did...has to be suspect." Estimates of Zain-stained cases range from twelve hundred to forty-five hundred.

Zain was tried but not convicted for his transgressions. In the end nature pointedly took care of this forensic trooper. It did to Zain what Zain's zany pendulum had done to so many others. On December 2, 2002 Fred Salem Zain died—albeit of colon cancer.

π

Ed Blake isn't afraid to use the "f-word" when critiquing a fellow forensic expert's pendulum. "[The prosecution expert] failed to notify the prosecutor or the trial jury that the conventional genetic marker traits found in the commingled semen stain evidence could all have been attributable to the victim and as a consequence could not be proved to be attributable to the semen source. This entire line of proof is based upon a fraud."

Herman Atkins spent twelve years in prison for rape because of this fraud. He was released two months after Blake's report was submitted to the court. When criticized that his use of the "f-word" was a bit strong because if referred to motivation, Blake responded, "Look, when you're dealing with professional people, you have a right to expect that they'll know certain things or should know certain things. And when they act in a way that's contrary to that, then it's reasonable to conclude that what they're doing rises to the level of fraud."

Edward T. Blake was graduated from the University of California in 1968, receiving a bachelor's degree in criminalistics. He remained in Berkeley to earn his PhD in criminology, which was conferred eight years later. Doctor Blake set up shop as a forensic biology consultant (Forensic Science Consultants) in close-by Emeryville, a small town north of Oakland between Berkeley and San Francisco Bay. Cetus Corporation, a biotechnology company, moved into the same building, which, except for Blake and his company, had been abandoned. Sharing the same after-hours watering hole, Blake became acquainted with a few Cetus employees. One was an eccentric chemist known for his weird ideas.

One Friday night after work, while Kary Mullis was driving to his cabin in the woods of Mendocino County, as was his custom most Friday nights, he pondered how to solve the most annoying problem of DNA chemistry—abundance and distinction. Isolating enough of a specific DNA strand for analysis was for the biotech scientist difficult at best. He had been theorizing a way to chemically make copies of a single distinctive DNA molecule. Like a lightning bolt, the solution hit him and made him pull off the road to scribble some notes. He calculated that he could turn one isolated molecule into one hundred billion similar molecules in an afternoon.

As with Einstein, it would take time for Mullis's theory to become fact. Einstein had to wait three years for a solar eclipse to verify his General Theory of Relativity, a consequence of which is that light does not travel in a straight line but is bent by gravity, a radical notion at the time. In 1919 scientists positioned their instruments at the point of a total eclipse and verified that the apparent positions of selected stars changed exactly as Einstein's theory predicted they would due to our massive sun's gravitational influence on the starlight. Einstein received the Nobel Prize for physics two years later.

For Mullis it took the better part of a year to demonstrate his discovery in the laboratory. Throughout the summer he researched and picked the brains of colleagues. Most thought it was another one of his weird ideas. But Mullis persisted. He designed and performed his first experiment one midnight in September. It was slow going but during three months of sporadic after-hours experimenting he managed to work out the kinks. On December 19, 1983 he achieved the world's first successful polymerase chain reaction. As he wrote in *Scientific American*: "PCR is easy to execute. It requires no more than a test tube, a few simple reagents and a source of heat. The DNA sample that one wishes to copy can be pure or it can be a minute part of an extremely complex mixture of biological materials. The DNA may come from a hospital tissue specimen, from a single human hair, from a drop of dried blood at the scene of a crime, from the tissues of a mummified brain or from a forty thousand-year-old wooly mammoth frozen in a glacier."

PCR revolutionized biotechnology. Scientists could now amplify into useful quantities selected strands of DNA previously too small to decipher. For his achievement Kary Mullis was awarded the 1993 Nobel Prize for chemistry.

Also working at Cetus was Dr. Henry Erlich. In the lab next to Mullis's Erlich used PCR to isolate and amplify the HLA-DQα segment of the human genome. He was interested in this gene because of its high variation between individual sources. In the late nineteen eighties Ed Blake presented Dr. Erlich with a forensic problem. Blake's prosecutor client suspected that an autopsy sample had been switched to cover up foul play. The sample had been stored in formaldehyde, rendering conventional analysis impossible. A PCR was done. The prosecutor's suspicion was just that. The test proved that there had been no monkey business with the autopsy sample. Nevertheless, Ed Blake became the first forensic scientist to apply PCR to the justice biz. Erlich and Blake successfully collaborated informally for the next five years. In time Blake outgrew his small Emeryville lab and relocated to larger facilities in Richmond, a few miles to the north.

Until Blake and PCR came along, restriction fragment length polymorphism was the standard DNA forensic tool. The drawback with RFLP was that it required large samples to yield meaningful results. In no time PCR replaced RFLP as the standard. Blake's achievement of applying PCR to forensics has given him mythical status, often causing the opposing side to accept his results without independent verification. Blake's brilliance in the lab has become legendary. He routinely achieves definitive incriminating or exonerating results from just a few telltale cells. His expertise is sought out by prosecuting and defending attorneys alike. Not infrequently he donates his services pro bono to the Innocence Project, a non-profit organization established and operated by Barry Scheck and Peter Neufeld, that takes on post conviction cases of worthy krones.

Uncomfortable being referred to as a "mythic figure" in the *The New Yorker* magazine, Blake responds, "The problem with this sort of characterization is that it reinforces the myth of the expert as a god. In forensic science you demonstrate your competency not by your reputation but by the quality of the work that you do for each case."

Blake's outspoken fidelity to forensic science and his complete immunity to pendulum pressures have earned him the reputation of being somewhat of a renegade in the forensic biz, critical of anyone and everyone who falls short of perfection. "The FBI," he contends, "has exerted Gestapo-like control over the field of forensics. One of the dicta coming out of their lab is that an adequate report need only contain results and a conclusion. The problem with this approach is that it doesn't put the work product in an intelligible context with the case facts. That's why the FBI's reports are largely incomprehensible—even to scientists. The FBI is one of the country's most dangerous organizations."

Dr. Blake prides himself on his comprehensive reports, in which he puts his lab results into a sensible context. But lawyers are not always sensible. Consider the Los Angeles prosecutor who tried Theodore Scott for rape/murder. After the jury hung, the prosecutor and the defense attorney agreed to have the semen evidence tested prior to re-trial. When the prosecutor's experts agreed with the defense's Ed Blake that the semen didn't come from Scott, you'd think that that would be the end of the story. Not so. Unable to fathom the forensic findings, the prosecutor theorized that Scott must have had an accomplice who did the raping while Scott did the killing. Sure enough, an individual who shared the same residence with Scott at the county jail came forward to testify that Scott had bragged about killing the elderly woman after his buddy raped her. Fortunately for Scott, there was no Nobel Prize for this obdurate prosecutor's theory. A fortuitous coincident led to Scott's acquittal. A scandal erupted within the Los Angeles District Attorney's Office over the questionable tactics that had been used to manipulate jailbird pendulums.

Blake has a phrase for this type of pig-headed denial of facts, which is not uncommon within the adversarial justice biz. "Lawyers," he said in commenting on the Scott case, "seem to think that under the umbrella of advocacy they can put aside their moral obligations as human beings and take positions that are independent of any objective reality. Just ask yourself, 'After already trying a case on one theory, who but an advocate could then come up with *the unindicted co-ejaculator theory?*'"

Blake prefers the unemotional, objective detachment of his lab. "In an early post conviction case," he relates, "I was in the courtroom when the judge overturned the jury verdict. It was an incredibly emotional scene. Everyone was weeping and I just didn't like being that close in. As a scientist, I don't think I should [be emotionally involved]. In the lab all of these cases are problem-solving exercises. It's only when I get home that I think of them as human beings."

That Blake is the epitome of what a forensic scientist should be was reinforced in each of my three visits to his lab. At one such visit I sat in while he and Plourd discussed sample 4B. Blake could not exclude Ray as the source of the DNA found on the victim's bra. Listening to him, I got the impression that he felt it highly probable that it was indeed Ray's DNA, especially if it were mixed with DNA from the victim. Over lunch, Plourd continued to question Blake. I don't know if he was simply trying to find out as much as he could about the problem evidence or if he was testing the water to see if there was any way he could get this prospective expert witness to put a favorable spin on the evidence. If the sample were a mixture between three or more individuals, then Ray was excluded. But Blake thought that possibility unlikely and held firm.

"Well, Jim, it is what it is," Plourd said as we walked back to the car. He had decided to drop Blake from the witness list and deal with prosecution expert Moses Schanfield's interpretation of Blake's results, that Ray could not be excluded from the bra sample.

When an expert is retained by one side he is off-limits to the other side. It's not unusual for an expert of Blake's caliber to be hired just to keep him out of the courtroom. This strategy may have been the reason why OJ Simpson's dream team hired Blake to do their independent DNA testing. When the dream team did not call Blake to testify, attempts were made by the prosecutors to force Blake to the stand. Judge Lance Ito rejected the attempts. "It's an absolute outrage,"

Blake said of his name's being dropped before the jury, "the way [prosecutor] Rockne Harmon, who is a friend of mine—somebody I've known for ten years—has been injecting me into this case." The name-dropping had seemed designed to imply that Blake thought Simpson was guilty.

Plourd certainly didn't hire Blake for the purpose of keeping him off the stand. He hired Blake because he wanted the best for his client and dropped him from the witness list only when the DNA results became problematic.

Although PCR was ten years old by the time of the first trial, its application to forensic science was still in its infancy. Only one marker, DQα, had been developed for PCR amplification. By the second trial, five additional markers, called polymarkers, had been developed. With each new marker, the degree of statistical certainty increases. Schanfield had assigned a probability of ninety-nine point four percent that it was Ray's DNA on the victim's bra. This high probability was troubling but not insurmountable. Because population frequencies of each marker had yet to be statistically determined, the accuracy of Schanfield's estimate was challenged and stricken from the record. Nevertheless, whatever the actual probability, Ray could not be positively eliminated as the source of the troubling DNA.

In a few years forensic DNA technology would advance to the point where even polymarkers would be relegated to the dark ages of forensic science. A set of thirteen highly definitive new markers would be developed which would push DNA comparison probabilities to near statistical certainty, to as high as one quadrillion to one. That's 1,000,000,000,000,000,000,000,000 to 1. Wow! Look at all those zeros. The total world population is not even 10,000,000,000. So when someone's DNA matches crime scene DNA nowadays, unless he has a twin, it's pretty much certain that he's the guy who left it there. Conversely, innocent suspects would most certainly be excluded.

When these thirteen new markers became available Dr. Blake would be called upon to revisit the bra sample. An absolute exclusion would no doubt help win Ray a third trial.

Largely due to Ed Blake's pioneering, the Innocence Project accepts cases where DNA testing can, as their book details, prove *Actual Innocence*. Students at the Benjamin N. Cardozo School of Law in New York City do the casework under the supervision of skilled attorneys. Since 1992 more that one hundred individuals convicted of serious crimes, primarily rapes and murders, have been proved innocent beyond a shadow of a doubt by the Innocence Project.

This noble success story has opened a Pandora's box containing an alarming set of statistics to support the fact that the Krone case is not an isolated instance of injustice. Prosecutorial misconduct occurred in half of the cases cited by the Innocence Project. Junk science was used in one-third of them. Incorrect microscopic hair comparison also occurred in about a third and incorrect serological inclusion (ABO blood typing) in more than half.

π

Hanging out on the fringes of a social event at one of the annual meetings of the American Academy of Forensic Sciences, I listened to Chris Plourd and Ed Blake discuss the state of the forensic justice biz. Dr. Blake keeps a low profile at such events, dodging criticism for his staunch unwillingness to play the game. He has not won many friends by refusing to allow his lab to submit to accreditation by such organizations as the FBI and the American Society of Crime Laboratory Directors. The FBI, which uses Blake's techniques, does not accept Blake's work. "Just because a lab has credentials doesn't mean it produces accurate work," he said, citing numerous problems and scandals within accredited labs. "What the FBI and crime lab directors are saying is that the only ones to be trusted are the ones they say should be trusted."

Some of the individuals prancing before us that evening were simply hired guns and cops in lab coats ready to jangle at the drop of some puppet master's jingle. Behind the scenes, there is another name by which Plourd, Blake and others refer to these forensic puppets. In a three-ring binder on a shelf in his office Blake keeps tabs on the ones who have crossed the line...and crossed his path. The notebook is labeled simply, WHORES.

Returning to our hotel rooms that evening, I asked Chris, "Isn't there something—anything—that can be done about this venal business?"

"Well, Jim," said Chris philosophically, "where there are whores, there's a..."

CHAPTER 18
WHOREHOUSE

udges officiate the justice game. They make the call when one of the adversaries cries foul. Like a boxing referee, the judge is there to separate the combatants when one of them hits below the belt. But unlike the referee, the judge rarely acts on his own initiative when there's a low blow. He waits for one of the fighters to say "ouch." For example, prosecutor Levy's low blow at the beginning of the first trial was met by defense attorney Jones's "Objection!"

Judges have wide discretion when considering objections. There are no instant replays. The game goes on. When a judge's performance is evaluated years later by an appellate court, wrong calls are not infrequently determined to be "harmless error." That is, the appellate judges agree that the trial judge was in error but feel that the prosecutor would have won the game anyway.

After a bit of mental masturbation lubricated with legal jargon, Judge Hotham overruled Jones's objection and allowed the last-minute videotape to play. This error in judgment gave Levy a weapon with which to bludgeon the virtually defenseless defense attorney. It was Rawson's slick video song and dance under the guise of science that most influenced the first jury to convict. That this blow was low and Hotham erred was affirmed by the Arizona Supreme Court when it overturned Ray's conviction and ordered a new trial.

I learned about Judge Jeffrey Hotham through the transcripts of the first trial. By and large he had sustained the prosecutor's objections and overruled the defense's. My first and only encounter with the man was in his chambers. It was also the first time I would meet prosecutor Noel Levy face to face. I was curious to see what kind of man would refer to me publicly as "a shady person." Levy had challenged Plourd's request that he be allowed to proceed with post conviction relief, a Rule 32, for his client. A debate between two attorneys doesn't require a courtroom. Judge Hotham invited the adversaries into his chambers to discuss the matter. I went along with Chris.

While Chris studied his notes, I looked about at the photographs on the walls. They were mostly beach and underwater pictures of the judge obviously enjoying vacations. After a ten-minute wait, Hotham and Levy appeared simultaneously from the judge's chambers. I thought it odd for them to have been chatting beforehand. It's highly inappropriate during litigation for a judge to meet with the attorney for one side without the attorney for the other side being present. Oh well, it was way before Ray would be—if indeed he would be—granted a second trial. Perhaps they were discussing old times at the county prosecutor's office…or maybe scuba diving?

Levy was trim, with graying hair. He looked fit for a man his age, which I guessed to be mid-forties. He was not a large man and seemed even smaller standing next to Chris's six-foot, one-inch, heavy-set frame. The two attorneys talked as the judge checked on the court reporter. Levy seemed to me, also a six-footer, to look even smaller as of necessity he had to look up while listening. I wondered if some Napoleon complex had prompted his attempted "shady" intimidation. Now he virtually ignored me. I stood close to sandwich him in between Chris and myself and cast as much shade upon him as I could until we were called into chambers.

Jeffrey Hotham was about the same size, shape and age as Levy. He had been an intelligence officer in the US Army before entering Arizona State University's College of Law in nearby Tempe. Thereafter he had been for thirteen years a Maricopa County prosecutor, during which time he'd gotten to know Levy. He was appointed superior court judge in 1987. His avocation had been revealed by the pictures on the walls in the waiting room.

We were only a moment in chambers before the court reporter arrived. I was introduced for the record, briefly mentioned as a suspected tamperer of evidence, and then once again ignored. I supposed that Levy was less concerned that I had looked at the evidence than that I had invited Dr. Campbell in to evaluate the bite mark material and render a second opinion.

Judge Hotham seemed attentive as Plourd outlined the tidbits of evidence that he'd already seen and asked the judge to be allowed access to all of the evidence then in storage. He showed the judge Campbell's affidavit excluding Ray as the source of the bite mark. Plourd wanted a copy of Ray's teeth cast and copies of all bite mark photos for other experts to evaluate. He also wanted copies of all crime scene photos in evidence as well as copies of any and all case-related photos in the police files. As for the DNA evidence in custody, Plourd told Hotham, "Essentially new genetic markers have come on line in the last year or so since Krone's trial. I believe there's a strong possibility, if not almost a certainty, that Mr. Krone would positively be excluded…and there's a chance, depending upon our ability to get reference samples from other people, that we may be able to identify somebody else…"

Showing obvious lack of interest in Plourd's suggestion that there might actually be a way to solve the crime, Levy gave his spiel about no one in Arizona's ever having proceeded with a Rule 32 while his appeal was pending and "therefore" Ray Krone should not be the first. He also wanted the evidence sealed because of his "concern about Mr. Rix's…allegedly fooling around with the exhibits."

In the end Judge Hotham couldn't figure out the fair thing to do. "Procedurally this is sort of a no man's land and quite complex," he said for the record. He ordered the exhibits sealed and dismissed the Rule 32. Plourd subsequently filed a special action with the Arizona Supreme Court questioning Hotham's judgment.

Logically one might ask, What harm could be done by allowing two independent processes to proceed simultaneously? An appeal dealt with errors that occur at trial, a Rule 32 with newly discovered evidence. If anything, a guilty man would be executed sooner or an innocent man would go free. In any event, Hotham ruled in favor of his old prosecutor buddy.

It would be months before the supreme court would agree with Plourd and allow him to proceed with discovery. In the meantime Plourd's concern about Judge Hotham grew. He discovered that the judge had the reputation of being a "prosecutor's judge." Two Maricopa County justice game insiders had actually referred to him as such in my presence. It was a rare event for Hotham to rule in favor of a defendant. Apparently he'd forgotten to remove his prosecutor's hat when he donned a judge's robe.

A Rule 32 is almost always heard by the original trial judge. If the judge is honest and objective, this custom makes sense because he or she's familiar with the evidence and therefore able to determine whether the new evidence would have made a difference in the verdict. The judge at his or her sole discretion can grant a new trial.

Troubled by Hotham's obviously jaundiced eye, Plourd filed a motion to dismiss with cause to try to have Hotham replaced. Plourd had discovered that the judge had made a procedural error at the end of the trial. Due to a clerical omission, Hotham had left out an important element of felony kidnapping in his instructions to the jury. The instructions should have read:

The crime of kidnapping requires proof of the following three things:
Number One, the defendant knowingly restricted another persons's movements; and
Number Two, the restriction was accomplished:

a) by physical force; and
b) by moving the person from place to place by confining the person [in a manner which interfered substantially with the person's movements]; and

Number Three, the restriction was with the intent to inflict death, physical injury or sexual assault upon the person.

The bracketed part had been omitted. The record showed that the jury had begun deliberations at 2:45 p.m. The chambers conference noting and correcting the error concluded at 3:05 p.m. The jury returned with its verdict at 5:20 p.m. In chambers Hotham had suggested that the bailiff read the amended instructions to the jury. But Plourd could find nothing in the record indicating that this had been done.

Plourd argued that the bailiff and even the judge himself would have to be called as witnesses to find out exactly what had happened and whether it affected the verdict.

It was a minor technicality that Plourd hoped would get the judge removed from the case.

Such requests are heard by another superior court judge. Presiding Judge Ron Reinstein got the call. It was a long shot that one member of the club would go against another, and Reinstein didn't. Plourd faced the grim prospect of having to face judge Jeffrey Hotham to try to convince him that an innocent man had been convicted in his court.

When the Arizona Supreme Court came to the rescue and granted Ray's appeal and ordered a new trial, Ray was fortunate that in the meantime Hotham had been transferred to the family law division.

Hotham types are not uncommon in the justice game. Of judges who rise from the criminal attorney ranks, former prosecutors outnumber former defense attorneys ten to one.

Ray was lucky that the Honorable James E. McDougall was selected to preside over his second trial. In 1981, after eight years as a court commissioner, McDougall had been appointed judge. He served in juvenile court and in superior court. In 1991 he became the first judge honored with the Freedom of Information Award presented by the Society of Professional Journalists.

This judge tried to see to it that Ray received a fair second trial— at times bending over backwards. A good example is his handling of Plourd's objection to Dr. Moses Schanfield's bombshell. Late on a Friday afternoon this expert had told the jury during prosecutor Levy's redirect examination that he was "ninety-nine point five percent sure" that the DNA extracted from the victim's bra belonged to Ray Krone. Plourd did not immediately respond. In fact, the weekend passed and on Monday morning another witness had completed his testimony before Plourd stood up to object.

Chris Plourd was always well prepared. But Schanfield's surprise use of population frequencies caught him off guard. He had no idea that the expert was going to testify to them. In fact, in pre-trial meetings it had been determined that the frequency data were not supported by scientific controls. One can only wonder how Schanfield came about to render a statistical guess.

During Plourd's cross-examination, Schanfield had been guided through the DNA results of the saliva swabbed from the area of the bite mark and, to the expert's own surprise, was led to agree that Ray Krone was excluded as its source. Levy was noticeably miffed that his own expert had helped the defense. Could it be that the prosecutor had subsequently pimped Dr. Schanfield into giving phony testimony to try to counteract Plourd's brilliant cross-examination?

Be that as it may, Plourd emphasized that "this [frequency data] evidence potentially has great incriminating force should the jury accept it" and moved that the court "either strike the [scientifically unfounded] testimony or in the alternative grant a mistrial."

Judge McDougall took the objection under advisement and allowed the trial to proceed. Dr. Rawson was halfway through his testimony when McDougall ruled. He not only sustained Plourd's objection but also gave the defense the option to either have the spurious testimony stricken from the record or to be granted a mistrial.

The DNA evidence was at worst neutral and at best favored Ray Krone. Had Plourd known at the time that this jury was destined to ignore the real science of DNA analysis in favor of the Ouija science of bite mark analysis, he most surely would have opted for a mistrial. Instead, he had the incriminating testimony stricken from the record.

Levy lost little. A bell once rung cannot be unrung.

π

George Schuester, McDougall's bailiff, remembers the judge taking the forensic testimony quite seriously. "I'd never seen him take so many notes." DNA was relatively new to the courts of Arizona. Not only did the spectators' gallery fill up with the county's crime lab personnel whenever Plourd was performing with a DNA expert on the stand, but McDougall would also leave the bench, notepad in hand, and take a vacant seat in the jury box for a more advantageous view.

After one particularly grueling afternoon of DNA testimony, I was standing in the front row of the spectators' gallery as the jury filed out. One conscientious, concerned juror lingered behind and buttonholed the judge as he passed in front of the jury box. The juror said something like, "You know, your honor, I don't understand any of this DNA stuff. Perhaps you should excuse me from the jury?"

It was late in the day. The judge's guard was down. Without thinking, McDougall responded to the effect, "Don't worry. Do the best you can. I don't understand it either." Then, immediately recognizing what he'd done, he rushed into his chambers. This faux pas caused McDougall to admonish the jury the next day. He told them to keep their distance from him, he wasn't one of them. Since it's natural for jurors to look to the judge for guidance, McDougall's inadvertent confession of his lack of understanding of the scientific testimony quite likely adversely influenced the bewildered juror and the other jurors who may have overheard it, and it may even have helped cause them to ignore the DNA evidence.

The fundamental lack of scientific savvy within the justice game is not uncommon. As Barry Scheck of the Innocence Project has observed, "The reason many individuals choose a career in law is because they do not possess an aptitude for science."

Indeed, understanding science quite possibly hinders ambitious prosecutors by creating a moral dilemma when their cerebral cortex informs their conscience that they are prosecuting an innocent person. For prosecutor Levy there would be no such dilemma.

Other than the actual trial and the Rule 32 hearing in judge Hotham's office, I observed Levy in action on only one other occasion—during his pre-trial interview with Chris's DNA expert. Any notion that he was going to understand the science was dispelled ten minutes into the meeting.

I had driven from my High Sierra home to Oakland to pick up Chris at the airport and take him north to Ed Blake's Richmond lab, where Levy would already be waiting. Plourd had dropped Dr. Blake from the witness list because of concerns surrounding the problem DNA Blake found on the victim's bra. For this reason, it was unwise to let Levy have access to Blake. Nevertheless, an expert was needed to present the favorable serologic evidence, and senior forensic serologist Gary Harmor had been selected. The company he worked for, Serological Research Institute, was separate and independent from Blake's, but it occupied the same office building and shared Blake's lab. The meeting was held in the common conference room.

As a defense attorney skilled in forensic science, Chris Plourd frequently found himself having to educate scientifically challenged prosecutors on DNA. While I had some trouble with Harmor's technical explanations, Chris converted them into terms easy for a layperson to understand. Evidence of Ray Krone, he explained, was nowhere to be found in any of the bodily fluids Harmor had analyzed. Levy *seemed* to be listening to Chris, but when Chris reached a conclusion Levy didn't like, he would refuse to accept it and go back to dispute Harmor's findings, probing for holes in Harmor's analysis, however small, that he could exploit at trial.

"Is he dumb or what?" I thought to myself as I listened to Levy's circuitous "reasoning."

At one point, Chris and Harmor were called out of the room, leaving me alone with Levy. After an awkward silence in which I sensed that the prosecutor was uncomfortable in the company of a shady person, I offered some small talk. I wanted to ask him if he left the light on when he went to bed at night, but I rejected the sarcastic impulse and gestured toward the leather jacket that he'd draped over the back of his chair.

"Where'd you get the jacket?" I asked. It reminded me of the jacket worn by the World War I flying ace, the Red Baron.

"In the service."

"Which branch?" I expected to hear something to do with aircraft.

"Intelligence."

Fortunately, the others returned at this point, or I might have had to restrain myself again from saying something like, Right, you don't have to have it to be in it.

Until this point I had believed, as perhaps most Americans do, that justice is about discovering truth. Watching Levy at this meeting changed all that for me. It killed the last of my naïveté about the justice game. It was no longer possible for me to believe that Levy would eventually notice that Ray was innocent and do the right thing.

Okay, he didn't believe Chris's numerous bite mark experts who excluded Ray. But certainly, I had rationalized, when the DNA evidence is laid out before him he'll see the light. Well, it had been laid out at the meeting, and he hadn't seen any lights.

After the meeting was over, I repeated out loud for Chris to hear, "Is he dumb or what?"

Chris disagreed that Levy was stupid. He'd seen it before, a prosecutor so wrapped up in his belief that the defendant is guilty that he can't help but believe his own procured whores and reject any contrary evidence. Chris thought Levy a formidable opponent who was focusing his intelligence exclusively on navigating his prosecutorial yacht through the waves pushed out by the defense's barge. As it turned out, it was relatively smooth sailing for prosecutor Levy because he was able to fill his sails with forensic hot air.

π

You might wonder, how does bad science stay afloat anyway? Well, it has managed to sail around the two standards by which Ouija science might otherwise be sunk. The first, known as *Frye*, has been around since 1923 and puts the onus on the scientific community, when forensic science is challenged in court, to convince the judge that he should accept it because it is generally accepted within the scientific community. *Frye* has been a dismal failure because a pimp attorney who can find one whore to espouse Ouija science can find still other whores to vouch for it.

In a 1993 decision the United States Supreme Court created a second standard for judging Ouija science. *Daubert*, as it is known, goes beyond the general acceptance standard of *Frye* to consider the error rate of the science in question, as established by bona fide testing. It also requires that the challenged forensic science be subjected to peer review.

Unquestionably, bite mark analysis would fail *Daubert* because of the only test done had produced a sixty-three percent error rate and the majority of board-certified odontologists voted down peer review. (The vote wasn't a big surprise. What Ouija scientist wants someone looking over his shoulder while he's playing with his pendulum?)

Bite mark analysis has yet to be subjected to *Daubert*. Whenever an attempt is made, the opposition counters that it has already been accepted under *Frye* and, anyway, *it's really not a scientific procedure at all* but simply a comparison of one thing with another for which the odontologist is merely the guiding light for the jurors—who, it is assumed, are able to see for themselves.

This scenario is essentially what happened with Ray Krone's jury. After ignoring the evidence they couldn't understand and being blinded by the crisscrossing lights, the jurors sequestered themselves with the bite mark evidence and guessed for themselves.

Daubert, if properly applied, provides a suitable tool to keep junk bunk Ouija witchcraft out of the courtroom. *Daubert* fails primarily because in the justice game trial court judges are the gatekeepers. And they are not infrequently biased, afraid to rock the boat and/or bewildered by science. It's no wonder that quackery of all sorts routinely surfaces in court. We can't expect a judge who foisted nonsense like the barking dog hocus pocus onto a jury when he was a prosecutor to be very receptive to a *Daubert* hearing in his court. Nor can we expect it of the conscientious, job-fearing, scientifically challenged judge whose standard rationalization might well be, "Oh well, I don't understand it so I'll let the jury decide."

It stands to reason that judges by and large pay little attention to board certification (or to any certification for that matter) in qualifying expert witnesses—otherwise why would a guy like Dr. Michael West, who resigned before he was booted out of two professional organizations and suspended by a third, be allowed to testify? Yet despite these sanctions he remains in high demand and continues to be procured and allowed into the house.

My impression is that a doctor of something will qualify as an expert on almost anything in most courts. And almost anybody can qualify as an expert on something or other if some attorney wishes it.

Consequently, judges more often than not turn a blind eye to pimp attorneys who procure and parade a steady stream of whores through their house. These tacit madams pretty much leave it up to the pimps to display their stable of whores and to challenge their adversaries' stable in front of the jury johns. The pimp whose stable most arouses the johns has the best chance of winning the game.

James Kemper, who would become Ray's next attorney, expressed this sorry situation this way: "I can get someone to qualify as an expert in court to testify that the sun rises in the west and sets in the east."

Chris put it best. "Jim, even you could qualify as an expert!"

π

Courts don't really need "standards" or even an aptitude for science if they would simply behave decently, muster some courage and employ a little old-fashioned horse sense. Trial judges routinely observe the prosecutor's expert confidently frothing scientific jargon and swearing that something is true and then watch the defense's expert swear with equal confidence, froth and jargon that exactly the opposite is true. It doesn't take an aptitude for science to figure out that at least one of these guys is full of shit. And in some cases, from a scientific perspective, both of them are. Just guys jangling for jingle, parading as doctors rendering opinions.

When confused by contradictory technical testimony, all that conscientious but bewildered jurors seem to be able to do is to give the Academy Award to the song and dance man they think gave the best performance. This penchant explains the success of charismatic whores whose confident, down home performance wins the Oscar more often than the cerebral out-of-towner's straight, plain presentation of the truth.

The pawn in this horse senseless game can only hope that the jury awards the witness who happens to be guessing in his favor. If not, the guilty pawn is duly punished while the innocent pawn suffers a gross injustice and must helplessly sit out the rest of the game hoping that his team will play on and somehow find a way to win.

> *The cloak and dagger dangles,*
> *Madams light the candles.*
> *In ceremonies of the horsemen,*
> *Even the pawn must hold a grudge.*
> – Bob Dylan

π

Having to wait to be sentenced, pawn Ray Krone wasted away in the county jail an additional nine months after the battle was lost. On December 9, 1996 Judge McDougall read his seventeen-page special verdict in open court. He sentenced Ray to twenty-one years for kidnapping and to "life, without the possibility of release on any basis until the completion of the service of twenty-five years," for felony murder. He also ordered that the sentences run consecutively.

Bailiff George Schuester believed that Judge McDougall agonized over the guilty verdict and in his heart believed Ray to be innocent. If you read his special verdict, you can sense McDougall's angst:

> ...although there was sufficient evidence upon which twelve people could and did render a verdict beyond a reasonable doubt, there were still many unanswered questions.

Doesn't "unanswered questions" seem a hedge on "beyond a reasonable doubt"?

> The court could find only five facts which could be used to establish the defendant's guilt:

> 1. That when first questioned the defendant seemed to distance himself from the victim by claiming never to have associated with her outside the bar. [Detective Gregory's version of the relationship between the victim and the defendant.]
> 2. A witness testified that the victim told her "Ray," whom the witness understood to mean Ray Krone, was coming by to help the victim close that night. [Barmaid Kate Koester's hearsay testimony.]
> 3. The size of the footprints found in the kitchen and the bathroom were consistent with the size of the defendant's

feet. [The second police report pertaining to shoe size. The first police report in which the shoe size didn't fit Ray's feet was ignored.]

4. Ray Krone could not be excluded as the donor of the DNA evidence found on…the victim's bra if it was a mixture of the victim's DNA and someone else's DNA. [Moses Schanfield's bell unrung.]

5. Dr. Rawson and Dr. Piakas testified that in their opinions the bite marks on the victim's breast were made by Ray Krone. [The evidence upon which the jury hung its hat.]

McDougall then elaborated on the state's bite mark experts:

In this court's opinion, serious issues were raised by the defense regarding the credibility of the testimony of Drs. Rawson and Piakas.

Doesn't an incriminating expert's lack of credibility add up to "reasonable doubt"? As if to remove his own doubt, McDougall again used that phrase:

The court feels strongly that there was sufficient evidence upon which the jury could make a decision of guilt beyond a reasonable doubt in this case and their verdict will not be overturned by this court.

It would be political suicide in Arizona for a trial judge to overturn a jury's verdict. That McDougall considered it at all is telling. However, the most compelling indication that he was torn between the findings of his cerebral cortex and the jury's verdict came after he finished reading his rationalizations. Choking up trying to hold back his tears, McDougall abruptly switched from referring to himself as "the court" to using first person pronouns:

This is one of those cases that will haunt me for the rest of my life wondering whether I have done the right thing. Having reviewed all of the evidence presented in this case, I cannot find that it clearly supports the sentence of death and, therefore, it will not be given.

It was the best the Honorable James E. McDougall could do for Ray.

π

Chris Plourd was distraught at his client's conviction. Months after sitting through the sentencing, his last official duty as attorney of record, Chris was still noticeably upset. Always sensitive to others,

Ray attempted to cheer up his friend with a bit of whimsy. "Oh well," he said, patting Chris on the back, "I guess life is the consolation prize when you're innocent."

Ray maintained a sense of humor through it all. But privately he must have felt little consolation. Even with credit for time served, he faced at least forty-one more years in prison. At his age, he would be at least eighty years old when released—if he should live that long. The life sentence was in all probability another sort of death sentence.

π

The wisdom of our founding fathers cannot be overestimated. After whipping a vastly superior enemy in a revolutionary war that was not fought for land, wealth or power, but for a revolutionary idea called "Liberty," they created a government focused on preserving that ideal. They understood that it is difficult at best for a public servant, whether a magistrate, commissioner or judge, to behave fairly and objectively when fearful of losing his job by periodically having to face the electorate. They knew that justices, in order to dispense true justice, must be removed from politics and be allowed to rise above it. That's why the constitution they created set the term for supreme court justices and all federal judges at life without the possibility of removal unless impeached and convicted of a high crime or misdemeanor.

In 1911 the people of the prospective State of Arizona submitted their constitution to Washington for consideration. Congress approved and voted Arizona into the Union. However, President William Taft did not approve. He vetoed the resolution for statehood because Arizona's constitution provided for the recall of judges. This provision was subsequently removed and the constitution resubmitted. On February 14, 1912 Arizona became the last of the lower forty-eight states to be admitted to the Union. But it didn't take Arizona's pioneers long to restore their original intent. Before 1912 was history its constitution was amended to reinstate the recall provision, thus guaranteeing that Arizona courts would be staffed by quasi politicians wearing judge's robes.

Unlike federal judges, who are appointed for life, Arizona judges (and most state judges now) must periodically face the electorate. It is only natural that they pander in varying degrees to those who demand that their elected officials be tough on crime. "Doing the right thing" is likely to be construed as being soft on crime and lead to loss of job. It is unlikely that Judge McDougall would have survived the headline, JUDGE FREES CONVICTED MURDERER, despite the fact that the accompanying article might reveal a case of serious railroading to those capable of reading between the lines.

Rudy Gerber knows this situation well. He spent twenty-two years as an Arizona trial and appellate judge and has written numerous articles and books on his adventures working on the Arizona judicial railroad. In his book, *Cruel and Usual: Our Criminal Injustice System*, a very informative title, he writes: "Unpopular decisions in capital cases...may cost a judge the bench..." He gives the example of a judge who "was voted off the court...after he recommended that a death sentence be set aside due to prosecutorial misconduct."

In Arizona and elsewhere you don't want to mess with the prosecutors who engineer the train.

Judge Gerber and some of his colleagues who intimately understand the reality of Arizona justice agree that they would rather be tried in any European court than in an Arizona court—even one over which they themselves preside. Their fear of having their robes stripped away for making unpopular decisions makes them essentially puppets of those in charge of finding, prosecuting and punishing criminals. Gerber writes:

> Our judicial robes hinder frank evaluation of policies that create [injustice]. While many Arizona judges privately are critical of our justice system, their public silence is profound.

Consider Yuma County Superior Court Judge Thomas A. Thode, who presided over *Arizona v. Bobby Lee Tankersley.*

Not long after my first visit to Death Row, Ray told me, somewhat excitedly during one of his monthly telephone calls, "There's another guy down here [on Death Row] who was convicted on a bite mark."

"Really."

"And Rawson was the expert," continued Ray. "And there was a videotape."

"Really!" I said, catching his excitement. "What's his name?"

"Bobby Tankersley."

After the conversation I called Chris, who at the time was feverishly preparing Ray's case. He was very interested in the information and wanted to get a copy of this Rawson videotape and the associated transcripts. I immediately wrote Bobby that I was working on Ray's case and would like to be put on his visitation list. When he said yes, I made plans to visit both him and Ray.

After an hour with Ray, I remained in the private booth waiting while the guards ushered Ray back to his cell and Bobby from his.

Though I was just a family member of Ray's, I was listed as being on his legal team and therefore afforded the attorney's private booth for visits. In time Bobby showed up. We chatted in depth about his case.

A month and a half before Ray was arrested, Thelma Younkin had been found dead on the floor of her bedroom in her apartment at the Post Park Motel—no longer a motel but a rundown flophouse in downtown Yuma. An obvious struggle had occurred. Her body was partially covered by her housecoat. Her panties were found on the floor near her legs, her bra pushed up, exposing her breasts, which displayed numerous bite marks.

The decaying motel turned flophouse was the residence of many Yuma down-and-outers. One was Bobby Tankersley, who lived at the other end of the building. He didn't remember much about the weekend because he was drunk most of the time back in those days. He was one of several people milling around as the police investigated the crime scene. He gave a statement to one of the officers. The crime was not immediately solved. Bobby moved to California. Nine months later, in San Diego, he was arrested for the murder.

I suppose it was just a coincidence that "the snaggletooth murder" had occurred in the interim. It couldn't be that the ambitious Yuma prosecutor had gotten wind of the fine work done by her Phoenix colleague in solving a bite mark case, could it? It couldn't be that a corollary of the then unknown West Phenomenon had come into play, whereby *anyone* charged with inflicting a bite mark is going to be pointed at by some hired gun's pliable pendulum, could it? In any case, Rawson was hired. Bobby was located and forced to provide his bite impression. He was then shipped back to Yuma to stand trial. In short order Bobby joined Ray on Death Row.

Throughout the visit Bobby maintained his innocence. Before leaving, I asked, "Any other trouble with the law?"

After a pause Bobby looked directly into my eyes and said, "I have a rap sheet as long as my arm. I'm a drunk and a petty thief. But I didn't kill anyone."

A straightforward answer, I thought.

My mission the next day was to go to the Yuma County courthouse and make a copy of the videotape and then meet with Bobby's defense attorney and get a copy of the bite mark testimony. Before making the four-hour drive to Yuma, I swung back through Phoenix and stopped into a video rental store for a TV and two tape players for the evening.

My experience with Maricopa County's evidence department had prepared me for this caper. Viewing a videotape there required that the viewer provide his own TV and tape player. Making a copy was out of the question without some higher-up's approval, which most likely would not be given to a layperson like me. To get a copy of Rawson's Krone videotape, Mike Pain had had to schmooze Ray's appellate attorney, John Antieau. The easiest way for me to get a copy of Tankersley's videotape would be to do it surreptitiously.

I checked into my Yuma motel room about eight in the evening, had a bite to eat and then stopped by a Blockbuster to purchase a blank tape and rent a movie for testing. I hadn't thought to do a test back in Phoenix. Instead of renting, I purchased a used copy of Woody Allen's "Shadows and Fog," filmed in black and white à la Fellini's "La Strada." Both films are about circus misfits, but Woody's is a farcical murder mystery in which the strangler magically escapes. As I watched it, I thought of Thelma Younkin. She had been strangled to death. The murder weapon was the plastic tubing attached to her oxygen canister. Younkin was sixty-five and suffered from emphysema and heart disease.

I set up and tested the equipment so that the taping process might go unnoticed. The TV had a VCR player/recorder innocuously positioned inside the unit, under the monitor. It would serve as the recording device. I loaded the blank tape so all I had to do was hit the record button before playing the Tankersley tape on the external VCR.

"I'm investigating the Tankersley case," I told the clerk, "and would like to take a look at the exhibits." I'd learned to watch my phraseology. Claiming to be a *private* investigator when not properly licensed was not advisable.

The clerk showed me a list of all the exhibits in the case. I jotted down a dozen or so exhibit numbers, which included the one for the videotape, all the while engaging her in small talk by asking her about the dolls sitting on the ledge next to the counter.

"I make and sell them for gifts," she said.

Before handing her my list of selected exhibit numbers, I bought a doll for my daughter Aisha.

She compared my list with the master list and said, "This one won't do you any good, it's a videotape. We don't have equipment."

"That's okay. My own equipment's in the car. Where do I set up?"

It was obvious she hadn't dealt with such a request before because she had to disappear for a bit. She returned and directed me to a forlorn room that appeared to be a library of sorts.

As she fetched the exhibits, I fetched the equipment.

She watched about half of Rawson's version of *Shadows and Fog* with me, the doll poised in front of the TV to hide the recording indicator light.

Just before leaving me to my devices, she remarked, duly impressed, "It's amazing what they're doing with science nowadays."

"Yes, it is," I agreed. She did not notice my sarcasm.

Familiar with the illusions used in the Krone videotape, I watched closely for similar legerdemain. It didn't take long to detect the prestidigitation. In this video Rawson compared the left half of the arch of a bite mark with the left side of Bobby's upper teeth cast then faded out and back in to compare the right side—after repositioning the dental model. This procedure was repeated several times on several bite marks. Overall, the tape was no more convincing than the one used to convict Ray.

But there was more evidence against Bobby, which I would learn about that afternoon.

After lunch I met with Kirby Kongable, Bobby's defense attorney. As promised, he had copies of the bite mark testimony for me. We talked the better part of an hour about the case. My lunch hadn't fully settled—and wouldn't after I learned that splotches of fecal matter had trailed from the victim's perineum all the way into the bathroom. Apparently Ms. Younkin's bowels had voided during the attack and her assailant had had to clean himself up. A brown-stained washrag was found in the sink.

Four hairs were detected in the washrag. But they were of no definitive use because their follicles were missing. The police criminologist who compared one of these hairs with a sample hair taken from Bobby concluded, "The hairs were not similar, but also they were not so dissimilar as to exclude the suspect." Orwellian doublespeak.

However, another hair was found near the sink, its root intact. This hair was sent to Ed Blake's lab for analysis. Blake determined the DQα marker to be (1.1,4), the same as Bobby's. Though four percent of the Caucasian population share this allele, it did not bode well for Bobby, especially when someone the caliber of Blake was working for the prosecution.

When I asked Kongable if he had retained a bite mark expert for the defense, he drew back seemingly offended. Apparently he, like Ray's first attorney, and Ray himself, had believed Rawson. Perhaps he didn't fully understand the justice game, whereby even if it were

Tankersley's bite mark on the victim, he could easily have procured some board-certified forensic whore to say it wasn't. For he had made no effort to find one.

Yet this attorney talked with pride about his work on Tankersley's case. "If I get one more death penalty case like this one," he told me, "I could be appointed judge." Well, he must have lost another one because Kirby Kongable is now a superior court judge for Yuma County. And Chris assured me that losers are promoted in other places besides Arizona also.

Convicted on bite marks and a single hair, Bobby had by 2004 languished on Death Row for twelve years while his attorneys worked to discover new evidence. He had kept me informed of progress on his case. I in turn had informed Chris. As the information accumulated, Chris on his own volition volunteered and worked behind the scenes educating Tankersley's attorneys on the best way to approach the untouched DNA evidence known to be in storage. These attorneys hadn't even had the savvy to look at the lab notes for clues. When they did, under Chris's tutelage, much was discovered. Chris particularly liked the blood noted to be on the victim's fingernail clippings.

On October 14, 2004 a motion to exonerate defendant based on new DNA evidence was filed in the Yuma County superior court. The original trial judge, the Honorable Thomas A. Thode, was assigned to hear and rule on the motion.

At the evidentiary hearing held a month later, Judge Thode learned that (1) the DNA found on the murder weapon, the oxygen tubing, came from three individuals, one the victim and *neither* of the other two Bobby Tankersley, (2) the DNA extracted from the victim's fingernail clippings belonged to the victim and a male who was *not* Bobby Tankersley and (3) the DNA swabbed from several bite mark wounds did *not* belong to Bobby Tankersley or the victim.

Bobby could not be excluded by the stray hair found in the sink. However, he was known to have befriended the victim and to have given her a ride in his car to do errands on at least three separate occasions. He could quite possibly have used her bathroom on one or more of those occasions. The defense argued, "Hairs can and do transfer from people to vehicles, and then can be picked up on another person's shoes or clothing. If the state must rely on this hair, no conviction would result."

Of defense attorney Kirby Kongable, Judge Thode wrote in his opinion, "Counsel was ineffective for several reasons, including, most egregiously, counsel's disclosure of privileged information to the court." Kongable had disclosed that he essentially believed his client to be guilty even though he refused to accept a plea bargain, and that he shouldn't be blamed if his client was found guilty.

Lucky Bobby, you might think. The judge is going to turn it around for him.

Afraid not.

You're probably going to wonder what Judge Thode's free hand was doing as he wrote, "The court finds that the evidence presented is insufficient to exonerate the defendant of this crime...The evidence does not present newly discovered facts which probably would have changed the verdict. The guilt of this defendant shall remain undisturbed."

Thode could not even find it in his heart to give Bobby a new trial, merely ordering that he be re-sentenced. All this pussy could do—on the eve of his retirement no less—was to give Bobby a shot at life in prison.

I guess there's more than a little truth to Ray's whimsy that in Arizona, innocents convicted of murder get life in prison instead of death.

π

These personal observations suggest that in the pusillanimous milieu of Arizona's courts all a job-fearing (or retirement-fearing) judge can do is gingerly toe the rope, shed a tear and compliantly watch the railroading.

Ray, Bobby and who knows how many countless other innocents have had their passports to freedom painted out of existence the moment they were locked up in the caboose of Arizona's Injustice Express, which is operated by puppets and clowns and headed with some fanfare but essentially without detour to the hoosegow, accompanied perhaps by a mournful choir singing the prophetic Dylan jingle:

> *They're selling postcards of the hanging*
> *They're painting the passports brown*
> *The beauty parlor is filled with sailors*
> *The circus is in town*
> *Here comes the blind commissioner*
> *They've got him in a trance*
> *One hand is tied to the tight-rope walker*
> *The other is in his pants*

CHAPTER 19
THE COLOR OF JUSTICE

Ray Krone was broke but not broken.

In January 1997 he was escorted from the county jail and taken back to the state prison in Florence. It was the first time in fully a year and a half that he had seen sunshine. He had survived the roller coaster ride of the second trial. He had endured five years of incarceration, about half of them on Death Row and the other half split between his two trials in tough sheriff Joe Arpaio's even harsher custody. The only gain for his second stint in the county jail was life in prison rather than death by lethal injection.

Ray quickly adjusted to his confinement in the general prison population. His morale soon improved over what it had been during the low period of his confinement between his second conviction and his return to Florence. His spirits were buoyed by the knowledge that his family, though financially broke, were spiritually unbroken. In time everyone would recover and continue the fight for his freedom. For now, out of necessity, Ray's cause proceeded on a shoestring.

The justice system advertises equality with the statue of a blindfolded lady holding a scale evenly balanced. The import of this symbol seems lost in Arizona's justice game, where county attorneys don't seem to be constrained by the due process guarantees of the United States Constitution. Not only can they budget as much to prosecute a case as they see fit, but they also control the funding of the defense when the defendant is indigent. The defense investigator approved by the court for Ray's first trial put in a mere twenty-eight hours total while the prosecution had the Phoenix police department and its crime lab at its disposal.

The landmark 1985 United States Supreme Court decision *Ake v. Oklahoma* guarantees the right of the indigent defendant to have expert assistance. But *Ake* caused no pain for the Maricopa County Attorney. *Ake* does not guarantee that an indigent defendant have *competent* expert assistance. When asked by Geoffrey Jones for funding to retain a bite mark expert for the first trial, job-fearing Judge Hotham told the defense, "The county attorney is not going to be funding any extraordinary amounts of money." A paltry two thousand dollars was allotted for a defense expert. With it Jones retained a friend of the family, Bruce Etkin, a qualified prosthodontist but unqualified odontologist, who simply agreed with the prosecution's expert. For the first Krone trial, Dr. Ray Rawson was awarded ten thousand dollars.

The people of Maricopa County did not get off so easy the second time.

At the annual meeting of the American Academy of Forensic Science, held in Nashville just one week after Ray's second trial had begun, Dr. Rawson was confronted in his hotel room by a half-dozen fellow board-certified odontologists. Before the trial, prosecutor Levy had pressured Rawson to find a colleague who would support his position. He couldn't do it. Word was out to avoid Rawson's overtures like the plague.

Now Rawson was under pressure by some friends, odontology colleagues, to withdraw from the case. He was just weeks away from testifying when Dr. Richard Souviron advised him to "get out while you can. You know this is a bad case."

Rawson rejected Souviron's advice. "I'm in too deep."

Ten large was not enough to keep Rawson afloat a second time. The county attorney had given the order to do what was necessary to convict Ray Krone. But Levy needed more than this directive to procure the necessary funding. Someone somewhere within the county attorney's office must have balked initially at Rawson's price tag because Levy wrote an internal memo claiming that Krone's defense team was funded by some east coast anti-death penalty group with deep pockets—a barefaced, if imaginative, lie. The only logical explanation for this memo was that Levy sought to justify Rawson's demands. The hired gun received upwards of fifty thousand dollars jingle for his second trial jangle.

Not only did Levy have the county treasury at his disposal, he also had a strategy to bankrupt the defense and even recoup some of his own expenses in doing so.

For the second trial, Ray received no public funding. That burden was born by his family. When finally ordered to release the evidence, Levy did so...for a fee. One day, when I was asking Mike Pain, within Levy's earshot, if he'd received the necessary twelve hundred dollars from Ray's parents to pay for copies of some four hundred police crime scene photos, I noticed Levy's second smile—a big one. Ray's parents, Jim and Carolyn Leming, were charged four dollars per copy, ten times the rate at the nearest Photo Mat. The prosecutor seemed delighted that he'd been able to extort more than one thousand dollars profit from the defense.

Another such instance occurred when Judge McDougall ordered that the cost of having transcripts made of Moses Schanfield's stricken testimony be split between the prosecution and the defense. Jim Leming was called out of the courtroom to meet with a representative of the county attorney's office, who was in the hall with the court reporter with the transcripts modified to exclude the court-ordered stricken testimony. Leming was told that to get the transcripts he would have to pay the full amount then and there. He was told that it would take some time for the county's accounting department to release the funds and he was assured that if he paid the full amount he would be reimbursed one-half. Not wanting to delay the trial, Jim Leming dutifully wrote a check for the full amount. To this day, he has been refunded nothing.

Chris Plourd too was gouged. To interview and depose Ray Rawson he was required to pay the doctor his required one hundred and fifty-dollar hourly fee in advance. Just to get copies of Rawson's videotapes, acetate overlays, slide photos, and computer disks, he had to pay Rawson for fifteen hours merely to assemble these items (two thousand, two hundred and fifty dollars). The computer disks containing the CAT scan data were worthless. They were in some obscure format that only Rawson's computer could read. In all, Plourd was forced to pay Rawson more than four thousand dollars out of his own pocket.

Bankrupting the opponent is a common strategy in civil cases, where making it costly to litigate often facilitates a settlement. In criminal cases, however, it is one-sided. It would be virtually impossible to bankrupt the government. And if a capital defendant is offered a settlement what are his options? Life v. death! You might as well spend all you've got and then some.

Levy's strategy worked. When it came time for the appeal, not only was there no money to pay for it, but also Ray's family and Chris were still trying to pay off the debts incurred during the trial. Chris had to pony up about fourteen thousand dollars and the Lemings about half that.

Because Ray was consigned to a life sentence instead of death, there would be no automatic appeal. He would have to initiate his own. With Chris's help Ray filed his notice of appeal then petitioned the court to appoint an attorney for him because he was indigent. The court had no alternative but to appoint Ray an appellate attorney.

James Kemper was a well-respected veteran of the Maricopa County Public Defender's Office. In his late fifties, he was nearing retirement when assigned to do Ray's appeal. I volunteered to be point man and kept Ray, his family and Chris informed of Kemper's progress.

Compared to a trial, an appeal is relatively straightforward. Kemper essentially locks himself up with the trial transcripts and digests them, looking for errors in overruled defense objections or sustained prosecution objections. Then he formulates arguments claiming that those errors were harmful to his client, the appellant. Finally he prepares an "opening brief" in which he defends his arguments with points of law and concludes that the appellant did not receive a fair trial. It's a cerebral exercise committed to paper. The appellee, the people of Arizona represented by the state's attorney general, responds with an "answering brief" challenging the appellant's arguments and defending the conviction. Kemper has the last word with a "reply brief" answering any new issues raised by the appellee. When this reply brief is filed, Ray's appeal enters the queue with all the other appeals that are waiting to be considered and adjudicated by the court of appeals. At its discretion, the court may call for oral arguments to clarify any of the issues. Ray's case did not require clarification.

After my initial meeting with Kemper, I contacted Chris and asked if he would like to sit in on the next one. I wanted Chris's opinion as to whether Ray was well represented. Chris jumped at the opportunity. A good defense attorney frequently objects during a trial to create issues for consideration on appeal. An error to which the defense attorney fails to object cannot be considered at this stage but must wait for the next phase, the Rule 32, which, in addition to any new evidence, may raise the issue of ineffective assistance of counsel.

For Chris the trip to Phoenix was a simple commute. He was close to the airport in San Diego and seventy-minute flights leave and return almost every hour of the day, everyday. For me, connections were not so convenient. After a ninety-minute drive to the Reno airport and an hour to check in, I had a ninety-five minute plane ride to Phoenix—if I was lucky enough to get a nonstop flight. A stop in Las Vegas would add another hour to the trip. The only outbound nonstop morning flight was at 6:40, which meant that I would have to be up and at it by 3:00 a.m. I never took this flight but always came into Phoenix the night before I needed to be there and usually stayed at my old friend Gene Burdick's place.

Though Gene lived twenty-five miles from downtown Phoenix, Sky Harbor Airport was on the way, and I picked Chris up there late the next morning. We met Kemper briefly at his office then we all went to lunch at Crazy Jim's, a Greek restaurant within walking distance. Back in Kemper's office, the two attorneys seemed to hit it off. Chris was well prepared as usual and laid out all the issues he had set up with the appropriate objections at trial. Kemper seemed to be taking extensive notes and offered well-thought-out suggestions of his own. The meeting lasted most of the afternoon. At one point, when Kemper was out of the room, Chris leaned over and whispered, "I like this guy."

This comment was quite comforting. We would do what we had to do to help Ray, but the thought of having to retain a private attorney to do the appeal, should Kemper not pan out, was fiscally distressing.

Back at the airport Chris expressed his satisfaction with Kemper and assured me that Ray's case was on the right track. He caught the 6:15 back to San Diego. For me, the outbound flight was no less inconvenient than the inbound. The 6:50 flight through Vegas arrived in Reno a half-hour later than the 8:15 nonstop, so I waited for the latter and rolled into my driveway just before midnight. Chris had gotten home before I left Phoenix.

π

Nineteen ninety-seven was the year of the appeal. For Kemper and the rest of us it was mostly a waiting game. To do his work Kemper needed copies of the trial transcripts. All but five of sixty-three were in his possession by mid August. Those five hadn't yet been produced by the court reporter. It wasn't only Ray's case that was affected. Numerous other transcripts from seven other cases on appeal were also in this court reporter's limbo. Kemper finally realized that the missing transcripts might be a long time coming so he decided to try to proceed without them. It was a good decision. He didn't receive the final five transcripts until several months after he filed the appeal—and then only because the court reporter had been tossed into jail with her typewriter and notes and not allowed to leave until she finished. The transcripts delivered post-appeal to Kemper were essentially gibberish. The reporter seems to have been sleeping in court.

For some reason, Kemper's frustration soon became directed at Chris Plourd. I sensed that Kemper had a bit of an ego and had come to resent Chris. I suspect that he believed Chris was a highly paid defense attorney who continued to receive big bucks to advise on the case while Kemper was doing the dirty work on a measly public defender's salary. I didn't think it appropriate for me to let him know that Chris had taken a heavy loss and still continued to work on it pro bono. Anyway, it wasn't any of Kemper's business.

Kemper wrote Chris several letters asking for clarification of certain issues. Chris always responded with a phone call but always seemed to get Kemper's answering machine. Kemper, on the other hand, didn't return long distance calls. Apparently the public defender's office didn't have as copious a budget as the prosecutor's office. Perhaps Kemper had to account for all of his long distance calls and consequently chose not to make any.

On my frequent visits to meet with private investigator Mike Pain I observed another clue that public defenders aren't well funded. Mike's office was in the same building as Kemper's. The door next to Mike's had the sign "Public Defender's Training Facility" painted on its window. On my many trips to Mike's office from 1993 to well after the second trial in 1996, I can't recall ever seeing the lights on in that office.

In August Kemper wrote me of his impatience over the missing transcripts and of his irritation with Chris, "I know you paid this guy a lot of money and all that but I'm beginning to wonder if he is some sort of a flake."

Kemper's ego was getting the best of him. I tried to schmoose him. He didn't seem to understand that Chris's bills were being paid by other cases he was working on. Chris would always respond to help Ray and I understood that sometimes he would have to sandwich it in among his active cases. I always asked him what he was up to. I knew how focused he would get on a case. When he was involved in a trial, I would wait until after he had given his final argument to disturb him, unless I had something extremely important.

It took a bit of good luck to get Kemper and Chris together again.

One Saturday in November, the country rock group .38 Special was playing at one of the Stateline, Nevada casinos that butted up to California. After watching the California Golden Bears win their football game that day, I decided to take in the show after I collected my winnings. My daughter and older son had both attended Cal Berkeley on athletic scholarships. Vanita competed in gymnastics and crew, Lee played football. I had consequently become a Bears fan and during football season I couldn't resist the temptation to stop into a local casino and place a wager on them. I collected my one hundred-dollar take and, with an hour on my hands before the rock show started, I decided to play Pick-the-Pros.

For a five-dollar bet I bought a chance to win the progressive jackpot. All I had to do was pick all thirteen winners of the Sunday and Monday night professional football games. I also had to predict for two of the games whether the total score would be over or under a particular value. The pot accumulated each week that no one picked all fifteen items correctly. That week the jackpot was just over twenty-seven thousand dollars. I came up with ten selections that I felt pretty sure would be winners. Applying simple math, I calculated what it would take to wheel the remaining games. "Wheeling" is gambler's lingo for covering all possible combinations. Two to the fifth power, or thirty-two, was the number of plays necessary to wheel the five remaining propositions. But a hundred and sixty dollars was more than I wanted to invest. "Invest" is gambler's rationalization for "bet." I selected the Seattle Seahawks as my eleventh "sure thing," mainly because my younger son Marlon, who was born in Seattle and followed the Seahawks, had told me earlier in the week that they were due for a win. Wheeling only four games cut the necessary investment in half. Accordingly I marked sixteen tickets, plunked down eighty bucks and went to the concert.

The next day, while most of the games were being played, I worked in my office with brother Dan, catching up on some company business. Our computer company supported software I had written in the 'eighties to manage the practice of medical and dental offices. On Dan's impetus the company had expanded to include electronic claims submission whereby insurance claims for our clients were processed via computers over telephone lines, eliminating the need for paper claims. Today we process claims over the Internet, but back then telephone modems and communications software were used.

It was Dan's day-to-day management of the office that afforded me the freedom to gallivant about the country looking into Ray's case. Dan was also more than willing to help Ray. Our expenses were relatively small, mostly for travel. Though they would add up over the years, they were about the same as the contribution of Ray's parents, Jim and Carolyn Leming, and of Chris Plourd.

I had no idea at the time just how much Chris had contributed. He quickly went through the money the Lemings had raised to retain experts and do the investigation. After their funds ran out, Chris used a significant amount of his own money to keep the case alive. Not only was this a financial loss for him, but he wasn't paid a single dime for his time.

At the end of that Sunday workday, Dan and I walked a few doors down to Sam's Place for something to eat and a few beers. The TV in the sports bar was recapping the day's games. We watched together. Dan had also played Pick-the-Pros that weekend.

"You know," I told Dan, "I don't think I've missed any games so far."

I watched the results a second time and became a little more excited. I cut the evening short to get home and check my tickets. Dan lived just up the hill, I ten miles away. I rushed home and turned on the Sunday night game. The third quarter had just started. I don't remember now who the Jets were playing. As the results of the afternoon games ticked by on the screen below the action, I checked my tickets and weeded out the losing spokes of the wheel one by one. Eventually I ended up with one ticket that sure enough had no losers— at least not yet. On it I had taken the Jets to win and I also needed the over. I rarely watched pro football but now with a vested interest I watched in earnest.

At the point the magic ticket had surfaced, the Jets were losing and it had been a low-scoring game. The game remained close as the total score gradually increased. At the two-minute warning, the Jets were ahead and one score would give me the over. The other team had the ball. They drove down the field and, with less than one minute left to play, scored. I now had the over but the wrong team was winning. I tensely watched the final seconds of the game and saw the Jets, bless their hearts, drive down the field, score and win the game. The ticket was still alive.

I hadn't won yet. I needed one last event to occur—the Cowboys to win Monday night's game. I spent the rest of the evening on the phone sharing my excitement. I went to bed wondering how many other Pick-the-Pro players had the same picks and would share my prize if the Cowboys came through. After all, if I, who didn't really follow football, had a winning ticket, how many others who did follow the sport also had one?

The next day, on my way to the office, I stopped into the casino shortly after the sports book opened and checked the situation.

"There's one guy going into tonight's game," the clerk said, not knowing that he was talking to *the* guy.

Continuing to the office, adrenaline flowing, I couldn't help but think of Marlon and his advice. Apparently nobody else had expected the Seahawks to win.

Needless to say, the situation generated quite a bit of excitement at the office. "You should hedge the bet," my brother advised. By betting approximately half the amount of the jackpot on the opponent, I would win that amount no matter the outcome of the game. But because the Cowboys were favored by nine points, there was a third possibility. By taking the Eagles and the points I would win both bets if the Cowboys won by fewer than nine points.

Betting exactly half would be sufficient if it weren't for the vigorish, more commonly known as "the vig." It's equivalent to Shylock's pound of flesh. It's the "interest" charge required by a bookie to take a wager. The vig for a straight bet is "eleven pays ten"; that is, for every eleven dollars bet the casinos pay winning tickets ten dollars plus the amount of the bet. The casinos set the point spread so that roughly the same amount of money will be bet on each opposing team. Every eleven dollars bet on one team is balanced by eleven dollars bet on the other. Of the twenty-two dollars bet, the winner receives twenty-one dollars and the house keeps the extra buck as its vig. That's how sports books make their money. They don't care who wins. While it seems that you're betting against the casino, you're really betting against those who took the other team. I spent the rest of the morning calculating the optimum amount of the hedge bet. It came out to be more than my bank account could handle so I settled upon $9,900. That amount could win a round $9,000.

At lunch I went to the bank and withdrew the money. Except for my visit to Tex in Albuquerque, this was the most cash I'd ever carried. I spread it among three Stateline casinos, at each one betting a third on the Eagles.

Should the Eagles win, I would take the Pick-the-Pros consolation prize, a few hundred dollars, and net nine thousand dollars from the hedge bet. Should the Cowboys win by more than nine points, I would collect the big jackpot but lose the hedge bet, netting about seventeen thousand dollars. But should the Cowboys win by less than nine points, I would garner both prizes for a grand total of thirty-six thousand dollars. I spent the rest of the afternoon trying not to think about the possible outcomes of the evening's event.

My daughter's in-laws were in town for their annual Thanksgiving visit and I planned to have dinner with them that evening. Vanita and her husband Roger lived over the hill east of Lake Tahoe in Carson Valley. Dinner was at a nice restaurant near where they lived. I didn't let the game interfere with dinner. Only the final score mattered. How it was arrived at was of little importance. I enjoyed the company. But

Roger left the table several times to go to the TV in the bar to see how the game was going. His reports indicated that the Eagles were dominating. I resigned myself to accept the worst-case scenario.

The check had been paid and I remained at the dinner table visiting with Vanita and Roger's parents and waiting for Roger to return with the final score. Suddenly he rushed in and exclaimed, "The Cowboys just went ahead with a field goal!"

Just sixty game seconds away from my winning thirty-six thousand dollars, the five of us rushed into the crowded bar to watch. Our ecstasy turned to agony as we watched the Eagles take the kickoff and meticulously work their way down the field to just inside the ten-yard line. With only enough time left for one more play they took a time-out, then lined up for a virtually certain game winning chip-shot field goal. But the Cowboys prolonged the suspense by calling a time-out of their own.

Finally the Eagles center snapped the ball to the placekick holder, and he fumbled the snap! Attempting to run the ball into the end zone, he was tackled just short of the goal line. Our ten feet left the floor simultaneously.

At the same time two hundred miles away, as I later learned from Dan's son Zack, my son Marlon leapt up with hands in the air and took out his cousin's ceiling fan.

It had been an exciting thirty hours. My friends gave me an appropriate nickname and I really believed I had *the system*. How difficult could it be for "Mr. Football" to predict the winners of eleven games and wheel the rest every week? I tried it for the rest of the football season and came to the conclusion that the results of the magic weekend had been due to nothing more than blind-ass luck.

Anyway, as soon as my jackpot and hedge-bet winnings were safely in the bank, I once again turned my attention to cousin Ray. What better initial use of this windfall than to try to set the appeal in motion again by getting Chris and Kemper together in person? As it turned out, an odontology seminar was going to be held within the month at a convention center on the north shore of Lake Tahoe, twenty-two miles from my house as the crow flies. I called Chris, telling him first of my good fortune and then inviting him to Tahoe for the weekend of the bite mark conference. I had made the same offer to Kemper and was waiting for his reply. Chris relished professional meetings and was even more interested when he learned that Kemper might attend. When Kemper accepted, Chris did too. I also invited Jim and Carolyn Leming, but only Jim was able to make the trip.

I put Kemper and his wife into a nice room at a Stateline casino with a great view of the lake. Jim, Chris and I hung out at my house.

Forensic science is of no use to an appeal, so the conference was understandably of little interest to Kemper. I don't remember much about the conference itself except that John Piakas seemed a bit befuddled when the Krone "team" showed up. Taken aback by the appearance of the four of us at this out-of-the-way place, Dr. Piakas sauntered up to me and asked, "You live around here, don't you?"— perhaps as a way of explaining our presence. He knew more about this "shady person" than I would have expected of a simple-minded witness. I have little doubt that the continued interest in the Krone case was duly and dutifully reported back to his benefactor, Noel Levy.

Jim and I were most interested that Kemper's work on the appeal be completed. Chris was the only one who took an interest in the conference but he also wanted the appeal to get back on track. The two attorneys chatted non-stop on the drive to the north shore and then again on the return trip, as well as at the evening's dinner overlooking Lake Tahoe.

Mission accomplished. Within a month of his return home, Kemper completed and filed the appellant's opening brief. It raised six issues. Two dealt with the victim's hearsay in Kate Koester's testimony. One, that it was irrelevant, two, that it violated due process as protected by the Sixth and Fourteenth Amendments to the United States Constitution, which guarantee the accused the right to confront the witnesses against them.

Two other issues concerned the two charges of which Ray was convicted: kidnapping and felony murder. Ray had been acquitted of rape at the first trial and of first-degree (premeditated) murder at the second. Felony murder carries the same punishment as premeditated murder but differs in that the death must have occurred during the commission of another crime. Levy contended that Ancona was killed during the kidnapping, thus justifying the charge of felony murder. Kemper argued that the record nowhere showed that any evidence of kidnapping had been presented:

> What the state has attempted to do here is to create a legal Möbius strip that goes like this. "This lady was murdered. You can't murder someone without kidnapping them. Therefore by proving she was murdered we have proved, *ipso facto*, that she was kidnapped. By thus proving that she was kidnapped we are enabled to prove, under the felony murder rule, the murder that enables us to prove that she was kidnapped." This court

cannot lose sight of the proposition that the state always has to prove that a crime took place, as well as who did it, by proving the elements of that crime.

Levy had taken the lazy way out. But he didn't anticipate that Ray might be acquitted of first-degree murder. If the high court threw out the kidnapping charge then there could be no felony murder under the law and therefore there would be nothing left against Ray. It was a technicality, but if bitten upon by the high court it would mean that Ray would walk.

Another argument Kemper raised was that it was improper to impose consecutive sentences for felony murder and kidnapping. If this argument were to be accepted and all others rejected, Ray's sentence could be cut in half. He might possibly be paroled in fifteen years.

But Kemper hung his hat on the argument that the judge erred in allowing the original case agent, detective Chuck Gregory, to express his opinion that Krone was "lying." "If there is a bright line rule in criminal law in Arizona in 1997," he wrote, "it is that a witness may not express an opinion as to the truthfulness of another witness." The ink recording the decision of the court in *Arizona v. Reimer* reversing Reimer's conviction was barely dry when Kemper cited it. In this case the police officer had been allowed, over objection, to state his opinion that "I believed she was telling the truth" when a witness made a statement out of court that implicated her husband, the defendant. In court, Kemper emphasized, the witness had stated the opposite:

> [The] Krone [case] was prejudiced...because the prosecution under *Reimer*...was not entitled to have on its side the scale of Gregory's opinion that Krone lied. But this case is even worse than *Reimer*. Here is the original case agent, the man who put the case together, doing the opining, and it is the defendant, not a mere witness, who is the subject of Gregory's inadmissible opinion.

It took Arizona's high court to enlighten the lower courts of two obvious facts—that cops are by nature not very objective individuals, regardless of their level of integrity, and that jurors tend to give a good deal of credence to a policeman's testimony. Certainly not all cops are dishonest. But what cop is going to say, "Yeah, I believed the defendant, but I arrested him anyway"? If a cop believes the suspect and is honest he lets him go. An honest cop may of course mistakenly believe his suspect to be lying. Though unfortunate for the suspect, it is quite understandable. That's why it should be left up to impartial observers to decide. An honest cop, by definition, will not kluge up police reports to cover up honest mistakes.

The purpose of *Reimer*, as I see it, is not only to check and balance an honest cop's mistaken judgment but also to prevent a dishonest cop from further reaming the defendant with lies that are too indulgently referred to as "opinions." Under *Reimer*, testimony, whether that of a police officer or of a lay witness, is supposed to be limited to facts. While lay witnesses are rarely allowed to express an opinion in court, many superior court judges, fearful of incurring the county attorney's wrath, routinely allow cops to express their natural biases as freely as expert witnesses are allowed to express their own fast and loose opinions in court—simply because they are doctors of something or other.

Under a seemingly double standard, there are no laws requiring expert witnesses to stick to plain and simple facts, scientific or otherwise. While *Frye* and *Daubert* provide guidelines, in actuality no significant restraints are imposed upon expert witnesses to keep them from foisting their unbridled opinions upon juries.

Medical doctors are assumed to be naturally objective. But are they? Consider the strange thing that happens to a young person when he makes it through college and is awarded a medical doctoral degree. Immediately the new Doctor Somebody is by and large perceived by laypeople to know everything about something and something about everything. But most of what is learned in school is merely the foundation for the learning that follows. Nevertheless, it doesn't take young doctors long to learn that their educated guesses are accepted as truth by just about everyone who will listen. Those with big egos may, à la the West Phenomenon, even render guesses on things they know nothing about and actually believe that the guesses are Gospel truth. Medical doctors who deal with matters of life and death are often perceived by their patients—and not infrequently by themselves—to be godlike.

I have been to no fewer than six annual meetings of the American Academy of Forensic Sciences. As an outsider looking in, I found these meetings to be essentially egos on parade. This is not necessarily a bad thing. The lectures at these meetings are uniformly objective scientific presentations in which speakers, unencumbered by pressures on their pendulums, strive to present some forensic scientific truth. They are free exchanges of ideas whereby younger egos are not infrequently corrected by and learn from older, more experienced ones.

However, when these same egos' pendulums lead them into court, things change. It's a rare ego that doesn't spin its testimony to favor whoever is greasing its pendulum. The audiences for these in-court lectures include none of the critical colleagues who might very well stand up at a scientific meeting and say "Horseshit!" if the same lectures were to be given there. If a dueling expert greased by the other courtroom adversary appears to testify, the jury is then spun in the opposite direction. Forensic experts rarely criticize a colleague's performance before a jury.

The reality is that even medical doctors, notwithstanding their specific knowledge acquired through much effort, are just like the rest of us—ordinary people who need to earn a living. Since their livelihood pretty much depends on their opinions, it doesn't take them long to learn which ones pay the bills. When venality prevails, we as individuals may voluntarily find ourselves undergoing expensive treatments that do no good or taking pills that are not needed or electing surgeries that do more harm than good.

And some more unfortunate individuals, victims of the venality of Doctors of Something testifying in court, may even find themselves convicted of a crime they didn't commit.

When a court chooses to overrule an objection to something that obviously violates a decision like *Reimer*, and the objector persists, the judge routinely shuts down the objector by cavalierly saying, "Take it up on appeal." Irking the county attorney is more dangerous than sending an obvious error to an appellate court, which has the discretion to classify it as "harmless." Kemper attacked this scenario boldly:

> *Harmless Error Analysis:* The state, of course, will argue that this error [allowing Gregory to express his opinion] is harmless; the state before this court *always* says *every* error is harmless. But to find any error in this case harmless—and this case is shot through with error—would truly be a travesty. This is a case in which no sooner were the verdicts in than the forewoman herself exclaimed, "I wanted to find the defendant not guilty."...[T]his is a case where the trial judge himself, who saw the evidence with his own eyes, found that there was a lingering doubt as to Krone's guilt. How could he find otherwise? The rational mind cannot conceive of a case where there is less evidence and a man is in prison for life.

Kemper concluded his brief by asking the court "that [Ray Krone's] convictions be reversed." He then went one step further—unusual for an appeal. "This court should then remand to the trial court with instructions that it enter judgments of acquittal of felony murder and kidnapping."

In December the state filed its anwering brief. As predicted, it argued that all errors noted by Kemper were "harmless." And countering Kemper's statement of the facts based upon reality, the state presented a version of the facts "viewed in the light most favorable to sustaining the conviction," as allowed by *Arizona v. Atwood.*

The *Atwood* decision allows the state to sustain prosecutor Levy's fantasy that, for example, the innocuous ride to the Christmas party was enough "evidence" to establish the notion that the suspect and the victim had a budding relationship that went sour three nights later. Another instance of runaway fantasy is the fact that Levy felt it necessary to let both Krone juries know that Ray was not wearing any underwear while being interrogated. I was bewildered as to the purpose of this ploy when I read about it in the first trial transcripts. But the state as well felt compelled to mention the missing briefs in its brief for the court of appeals to ponder.

Kemper too was puzzled as to the implied link between the omission of underwear and the commission of a crime. He responded to the state's briefs briefing with "[W]e are informed Krone 'was not wearing any underwear' when he spoke to detective Gregory. It is not clear what inference the state would have drawn from this factoid."

Kemper was very confident that Krone's appeal, offered on the heels of *Reimer*, would be successful. Privately he predicted success. Everyone felt that he argued the issues well. We shared his optimism and together patiently waited for the wheels of justice to turn Ray's way.

On April 23, 1998 Kemper wrote to Ray that he'd received the "at issue" order from the court and explained its meaning to him:

> When a case gets to the front of the line it is assigned to a 'panel,' which consists of three judges of the court of appeals. These judges, presumably having at the bare minimum read the briefs, then meet to talk about the case and vote on it. The presiding judge then assigns one of the three—it might be himself—to write the decision reflecting their vote...[I]nstead of expecting a decision in the indefinite future we can now expect a decision in the foreseeable future, six to eight weeks

is my guess…[T]he order tells us who our panel is, Judges Patterson (presiding), Ryan and Thompson…I feel good about the first two and not so good about the last. But if we get two out of three, we win, which is what I want.

Ray, his family and friends waited anxiously and apprehensively for the decision. I hoped that the court would have the balls to go the distance and remand the trial court to issue a judgment of acquittal. Or they could simply overturn the verdict, in which case the rest of Mr. Football's nest egg would be but a drop in the bucket toward funding another trial. Anything less meant that more time would have to be done by Ray and his family as they waited on further appeals to the Arizona Supreme Court and possibly to the United States Supreme Court to gain court ordered access to the unanalyzed DNA known to be on the victim's clothing.

π

The OJ Simpson case is a classic example of the results that can be attained when the defendant has the financial juice to compete.

It is no secret that, since their emancipation a century and a half ago, blacks in this country have disproportionately suffered at the hands of the people—directly through lynching and indirectly through a justice system the people condone. Lynching is believed to have taken its name from Charles Lynch, a Virginia justice of the peace, who ordered extralegal punishment for acts of treason during the American Revolution. Before the Civil War, lynching was mostly reserved for white abolitionists. Afterwards lynching changed colors. Seventy-three percent of the four thousand, seven hundred and forty-three known victims of lynch mobs after the Civil War have been black. While outright lynching has virtually disappeared, many Americans are aware that it has metamorphosed into the death penalty. In a recent *Newsweek* poll about half of those polled believed that a black man is more likely than a white man to be sentenced to death for the same crime. For interracial crimes, whites murdering blacks—blacks murdering whites, ninety-five percent of those put to death are black. While nationally blacks comprise only thirteen percent of the population, forty-two percent of this country's Death Row inmates are black.

Lynching was the ultimate affront to due process. That blacks nowadays continue to suffer its effects is epitomized by the statement made by a Texas police officer to two janitors of the elementary school where a white female student was found murdered. "One of you two is going to hang for this. Since you're the nigger, you're elected." Clarence Brandley spent ten years on Death Row before being completely exonerated in 1990.

But there's another, equally significant factor that subverts due process. "[R]ace, ethnic origin and economic status appear to be the key determinants of who will, and will not, receive a sentence of death," says a report filed with the United Nations Commission on Human Rights.

The late, great defense attorney Johnnie Cochran put it more succinctly. After receiving much flack for "playing the race card" in defending The Juice, he answered his critics simply with, "The color of justice is green."

CHAPTER 20
DINGLE DANGLE

Before getting to know cousin Ray I had been aware that wrongful convictions do occur but was under the impression that they were few and far between—perhaps one in a hundred or fewer.

"Five percent," said Chris Plourd when I asked him how many convicted he thought were actually innocent.

That's one in twenty. Ray's case was the tip of the iceberg. Watching him get convicted the second time, I did not see how anyone could beat Maricopa County, innocent or not. Thanks to the taxpayer, the justice machine has a large bag of marbles with which to play the game: a police force to do the investigating, a crime lab to massage the evidence, a courthouse full of job-fearing cronies, a budget to buy top of the line junk science—to name a few. Sure, there are accused individuals who, like OJ, have the means to buy enough marbles to play and win and, like OJ, may even be guilty. But they are a small minority. From watching how easy it was to krone Ray, I thought Chris's estimate low and wondered what real number might accurately quantify the bottom of the iceberg. I dove in and took a look and found that Maricopa County's brand of justice is not unique.

Chris told me of a San Diego case, a cop killing, that revealed how prosecutors everywhere not only have copious marbles, they also have three marbles at their disposal that not even OJ's juice can buy.

The deceased officer had walked into the middle of a gang fracas. To get a conviction of Stacy Butler and his gang, the prosecutor enlisted the services of a jailhouse snitch. The prospective stool pigeon was in jail waiting trial for armed robbery. To get his attention the prosecutor pulled from his bag of tricks the "stick" marble. He told the jailbird that if he didn't cooperate he would be charged with killing the cop. Then he used his "carrot" marble and offered to plea-bargain the armed robbery charge to time served. But being able to walk after singing like a canary was not enough. The wheels of justice move at a snail's pace. To keep the snitch focused for the long haul the prosecutor played the "dingle, dangle" marble. He allowed the snitch and his wife to spend time together alone. No fewer than fifty such conjugal visits occurred in the prosecutor's office.

Butler and gang were convicted. The DA's office bestowed The Prosecutor of the Year Award on the prosecutor. The dingle-dangled snitch was released but in time was back in trouble with the law. The prosecutor said "sorry" until the wife flashed a get out of jail free card—a picture of her playing with her husband's marbles on the prosecutor's desk. The prosecutor succumbed to the blackmail and let the husband go, claiming the case was too difficult to prosecute. The police department balked and the case was taken over by the state attorney general. When her husband was sent to prison for life, the wife spilled the marbles. The picture appeared in the *San Diego Union-Tribune.*

Interestingly, in the justice game it's okay to bribe a witness. The prosecutor didn't get in trouble for doing it. He got in trouble because he didn't show the defense the picture. That is, he withheld the fact that he'd given the snitch special favors in return for favorable testimony.

The scandal ended when Butler and gang were released from prison, the investigator who shuttled the snitch to and from the prosecutor's office was fired and the prosecutor was, according to the press, "transferred to a less prestigious job," which really translates to "promoted." He continues to prosecute.

π

I learned from another case that snitch for snatch is not uncommon in the justice game. I'd taken an interest in the case of the Lake Waco murders because it was a bite mark case. But I found out that it was much more than junk science that did in David Wayne Spence.

In July 1982 the bodies of three youths were found brutally murdered near the banks of Lake Waco in Texas. The case garnered much media attention and went unsolved for several months. The break in the case came when Spence and Gilbert Melendez were sent to jail for assault. The night shift jailer was a self-styled sherlock named Truman Simons. Simons had recently been laughed out of the sheriff's department for coming up with a harebrained theory that the youths were victims of an elaborate murder for hire conspiracy. His conspiracy theory suspect passed a lie detector test with flying colors. Undaunted and with nighttime on his hands at the county jail, sherlock Simons continued to "investigate." Soon seven jailbirds claimed to have overheard Spence and Melendez confessing to the murders. The prosecutor took the case. Melendez was offered a deal, confessed and fingered Spence. For insurance the prosecutor enlisted his hunting buddy, who was coincidentally a dentist and odontologist, to do the Ouija work. Spence was convicted and sentenced to die.

Ten years later, Raul Shonemann took on Spence's case. In a monumental effort taken all the way to the United States Fifth Circuit of Appeals, Shonemann produced five bite mark experts who excluded Spence and demonstrated that Melendez's confession (later recanted) had been coerced with threats of punishment and promises of leniency and that all of the seven snitches had been given special favors, including sexual trysts. But in the justice game special favors are rarely given to bad dudes even when they happen to be innocent. The high court upheld Spence's conviction.

At the eleventh hour the case went before the Texas governor, who briefly (for thirty minutes) looked at the evidence. Through a spokesman he expressed surprise that the case had made it all the way to his office but regretted that there was nothing he could do. The condemned had had full access to the courts, the only criterion the governor considers. Pardoning someone based upon evidence of innocence is rare without corresponding evidence that it would also be good for reelection. The governor signed the death warrant. David Wayne Spence was executed on April 4, 1997. More details about the Butler case and the Spence case are provided in the appendix.

The Spence case caused Chris Plourd to observe, "The problem with the justice system *is* the justice system."

π

Prosecutors enjoy extensive immunity. The rationale is that prosecutors should be allowed to do their jobs without the fear of having to face a possible lawsuit. In theory this protection is a good idea. In practice less-than-reputable prosecutors can take their immunity to the limit and beyond. They get away with all sorts of dingle dangle because within their judicial club they are rarely chastised. As with *Texas v. Spence*, appellate judges ejaculate their "harmless error" bullshit and disregard judicial principles like "beyond a reasonable doubt" and "innocent until proven guilty" to ignore or indeed even excuse prosecutorial misconduct. It's only when caught with pants down outside the club, as in *California v. Butler* when the *San Diego Union-Tribune* headlined SEX IN THE DA'S OFFICE, that prosecutors are subjected to any real scrutiny. Then one of the prosecutor's puppets might take the fall and get fired while the real transgressor receives a catch-22 punishment like being promoted or winning an award. I wonder what accolades prosecutor Noel Levy is destined to receive?

Policemen too have implied immunities. They have one of the toughest jobs in the world. They are called upon to make rapid-fire decisions in tense situations. A good, honest police officer can't be praised enough. But in the reptilian law enforcement environment where truth is incidental, honest cops get little reward. Bailiff George Schuester related to me how he had overheard a Phoenix police officer say that he routinely randomly picks someone to take the rap who is not well-liked within the community, like a gang member or someone who has been in trouble with the law. This perverse cop stated that he then "does what it takes" the get the conviction. And it's easy to do when juries are more apt to believe a lyin' cop's jangle than a scapegoat's protestations of innocence. This mentality explains what happened to Spence. Spence was a high school dropout and street tough who had been arrested for wielding an axe while robbing a gas station before being arrested for the sexual assault of a teenager. He was definitely a bad dude. So, when you're unable to solve the crime, why not frame a bad dude for the Lake Waco murders?

Ray Krone too got caught up in this type of mentality, though he was by no means a bad dude. He was an honorably discharged veteran and a responsible member of society gainfully employed with not so much as a single traffic ticket on his record. But the detective said he was lying and the prosecutor noted that he didn't wear underwear. That's all that was needed to get the ball rolling. Gregory pre-pimped Piakas and Rawson before turning them over to master pimp Levy. The detective procured and massaged evidence. The prosecutor controlled it by withholding the exculpatory parts and doling out the rest at his discretion and then only when ordered to do so. Judge Hotham supported Levy until the state supreme court slapped his hand. Only then, for example, was Plourd able to get a copy of Ray's dental model, which Levy had confiscated from puppet Piakas after Plourd approached the doctor for it. Dr. Perjury also backed Levy's hard-to-believe claim that he was not at the meeting in which Piakas discussed his mentor Dr. Norman Sperber's opinion that the bite mark evidence was not very good. Neither coach Levy nor any of his team disclosed Sperber's exculpatory opinion to the defense.

Levy is not alone among prosecutors who take their immunities to the limit. Discovery violations are so common that numerous books have been written and many lectures given on how to deal with them.

"Isn't there anything that can be done about these guys?" I asked Chris after hearing of one of detective Gregory's fishing trips.

When no Converse brand tennis shoes could be found belonging to Ray, Gregory used Ray's pair of MacGregors as bait to hook an expert who would conclude that the wear pattern on them was the same as the wear pattern of the footprints found at the crime scene. The first expert to look at this evidence told Gregory that the wear patterns were different and that the telltale footprints were made from shoes much smaller than Ray's.

Obviously not all forensic experts are whores. In fact, most are responsible scientists. However, detective Gregory knew that if he trolled long enough in the forensic expert pond he would eventually hook a venal fish swimming there. Gregory switched bait, preferring the bite mark evidence. In no time Dr. Ray Rawson sunk his teeth into it. In a second police report Gregory settled for upgrading the shoe print size and obscuring this evidence as much as possible. The information from the unknown shoe print expert was another tidbit of exculpatory evidence never disclosed to the defense. This misconduct wasn't discovered until well after the second trial and would have to wait for another Rule 32 if Ray's pending appeal went south.

"Where's the harm?" Chris answered with a question.

"Why, Ray's in prison!" I said, thinking it was obvious.

"That's not how it works."

Chris went on to explain another catch-22 in the justice game, one known as *no harm, no foul*. So long as Ray remained convicted there was no legal harm, therefore there could be no foul. While Ray remained in prison, despite the fact that he was innocent, any police or prosecutorial misconduct that got him there, even if provable, was not punishable.

Jingle jangle…dingle dangle…no harm, no foul. Prosecutors have it all. So long as Ray remained convicted, Levy could skate unscathed. Had Ray been acquitted Levy might very well have taken a hard fall. The pressure to win a second conviction must have been great. I could only wonder what chicanery might explain the strange verdict. Could any of it have been directed at the jury? A good, however unscrupulous prosecutor will keep jurors as far away as possible from any real evidence. But defense attorney Plourd had skillfully brought the Krone jury up close. Yet this Arizona jury, as a colleague of Chris had prophesized, did its "strange thing."

CHAPTER 21
BABY BLUE

In the mid-eighteen hundreds, Othneil Charles Marsh was one of many who prospected the Wild West. Unlike most other prospectors of the time he was not rushing for gold or silver. He was looking for bones. Shortly after the California Gold Rush of 1849, the discovery of prehistoric fossils in the western territories generated a similar rush for bones. Before their extinction, dinosaurs roamed the American West. Marsh was one of several scientists who went west to uncover the fossilized evidence of those large reptiles. Their endeavor was every bit as competitive as the Gold Rush and became known as the Bone Wars.

As young men Marsh and his colleague Edward Drinker Cope were best of friends. But with the discovery of large quarries of dinosaur remains in the American West they became bitter rivals. Marsh was unable to keep secret his rich discovery at Como Bluff in southeastern Wyoming. It was a seven-mile long mound of prehistoric fossils. Cope horned in. Marsh sent out spies to observe Cope with binoculars. At night Marsh's men would fill in Cope's diggings, requiring him to start over the next day. Marsh even assembled bones randomly at Cope's site to confuse his competitor. Cope was easy to confuse. Before coming to Como bluff, Cope once assembled a dinosaur's bones perfectly except—much to his embarrassment—he put the head on the tail.

Marsh must have won the war because in 1866, at Yale University, he became America's first professor of Paleontology. His collection of dinosaur bones was displayed at the Peabody Museum of Natural History. George Peabody was one of the richest men in the country and was Marsh's uncle and benefactor.

In 1859, Charles Darwin published *The Origin of Species*. Marsh became a strong proponent of the theory of evolution. His scientific discoveries strongly supported Darwin. Marsh was well aware of the tremendous religious backlash to Darwin's ideas. One of his discoveries was an early ancestor of the horse. It was a touchy situation when he entered the settlement of Ogden, Utah, hoping to ship his find back east because this town's inhabitants were a homogenous religious sect whose beliefs included creationism.

As it turned out, the leader of this religious group, its prophet Brigham Young, was in town hosting a gathering. When Young learned of Marsh's discovery, he brought the scientist to the podium and asked, "Were there horses here before the white man came?"

"Yes," Marsh affirmed.

The crowd went wild.

This religious group had its own gospel. In 1827 Joseph Smith claimed that with the guidance of an angel named Moroni he had found, buried on a hillside near his home in upstate New York, several golden plates containing ancient Egyptian-like hieroglyphics. Miraculously, Smith was able to understand the symbols etched on the plates and he translated them into a book having marked similarities to the Old and New Testaments. These scriptures, however, were set in North America. After Smith finished translating, the metal plates mysteriously disappeared. Nevertheless, these newly translated stories became *The Book of Mormon*, who was Moroni's father, and were the foundation upon which Smith was able to attract a significant number of followers.

On April 6, 1830, the Mormon Church, also known as The Church of Jesus Christ of Latter-Day Saints, was founded and Joseph Smith became its first prophet. Claiming it to be "the only true and living church upon the earth," engaging in secret rituals only for the chosen few, hidden from public view within its temple, and condoning the heretical practice of polygamy, the Mormons became subjected to ever increasing persecution, which, in a period of less than twenty years, forced their migration from New York to Ohio, to Missouri, to Illinois and finally to the desolate Salt Lake region of Utah.

Critics of this unorthodox sect were quick to point out problems with their Holy Book. Second Nephi 12:7 tells of a "land...full of horses." Modernday horses had in fact been introduced to North America by Spanish Conquistadors only three centuries earlier. Brigham Young welcomed paleontologist Marsh because he appeared to support the horse story contained in his religion's scriptures. Marsh wisely did not elaborate that the horse of which he had found remains had been extinct for at least eleven thousand years. This contradictory bit of information would not have been well received by the prophet whose gospel also taught that the world was a mere six thousand years old. Marsh knew to keep the scientific truth to himself and was allowed to ship his bones back to Yale without incident.

This episode is not the first time science has butted heads with religion. In 1614, Italian physicist and astronomer Galileo Galilei concluded after scientific inquiry that the earth moved around the sun and not vice versa as the Catholic Church decreed. Galileo and his ideas were denounced by the church as heretical. Galileo responded with a lengthy letter strongly suggesting that the Roman Catholic faith should not stand in the way of scientific discovery and that the interpretation of the Bible be adapted accordingly. In 1616, the church issued an edict censuring all books that suggested that the earth was not the center of the universe. Cardinal Robert Bellarmine told Galileo that if he knew what was good for him he would keep his science to himself. Galileo did so until the cardinal died. Then he published *Dialogue on the Two Chief World Systems.* In Rome, Galileo was brought to trial for heresy before the Inquisition. To save his own life, Galileo was compelled to renounce his book. It was burned and he was sentenced to life in prison, which was subsequently commuted to permanent house arrest. Galileo's struggle to free scientific inquiry from religious interference was finally achieved two hundred fifty years after his death, when in 1997 the Vatican under Pope John Paul II acknowledged that its condemnation of Galileo and his work was an "error." It took this first church of Jesus Christ two thousand years to become at peace with science. The Church of Jesus Christ of Latter-Day Saints has been around for less than two hundred years.

π

Shortly after the second trial, Mike Pain was asked to interview as many jurors as he could to determine whether they had done anything improper in reaching their verdict. Had they considered any information not presented at trial? Had any of them surreptitiously visited the crime scene? Had they improperly considered any of the evidence?

Visiting the crime scene unless under the supervision of the court would be a gross error because it would be highly unlikely that the CBS Lounge would have been in the same state as it was the night of the murder five years earlier. Any inferences from such a visit would be suspect. Jury foreman Eileen confirmed that no one had visited the murder scene.

But juror Rebecca told Mike, "I would like to have known in advance whether or not Ray had been playing around with methamphetamines that day. After I found out all the friends he was playing around with used meth and I talked with my son who had used meth in his past and found out what effect it has on you, I thought I would like to have known whether he was affected by that...It would have explained why...whether he used meth or not, I don't know. Many of his friends did—the dart players."

Nowhere in the trial was any evidence presented about any drug usage by Ray or his friends. Where did Rebecca get such a notion? Was there some outside influence on the jury? This allegation, not presented at trial but considered during jury deliberations, was highly suspect. Further investigation in this area might prove useful if and when Ray's case reached the Rule 32, new evidence stage.

The DNA evidence was discarded as "inconclusive" according to jury foreman Eileen. "A lot of samples...of course excluded Ray. There was some doubt about...the one on the bra I think...it just didn't point either way. It excluded him as the donor but that didn't mean that he just didn't leave any of the [other] evidence too."

Juror Rebecca "wanted the cute little guy [Dale Henson] that washed the sidewalk in front of the building...[to be] more believable because he might have really seen whoever killed her [the one who] went in [to the CBS Lounge] and came out...There were some [jurors] that thought that he was totally not credible but I tended to believe him because I thought somebody had to get in and out of the place."

But in the end Rebecca and the other jurors ignored all the real evidence and considered only the bite mark. Eileen confirmed that they watched Rawson's videotape three times. Once the jury bit on this tidbit of irrefutable logic, "if he bit her he killed her," Ray was toast. The jurors were confused by the bite mark experts. They put their own pendulums into action and became bite mark experts themselves, performing experimental comparisons of and on their own. In the beginning about half swung one way, half the other. Finally, several votes were taken to see which teeth *might* be guilty. "...[W]e went through each...tooth mark and each tooth and we took a vote whether it matched or didn't," said Rebecca. "...[I]t was very emotional because a lot of us did not want him to be guilty...When...we realized that most of the teeth could have made those marks many of us were crying..."

Suspicions that this jury may have performed uncontrolled scientific experiments on their own and may have considered evidence not presented at trial was intriguing because if true it could help Ray down the line. A costly investigation to validate this possibility would have to wait for the appeals process to run its course.

Since the verdict I have been haunted by the statement made long before the trial by Chris Plourd's colleague, "Arizona juries do strange things." What had caused this jury, which had observed the same trail as I, to abandon old-fashioned horse sense and render its "strange verdict"? Listening to Mike Pain detail his interviews with the jurors only further mystified me as to the bizarre outcome.

Then, as I was about to leave his office, Mike as an afterthought casually mentioned, "You know, the jury is predominately Mormon."

π

Until he entered the Air Force at age seventeen, Ray attended church regularly. His grandmother Hazel, my mother's sister, had married Carl Latshaw. Every Sunday Ray's mother, Hazel's daughter, would gather her children and meet at the Latshaws' house. They would all then walk together to the nearby Lutheran church to attend service. Ray was in the choir and was selected to light the candles before each service began. Ray does not remember his Great Grandma and Grandpa Diller, my grandparents', ever attending church services.

My mother met and married George Rix in Pueblo, Colorado shortly after she turned thirty-two. My brother Dan was born within a year and I thirteen months later. Mom worked as a nurse in a Pueblo hospital. She quit to become a housewife after Dan arrived. I don't know what type of work my dad did in Pueblo. We moved to San Francisco, where brother Ken was born, nearly three years younger than I. There my dad worked as a machinist.

Dad was a member of the Episcopal Church and I learned as a teenager that he was also a 32nd-degree Mason. I remember very little about going to church with Dad, as he died when I was seven years old. When Mom remembered Dad it was always with great love and affection. But I don't remember much about him at all except that he as tall and wore a belt. I wasn't much for silent prayer because the few times I tried it, He never caused me to be spared from the wrath of the belt. The belt passed on to Mom when Dad passed away. With it in her hands my occasional prayers were no longer silent and were more akin to begging.

Soon after Dad's passing, Mom stopped taking her boys to church. I suspect my religious outlook would have been somewhat different had Dad lived awhile longer. However, his belt lived on to see that his boys behaved in a Christian-like manner.

There was little mention of religion in our household. When religion or a religion was discussed, it was always in a matter-of-fact, objective manner. In high school my friends were evenly divided between Catholics and other varieties of Christians. My Catholic friends seemed to be a bit more uptight than the rest of us, especially when the opposite sex entered their thoughts. But they always appeared much relieved after they returned from "confession." I never could understand the connection between sex and sin. *The Kinsey Report* had been out for ten years. How could something everybody did be sinful? I rationalized. Nevertheless my friends, who were more afflicted with guilt than I, told me that He always knew what I was thinking. Yet I noticed that there was no difference in my life when I was thinking good thoughts as opposed to when I was thinking so-called nasty thoughts—so long as I didn't get caught, like the time Mom found my stash of *Playboy* magazines. It wouldn't have been so bad except that I was using them at the time and exercising my thoughts to the max. It was somewhat embarrassing, but not all that bad. I don't know who was more embarrassed, me or Mom. She made some obligatory comment. I responded off the cuff by delivering the punch line to a Woody Allen joke, "It's not so terrible. After all—it's sex with someone I love." Mom chuckled more than a little bit and all was soon forgotten.

I had had the good fortune to grow up not being subjected to any brand of religious indoctrination. To me God and Nature seem to be equivalent and act randomly, explaining why catastrophic natural events are referred to as "acts of God." It had been my observation that whether someone was a good person or not had little to do with their particular religious upbringing or to the depth of their religious conviction. Even in the world of 1996, when we were already recognizing that many terrorist acts were the work of religious fanatics, I still naively asked Chris Plourd, "Why is that important?" after he asked that religious preference be one of the items on the jury questionnaire. Levy had objected and Judge McDougall had agreed that it was "irrelevant."

Chris's simple response was, "Because Rawson's a Mormon and they stick together."

Not disagreeing with McDougall, however, I thought nothing more about it until Mike made his casual observation. Then, with little to do but wait for the outcome of Ray's appeal, I began to look into this particular religious persuasion.

When I was fifteen years old, I received *The Complete Sherlock Holmes* as a gift. I read it from cover to cover, fascinated by how this private detective used his powers of deduction to solve crimes. It had been years since I'd pulled the book off the shelf but I had a vague recollection that there was something in it about "Saints." I dusted the book off and it didn't take long to discover that sure enough Brigham Young himself makes an appearance in Sir Arthur Conan Doyle's first novel, *A Study in Scarlet*, in which supersleuth Holmes is introduced to the world. The story is set in 1878 London and begins with Dr. Watson, the narrator's, meeting Holmes for the first time in a chemistry lab interrupting an experiment:

> "Why, man, it is the most practical medico-legal discovery for years," exclaimed Holmes. "Don't you see that it gives us an infallible test for blood-stains?"

Blood types were discovered in 1875. What better way to introduce Sherlock Holmes than to give him credit for discovering the first ever forensic test for determining whether a stain found at a crime scene is or is not human blood. Watson and Holmes become roommates and sidekicks. Holmes amazes the doctor when he introduces the "science of deduction." To demonstrate, Holmes identifies as "a retired sergeant of marines" a man they observe on the sidewalk below their apartment window, a revelation that causes Watson to ejaculate.

> "How in the world did you deduce that?" I [Watson] asked.
> "Even across the street I could see a great blue anchor tattooed on the back of the fellow's hand. That smacked of the sea. He had a military carriage however, and regulation side-whiskers. There we have the marine. He was a man with some amount of self-importance and a certain air of command. You must have observed the way in which he held his head and swung his cane. A steady, respectable, middle-aged man, too, on the face of him—all facts which led me to believe that he had been a sergeant."
> "Wonderful!" I ejaculated.

The sergeant is carrying an envelope. In it is a note from Scotland Yard requesting Holmes's assistance in solving the murder of two Americans, Enoch J. Drebber and Joseph Stangerson. Holmes does so in short order after merely surveying the crime scene with a magnifying glass and employing the services of the "Baker Street Irregulars...a half-dozen of the dirtiest and most ragged...little scoundrels" that Holmes uses because they "go everywhere and hear everything." Another American, Jefferson Hope, is duly apprehended and subsequently confesses, confirming all of Holmes's deductions to be true.

Watson in his narrative interestingly notes:

> The [press] commented upon the fact that lawless outrages
> of the sort usually occurred under a Liberal administration.
> They arose from the unsettling of the minds of the masses, and
> the consequent weakening of all authority.

Even a hundred years ago there was a common perception that
Liberals are soft on crime.

Part II of *A Study in Scarlet*, entitled "The Country of the Saints,"
details the events that explain Hope's motive for murdering Drebber
and Stangerson. It begins with two remaining survivors of a wagon
party headed west. They have succumbed to the harsh elements of the
Great Alkali Plain. Fortunately, John Ferrier and his daughter Lucy are
rescued from their grim situation by a party of emigrants on their
exodus to Zion, their prophesied religious haven.

Arthur Conan Doyle perhaps took an interest in Mormonism in
1840 after reading the newspaper published by thirty-nine-year-old
Brigham Young, who was in Liverpool as a Mormon missionary.
Young returned to America the next year with several hundred
converts, mostly from the urban working class. Prophet Smith
rewarded Young's success and devotion by making him president of
the quorum of twelve apostles, the Mormon's administrative body.
Brigham Young's authority was exceeded only by that of Joseph
Smith.

The Latter-Day Saints endured harsh treatment from the
beginning. Wherever they went gentiles, as the Mormons referred to
all non-believers, persecuted them beyond belief. It probably was not a
good idea to claim to be the only true church. Also there was
resentment of this tight knit group's economic success and political
clout. It did not sit well with gentiles that the saintly prophet could
bestow divinity upon his flock and allow obedient males to become
Gods and their associated females to become childbearing Goddesses.
To Mormons, God and Jesus Christ were material beings who
routinely intervened in human affairs. Add polygamy to the mix,
which prophet Smith and his disciples privately practiced but publicly
denied, and the Saints didn't stand a chance among gentiles.

In 1839, after several skirmishes between gentiles and Saints
escalated into destruction of property and outright murder, on both
sides, the Governor of Missouri ordered the Mormons to leave the
state or be exterminated. Fleeing to Nauvoo, Illinois, the prophet
traded the block of votes he'd brought into the area simply to be left
alone. For awhile the Saints prospered, erecting a temple and building
a city of ten thousand inhabitants that would become the largest city in

the state. But within five years the Saints had again offended just about every gentile in the neighborhood. Exacerbated by polygamist prophet Joseph Smith's announcement that he was running for the presidency of the United States, a mob of gentiles imprisoned the prophet and his brother Hyrum after they had incited a riot and attempted to destroy *The Nauvoo Expositor*, a newspaper that had exposed the Mormon practice of polygamy. The mob subsequently stormed the jail and brutally killed the Smith brothers.

The New York Herald reported that Joseph Smith's death signaled "the latter days of The Latter-Day Saints." This scenario might have come true had it not been for Brigham Young, who succeeded Smith and became the Saints' second prophet. To avoid further persecution, the new prophet realized that it was better to move than to be moved. He had read recent accounts of a Great Salt Lake basin, a land surrounded by mountains so desolate that no one would want to live there. He hoped that they would be left alone there. It was also "outside the ownership and jurisdiction of the hated American nation." It was the perfect place for Brigham Young to take his tribe. In 1847, with brilliant organization and leadership, he began to move his flock lock, stock, and barrel to this alkaline desert, setting fire to the recently finished Nauvoo temple they were leaving behind as an offering to God.

It was during this pilgrimage that Arthur Conan Doyle set the narrative of the rescue of John and Lucy Ferrier. Though Doyle wrote that they encounter a group of ten thousand emigrants, in reality the Mormon migration, known as the Trail of Hope, spanned many years. The first party to reach Utah's Salt Lake Basin was a group of about 200 individuals, including Brigham Young.

To be rescued, there's a catch. "It can only be as believers in our sacred creed," said the leader. Ferrier agrees and joins the band. On the way, much to the appreciation of the pilgrims, Ferrier proves himself a useful guide and accomplished hunter. When they reach Zion, Ferrier is rewarded with a substantially productive track of land. Most of the land in the desolate valley is initially rock hard and breaks the pilgrims' ploughs.

But with the ingenuity and guidance of prophet Brigham Young, streams that flow into the barren wasteland are damned and diverted, causing the land to be flooded. In no time the valley becomes fertile. As Salt Lake City flourishes so does John Ferrier. In a dozen years he has became one of the twelve richest men in the settlement. Though Ferrier shunns the practice of polygamy, remaining strictly celibate, he in all other aspects seems to conform to and embrace the religion and is considered to be "an orthodox and straight-walking man."

Lucy grows into womanhood and falls in love with Jefferson Hope, a silver prospector from Nevada who makes frequent trips to Salt Lake City to resupply and raise capital for his adventures. But there's a problem. Hope is a gentile. He is one of many fortune seekers who pass through Utah on their way to the California Gold Rush of 1849. Prophet Young wisely prohibits his flock from straying to the gold and silver fields.

Ferrier relishes the expectation that Lucy will marry a non-Mormon. He keeps it to himself that he believes marriage to a polygamist would be "a shame and a disgrace." Doyle writes:

> He had to seal his mouth on the subject for to express an unorthodox opinion was a dangerous matter in those days in the Land of the Saints. Yes, a dangerous matter—so dangerous that even the most saintly dared only whisper their religious opinions with bated breath, lest something which fell from their lips might be misconstrued and bring down swift retribution upon them. The victims of persecution had now turned persecutors on their own account, and persecutors of the most terrible description. Not the Inquisition of Seville, nor the German Vehmgericht, nor the secret societies of Italy, were ever able to put a more formidable machinery in motion than that which cast a cloud over the Territory of Utah.

Doyle then alludes to a secret organization, "Avenging Angels" who enforced the prophet's dictates. Those who went against church doctrine or simply wanted out of the church "vanished away." Suspicions were high that these angels often dressed as Indians to disguise their identity and also that they did not confine their clandestine nefarious activities within their own group.

> Strange rumors began to be bandied about—rumors of murdered immigrants and rifled camps in regions where Indians had never been seen.

Brigham Young shows up on John Ferrier's doorstep. A good prophet knows everything of importance that goes on within his flock. He has heard a rumor that Lucy is "sealed to some gentile." He is not happy about this and questions Ferrier's faith by chastising him for not taking a harem. But this transgression will be forgiven if Lucy marries a Saint. She must choose between Enoch Drebber and Joseph

Stangerson. Ferrier sends word to Jefferson Hope detailing the dilemma. Hope attempts a rescue. In the middle of their second day of flight they seem to be home free. With provisions running low, however, Hope must leave father and daughter in camp and go hunt for food. When he returns he finds that the Avenging Angels have struck. Ferrier is dead and there's no sign of Lucy. Hope tracks Lucy down about a week later and finds that she is married to Drebber. Heartbroken, Lucy dies within a month. Drebber feigns bereavement but has achieved his main objective: acquiring Ferrier's property. Hopeless against the Avenging Angels on their own turf, Hope bides his time and vows revenge. He returns to the Nevada silver mines. Time passes. Five years later he returns to Salt Lake City under disguise to find that both Drebber and Stangerson have defected and escaped the Avenging Angels. Drebber, the wealthier of the two, has employed Stangerson as his secretary. It takes Hope another fifteen years to track them down in London. He does away with Drebber first and then Stangerson, by way of a ritual involving two pills, one of which is poison. Hope forces Stangerson to select and swallow one of two pills, while Hope swallows the other. With righteousness on his side, Hope survives. Sherlock Holmes deduces the entire scenario, lays his trap and captures Hope. Hope dies the next day in his cell of an aortic aneurism.

Though suspenseful reading, there really is no "science of deduction" or we would hear about it today as a crime solving tool. It works for Sherlock Holmes because he is a fictional character. The author can and does manipulate the facts so that Sherlock's guesses are always right.

One lesson modernday sleuths can learn from Sherlock, though, is to resolve all the facts of a case before settling on a suspect. In that respect Detective Gregory and prosecutor Levy were no sherlocks. To them, in the Ray Krone case, only the saintly interpreted bite mark evidence was relevant. The rest they ignored.

It was a scarlet picture that Sir Arthur Conan Doyle painted of the Latter-Day Saints. But was it really more fiction than fact? I wondered. I turned to Mark Twain, who actually met prophet Brigham Young during his several years of "variegated vagabondizing," *Roughing It* in the "Far West" between 1861 and 1867. Twain, born Samuel Langhorne Clemens, jumped at the opportunity to accompany his brother Orion, who had been appointed Secretary of Nevada Territory by President Abraham Lincoln. Orion appointed his brother as his secretary.

They traveled together by overland stagecoach from Saint Joseph, Missouri to Carson City, Nevada, passing through Salt Lake City on the way. Twain writes that eight days and eight hundred miles out "we overtook a Mormon emigrant train of thirty-three wagons. Trampling wearily along and driving their herd of loose cows were dozens of coarse-clad and sad-looking men, women and children, who had walked as they were walking now, day after day for eight lingering weeks." The Mormon migration continued sporadically for more that twenty years, essentially ending when the transcontinental railroad was completed at Promentory Point, Utah in 1869. Twain observed this particular party to be "dusty and uncombed, hatless, bonnetless and ragged, and they did look so tired!" More that three thousand Saints perished on the Trail of Hope to Zion.

Twain's next encounter with the "peculiar institution" was at the outskirts of Salt Lake City when he took supper with "a Mormon Destroying Angel," no doubt what Arthur Conan Doyle referred to as an "Avenging Angel." Mark Twain wrote:

> Destroying Angels, as I understand it, are Latter-Day Saints who are set apart by the church to conduct permanent disappearances of obnoxious citizens. I had heard a deal about these Mormon Destroying Angels and the dark and bloody deeds they had done, and when I entered this one's house I had my shudder ready. But alas for all our romances, he was nothing but a loud, profane, offensive old blackguard! He was murderous enough, possibly, to fill the bill of a destroyer, but would you have *any* kind of an angel devoid of dignity? Could you abide an angel in an unclean shirt and no suspenders? Could you respect an angel with a horselaugh and a swagger like a buccaneer?...A lot of slatternly women flitted hither and thither in a hurry, with coffeepots, plates of bread and other appurtenances to supper, and these were said to be the wives of the Angel—or some of them, at least. And of course they were; for if they had been hired "help" they would not have let an angel from above storm and swear at them as he did, let alone one from the place this one hailed from.

On his first day in Salt Lake City, Twain:

> strolled about everywhere through the broad, straight, level streets, and enjoyed the pleasant strangeness of a city of fifteen thousand inhabitants with no loafers perceptible in it; and no visible drunkards or noisy people; a limpid stream

rippling and dancing through every street in place of a filthy gutter; block after block of trim dwellings, built of "frame" and sunburned brick—a great thriving orchard and garden behind every one of them, apparently—branches from the street stream winding and sparkling among the garden beds and fruit trees—and a grand general air of neatness, repair, thrift and comfort, around and about over the whole. And everywhere were workshops, factories and all manner of industries; and intent faces and busy hands were to be seen wherever one looked; and in one's ears was the ceaseless clink of hammers, the buzz of trade and the contented hum of drums and flywheels...The Mormon crest was easy. And it was simple, unostentatious and fitted like a glove. It was a representation of a Golden Beehive with the bees all at work!

Indeed, Brigham Young did a remarkable job of building such a city in a mere fourteen years since the summer of 1847 when he looked upon the desolate wasteland and declared, "This is the place." His chosen isolation, however, disappeared almost immediately. Within a year of his exodus out of the "hated nation," he found himself back in. The United States had won the war with Mexico and, as provided in the Treaty of Guadalupe Hidalgo, signed in February 1848, had acquired all Spanish territory from the Missouri River to the Pacific Ocean. In response Brigham Young instituted the "free and independent state of Deseret."

Congress snubbed Brigham's state and created the Territory of Utah. But it made the prophet its first governor. An enormous migration west precipitated by the Gold Rush poured through Utah. The Mormons obediently stayed put and prospered by catering to the Forty-Niners and those who followed. Twain observed that products and services that cost a nickel or a dime back east cost at least a quarter in Salt Lake City.

Governor prophet Brigham Young virtually ignored the authority of the United States and took his orders from a higher authority—Himself. As Mark Twain noted, his "official grandeur" did not stop with being a mere prophet. "There was but one dignity higher which he *could* aspire to, and he reached out modestly and took that—he proclaimed himself a God!" with "an heaven of his own" into which "all faithful Mormons will be admitted" and would be ranked "according to the number of wives and children."

Twain chronicled his and his brother's "state visit to the king":

He seemed a quiet old gentleman of fifty-five or sixty, and had a gentle craft in his eye that probably belonged there. He was very simply dressed and was just taking off a straw hat as we entered. He talked about Utah, and the Indians, and Nevada, and general American matters and questions, with our secretary and certain government officials who came with us. But he never paid any attention to me, notwithstanding I made several attempts to "draw him out" on federal politics and his highhanded attitude toward Congress. I thought some of the things I said were rather fine. But he merely looked around at me, at distant intervals, somewhat as I have seen a benignant old cat look around to see which kitten was meddling with her tail. By and by I subsided into an indignant silence, and so sat until the end, hot and flushed, and execrating him in my heart for an ignorant savage. But he was calm. His conversation with those gentlemen flowed on as sweetly and peacefully and musically as any summer brook. When the audience was ended and we were retiring from the presence, he put his hand on my head, beamed down at me in an admiring way, and said to my brother: "Ah—your child, I presume? Boy or girl?"

By all accounts Zion was a theocracy autocratically ruled by Brigham Young with the spiritual help of divine guidance and the secular help of an army of Avenging Destroying Angels. The most egregious and horrific example of this abusive power is known as the Mountain Meadows Massacre. When Mark Twain passed through Utah, he heard rumors "implicating the highest church dignitaries in the many murders and robberies committed upon the gentiles during the past eight years."

The ill-fated Fancher Party arrived in Salt Lake City at the wrong time. Named for Alexander Fancher, one of several prosperous Arkansas farming families who organized a wagon train to California in 1857. President James Buchanan had appointed a successor for Governor Brigham Young. The prophet scoffed at the appointment and the president sent an army to Utah to install the new governor.

Preparing for what would be known as the Mormon War, Brigham Young ordered all trading with outsiders to cease. The Fancher Party had counted upon restocking their provisions in Salt Lake City. Disappointed, they headed south some three hundred miles and stopped to camp in a place called Mountain Meadows. Several disillusioned and disgruntled Saints had joined the wagon train, seeking its safety for their escape from Mormondom. Hatred for the

Arkansas travelers escalated when news arrived in Salt Lake City that devoted Mormon Missionary Parley Pratt had been murdered in Arkansas. These events were enough for Brigham Young to take action.

The Fancher party also possessed a significant amount of cash, arms and livestock, including a thousand head of prized longhorn cattle, which had never before been seen in Utah. There are many accounts of the details of the slaughter. One gentile version offered by C. V. Waite in her book, *The Mormon Prophet*, is as follows:

> A "revelation" from Brigham Young as Great Grand Archee or God, was dispatched to [Mormon leaders including] J[ohn] D Lee (adopted son of Brigham), commanding them to raise all the forces they could muster and trust, follow those cursed gentiles (so read the revelation), attack them disguised as Indians, and with the arrows of the Almighty make a clean sweep of them, and leave none to tell the tale; and if they needed any assistance they were commanded to hire the Indians as their allies [by] promising them a share of the booty. They were to be neither slothful nor negligent in their duty, and to be punctual in sending the teams back to him before winter set in, for this was the mandate of Almighty God.

The Fancher Party circled their wagons in the serene mountain meadow and valiantly held off the mock Indian attack for five days. Stifled, John D. Lee approached the besieged wagon train and offered help. He claimed to have made a deal with the Indians. If the Fancher Party threw down their weapons, Lee's angels would take them to the safety of their settlement. Trustingly they agreed and one armed angel was assigned to escort each male as they walked out in single file. A signal was given. In a few short minutes the massacre was over. One hundred and twenty men, women and children had been shot dead. There were seventeen survivors—not one of them over the age of seven. The victims were stripped naked and left where they fell to rot or be ravaged by indigenous varmints. Years afterward the surviving children testified that they saw their "benefactors" wearing clothing and jewelry that had belonged to their parents.

Without incident, the US Army replaced the prophet governor and installed an assortment of other federal officials in Utah. But, as Mark Twain wrote:

After they were in office they were as helpless as so many stone images. They made laws which nobody minded and which could not be executed. The federal judges opened court in a land filled with crime and violence and sat as holiday spectacles for insolent crowds to gap at—for there was nothing to try, nothing to do, nothing on the dockets! And if a gentile brought a suit, the Mormon jury would do just as it pleased about bringing in a verdict, and when the judgment of the court was rendered no Mormon cared for it and no officer could execute it...

Up to the date of our visit to Utah, such had been the territorial record. The territorial government established there had been a hopeless failure, and Brigham Young was the only real power in the land. He was an absolute monarch—a monarch who defied our president—a monarch who laughed at our armies when they camped about his capital...

The horror of the Mountain Meadows Massacre did not go unnoticed or unpunished, but it would take twenty years. Efforts were made to link Brigham Young directly with the massacre but to no avail. However, it is highly improbable that he was not involved in some way because he clearly commanded and controlled every aspect of his domain. While he might not have been aware of the exact details of the raid, it is unlikely that he did not give the order himself. John D. Lee was a loyal angel. It is doubtful that he would have initiated such an attack unless ordered to do so. Had it been a rogue act, I would think that Brigham Young would have dealt with it accordingly. But, in a Watergate-like cover-up, Salt Lake City's Mormon-controlled newspaper, *The Deseret News*, did not report it. When the prophet himself finally first spoke of the massacre, seven years later, it was in support of the contention that the Indians had done it alone.

In the end, John D. Lee took the fall. His first trial ended in a hung jury. Public outcry forced Brigham Young to abandon his support of Lee. Lee was subsequently convicted by a second all-Mormon jury. On March 23, 1877 he was executed by firing squad at Mountain Meadows. While Lee did not directly implicate the prophet, one account of his last words is:

I am a true believer in the gospel of Jesus Christ. I do not believe everything that is now being taught and practiced by Brigham Young. I do not care who hears it...I believe he is leading the people astray, downward to destruction...I have been sacrificed in a cowardly, dastardly manner. I cannot help it. It is my last word—it is so.

Brigham Young died later that year.

π

That the prophet controlled the votes of his religious family is indisputable. In 1862, Congress outlawed the practice of polygamy in the United States and its territories. Brigham Young defied the law and blatantly continued to take plural wives, eventually totaling at least twenty-seven. He was brought to trial in 1871 for polygamy but was acquitted by loyal hometown jurors.

Joseph Smith had privately taught and practiced polygamy. His first wife, Emma, did not embrace the notion. In a biography of Emma Hale Smith, *Mormon Enigma*, authors Linda King Newell and Valeen Tippetts Avery write:

> Observers and writers have speculated about Joseph's motivation for initiating a practice that violated local laws and went against the prevailing Christian teachings of his time, postulating that he was either a brilliant imposter or that he suffered from some mental disorder. Many concluded that the practice of polygamy stemmed from his own insatiable sexual drive, fueled by a quest for power…The majority of faithful Mormons would give little consideration to Joseph's own physical drives or to other charges. With "an almost compulsive emphasis on unquestioning loyalty to the Priesthood authority as the cardinal virtue," they would maintain simply that God commanded plural marriage through the prophet Joseph Smith.

Smith kept knowledge of his thirty plus additional wives from Emma as much as possible. Publicly he denied that he and fellow Mormons were engaged in the practice. Shortly after arriving in Utah, Brigham Young ended Smith's hypocrisy and went public with the first prophet's revelation that polygamy was a good thing and entered it into the Doctrines and Covenants of the church. Polygamy formally lasted until 1890, when the church abolished it once and for all under pressure from the United States government as a precondition to statehood. Utah became the forty-fifth state in 1896.

There is little doubt, however, that polygamy has had a significant impact on Mormonism. As Cal Tech History Professor Martin Ridge observed during an episode of the History Channel's documentary series "The Real West" detailing "The Mountain Meadows Massacre":

Polygamy is a perfectly logical extension of what Mormonism is all about. Mormonism is a primitive Christian religion. If you are going to go back to this Old Testament belief that everyone marries into every other family, you have only one family.

And families do stick together.

π

Mark Twain left Utah with some reading material:

> All men have heard of the Mormon Bible, but few except the "elect" have seen it, or, at least, taken the trouble to read it. I brought away a copy from Salt Lake. The book is a curiosity to me, it is such a pretentious affair, and yet so "slow," so sleepy, such an insipid mess of inspiration. It is chloroform in print. If Joseph Smith composed this book, the act was a miracle—keeping awake while he did it was, at any rate. If he, according to tradition, merely translated it from certain ancient and mysteriously engraved plates of copper, which he declares he found under a stone in an out-of-the-way locality, the work of translating was equally a miracle, for the same reason...
>
> The book seems to be merely a prosy detail of imaginary history, with the Old Testament for a model; followed by tedious plagiarism of the New Testament. The author labored to give his words and phrases the quaint, old-fashioned structure of our King James's translation of the Scriptures; and the result is a mongrel—half modern glibness, and half ancient simplicity and gravity. The latter is awkward and constrained; the former natural, but grotesque by the contrast. Whenever he found his speech growing too modern—which was about every sentence or two—he ladled in a few such scriptural phrases as "exceedingly sore," and "it came to pass," etc., and made things satisfactory again. "And it came to pass'" was his pet. If he had left it out, his Bible would have only been a pamphlet...
>
> The Mormon Bible is rather stupid and tiresome to read, but there is nothing vicious in its teachings. Its code of morals is unobjectionable—it is "smouched" [John Milton] from the New Testament and no credit given.

Mark Twain wondered:

I left Great Salt Lake a good deal confused as to what state of things existed there—and sometimes even questioning in my own mind whether a state of things existed there at all or not.

The tragedy at Mountain Meadows, in which ordinary God-fearing people obediently committed cold-blooded murder, occurred a century and half ago, when the law in Utah was Brigham Young and order was enforced by a loyal band of obedient angels. The theocracy observed by Mark Twain has ostensibly been replaced by constitutional law. To what extent, I wondered, could these past saintly, sultry influences still be alive today?

π

The slogan that greets everyone who enters the tallest building in Utah, which dominates Salt Lake City's skyline and which houses the headquarters of the modernday Church of Jesus Christ of Latter-Day Saints, is:

THE COURSE TO WISDOM IS THE COURSE TO OBEDIENCE

Writes Ed Decker in *The God Makers*:

How well Mormons know the truth of that slogan! It has been drilled into their consciousness since earliest childhood...to conform to a power that insists upon overriding both conscience and God...[and those who] do not submit obediently...are "gentiles" outside the true church...and are without salvation.

That Mormons are obedient by nature is supported by the fact that both the FBI and the CIA, according to an article in *Time* Magazine (August 4, 1997), actively recruit Mormons because of their "seemingly incorruptible rectitude." But to whom are they ultimately obedient?

The Mormon Church states that its president, supported by two counselors (collectively known as the first presidency) and the quorum of the twelve apostles, "receive revelations and directions from the Lord" and "communicate God's will to all people." Justice of the Utah Supreme Court Dallin H. Oaks resigned in 1984 to join the quorum. Apostle Oaks teaches:

Criticism is particularly objectionable when it is directed toward church authorities, general or local. Evil speaking of the Lord's anointed is in a class by itself. It is one thing to deprecate a person who exercises corporate or even governmental power. It is quite another thing to criticize or deprecate a person for the performance of an office to which he or she has been called of God. It does not matter that the criticism is true.

In other words, put your faith in Us and you can't go wrong.

π

Juror Rebecca may have obediently done just that. "I'm very religious," she volunteered not long after voting to convict Ray Krone, "and I'm a Mormon. I had the jury's name's put in the prayer roll at the temple while we were in trial so that we would make proper decisions."

The accused was a gentile "without salvation" and one of the accusers was a high-ranking family member. What was the church going to tell Rebecca to do, Vote your conscience, acquit Ray Krone, and make one of our anointed stake presidents, Ray Rawson, look like a nincompoop!? (The Mormon Church is divided into areas, stakes and wards.)

Of course, if such instructions were given they would not have been conveyed in such direct terms. But they could easily, subtly be made known. Prayer seems to be the way the church communicates its directives.

"We were in deliberations this one day," Rebecca continued, most likely referring to the day before the verdict was rendered. "I asked everyone if they would pray about it. They came back the next day saying that they had done so. I felt very relieved that we were trying to do the right thing and that we would be guided to do that so that I would feel good about it afterwards because it wasn't an easy thing to do."

"It" presumably was voting to convict and innocent man. Perhaps "it" explains the tears shed in unison by many of the jurors as the verdict was read?

Rebecca turned out to be the last holdout for acquittal. I remember sitting just outside the jury box three seats away from her, watching Levy perform on the final day of the trial. On the few days prior, the prosecutor had floundered a bit, struggling to keep up with Chris Plourd's aggressive defense. But Levy's final argument was smooth and polished. At one point he sauntered up directly in front of Rebecca and took his best crucifixion stance—arms out, palms open—and said something to the effect that the defense had made accusations that someone deliberately withheld evidence and then asked, "Who would that [someone] be? Who would that be?"

At the time I thought this parody odd. Yes, Plourd had battled Levy for access to the evidence. But these encounters occurred only during pretrial hearings to which the jury was not privy. As I thought about this event over the days to come, I wondered why Levy wanted to introduce and call attention to the fact that he had been accused of wrongdoing? Was it only a coincidence that he sanctimoniously parked himself in front of Rebecca to deliver this revelation? Couldn't it possibly have been that he had some forewarning that Rebecca might be trouble? Was he appealing to her faithful obedience and attempting to ride Rawson's coattails by pointing out that not only had the defense attorney deprecated Saint Raymond, he had accused "me too."

As Appellate Attorney James Kemper rounded up the trial transcripts, I had a copy of them routinely made for my own personal reference. I particularly wanted to revisit Levy's final argument. When I did read it, I could not find Levy's revelation or anything close to it anywhere in the transcript. It seems to have disappeared as mysteriously as Angel Moroni's golden plates after prophet Smith was done with them. Perhaps I too had been dreaming?

π

Jury selection is *the* most important aspect of the game. The original jury pool for the Krone trial contained about one hundred individuals. They were crammed into the spectator's gallery to hear the judge's instructions, fill out the jury questionnaire and submit to brief questioning. The judge did most of the inquiry: prior knowledge of the Krone case (aware that Ray was convicted once before and that this was a retrial), prior contact with law enforcement, attitudes toward the death penalty, familiarity with any participant in the trial, occupation, attitude toward scientific evidence, particularly DNA, attitude toward the defendant should he choose not to testify, etc.—general information really.

Chris Plourd had just one evening with a copy of each prospective juror's questionnaire. After jury selection, the questionnaires were to be returned to the clerk of the court. That evening we all, Jim and Carolyn Leming and I, sat around a table with Chris and helped him evaluate the prospective jurors, going through each questionnaire one at a time. Chris then summarized each juror's information onto a three-by-five index card, which he color-coded with sticky dots: green for good, yellow for okay, red for bad. He ordered the cards by each juror's seat number. The ones who ended up in the first sixteen seats would comprise the jury.

Jury selection procedure allows each attorney twenty strikes—opportunities to remove a juror. The next juror in line takes the vacated seat. The attorneys alternate striking jurors and may pass if they choose, saving one of their strikes for later. The jury is set when each attorney exhausts his twenty strikes or when there are two passes in a row. Saving a strike for later by passing is dangerous if the jury is not to the attorney's liking because if his opponent passes the jury is locked.

Chris was looking for those jurors with an education, preferably in science, particularly those who were knowledgeable of DNA. The jury was all yellow dotted and contained two physical therapists, two registered nurses, two medical lab technicians, and two computer analysts. Ten indicated that they would be favorably receptive to DNA evidence. On the surface at least it seemed that the jury was by and large an intelligent lot. What had gone wrong?

The following year (1997), in Philadelphia, Jack McMahon got into hot water. He was running for the office of district attorney. His opponent incumbent, Lynn Abraham, released a videotape made ten years earlier of McMahon, then a successful prosecutor with thirty-six successful murder convictions to his credit, giving a talk to neophyte prosecutors in training on jury selection. McMahon was asked to give the presentation at the last minute. Without preparation, "straight shooter" McMahon extemporaneously told it like it was, making statements like:

> The blacks from the low-income areas are less likely to convict...
>
> Young black women are very bad. There's an antagonism. I guess maybe because they're downtrodden in two respects. They are women and they're black...so they somehow want to take it out on somebody and you don't want it to be you...
>
> In selecting blacks, you don't want the real educated ones.

These seemingly racial remarks caused the instructional videotape to disappear into the archives until McMahon's opponent needed it for political purposes. But McMahon's taped comments were hardly racial. They were realistic. He also said:

> Older black men seventy to seventy-five years old are very good jurors generally speaking. They are from a different

era, and a different time. And they have a different respect for the law.

Blacks from the South [are] excellent. I don't think you can ever lose a jury with blacks from South Carolina. They are dynamite. They just have a different way of living down there, a different philosophy. They are for law and order. They are on the cops' side. Those people are good [jurors].

McMahon made no bones about the essence of the justice game:

You are there to win. The only way you're going to do your best is to get jurors that are unfair, and more likely to convict than anybody else in that room. The case law says the object of getting a jury is to get a competent, fair and impartial jury. Well, that's ridiculous! You're not trying to get that. Both sides are trying to get the jury most likely to do whatever they want them to do. If you go in there and think you are going to be some noble civil libertarian, that's ridiculous! You are there to win. If you think that it's some noble esoteric game, you're wrong and you'll lose. You'll be out of [a job].

Throughout his talk McMahon emphasized that "The defense is there to win, too." He left the prosecutor's office to become a successful defense attorney. I know that if I were a defendant in some Philadelphia court I would not want to face prosecutor Jack McMahon. But I would want defense attorney Jack McMahon sitting at my table. McMahon advised the aspiring prosecutors:

You do not want smart people. I wish we could ask everyone's IQ. If you could know their IQ, you could pick a great jury all the time. You don't want smart people because smart people will analyze the hell out of your case. They have a higher standard. They hold you up to a higher standard. They hold the courts up to a higher standard...They take those words "reasonable doubt," and they actually try to think about them.

Chris Plourd, too, knew how to play the game and seemingly had done his job well. The impaneled jurors appeared to be reasonably intelligent. How had Levy been able to discern this jury's imperceptible lack of horse sense, its willingness to ultimately ignore "reasonable doubt"? Perhaps selecting a jury in Arizona is not simply a black and white matter as it is in Philadelphia? And perhaps, relative to the prosecutor, Plourd was flying blind? Mark Twain observed:

Let it be borne in mind that the majority of the Mormons have always been ignorant, simple, of an inferior order of intellect, unacquainted with the world and its ways.

Even Mormon president (1985-1994), prophet Ezra Taft Benson observed:

[Those]…who have the greatest difficulty in following the prophet are the proud who are learned.

Perhaps Levy had a simple IQ test available only to him. Is there any doubt that Levy could have learned each prospective juror's religious affiliation if he really wanted to? After all it was his hometown.

π

In 1846, while camped in Iowa on the way to Zion, Brigham Young volunteered some five hundred young Mormons to enlist in the United States Army to fight in the Mexican War. The volunteers donated their pay to help finance the exodus. The Mormon Battalion, as it came to be known, served with distinction, cutting a trail from New Mexico to the California coast through southern Arizona. Many who rejoined their families in Salt Lake City after the war reported a fertile land to the south. The completion of the transcontinental railroad brought pressures on the Mormons to expand beyond Utah. The first settlers reached Mesa, Arizona in 1877. Many of them entered the territory on Lee's Ferry, which was operated by the same John D. Lee who had served in the Mormon Battalion before leading the Mountain Meadows Massacre. Lee had been excommunicated because of his involvement in the tragedy and subsequently earned his living ferrying travelers across the Colorado River at the eastern end of the Grand Canyon—until he took the fall for the Mountain Meadows murders.

Mesa flourished. A Mormon temple was erected there in 1927. It lies twenty miles east of Phoenix in the heart of Maricopa County. Mesa is the fortieth largest city in the United States, the third largest city in Arizona and is still dominated by Mormons.

However, in Maricopa County at large Saints are in the minority. It would be expected that a jury selected randomly would reflect these demographics. But, many Ray Krone jurors were from Mesa and its outlying areas. To win with this saintly jury, all prosecutor Noel Levy needed to do was to let them know that the star witness was family and that the defendant wasn't.

A Mormon temple is not for everyone, not even for every Mormon. It is not a place where the rank and file Saint worships regularly but a place where periodic rituals known as "ordinances" are reserved only for the "worthy." To be worthy one may simply die. The Mormons who believe that they are the saviors of the world baptize by proxy everyone who has ever lived. For the living to be worthy, a celestial income tax must be paid on time. With most churches tithing is optional. However, for Mormons to be admitted into the temple a mandatory ten percent donation is required. Also, the worthy must believe without question everything every prophet has ever said, ignoring contradictions, accepting the most recent revelation. Polygamy once was good, now it is bad, for example. The worthy must pay to play and leave horse sense behind.

Once inside the temple they strip down and don a special garment before proceeding to the "endowment ceremony." The garment is laced with special markings suspiciously similar to Masonic symbols. The link between Masonic rituals and temple ceremonies are parallels that the worthy must reject despite the evidence: that Joseph Smith initiated temple ordinances shortly after he became a Freemason, that they share similar blood-death oaths of secrecy, that they use special handshakes, that they require similar initiation garments, that they anoint in oil, and that they share similar symbols—an all-seeing eye, a beehive, clasped hands, sun, moon and stars, to name a few. The Masonic square and compass adorn the Mormon garment, one sewn over each breast.

Until recently the garment was left open in several places. For Masonic rituals it was necessary to determine gender, presumably by reaching in and down. Ladies were not allowed to become Masons. Mormon ordinances required that important body parts be hand anointed with oil by a temple headmaster and blessed so that they would perform properly. Procreation is believed to continue into the afterlife, where rank is determined by fecundity.

Responding to numerous freak-outs by modernday Saints while being fondled during the endowment ceremony, the Mormons have zipped up the garment to prevent access to the participants' endowments during the ceremony. Anointing is now confined to the top of the head. Nevertheless, those endowed, like their forbears, are required to wear a similar garment twenty-four/seven to demonstrate, as church elder Carlos Asay writes, "faith in God, faith in self, faith in one's cause and faith in one's leaders."

Asay also points out that the saintly underwear has magical properties "enabling us to withstand the fiery darts of Satan."

I was told that family members recognize each other by discerning an everyday version of the garment being worn under regular clothing. I wasn't savvy enough at the time of Ray Rawson's testimony to check him out for magical underwear, but subsequently I did notice the garment being worn by others in the Phoenix area. Under a dress shirt it appeared as a hemline similar to that of a long sleeve undershirt. The "hemline" also showed under the trousers, especially while sitting— about a third of the way down the thigh. If the jurors weren't able to ascertain Rawson's family ties by his dress they certainly could have determined it from his curriculum vitae, which Levy had entered into evidence.

But, how was Levy able to let the jury know that the defendant was not one of them? Did he have an ulterior motive in pointing out to them that when Ray Krone was arrested he wasn't wearing any underwear? Farfetched? Perhaps. But then, what is the explanation for Levy's fixation on the dart-playing defendant's absence of protection?

π

Jury selection à la McMahon depends upon demographics. In Philadelphia it's one way, in Phoenix another. I learned from Dr. Richard Souviron what it is in Mississippi. We were sitting together in the back row of a forensic lecture waiting for the next speaker to set up his slide show and we chatted about his fellow bite mark experts. Dr. Souviron detailed his encounter with Ray Rawson at the Nashville AAFS meeting at which he buttonholed Rawson and strongly advised him to bail out of the Krone case because "you know your analysis is no good." To which he said Rawson dejectedly replied, "I can't. I'm in too deep."

I asked Souviron about his testimony at Kennedy Brewer's trial. He flat-out stated that the marks that Dr. West had said were made by Brewer's teeth were in fact not bite marks at all but insect bites.

"Why do you suppose the jury believed West's bite mark nonsense?" I asked.

Without batting an eye, Souviron responded in effect, "It wouldn't have happened outside the Bible belt. Those Southern Baptists will believe anything."

I then asked if he'd heard about West's response in another case in which the defense attorney had the goods on West's numerous forensic boners and was ready to lay them out for the jury.

I told Souviron that the defense attorney asked, attempting to set the expert up, "How many times have you been wrong, Dr. West?" To which West pompously, piously responded,

"Slightly less than my Savior Jesus Christ."

Eye-Brain Coordination

The defense attorney was left speechless. From then on he would have appeared to the jury to be challenging the Lord Himself.

π

Prosecutor Jack McMahon got into trouble because of his seemingly racial remarks regarding jury selection. According to the 1986 US Supreme Court decision, *Batson v. Kentucky*, it is illegal to eliminate jurors based upon race. "The harm from discriminatory jury selection," the court ruled, "extends beyond that inflicted on the defendant and the excluded juror to touch the entire community." It's a law with good intentions but difficult to enforce. McMahon claims, and rightly so, that it is not race per se that he used to select jurors. It's "life experiences" that count. It's just that in his jurisdiction, "blacks from low-income areas are less likely to convict...people from 33rd and Diamond stink..." But, McMahon also avoids "intelligent doctors."

And it's not that the jurors are out to get a particular defendant. He's merely a pawn in the game and they are simply tools of the trade. Maricopa County prosecutors, Levy included, no doubt have discovered what works in their hometown. Suggesting that jury discrimination may have occurred based upon one's religious life experiences or lack thereof is touchy in this country, which was founded upon separation of church and state.

Yet the age-old struggle between science and religion seems to be alive and well in the courtroom. In the beginning I had difficulty understanding how Levy could go forward with the trial. All he had was a bite mark disputed four experts to one, no fingerprints, no eyewitnesses, and was up against solid DNA evidence. Yet he persisted and won. As I think back on the whole experience, the courtroom drama seemed more akin to a church service than to an academic pursuit of the truth. Both rituals are presided over by well respected men wearing robes, one wielding a cross, the other a gavel. Many spectators engage in prayer throughout both ceremonies. For the Krone service, Plourd's final argument was a lecture on scientific truth. Levy's was more like preaching to the choir. The ceremony ended with wailing when the verdict turned out to be that prophesied by the not-so-obedient Mark Twain:

Faith is believing what you know ain't so.

π

For several years after Ray Krone's conviction, I would occasionally bring up my ruminations about the jury's "strange verdict" with Chris. Whenever I did, he would abruptly change the subject. At first I thought it was a sore point with him. Eventually he did acknowledge that he lost the trial at jury selection. My assumption about Chris was wrong—I came to appreciate that he was not one to dwell on the past and waste time in areas that would be of no help to his client. He stayed focused on the task at hand, pursuing the unknown DNA known to be on the victim's under garments. Even if it could be proved that the jury was intentionally salted with Saints, it would go nowhere. There is no court in this land that would prevent discrimination based upon magic underwear.

Nevertheless, I believe that I could convince this Arizona jury that Bob Dylan's *Mr. Tambourine Man* is about Ray Krone—despite the fact that Dylan himself would testify that he wrote the song while in New Orleans when Ray Krone was but a lad of seven and that he was inspired, among other things, by a tall, lanky band member who played a gigantic tambourine and by images of Fellini's *La Strada*. I would simply explain to this jury that Dylan, in addition to being a poet, is also a prophet:

> *Look out the saints are comin' through.*
> *And it's all over now, Baby Blue.*

CATCH-22
THE GILA

From southwestern New Mexico, a river born of the waters of mountain tributaries enters Arizona and travels westward across the state. The first part of its journey is mostly through mountain valleys. At Florence, its halfway point, it passes so close to Arizona State Prison that Ray would have had a view of the Gila—if his cell had had any view at all. Then it moves northwest, passing through Maricopa County south of Phoenix before turning southwest toward Yuma, where the waters that survive the Sonoran Desert join the Colorado River and eventually return to the Pacific Ocean through the Sea of Cortez.

The Gila River shares its name with a monster of sorts, a poisonous lizard indigenous to the desert southwest. When the Gila Monster bites its prey it rolls onto its back to allow the venom stored in glands in its lower jaw to trickle down grooves in its teeth into the wound. Unlike its cousin the snake it does not have the ability to inject its poison. The Gila Monster must hang on tenaciously until its victim dies. Its reptilian brain is programmed only for survival. Should the Gila Monster bite off more than it can chew it has no intelligence to tell it to let go. So when it bites a human being it doesn't know any better than to hang on until its own death. Fatalities among humans are rare, although it does take a pair of pliers to release the reptile's jaws.

The brains of the great dinosaurs that dominated the earth for hundreds of millions of years were ill-equipped to deal with the climate changes that were triggered by the impact of a huge meteorite on the Yucatan peninsula around 65 million years ago. As a result, the dinosaurs became extinct. Among the survivors were birds—the only direct descendants of the dinosaurs—and budding mammals from which humans evolved.

For all species of life survival is paramount. We human beings are no exception. Our brain begins where the reptilian brain ends. At the top of our spinal column resides the remnant of our reptilian ancestry known as the reptilian-complex—R-complex for short. It is the seat of aggression, territoriality, ritualistic behavior, the establishment of social hierarchies, the willingness to blindly follow leaders, etc.

Surrounding the R-complex is the cerebral cortex, which in us humans accounts for eighty-five percent of our brain mass. It is our highly evolved cerebral cortex that distinguishes us from all other animals and has allowed us to become the dominate species on the planet. It is where we reason rationally, ponder objectively, pursue science, compose music, create art, build machines, raise skyscrapers, erect bridges, develop technology, communicate with each other and accumulate knowledge by writing books.

Another important function of the cerebral cortex is to reign in the R-complex, which is still programmed to behave like our cold-blooded ancestors. When it fails, strange dinosaur-like things happen: innocence is crucified, thousands perish blindly following a leader, groups of people exterminate other groups of people, planes fly into buildings, bombs explode on crowded busses, wars are fought under false pretenses, OJ is acquitted and Ray Krone is convicted.

There is no doubt that the Constitution of the United States— including its first ten amendments, the Bill of Rights—was conceived in the cerebral cortex. But it is by and large administered by the R-complex. "Despite welcome exceptions," writes Carl Sagan in *The Dragons of Eden*, "[reptilian mentality] seems to me to characterize a great deal of modern human bureaucratic and political behavior." Survival for the bureaucrat means kissing the ass of the politician who keeps him on staff. Survival for the politician means reelection. And reelection for the politician who occupies the Maricopa County Attorney's Office means a high rate of convictions. "It's a numbers game," observed George Schuester in explaining the strange verdicts he'd observed during his career as a court bailiff.

Richard "Rick" Romley served with distinction in the Vietnam War. He was born in Tucson in 1949 and joined the Marines just out of high school. In April 1969, while leading his squad through the jungle, he stepped on a land mine and lost both legs. He was awarded a Purple Heart. After a lengthy recuperation and rehabilitation in which he learned to walk with prostheses and a cane, Romley returned to Arizona and entered Arizona State University. He was awarded a degree in business management, with honors, in 1974, then he started a retail business. He sold his business in five years and returned to ASU and earned a law degree in 1981. From there he became a deputy Maricopa County prosecutor. In 1988, he was elected district attorney, the district being Maricopa County, and was in his first term of office when Ray Krone was convicted the first time.

According to his own standards, Rick Romley was a very good county attorney. "As you can see in the statistical section," he wrote in one of his annual reports, "we achieved an 89.9 percent criminal conviction rate, five percent higher than the national average." How did he do it?

Before becoming a professor of law at ASU, Gary T. Lowenthal was a criminal defense attorney, defending more than thirty clients before a jury. At one point he had a string of eight consecutive "not guilty" verdicts. After twenty years in the academic world he felt that he had gotten out of touch with the real world of criminal justice. He took a sabbatical and was allowed to intern as a deputy county prosecutor, provided that he "agree to follow all office policies, *always,*" as dictated by his boss—Maricopa County Attorney Rick Romley. Incidentally, Romley had been a student of Lowenthal's at ASU. But now he was the teacher and Lowenthal had to relearn how the justice game is played.

One policy was known as the "reasonable likelihood of conviction" rule. Writes Lowenthal in his book *Down and Dirty Justice*:

> Since the county attorney was a locally elected official, high conviction rates would demonstrate to the voters every four years that [this official] was doing his job well...What would be politically troublesome...was not a refusal to file charges, but instead the risk that a significant percentage [might result] in either an acquittal or a dismissal. The need to drive up aggregate conviction rates translated into a policy of rejecting prosecutions when the evidence was a little shaky—or the facts lacked "jury appeal"...Filing charges in cases unlikely to result in conviction was a path to professional oblivion in the county attorney's office.

Because of this policy, Lowenthal tells an interviewer, "very often people who commit serious crimes are never prosecuted. The reason I call my book *Down and Dirty Justice* is that it's all about that kind of bargain justice. It's a system that's run for administrative efficiency, to get the messy cases out of the system, to just go with the slam-dunks...and [prosecutors will] plea bargain as many cases as they can to make it look like they're winning even more [cases]." Statistically, a plea bargain has the same effect as a conviction.

Ray Krone enlightened me on another way Arizona prosecutors jack up conviction statistics. Many of his inmate acquaintances reported that in order to get a favorable plea bargain for the crime they committed, they must also confess to similar unsolved crimes that they had nothing to do with.

Ray was initially offered a plea bargain. But it wasn't much of a deal—life in prison instead of death by lethal injection—especially for an innocent man expecting "up and clean justice." He rejected the plea bargain and maintained that he was innocent. Lowenthal notes that a corollary to "down and dirty justice" is that "innocence isn't always the best defense." When the police department presents its candidate to take the rap for a crime, guilt or innocence seems to be of less interest to the county prosecutor than convictability.

Ray Krone was a slam-dunk. In October a postal worker in Wayne, New Jersey killed his former supervisor and two fellow employees. In November a postal worker in Royal Oak, Minnesota killed four supervisors and wounded five fellow employees before killing himself. In December news was abuzz with postal workers going postal when postal worker Ray Krone was arrested for the murder of Kim Ancona. He was trumped up by the lead detective to be her lying boyfriend. The evidence whittled down to a single bite mark ripe for some forensic whore to step in and validate. The defendant, unable to afford competent counsel, accepted a court appointed good 'ol boy who squandered on a dentist buddy the paltry funds allocated for a defense expert.

The case had "jury appeal." An attractive victim brutally killed by someone who went postal and left a telltale bite mark. Her postal worker "boyfriend" who had crooked teeth and didn't wear underwear. It was another quick and easy statistic for the ambitious county attorney.

But then Ray's conviction was overturned. Had this event awakened the entire brain, the cerebral cortex would easily have discerned that the case boiled down to dueling experts, and this "reasonable doubt" would have compelled the reptilian-complex to let go. But the county attorney and his loyal band of followers were in charge. Once their bite is on they can't be woken up, and "reasonable doubt" disappears, the bitten having become merely a number in the game, a statistic to make a county prosecutor shine.

Word was that Romley was furious that the supreme court had given a new trial to a mere statistic. However subtle or implied, the Machiavellian order came down to "do what it takes to convict [94877, which was the number assigned to Ray Krone by the Arizona Department of Corrections when he first entered prison]." Although it wasn't so easy the second time around, taking eight weeks instead of eight days, Romley's crew nevertheless got the job done and preserved their precious statistic.

Perhaps contributing to the decision to krone Ray Krone once again was the egg lingering on Romley's face from a much bigger case. He had taken a big hit with his handling of "the temple murders." To take a second hit by acknowledging that an innocent man had been convicted on his watch would quite possibly have doomed his reelection.

Four months before the murder of Kim Ancona, the worst mass murder in Arizona history had occurred on the far west side of Phoenix, at the Wat Promkunaram Buddest Temple. The bodies of six monks, two temple acolytes and a nun were found cloistered together in what appeared to be an execution style hit. The nine unfortunates had been sprayed with several shotgun blasts and then, as they lay on the floor, shot in the back of the head one to three times with a .22-caliber rifle.

News of the temple murders was received with horror in Thailand. The murder of a Buddhist monk—let alone six—is one of the worst crimes imaginable. The country observed a national day of mourning. The Thai ambassador to the United States was sent to Phoenix to get to the bottom of the tragedy. Sheriff Tom Agnos, Arizona Attorney General Grant Woods and Maricopa County Attorney Rick Romley attended a dinner party given for the ambassador. Throughout the evening, as the luminaries dined, word spread that the case had been solved. In Tucson a young man was arrested in a psychiatric hospital who Maricopa County Sheriff officials said had information about the crime. Soon three of his friends were arrested and all were subsequently indicted. They became known as "the Tucson four."

In no time after being subjected to the interrogation procedures of the Romley complex, each of the Tucson four made incriminating statements linking himself and the other three to the temple murders. But shortly after being released from "the Miranda room," all four recanted.

The *Miranda v. Arizona* decision had done little to slow down Maricopa County inquisitors. Indeed, false confessions are not uncommon in the justice game. Of those individuals who have been exonerated by DNA analysis nationally, false confessions played a roll in more than twenty percent of the cases.

Why would someone confess to a crime he didn't commit? According to the Capital Post Conviction Project, false confessions occur when the suspect is vulnerable and the interrogator employs psychological coercion. Youths are particularly vulnerable. Juvenile exonerees had confessed forty-four percent of the time. Mental disability accounts for sixty-nine percent of all bogus confessions.

Coercing a false confession begins with the interrogator's engaging the suspect in small talk about the crime, seeming to seek his help. Then the interrogator demonstrates his willingness and ability to punish the suspect if he doesn't cooperate. Rewards like food, sleep, and medical care are withheld for hours on end while the interrogator feeds the suspect details of the crime interspersed with suggestions of how the suspect might be implicated in them.

Securing "confessions" from the Tucson four was straightforward: youth and mental disability. But the Maricopa County Sheriff's Department had too hastily selected the Tucson four. Tucson is a hundred eighty miles south of Phoenix. Employers for two of the four produced time cards showing that they had punched in and out on the day of the murders, rendering the logistics of the confessed crime virtually impossible. The suspected murder weapon, a rifle belonging to a brother of one of the four, could not be tied to the crime. It failed ballistic tests.

In two months, the case against the Tucson four unraveled so completely and publicly that the Romley complex was forced to let go and put its bite on the taxpayers' wallets instead. The four youths were awarded $8 million in damages.

After the Tucson four fiasco, two Phoenix youths Alex Garcia and Jonathan Doody were next in line. They were spirited off to the Miranda room. Doody, a seventeen-year-old Thai with a marginal understanding of English, made incriminating statements and after fourteen hours of non-stop interrogation Garcia "confessed":

> ...[I]n June of 1991, Jonathan Doody and I got together and planned to rob and burglarize the Thai Buddhist Temple. Part of our plan was to leave no witnesses. On the evening of August 19, 1991, we started to put our plan in action. Jonathan and I drove to the temple. I was armed with a 20-gauge pump shotgun. Jonathan was armed with a .22-caliber semiautomatic rifle...Before leaving the temple, Jonathan told me, "No witnesses." I told him, "Robbery is one thing, but murder is another." Jonathan repeated to me that there could be no witnesses. He then stepped to my right and, while armed with the .22-caliber rifle, began shooting the nine occupants while they were lying on the floor. I began firing my 20-gauge shotgun, but fired not to kill anyone. I fired four rounds from my shotgun toward the nine people lying on the floor.

A signature of coerced false confessions is that they do not add new details and they contain information contrary to the facts. Such was the case with Garcia's "confession." The medical examiner reported that the victims were standing when they were shotgunned.

Once outside the Miranda room, both Garcia and Doody quickly recanted—but to no avail. Based upon their "confessions," the Romley complex now promoted a new motive. The murders were no longer a "hate crime" but a "robbery gone bad".

Garcia and Doody were duly tried and convicted of the temple murders and sentenced to life in prison. But suspicions lingered that they had been kroned. Ray's bailiff, George Schuester, was also bailiff for the temple murders trial. He personally expressed to me his skepticism that Doody had committed the crime.

The Grapevine, a small local newspaper, reported the strong possibility that the temple murders were drug related. Much of the world's heroin comes from Thailand, and Buddhist temples in the United States have long been suspected to be fronts for heroin trafficking. (More details about the temple murders are provided in the appendix.)

The state's leading newspaper, *The Arizona Republic*, made little of the Thai heroin connection. Instead it reported the version of events promoted by politician Rick Romley, an Arizona Republican in good standing.

π

Ray's first trial received a fair amount of press coverage. The second trial, however, was barely mentioned in the local newspapers. Early on, shortly after my eye-opening meeting with Dr. Campbell, I stopped into the lobby of *The Arizona Republic* and asked the receptionist to see a reporter who might be interested in new evidence that strongly suggested that an innocent man was on Death Row. I was met by staff writer Susan Leonard. I spent half an hour or so laying out the case for her, showing her the bite mark photographs, and emphasizing Dr. Campbell's exculpatory opinion. She seemed quite interested and gave me her private number to keep touch.

From then on, each time Chris made an important discovery, we wined and dined Susan and fed her the new information. Her initial enthusiasm gradually turned into skepticism, however, which I assumed was due to a supervisor's being in her ear playing devil's advocate. When asked when she was going to write a story, she put us off with a flimsy excuse. I sensed that her initial enthusiasm had been tempered by her boss.

Finally, a month before the trial was scheduled, her article appeared. It was a good article, detailing both sides of the case. But it would be her only article and *The Arizona Republic* would cover only the opening of the trial and the verdict. After hearing Chris Plourd's opening statement, the lone local reporter present left the courtroom shaking his head and commenting, "You mean, all they've got on this guy is a bite mark?" His short, innocuous article was buried in the B section of the Saturday edition. What happened during the following eight weeks, up until the verdict, went unreported to the people of Maricopa County, who, without having been able to watch the game, were then shown the victory celebration—ho-hum, just another job well done by the hometown team.

Susan Leonard's article did however produce one important benefit –Teri read it and made contact with Chris Plourd relating her biting encounter with Tennessee Mike subsequently becoming an important defense witness.

In sharp contrast to Phoenix's coverage of the second trial, Ray's hometown newspaper, *The York Daily Record*, took an active interest due to the lobbying of Ray's stepfather, Jim Leming. After talking with prosecutor Noel Levy, the newspaper's editor, Dennis Hetzel, was moved to write an editorial, "Cinic of Skeptic," critical of the prosecutor's comment, "Everyone in prison is innocent. Just ask them."

Hetzel dispatched two reporters to cover the day-to-day proceedings of the second trial. Newspaper readers in the small Pennsylvania town of York were as flabbergasted at the trial's outcome as almost every television watcher in America had been some months earlier at the outcome of the OJ trial.

I guess the contrast in each hometown's coverage was that it was just that.

π

The Romley complex, like most district attorney operations, is allowed to control and hoard the evidence in criminal cases. This situation frustrated Ray's team no end. The hoops Chris had to jump through to gain access to it were staggering. Not only did the game have to be played on the hometown court, the hometown team owned the ball. Most of the time the defense was forced literally to play defense. Should the ball finally be wrested away, it was often not the one play started with. The excised bitten breast tissue disappeared before the game even started, replaced by a simple plaster cast. The cotton swab of the bite injury became a cottonless stick. Altered detective notes didn't come into play until the last quarter. A second police report popped up with a shoe size inflated to fit the defendant. A one-bite bite mark report was puffed up by eye-brain coordination into a report claiming multiple bite marks. A serology ball was turned inside out.

With this reptilian control over the evidence, it's a wonder that DNA from Ray's reference sample didn't simply turn up all over the victim's clothing to really make a slam-dunk of it. I guess the Romley complex didn't think it needed to do that for the first trial, and such ball tampering as that would have been a serious foul if true and discovered. But who would have caught 'em anyway? Besides, they were protected by the "no harm, no foul" rule. And what would the Romley complex do if caught—prosecute itself?

π

When I told my older daughter, Vanita, some of the things the Romley complex did to convict and keep our cousin Ray convicted, she asked, "How do those people sleep at night?"

A good question, which Gary Lowenthal answers in *Down and Dirty Justice*. When he was handed the Garry Espinoza case, his cerebral cortex didn't want to prosecute Espinoza, who was charged with prohibited firearm possession and drug possession for sale with intent to assist a street gang. Espinoza insisted that he was innocent and refused to accept a plea bargain. The evidence against Espinoza consisted of the fact that his birth certificate and social security card were confiscated along with cocaine, marijuana, cash, an assault rifle and a sawed-off shotgun from the rear bedroom of an inner city home.

Espinoza was outside the house with a beer in his hand and $1,450 cash in his pocket when the search warrant went down. A twelve-year-old girl who lived in the house with her family told the investigating detective that Espinoza and Tony Montoya lived in the back bedroom. True, Espinoza had lived there in the past. Juanita Sanchez, the resident owner and landlord, would testify to this fact, which could explain Espinoza's forgotten birth certificate and social security card's being in the same room as drugs and guns. Sanchez stated that Espinoza was merely a visitor at the time of the raid.

Montoya, the current occupant, confessed and received six months in jail. He claimed that the drugs and the weapons were his alone and that Espinoza knew nothing about them. Having served his time, Montoya was set to testify in Espinoza's defense. Espinoza produced a lease confirming that he had for some time been living elsewhere. "The case reeked of reasonable doubt," wrote Lowenthal.

Enter gang squad detective Tom Kelly. He'd been out to get Espinoza for some time. He showed up in Lowenthal's office with a pile of material a mile high. It contained eight years of police reports and associated photographs, fat scrapbooks filled with letters and gang-related drawings and a detailed dossier on the Lado Sur (Southside) gang's leader, Garry Espinoza, a.k.a. "Joker," the gang's nickname for him. It was not a mere drug possession case, Kelly emphasized, but the story of a gang leader. "I *guarantee* you won't lose this case...All you need is twelve good citizens." The facts of the case didn't really matter so long as Espinoza's gang activities came before the jury.

Lowenthal watched from the sidelines because his tenure expired before the trial could begin. Another prosecutor stepped in. Officer Kelly's gang presentation was toned down so the prosecution wouldn't look so much like a persecution. The prosecutor used one of Kelly's photographs to produce a large poster showing Espinoza posing with other gang members brandishing assault rifles.

Defense witnesses testified that Kelly's material was at least two years old. Espinoza acknowledged his past Southside gang membership but testified that he'd left the gang some months before his arrest. The defense attorney, either through incompetence or overconfidence, hadn't struck a single juror. The first twelve good citizens determined by the prosecutor were seated. Sure enough, as Kelly predicted, the jury convicted Espinoza, deliberating less than eight hours.

Though Espinoza was innocent of the specific charges against him, it would have been far better for him to have taken the plea bargain of simple drug possession and spending a few months in the county jail than to have gone to trial. He spent several long years in the state pen.

Chris knows what it's like defending innocent clients who are not well liked. In one of Chris's cases where the defendant was obviously innocent, the judge wouldn't give Chris a break, ruling against him at every turn. Frustrated, Chris caught the judge on the side and asked, "What's going on? You must know my client is innocent," to which the judge curtly responded, off the record, "Yes, but he's a bad dude."

So long as the defendant is a bad dude, members of the Romley complex sleep like a baby at night, no matter what shenanigans they might pull in the process. If they lose any sleep at all it's over their cerebral fear that their reptilian high jinks will be discovered and they'll be punished, not over the possibility that some innocent, albeit bad dude has been harmed.

Garry Espinoza didn't stand a chance. It didn't matter that the gang related material presented by Officer Kelly was two years old or that the real perpetrator of the crime testified that he alone had committed it. He was a bad dude and easily convictable by twelve good citizens. But what if, as in Ray's case, the dude is really not bad at all. No matter, so long as he's *perceived* to be bad. For the R-complex, simply being different qualifies you—having a different skin color or being a member of different ethnic group or wearing a different brand of underwear or none at all.

Newspapers devote paragraphs to arrests made for violent felonies detailing the horrors of the crimes and the police/prosecution version of the facts—"the victim was bitten and her 'boyfriend' with crooked teeth has been arrested." The suspect's version of the story becomes the one-liner, "The boyfriend denies any involvement," and gets lost in hyped Levy type cynicism, "Everyone in jail is innocent. Just ask 'em."

Certainly not all bright-eyed lawyers emerging from law school and entering the Romley complex training program are cynical. As Lowenthal reports in *Down and Dirty Justice*, there's a tremendous turnover of deputy county prosecutors. He found that twenty-five percent of the prosecutors working for Rick Romley had been employed for less than one year and forty percent for less than two years. In a one-year period, one prosecutor resigned weekly, on average.

Lowenthal attributes the attrition to two factors. The compensation for recent law graduates who have passed the bar was one third that offered by most major law firms in most major cities, including Phoenix. But the principal factor was "the rigidity of office policies that restricted the ability of prosecutors to do what they thought was right in each case." Once the indictment department decides to put the bite on a particular individual, that's it. A prosecutor with brains who finds that the evidence against the accused doesn't pan out and has the balls to speak up gets weeded out.

What's left? Not too bright prosecutors completely loyal to the boss whose message is "prosecute or perish." Career prosecutors with this mindset who eventually move on to become judges along with their other scientifically challenged colleagues perhaps account for the bizarre ejaculations such as "eye-brain coordination" and "the unindicted co-ejaculator theory" that get into the courts. It's no wonder that these courts buy all types of ridiculous arguments espoused by loyal Levy types, the more powerful members of the club, and serve to keep bad dudes down, guilty or not.

π

If you happen to be an innocent dude on Death Row reading these words, I wish I could offer you some encouragement. But from what I've seen of the justice game, there's no encouragement to offer. My advice to you is to take up yoga. For unless there exists exculpatory DNA in your case *and* some asshole has not already destroyed it *and* an organization such as the Innocence Project is willing to take up your cause *and* is able to uncover the hidden truth *and* the court has the brains to understand it *and* the courage to act upon it, you might as well bend over and kiss your ass good-bye.

It's unlikely that the justice system as it exists today will on its own volition come to your rescue. Should you find some new evidence, the assholes who put you away are more likely to cinch up their blinders and fight you tooth and nail than to take an objective look at your new evidence.

And if, after your lengthy incarceration away from your family and friends, with the prospect of death looming over your head the whole time, you are able, by some miracle of miracles, to walk out of prison a free man, those same assholes will ignore the fact that they have ruined your life and will use your success to try to convince anyone watching that "the system works," after which they'll go back unscathed to business a usual.

π

Ray Krone was no longer on Death Row but he had essentially been sentenced to death in prison, for unless Boss Romley and his complex could be beaten, Ray would most likely die there. In 1998, nearly two years after the second conviction, his battle was being fought in the Arizona court of appeals. The case was in the hands of a three-judge tribunal comprising the Honorables Jon W. Thompson, Michael D. Ryan and Cecil B. Patterson, Jr. (presiding). Ray's court-appointed appellate attorney, James Kemper, rested cautiously confident that his arguments would penetrate at least two of the three cerebral cortexes. For some reason he was concerned about Thompson, who, ominously, would write the panel's opinion.

On the surface, appellate judges don't consider guilt or innocence. However, the Arizona Supreme Court judges who gave Ray a second trial were clearly influenced by the evidence of innocence that was slipped under their noses. The petition for special action defended

Ray's right to proceed with new evidence discovery. It detailed the exculpatory evidence Chris had been able to discover before Judge Hotham shut him up and down. It was being considered by the supreme court in tandem with Ray's appeal.

An appeal is at best a crapshoot. If a judge has the courage and wisdom to question whether the appellant is really the bad dude that the prosecution made him out to be, he may lean toward the appellant's arguments. But if he believes the opposite, the perceived bad dude is most likely screwed, however meritorious his arguments. There is little doubt in my mind that without Plourd's thoroughly prepared petition, the late discovery of the videotape would have been ruled to be "harmless error," the appeal of Ray's first conviction would have failed...and he would most likely have been executed.

Hope was that the tribunal would respond favorably to Kemper's realistic interpretation of the facts, which concluded, "The rational mind cannot conceive of a case where there is less evidence and a man is in prison for life," and frown on prosecutor Levy's trumped up interpretation for the facts.

The tone of Thompson's opinion, handed down on July 2, was set right off the bat, "We view the evidence in the light most favorable to sustaining the conviction, resolving all reasonable inferences therefrom against the defendant." This legally permissible rationalization justified Thompson's rendition of the facts of the case, which couldn't have been stated more one-sidedly by Levy himself. Not only did he parrot Levy's version, he used Levy's lingo in doing so. Instead of phrasing Ray's statements to detective Gregory neutrally, such as "the defendant stated...," Thompson used the phrases "the defendant admitted..." and "the defendant denied...," obviously designed to imply guilt. Thompson made no mention of the abundance of exculpatory DNA evidence, emphasizing rather that "the defendant could not be ruled out as a contributor to a 'mixed' substance found on Kim Ancona's bra." Thompson must have sided with Levy's bite mark experts because, while he did note that defense experts had disputed the bite mark evidence, he failed to mention that trial Judge McDougall had "serious issues...regarding the credibility...of Drs. Rawson and Piakas."

Thompson dispatched the strongest argument of the appeal, that it was improper to allow the jury to hear detective Gregory's opinion that Ray was lying about his relationship with the victim: "[it was] absent a clear abuse of discretion"; and, of course, "even assuming that the testimony was inadmissible, any error was harmless." The other issues, the victim's hearsay statements, the insufficiency of the kidnapping evidence which supported the charge of felony murder, and the permissibility of imposing consecutive rather than concurrent sentences were similarly dispatched. Thompson ended by stating the foregone conclusion, "Defendant's convictions and sentences are hereby affirmed." It was unanimous.

As I read this jaundiced decision I couldn't help feeling that a prosecutor had written it. Who was this guy Jon W. Thompson anyway? His name seemed awfully familiar to me.

A little research soon discovered that Thompson was born in 1954 in Santa Monica, California, earned a bachelor's degree from Northern Arizona University in 1975 and a law degree from the University of Colorado in 1979, was an Arizona prosecutor in Yuma and Coconino Counties from 1980 to 1988 before becoming a superior court judge and was an elder and a deacon in the Flagstaff Federated Community Church.

A prosecutor in Flagstaff—BINGO—*Arizona v. Abney*! Thompson was one and the same prosecutor who brought Abney to trial. The only evidence in that case was a mark found on the victim and his expert was none other than Dr. Ray "Walksonwater" Rawson, who of course said that the mark was made by defendant Abney's teeth. Dr. Homer Campbell testified for the defense. He said that the injury was in fact a knife wound. The jury sided with Campbell and acquitted Abney.

How could Thompson objectively consider Ray's appeal when Levy's whore had previously been Thompson's whore? Should not this obvious conflict of interest have been enough for Thompson to recuse? But he didn't and nothing could be done about it until the appellate process had run its course. Round one of the appellate battle to the Romley complex.

I would like to believe that prosecutors would leave partiality and cronyism behind when they become a judge, that they would become a cerebrally objective adjudicator of the law. But this fantasy seems to be the exception rather than the rule in the justice game.

Michael Ryan too worked nine years as a Maricopa County prosecutor before becoming a judge. The three-judge tribunal is supposed to be selected at random from the state's fifteen sitting appellate judges...I wondered...Was it simply bad luck for Ray that two of Levy's cronies had been selected to decide the first round? Be that as it may, it's human nature to not want to make a crony look bad.

Survival in the Romley complex resembles survival along the banks of the Gila River...where snakes don't bite other snakes.

Whether Thompson's failure to recuse himself was a boner under the law would have to wait to be exposed along with the presentation of any and all other newly discovered evidence during post conviction relief, as provided by Rule 32. We could not fight the post conviction relief battle until the appellate battle was over. That would take another year. James Kemper continued the fight. The next step was to appeal the appeal. In record time (within a month) Kemper filed with the Arizona Supreme Court a petition for review asking the high court to overturn the decision the court of appeals.

Whether to consider such a petition is discretionary. Arizona's high court had been Ray's only friend in the past, granting him the second trial. There was hope that it still was. But things had changed. In March 1999 Kemper received word that this time round the state's high court declined to review the appellate decision. Round two to the Romley complex.

At this point, Ray could have thrown in the towel and ended the appellate battle, but Kemper thought that allowing Kate Koester's hearsay testimony of victim Ancona's possible belief that she expected Ray *Krone* to help her close the bar the night of the murder violated the United States Constitution's Sixth Amendment, which gives the defendant the right to confront all accusers. Taking this esoteric issue to the highest court of the land was a long shot but it would cost Ray nothing except time. He could still proceed with new evidence discovery and more time could help because more genetic markers were being developed that would be able to extract more definitive results from the DNA evidence. At the end of May 1999 Kemper filed a petition for writ of certiorari with the United States Supreme Court. Such a petition asks a higher court to review the findings of a lower court. Four months later the high court exercised its discretion and also declined to hear the hearsay issue. Final round, and bout, to the Romley complex.

The clock was now ticking for the next battle to begin. Ray had thirty days to file notice that he would seek post conviction relief, which would include extensive DNA testing.

Then Kemper did a strange thing. He advised Ray to skip post conviction relief and go directly to federal habeas corpus. Kemper wrote me a letter saying, "I do not think—*based on what I know at this time*—that Ray has a chance of winning [post conviction relief]."

Personally, I couldn't disagree. Certainly Ray could not beat the Romley complex with what was known at that time. He'd tried that at the second trial.

"The [post conviction relief] process," Kemper continued, "will be very expensive, if you are going to hire a lawyer, and very, very time consuming, whether you hire one or not. The question then is what is the point of exhausting one's resources and one's time in a quixotic endeavor? There is no point." Further down in the letter he added, "To go straight to federal court without going through the state [post conviction relief] process is, I am well aware, putting your eggs in one basket. Yet sometimes putting your eggs in one basket is the wisest thing to do because it enables you to maximize your resources."

What Kemper was referring to was that by going straight to federal court, Ray would forever waive his right to have more advanced DNA testing done on the evidence in his case.

What was Kemper thinking? He knew that blood stains had been found on Ancona's panties at the last minute during the trial and had yet to be tested. Sure, there was a strong possibility that the blood belonged only to Ancona and would be of no use to Ray. But why take that chance? It was possible that it belonged to someone else and, if so, the true explanation for its presence could surmount any "co-ejaculator" theory that the Romley complex might dream up. There was also the bra sample. All that could be presented in federal court was that Ray could not be excluded from the mixture. New testing would at the very least exclude Ray from this last significant bit of unfavorable evidence.

Kemper's letter seemed suspicious to me—as if it had been written by someone in the Romley complex. Pursuing the truth is not what such organizations do. That's why important evidence sometimes goes missing or gets destroyed. Chris, however, thought that Kemper might simply have wanted to be retained to do the federal habeas corpus. Arizona certainly wasn't going to pay for Ray to go into federal court. It was a chance for Kemper to make some extra money.

Kemper remained Ray's attorney of record but he was not the one Ray or the rest of us wanted to do the post conviction relief. It was clear he had little appreciation for forensic science. In my conversations with Kemper, I had the distinct impression that science bewildered him. Ray wrote Judge McDougall asking that Kemper be replaced. McDougall did not respond. Up against the deadline and respecting his client's wishes, Kemper filed his final motion on Ray's behalf. It read:

Deputy public defender James H. Kemper advises the court that he has searched the record in this case and is unable to find a tenable issue to submit to the court in a petition for post conviction relief. He asks the court to allow Mr. Krone to proceed pro se, and to grant Mr. Krone a 30-day extension of time in which to file a petition.

The motion was granted. As Y2K approached, Ray was acting as his own attorney. He filed his petition on time. But it was virtually impossible for him to do his own post conviction relief. He was in prison. Chris couldn't do it because as his trial attorney he would have a conflict of interest. IAC (ineffective assistance of counsel) is always an issue raised in post conviction relief. An attorney cannot be expected to objectively raise IAC issues against himself.

After New Year's Day, Ray wrote a second letter:

Dear Judge McDougall,

Some months have passed since I last wrote asking you to please appoint me a new attorney for my Rule 32 [post conviction relief] …Because of my indigence, I have no way of undertaking this task. I have absolutely no ability to represent myself as Mr. Kemper recommended when he requested to be withdrawn as my counsel. Besides the inability to conduct any investigations, there isn't even a law library here where I could, at least, research case law…I need an independent legal counsel to review my issues. I need help, Your Honor. As you may recall, there was biological evidence uncovered for the first time during the trial. No DNA testing has ever been done on that sample. You may recall that with the exception of one DNA sample of mixed origin, all other DNA excluded me. That mixed DNA sample was cited by the prosecutor as evidence of guilt and you yourself listed it as such in your special verdict. New DNA tests are now available that can clear me completely as any donor of that sample. I did not kill Kim Ancona, I was not there! I have complete faith that there will not be any of my DNA present. I've spent 8 long years in prison so far while trying to correct this miscarriage of justice. I can do little without reasonable legal representation. I am begging you to please appoint me new counsel so that we can pursue legitimate Rule 32 issues. Thank you for your time and consideration.

Respectfully, Ray M. Krone

π

Well, that's the justice game as I observed it while trying to help cousin Ray. It's an adversarial contest in which the hometown team owns the ball and the field and gets to play going downhill with seemingly unlimited resources, in a game refereed by intimidated officials—mostly home team cronies—before a hometown crowd.

I had believed that, as advertised, a defendant was presumed innocent until proven guilty beyond a reasonable doubt, and that prosecutors had the burden of proof to prove otherwise. But nothing is further from the truth. It's clear to me why lady justice is blindfolded—so that she can't see just how woefully out of balance the scales are that she's holding.

Mark Twain put it aptly:

The jury system puts a ban upon intelligence and honesty, and a premium upon ignorance, stupidity and perjury.

Little had changed in the century and a half that began with that observation in *Roughing It* and ended with cousin Ray a krone roughing it.

How were we ever going to beat Boss Romley? I pessimistically wondered. The catch-22 for Ray to escape the banks of the Gila was that *he* had the burden of proof, not simply to prove his own innocence beyond a reasonable doubt, but also to find out who actually killed Kim Ancona and to prove it beyond *all* doubt. So far, all efforts to discover a cerebral cortex in the Romley complex had failed. A new direction was needed. Chris Plourd knew the way...

PART THREE
JANGLE JINGLE

We must find out who killed Kim Ancona and shove it up their ass with a hot poker.

– Christopher J. Plourd

CHAPTER 23
UNTIL TOMORROW

A fter Ray Krone was granted a second trial, he wanted to stay on Death Row until it began. He knew what the county jail was like and preferred The Big House. But that wasn't possible. He was returned to the Madison Street jail in mid-summer 1995.

The trip from Florence to Phoenix wasn't pleasant. Because he was charged with murder he rode in the back of the bus in a separate compartment reserved for violent offenders. The air conditioner was at the front of the bus and useless to the back, especially in Ray's cubicle. It was barely bearable so long as the bus was moving. Ray was able to crack the window enough for the outside air to circulate. When the bus stopped it quickly became an inferno.

One stop lasted longer than usual. After a half-hour Ray was sweating profusely. His shirt and Levis were thoroughly soaked. Ray is not a complainer but this heat was serious. He began to fear for his life. He became dizzy and was on the verge of passing out. He started screaming and banging on the side of the bus. Finally the guard let him out. Stepping into the 113-degree heat, he felt cool. He was allowed to ride up front for the rest of the trip. Nevertheless, he arrived for his first pre-trial hearing a bit worse for the wear.

It would be a miracle for any Maricopa County judge to grant bail to someone charged with murder. All the same, Chris Plourd made the attempt, taking the opportunity to introduce Ray's case to Judge James McDougall and noting the exculpatory DNA evidence and the fact that four board-certified bite mark experts would dispute the state's only incriminating evidence. Predictably bail was denied and Ray resigned himself to endure Sheriff Joe Arpaio's hospitality once again.

A year and a half later (ten months awaiting trial, two months in trial and six months to be sentenced) Ray returned to Florence. It was the first time since he'd left Death Row that he was able to see the sun shine. It was mid-winter and he enjoyed the ride, happy, to say the least, to be rid of Maricopa County jail, where he always had to be on his toes. Unlike prison, jail inmates change frequently and many are neophytes who have yet to learn the discipline necessary to survive long-term incarceration. Back "home," Ray this time would not be isolated on Death Row and would have to make the adjustment to a maximum security prison yard. He would have to deal with Arizona's baddest of the bad.

The first prison in Arizona, Yuma Territorial Prison, was built in 1876, initially housing the seven convicts who built it. In all it confined three thousand, sixty-nine prisoners, including twenty-nine women until it was abandoned in 1909. No one was executed there, but one hundred eleven persons died while serving time, mostly from tuberculosis, a widespread ailment in the wild desert southwest. The most commonly punished crime at Yuma was grand larceny but the territorial prison housed offenders from innocuous polygamists to dangerous murderers. There were twenty-six successful escapes.

To flee overcrowded, deteriorating facilities, Arizona built a new prison centrally located fifty-five miles southeast of the soon-to-be-state's intended capital, Phoenix. The state prison unofficially became known as "The Walls" and served as Arizona's only prison for sixty-nine years. A second cellblock, CB-2, was opened in 1930. The Walls eventually grew to accommodate six cellblocks.

Then, with the legislation of mandatory sentencing in 1978, Arizona's prison population exploded. In the decade prior to 1978, the number of prisoners merely doubled from 1,675 to 3,211. But in the next decade it increased fourfold, to 12,167. The Arizona Department of Corrections (ADOC) responded by opening seven new prisons in almost as many years. The seventh opened in Yuma in 1986. Today, sixteen Arizona prisons hold more than thirty thousand inmates.

The ADOC classifies inmates in two ways, the first by their behavior inside prison and the second by the felony for which they were convicted. The scale for both is one to five. Within each prison, inmates are separated based upon their paired classification. Ray was worst case, a five-five. He could do nothing about the second five, the classification for murder. In time, with good behavior, he could reduce the first number and be transferred to a lower-security yard.

Ray entered the maximum security of The Walls on January 25, 1997 to continue serving his twenty-five years-to-life sentence.

Cellblocks One and Three were for hard-core prisoners requiring special management. Four was for sexual offenders, segregated for their own protection. Rapists and especially pedophiles are treated harshly by other inmates. Ray was lucky he was acquitted of rape and for his own good he never mentioned that he'd been charged with it. Cellblocks Five and Seven were the workers' pods. Cellblock Six was Death Row, separate and independent from The Walls. Cellblock Two housed new arrivals waiting to be classified and those who didn't fit anywhere else. Inmates within a cellblock dined together and took recreation together, in isolation from the other cellblocks.

Ray's new home, CB-2, was your classic Hollywood prison and has appeared in several movies. "Stir Crazy" was one, with Gene Wilder strutting down the cellblock and Richard Pryor boasting, "I'm, bad! I'm bad!" "Raising Arizona" with Nicholas Cage and Holly Hunter was another. The prison yard is about the size of a football field but more of a square. It's enclosed by old stone walls thirty feet high, which give the whole prison its nickname. There's a guard tower at each corner and a walkway atop each wall, from which armed guards patrol the yard below.

Ray called CB-2 "a dungeon type cellblock." His "house" had double-thick stone walls on three sides. He could easily touch the side walls simultaneously with outstretched arms. A narrow bunk butted up against one of them. There was a sink in the back corner, adjacent to a toilet. Sitting on the commode, Ray could rest his feet on the bed. When he stood up he was half-way to his front door. It was just two steps from the commode to the bars.

The cellblock consisted of three tiers of two parallel, facing rows of cells, forty feet apart. There were no windows to see outside. Ray's only view was through his front door into the opposite cells. There was no privacy at any time—not even while on the commode.

In the summer Ray would soak his shirt and boxer shorts, remove the sheets and sleep directly on the vinyl-covered mattress. The heat was miserable from July through September. The ancient swamp coolers were worthless and added unneeded humidity. In the winter Ray slept in his sweat clothes under a single blanket. He was allowed a TV, a small radio and writing materials. Only his legal papers were off-limits to periodic unannounced searches, protected by law.

It was hard time, but Ray was allowed out of his cell three times a day for meals. He enjoyed the walk to and from chow hall. He was a non-smoker before entering prison, but took up the habit. He smoked only in his cell or outside in the yard and appreciated that smoking was prohibited during meals.

He was allowed into the prison yard three times a week. It was the largest area that he'd been free to roam since his arrest five years earlier, and he relished it. On Death Row he had been able to work out his upper body by curling books and doing pushups. But his lower body suffered. He couldn't remember walking more than one hundred feet at a time before he reached The Walls. He'd been allowed exercise on Death Row but was isolated in a caged area about half the size of a basketball court.

He remembers that upon entering the yard for the first time he had to readjust to distance focusing. His eyesight had deteriorated. He didn't know whether it was from his incarceration or his advanced age.

At first he could barely make it twice around the yard running and walking. But before long he was able to jog six times around without stopping. In summer he could take off his shirt and take in the rays. He no longer needed vitamin-D supplements. He could play volleyball, softball and basketball and toss (rubber) horseshoes.

It was the first time at Florence that Ray came in direct contact with other inmates. Isolated on Death Row he'd never been tested. Nevertheless, he'd learned by osmosis what it was like being in a general prison population. Each new arrival is initiated. The weak are badly abused. Ray knew that he must stand tall and be strong at all times in order to survive. You never back down from a fight. "Bring it on. Do me a favor. Kill me!" was Ray's approach to hostile encounters. He was somewhat lucky, though, in that he had arrived at The Walls with some clout. Word spread rapidly that he'd done time on Death Row. Nevertheless he had to establish a reputation.

During one of Ray's first times in the yard, a guard who knew Ray from Death Row approached him in a friendly manner within in earshot of other inmates. Ray lit into the guard and cussed him up one side and down the other. Stunned, the guard took Ray off the yard to a private detention room. Ray knew that what a guard might do to him paled in comparison with what would happen to him at the hands of fellow inmates who thought he was sociable with a guard.

Before the guard could get in word one, Ray told him, "Why did you put me in that position? You know we can't be friends!"

He then elaborated on the potential danger the guard had put him in by appearing chummy. The guard softened almost to the point of an apology and the two acquaintances chatted for awhile, mostly about what had happened during Ray's absence. The guard may simply have been surprised to see Ray after knowing him on Death Row and learning that he'd been given a second trial. The convicts who witnessed the encounter between Ray and the guard were impressed to see Ray reappear in the yard before the recreation period was over.

Fighting is a fact of prison life. Ray knew when he could talk his way out and when he couldn't. When confronted one-on-one in the yard he didn't spend much time arguing, he started swinging. Certain keywords, like "punk," started immediate fisticuffs. While Ray had his share of black eyes and bloody noses over the years, his 6'2" height, his intelligence and his reputation kept skirmishes to a minimum.

Ray would watch newcomers being initiated and on occasion take it upon himself to offer survival training to the ones who floundered. In particular need of instruction were those who didn't understand the racial nature of prison. On the outside, they may have had interracial friends, but on the inside, if they attempted to intermingle they were invariably beaten back. In prison blacks stick with blacks, whites with whites, Mexicans with Mexicans, etc. There's strength in numbers. Ray estimated that the general prison population was half white, a quarter Hispanic, twenty percent black, and the rest Asian and American Indian. Of necessity Ray joined the appropriate group but remained on the fringes as much as possible.

Problems within your own group are easily handled. You assemble several others experiencing the same problem and confront the offender. Going one on one with your own kind, however trivial the dispute, means getting into a fight. And you really don't want to confront a member of another race directly or his whole group will be down on your ass in no time. Protocol is different for interracial disputes. First you go to the leaders of your group, who then take the matter to the leaders of the offender's group, and then you hope that there's a meeting of the minds. If not and the problem cannot be tolerated or ignored a major confrontation erupts.

Such confrontations require a "shank." Shanks are makeshift weapons fashioned from any material that can be made sharp enough to cut or stab. Glass was hard to find because the ADOC didn't allow it inside The Walls. Plastic from pens and cassette cases could be melted down, poured into a magazine cover rolled into the shape of a cone and then further sharpened when dry. The most common shank and easiest to make was a toothbrush broken off at the end and sharpened in a pencil sharpener. Shanks are prized possessions and a good one is always available when needed.

Ray told me matter-of-factly that one time he was stabbed in the back just below the shoulder with a pencil. The lead broke off and the wound festered and refused to heal. Because of its location he needed a fellow inmate's help to lance the wound and remove the lead. Inmates attended to such injuries themselves whenever possible. Medical attention was marginal at best. Going to the infirmary attracted too much attention and required a report. The few times Ray did have to see the prison doctor, he said he'd fallen in the shower. The official taking Ray's report knew that he'd been in a fight but also knew that Ray wasn't going to fink on his assailant. On the record, "shower fall" was the euphemism for "fight."

One time Ray legitimately broke his arm playing softball. An opponent body blocked him while sliding into second base and Ray fell on his arm. He had to wait three days to be X-rayed. A cast was applied and the arm healed okay. Serious cases like drug overdoses and major shank wounds were taken to the downtown Florence hospital. Ray once saw an inmate helicoptered out. Dental care was virtually nonexistent. There was no periodic prophylaxis. A tooth aching for any reason was simply extracted.

The first major confrontation Ray witnessed at The Walls took place in the chow hall. He sensed that something was in the air because there wasn't the usual chatter. It was like the calm before the storm. As he sat down with his tray someone said, "Watch your back. Something's going down." Ray ate hurriedly then watched and waited. His group sat at the tables along one wall, the Mexicans at the middle tables and the blacks along the far wall. A white inmate set his tray down and walked to the alcove where the juice and milk dispensers were located. He took something out of one of the machines. Ray though it might have been a shank left there by a confederate.

Instead of returning to his seat the white guy walked over to one of the blacks' tables and said something to one of them. The black dude stood up immediately, followed by the rest of the table. The whites cleared their benches and about twenty or so who knew what was up rushed the blacks. The mêlée was on. Ray followed his group but didn't throw any punches. He picked up two of his comrades who had been knocked down in the brawl. The guards in the chow hall disappeared. Tear gas came in from the guard tower in the corner. When Ray heard shots over his head he moved to the side out of the line of fire. In the yard, guards were allowed to shoot to kill if a weapon was involved in a fight. But in the mess hall, because of the threat of ricochet, wooden bullets were used.

The guards reappeared, reinforced and decked out with face masks and shields, wielding batons and firing pepper spray. Guards never carried guns when in with inmates for fear they might be wrestled away. Calm was restored without any fatalities. The black dude ended up being the one most severely beaten. One participant suffered a broken ankle from being hit by a wooden bullet.

Ray spent the rest of the afternoon lying face down on the grass in the yard along with other participants. The bloodied and battered were taken away first. Ray didn't get back to his cell for four hours. He and several others suffered severe sunburn that hot May day.

Whites seen running from the chow hall when the fight began later received for their cowardice a beating from their own kind.

The fracas had been over a fan at the end of the cellblock. The black dude would point it toward his and some of his fellow black inmates' cells whenever he passed it. The white guy (the one who initiated the fight) would move the fan to its original position when he passed it on his way to work detail. The white leaders approached the black leaders and told them to leave the fan alone. The warning was ignored and the white guy was told to take care of the situation and assured that he would have back up.

π

Ray settled into The Walls. Except for an occasional skirmish here and there, each day was pretty much the same as the one before.

On the outside, public defender James Kemper had been assigned to his case and Ray's appeal was progressing. It was out of the question to do new evidence discovery, a Rule 32, simultaneously with the appeal as had been done after Ray's first conviction. Ray and his family were not only out of money but were in significant debt from the second trial. Because Ray was destitute the state funded his appeal.

Like the rest of us, Ray was curious about the unanalyzed blood discovered on the victim's clothing during the second trial. He wondered whether the Innocence Project might take an interest in his case. The project takes cases pro bono where DNA evidence can show definitive proof of innocence. So Ray in his copious free time took it upon himself to apply.

Six months after entering The Walls, Ray received a response. "We only take cases where DNA testing can provide dispositive proof of innocence. In your case, because the testing has already been conducted (and Dr. [Ed] Blake is generally the expert we use), there is nothing that additional DNA testing will show that has not already been considered by the courts." I wondered whether the DNA found on Ancona's bra contributed to the decision. Dr. Blake was likely consulted by the Innocence Project in considering Ray's application. Blake had been dropped as a defense witness because he had the same "not excluded" opinion as state witness Dr. Moses Schanfield.

Privately Schanfield believed that the DNA was without a doubt Ray Krone's. I learned this fact firsthand. Prior to Ray's second trial I'd attended two meetings of the American Academy of Forensic Sciences. After his conviction I continued to attend, accompanying Chris to lobby members of the odontology section on Ray's behalf. We had hoped that Doctors Rawson and Piakas would be sanctioned by their peers. They weren't.

Nevertheless, hanging around with Chris at these meetings afforded me the opportunity to rub elbows with some heavyweight forensic scientists. One evening in Seattle, after a day attending forensic seminars, I sat down to dinner with Chris and a half-dozen or so well respected forensic experts. Dr. Michael Baden was there. He's a forensic pathologist of legendary proportions, the star of Home Box Office's *Autopsy* show, which takes the audience through murder cases in which Baden's expertise solved the crime.

By chance none other than Dr. Moses Schanfield sat down in the chair next to mine. Not recognizing me, he introduced himself and asked my forensic expertise. I told him that I was interested in bite marks. I said I was Ray Krone's cousin, there with Chris working on Ray's case. He was taken back and wanted to know why I was wasting my time since Ray's DNA was on the victim's bra. Chris abruptly but politely interrupted and changed the subject before I could mention that Dr. Blake was on call to rerun the telltale sample when more DNA markers became available. More markers would yield more definitive results that could positively exclude Ray from the bra sample.

I sat quietly the rest of the evening listening to the table talk and enjoying dinner. There was no way Ray's DNA could be on Ancona's bra, I thought. Maybe, when Blake proved Schanfield wrong, Ray's application to the Innocence Project would be reconsidered. For the time being, however, they declined to tackle Ray's case, no doubt believing that discovering DNA of unknown origin would have little effect so long as Ray was linked to DNA found on the bra.

π

Inmates were evaluated every six months. Even if there were no incident reports on an inmate's record it usually took several evaluations to lower a classification. At his first reclassification hearing, Ray was quick to point out that although he'd been at The Walls for only six months, he'd been on Death Row for nearly three years without incident. The officer was impressed, checked Ray's background and found him a job as an ice porter.

It was a good job and Ray liked it. It got him out of his cell an extra four hours each evening. It also gave him extra spending money, but money was the least of Ray's worries in prison. His mother saw to it that Ray's prison bank account always had sufficient funds.

Ray would have dinner during the first shift and then sit by the ice machines outside the chow hall and distribute bags of ice to inmates to take back to their cells. Each inmate was allowed three bags per week. Ice tickets were purchased through the commissary. Ray would exchange one bag of ice for each ticket. It was easy work and great to be outside at that time of day.

Because every inmate passed the ice machines, Ray inevitably became an informal postal service between the cellblocks "Here, give this to so-and-so," Ray would be instructed as someone attempted to hand him something surreptitiously. Usually it was a note scribbled on a scrap of paper but it could be another small item such as cigarettes. Ray avoided passing items between prisoners as much as possible. Getting caught would mean losing his job. But sometimes, to keep on good terms, he would accommodate hard-core prisoners who had significant influence with an illegal exchange. On occasion he would even sneak them a bag of ice.

When the guard was collecting tickets, there was not much Ray could do but pass out ice. When the guard was distracted, usually by the nearby phone, Ray would collect the tickets and pass out the ice. It was then he could make an illegal exchange or schmoose a "friend" with a free bag of ice. Upon the guard's return, Ray would hand in the tickets and the guard would be none the wiser.

On one occasion a black inmate handed Ray a ticket and picked up a bag of ice. Noticing the guard turn away to answer the phone, he snatched the ticket back. The guard turned around to see him walking across the yard with a bag of ice and asked Ray for the ticket. Ray didn't want to fink on the guy but he didn't have a ticket to give the officer either. He did the only thing he could do in that circumstance. "He didn't give me one." The guard got on the phone and told his counterpart at the other end of the yard to stop the inmate and get an ice ticket. "I gave it to Ray," said the inmate. It went round and round but no ticket was produced. Ray and the inmate were escorted to detention. Ray was vindicated and released after both were strip-searched. The ticket turned up on the other guy.

The next day Ray was called into the captain's office and asked if he wanted protection. The black inmate had made threats that he was going to kill Ray. Ray declined, telling the captain that he could take care of himself. Accepting protection from prison officials was a sure way to a fight with your fellow inmates.

The black inmate continued to say that Ray had snitched him off to the guards. Being thought a jailhouse snitch is the worst rap and is dealt with severely. Ray went to the leaders of the whites and explained what had happened. Word went out that the whites were backing Ray. It was a tense situation for about two weeks. Ray waited anxiously, expecting the inmate to attack him with a shank. But Ray got lucky. Before the inmate could make his move, he assaulted a guard and was taken off to SMU (Special Management Unit), a cellblock where violent inmates are isolated in a way similar to Death Row inmates. The inmate was not heard from again.

Ray lost his job over the incident. But he avoided having a ding put on his prison record.

At The Walls, there was one job for every three inmates. Having a job was a privilege. Ray had been moved to CB-5, the workers pod. The cellblock was newer and the cells much nicer. It was more lenient and the workers were treated a little better. They were able to shower everyday as opposed to three times a week. Ray liked it. He didn't want to go back to CB-2 and wasted no time finding another job.

Ray next worked in the law library. It was an opportune job because some of the inmates who used the library were quite knowledgeable and he learned a great deal about the law. He in turn was able to help those who knew less than he.

Communication was through a wire screen that separated the inmates in the study room from Ray and the shelved books. Books and materials were passed back and forth one way at a time through a secure chute. Ray had access to a copy machine and could make copies for the inmates. All copies were supposed to be pre-approved by a guard. But Ray was not above bending the rules now and then and he was smart enough get away with it. It benefited him not to piss off the wrong inmate, so on occasion he would make unauthorized copies.

Requests took the form of "Take a look at page 85" accompanied with a nod or a wink as a book was passed through the chute. Copies were returned the same way. One time a tenderfoot asked Ray to make a copy of something within earshot of a guard. Ray loudly declined and chastised the inmate for the guard's benefit. Later in the week the guy attacked Ray in the yard, cutting him superficially in the side with a shank. Ray responded accordingly. The new guy learned the hard way how prison worked. He didn't bother Ray again.

The library job in time ended too because not all inmates were as cool as Ray. Ray continued to be a covert prison postman. He was given an ice ticket from a guy in one cellblock to deliver to a guy in another. The ticket was passed smoothly through the chute. Ray cringed as the recipient carelessly pulled the ticket out of the book and put it in his pocket. A guard saw it too.

"Give me the ice ticket," demands the guard.

"I don't have a ticket," lies the inmate.

"I know you do and I'll search you if I have to!"

"Oh, you mean this ticket," says the inmate as he pulls it out of his pocket. Then he sticks it in his mouth, chews it up and swallows it.

This messes the guard up because now he doesn't have the ticket. Of course, he's going to win the dispute whether there was a ticket or not, and after he takes care of the inmate he goes up to Ray.

"Who gave you the ticket?"

Ray isn't about to snitch off an inmate and says, "I don't know what you're talking about."

"Yes, you do and you'd better tell me."

Well, Ray didn't tell and was sent back to his cell. Jobless.

A week later the job control officer needed a clerk in the commissary. Ray was offered the job and was surprised because technically he wasn't allowed to work while disciplinary action was pending. For the first week every time the phone rang, Ray thought he was going to be yanked. Somehow he skated.

Inmates were not allowed in the commissary. To shop, an imnate filled out an order form. Ray would pull the ordered items off the shelves and bag them. After the manager, an outside contractor, rang up the order Ray would staple the bag shut and deliver it to the inmate's cellblock.

Other store clerks would steal items, mostly toiletries, off the shelves for their buddies and drop them into their bag before it was stapled closed. They would put larger items like radios and sweatshirts into the trash cans to be retrieved by a cohort at the dumpster end. Ray did not participate in this pilfering, nor did he fink on those who did. The "kids," as he called them, offered to pay him a percentage of the take. Ray wanted to keep the job. He declined and warned the kids to stand tall and take the rap if their thieving were discovered.

In time the lady who managed the store came to trust Ray and gave him a job in the back room doing the accounting. It was his responsibility to see that the inmates had enough money on the books to make purchases. Also he would etch the inmates' ADOC number onto purchased items like radios and TVs.

This job lasted three months. The manager learned that two tubes of a hair gel she had ordered specially for the black inmates were missing out of a freshly opened case. She had Ray look back through a month of receipts to see if the hair gel had been purchased. It hadn't and Ray couldn't fake it. He and all the clerks were called on the carpet. The thief did not fess up and all were fired.

"The guy [who took the gel] got taken care of," Ray assured me.

Ray was next told to go work in the mess hall. He initially declined. Sixty to seventy inmates worked the kitchen, creating unavoidable racial tension. The workers were rude to each other. It was hot, sweaty, dirty work. You had to start at four in the morning to get ready for the eight o'clock breakfast, or work until eight o'clock in the evening cleaning up. Anyone could get a job in the kitchen. It was "a real fucking ball buster," as Ray put it.

Told that if he refused the job he wouldn't be able to get work for six months, Ray acquiesced. He was a fast learner and wasn't lazy. When not busy Ray would help other workers do their jobs. Soon he advanced to the easier position of storeroom clerk. It was a job that required tact to keep both management and inmates happy. The feeding of inmates was contracted to an outside company. Ray saw to it that the chow hall was profitable.

To keep fellow inmates happy Ray had to turn his back. If he were in the storeroom and unauthorized inmates came in, he wouldn't tell them that they couldn't be in there. He'd leave. He didn't want to know what they were doing.

Ray didn't get involved with drugs. He didn't think many drugs got in during contact visits. Too risky. When I visited Ray, I was required to stand in front of a chicken wire fence while trained drug sniffing dogs were brought up behind me. If caught smuggling drugs, you faced five to seven years in prison. The most likely source was prison workers. Outside contractors who worked in the kitchen and in the commissary made eight to twelve dollars per hour. They had direct contact with inmates. There was big money to be made selling dope to prisoners. Dishonest guards too could make big bucks.

Ray knew when drugs were around. The sound of inmates barfing in their cells indicated that a bag of heroin had hit the yard. Needles were scarce and had to be shared. Ray knew that sharing needles was a good way to contract a blood-transmitted disease. Sixty percent of the prison population had hepatitis C. Other ways to become infected included being stabbed during a fight by a shank that had already stabbed someone else and by engaging in sex acts.

Ray kept this job as kitchen storeroom clerk until he was moved to the Santa Rita unit of the Tucson prison complex in September 1999. Of his transfer Ray said: "They finally got my classification right. I skipped [having to do time in] a four yard and was moved to a [medium security] three yard. It was more laid back—not super easy, not quite as political, not quite as dangerous [as The Walls]. People still got beat up and the sex stuff was still going on but not as much."

In my talks with Ray he was candid and detailed about all aspects of prison life except sex. If he mentioned it at all it was in passing and on a superficial level and I didn't ask about it. It's common knowledge that rape is not an uncommon occurrence in prison. Even though I visited Ray many times, I still had only an inkling of what it must truly be like inside such a haunted, frightening place. I often wondered what accommodations Ray had to make to survive.

Ray arrived at Santa Rita late one Friday afternoon and was surprised and delighted to see inmates still walking freely about the yard. Some were even driving golf carts. They weren't playing golf but doing their jobs, making deliveries between cellblocks. It was a welcome change from The Walls. Entering a new yard, Ray knew that he must reestablish his reputation. It turned out to be simple because several inmates at Santa Rita knew Ray from The Walls and word spread quickly.

Sporting activities were more organized. There were softball leagues and regular weekend tournaments between cellblocks on the "big" (regulation) field. Teams were required to be integrated to keep racial conflict to a minimum.

Compared with what he had been through so far, Santa Rita was like Disneyland. The majority of the inmates were short timers cruisin' to finish their sentence and be released.

Ray was assigned to a working yard where eight hundred fifty of the nine hundred inmates had jobs. He interviewed for and was immediately offered a position as work coordinator reporting to the job control officer. It was a great job with much clout. Anyone who wanted a good job had to brown nose Ray. He worked eight hours a day in an air-conditioned office. He was even able to use computers because he knew more about them than his boss did.

The most common way to lose a job was to fail a drug test. That was of no concern to Ray. Another possibility was to be drawn into an altercation and be put on report. Ray stayed out of trouble and held onto this job.

Even though he had to put up with a cellmate, life was much better here. When his cell door opened in the morning he strolled directly out into the yard, went to chow when it was time for his cellblock, then went to work. He would always finish what he needed to do for the day in about two hours, then with his boss's permission went outside into the yard for a cigarette. On nice spring days, he would frequently help others with their work just to stay outside longer. Ray's boss cut

Ray slack because Ray's skills and work ethic made the boss's life easier.

Ray was paid a whopping fifty cents per hour, the highest prison wage possible. It didn't take much money to live in prison and when Ray had a good job he always had more than enough money saved for Christmas. Then he would spend two to three hundred dollars at the commissary when an assortment of holiday items were added to its shelves. Ray would always share his Christmas cheer with less fortunate inmates.

Santa Rita was the best place in which Ray had done time so far and he hoped he could do the rest of his time there. But it was not to be. Gradually each of Santa Rita's four yards became overrun with Hispanics. Half were US citizens and half were illegal Mexican nationals. They formed gangs and fought amongst themselves. Ray watched one of their brawls break out in his yard. The whites and blacks moved out of the way and watched the gangs go at it. When it was over many lay motionless on the turf. A few were dead.

To manage the growing problem and because there was a Mexican consulate in Tucson, the ADOC closed Santa Rita to non-Hispanics. In October 2001, Ray and thirty others were put on the last bus to Yuma State Prison, where there had recently been a major race riot. Ray heard that it had been "a well-planned, all-out war." Several blacks had been killed and many badly injured. Most of the survivors had been moved to various other prison complexes with maximum security yards, thus creating vacancies for the Santa Rita exiles.

The entire Yuma unit was under lockdown when Ray arrived. He could not leave his quarters for six weeks. His new "house" was in a barrack type building that was little more than a wide hallway in which thirty guys lived dormitory style. Half resided along one wall facing the other half. Ray was given a space to call his own that was smaller than his Death Row cell. Two feet away from the side of his bed he had a small table and a waist-high shelving unit with a small cabinet to lock up personal items. His bed butted up against the back of the table and shelving of the inmate next to him. He was allowed his own TV and radio and was permitted to listen to them through headphones only. The residents shared three commodes, three sinks, and two showers. It was unpleasant to say the least. Not everyone shared Ray's attitude toward hygiene. To pass the time Ray continually played card and board games. The constant racial tension made it difficult to relax. When lockdown ended and Ray was allowed to go outside, he found the prison yard nothing like Santa Rita's.

Because it was an administrative transfer, Ray was supposed to be given an equivalent position. But not that many jobs were available at Yuma and Ray soon found out that "Yuma followed half of the ADOC rules half the time. It was the worst organized and most poorly administrated prison I'd been in."

He was given busywork raking rocks all day long, everyday, over and over again for fifteen cents per hour. He signed up for a carpentry class so that he would only be on rake rock detail half the day. He took high school over again because his diploma had been lost in the shuffle and the Yuma officials didn't care that he'd already taken college courses on Death Row, at The Walls and at Santa Rita. The instructor wondered why Ray was in his class. For Ray, going back to high school was better than vegetating.

Ray thought the original Yuma Territorial Prison must have been hell on earth if it were worse that the new Yuma prison outpost. Yuma was miserable. The brick barracks were unbearably hot in the summertime. The work was hot, dirty and demeaning. Sharing facilities with twenty-nine others was less than sanitary. Privacy did not exist. Racial tension was everpresent.

Because he was in for murder he could never go below a three classification for behavior and Yuma was a class three medium security yard. Ray dreaded the prospect that he would be there a long long time, conceivably having to serve out the rest of his sentence.

Ray adjusted to the tense routine of his new digs as best he could. Having a routine is requisite for survival in prison. It makes time pass quickly. Time is the one thing all inmates have in common. For some it's all they have.

It had taken five years for the appeals process to run its gamut. Ray's fate now lay in the Rule 32 process, which would hopefully uncover some significant new evidence. Arizona had paid for Ray's appeal. It would not pay for a new evidence discovery proceeding. Although not fully recovered from the huge expense of the second trial, Ray's family rallied to see that his Rule 32 was funded. A private investigator recommended by Chris had been hired and a Phoenix attorney recommended by the investigator had been retained. Dr. Ed Blake was given the go-ahead to retest the bra sample DNA. A positive exclusion would be a huge plus, especially if it pointed to someone else. But that fact in and of itself most likely would not be enough to skate past a hometown, reptilian-concocted, unindicted co-ejaculatory theory that would no doubt be forthcoming from the Romley complex.

But if the actual perpetrator of the crime could be identified...

π

Helplessly fenced from fighting his own battles, Ray was not without hope because his family and friends had not given up. He was determined to survive. His habit each evening before retiring to his cramped cubical was to gaze out a bar-studded window, watch the hot sun end its mad dance across the sky and let another done day disappear through smoke rings circling above as cigarette induced reverie once again numbed his senses. Ray no longer remembered the last dart vanishing from his hand, hitting the wire surrounding the bull's eye and falling foul to the floor to lose the game—he'd been distracted by the image of a detective waiting outside the bar to strip away his freedom and cast him into a more serious game.

He's more weary from his nine-year ordeal than sleepy from another day's grind. He has no place to go, no one to meet. Ray stands frozen in time framed in the barrack's window, staring blindly across the sun long after it has set. He's unable to feel his hands gripping the bars or his toes waiting for his boot heels to go wandering somewhere, anywhere—to fade back into his own parade, into the ordinary life he lived before twisted fate cast him into this place of crazy sorrow.

The evenings when he ruled Phoenix's dart empire are ancient history now, obscured by foggy ruins of time too dead for dreaming. Ray avoids sleep to evade the inevitable recurring nightmare in which he is a ragged clown dragged relentlessly round and round by a reptilian ringmaster through the circus sands of justice.

He wonders if he will ever again see a sky unobstructed by barbed wire fences and he fantasizes escaping on the run, chasing his shadow all the way to Rocky Point, a Mexican beach on the Gulf of California, a mere one hundred miles away as the crow flies. It was there, camping out under a diamond sky with his girlfriend and Air Force buddies, that Ray had last been able to dance silhouetted by the sea hands waving free. If on some magic swirling ship he were able to escape the circus sands of his nightmare and return to this windy beach, he would dance, one hand waving free, until all memory and fate of having once been branded a cold-blooded killer were buried deep beneath the waves.

Ray forgets about today and wonders if tomorrow will bring the morning he will hear the sweet jingle jangle sound of keys approaching to set him free.

The barrack grows quiet except for the squeaking of an overworked swamp cooler. And no one pays it any mind as it resonates like a tambourine keeping time to vague traces of Dylan's skipping reels of rhyme…

Hey! Mister Tambourine Man, play a song for me,
I'm not sleepy and there is no place I'm going to.
Hey! Mister Tambourine Man, play a song for me,
In the jingle jangle morning I'll come followin' you.

Though I know that evenin's empire has returned into
sand,
Vanished from my hand,
Left me blindly here to stand but still not sleeping.
My weariness amazes me, I'm branded on my feet,
I have no one to meet
And the ancient empty street's too dead for dreaming.

Take me on a trip upon your magic swirlin' ship,
My senses have been stripped, my hands can't feel to grip,
My toes too numb to step, wait only for my boot heels
To be wanderin'.
I'm ready to go anywhere, I'm ready for to fade
Into my own parade, cast your dancing spell my way,
I promise to go under it.

Though you might hear laughin', spinnin', swingin' madly
across the sun,
It's not aimed at anyone, it's just escapin' on the run
And but for the sky there are no fences facin'.
And if you hear vague traces of skippin' reels of rhyme
To your tambourine in time, it's just a ragged clown
behind,
I wouldn't pay it any mind, it's just a shadow you're
Seein' that he's chasing.

Then take me disappearin' through the smoke rings of my
mind,
Down the foggy ruins of time, far past the frozen leaves,
The haunted, frightened trees, out to the windy beach,
Far from the twisted reach of crazy sorrow.
Yes, to dance beneath the diamond sky with one hand
waving free,
Silhouetted by the sea, circled by the circus sands,
With all memory and fate driven deep beneath the waves,
Let me forget about today until tomorrow.

CHAPTER 24
"BURY IT!"

hris thought that Svengali had done such a great job digging into a child murder case that he was the man to hire to investigate Ray's case now that the appeal was over and it was time to proceed with post conviction relief provided by Rule 32, the discovery of new evidence.

Chris met Svengali while he was defending the 21-year-old boyfriend of the murdered child's 18-year-old mother. Shortly after the mother left her 18-month-old baby boy in the hands of the boyfriend, the baby died. The autopsy showed that the cause of death was severe trauma consistent with shaken baby syndrome. The boyfriend was charged with first-degree murder based upon the medical opinion that the injuries had occurred at the time the child was in his care. He was head over heels in love with the young mother and had recently moved in with her and her child. He worked as a guard in the county jail. His dad was a deputy sheriff who knew Svengali when Svengali was a patrol officer for the San Diego sheriff's department. Svengali had since earned a doctoral degree in human behavior and had changed careers to become an expert witness consultant and private investigator. The dad asked his old friend to look into his son's case.

Svengali soon discovered that the young mother had a history of child abuse that predated her involvement with the defendant. She wrote love letters to her boyfriend in jail. Svengali believed she was stroking him to cover up for her and take the rap. The boyfriend said he'd heard the mother in the child's bedroom yelling and screaming at her little boy just before she left them alone together in their apartment. Because he was madly in love he at first would not believe that the mother had caused her child's death. He believed the babysitter had shaken the baby. Soon Svengali convinced the boyfriend that he was being played for a sucker. The boyfriend eventually turned on the mother, causing her to write:

Well...

Yes. I kill my baby. So what the fuck are you going to do about it. You fucked up when you turned on me you son of bitch. My Atorney already told me about you and that you *are* blaming me. He also told me that I have the Police and the atorneys on *my* side. So huh!…Im the smart one and your the stupid one. I can get away with murder. So what are you fucking going to do about it? *Nothing…*

Chris, with this and other incriminating letters in hand, was under no obligation to disclose them unless he intended to use them at trial. Of course he wanted to use them but feared if the mother was not called as a witness the judge might disallow them. And if he disclosed them too soon the prosecution might simply drop the mother as a witness.

While the prosecutor was giving the opening argument stating that the mother would be the key witness, Svengali delivered copies of the letters to the district attorney's office. The D.A. himself and two other high-ranking prosecutors showed up in court in no time. Chris was setting up his displays when the judge stopped the proceedings, moved the jurors into a waiting room and gathered the attorneys into his chambers. The heated discussion lasted three hours, after which the judge called a three-day recess to give the prosecutor's office time to evaluate their star witness's letters.

In preparation for his opening statement, Chris had had the letters blown up to poster size and they were resting on easels in open court. While waiting for the proceedings to continue, the press copied the letters verbatim. Back in court the following Monday, the judge realized that he had failed to admonish the jury not to read the newspapers over the weekend. When the judge asked the jurors how many had read the letters in the sunday edition, eleven of the twelve jurors raised their hands. The judge had no choice but to declare a mistrial. It was a brilliant use of the press.

Chris then sent the envelopes containing the letters off for DNA testing. The prosecutor's office was not impressed that the mother was definitely the one who licked them shut. They believed that the original letters had been replaced with fakes, so they sent the suspected fakes to the FBI's crime lab for handwriting analysis. If they were forgeries they were darn good. The FBI's handwriting expert opined that the handwriting matched that of the mother. (The reliability of handwriting analysis falls in between fingerprint analysis and bite mark analysis. In one test laypersons were as good as the handwriting experts and both groups were correct only fifty-two percent of the time.)

Three weeks after the mistrial, the boyfriend was released. Die-hard prosecutors investigated Svengali's background and found that his published doctoral dissertation was titled *The Relationship of*

Hypnotic Susceptibility to Articulated Perceptual Style. Eyewitness testimony (articulated perception) is known to be extremely unreliable. It contributes to at least one-third of all wrongful convictions. Svengali earned his PhD testing whether forensic hypnosis improves eyewitness reliability. The prosecutor's theory, however, was that Svengali used his skills to hypnotize the mother into writing the letters. She remembered writing parts of them but denied writing the incrementing (hypnotized) sections.

It was Chris who came up with the nickname. Upon hearing the prosecutor's mind-bending theory, Chris whimsically told his ace investigator, "You're a regular 'Svengali.'" Svengali was the villainous hypnotist in the early nineteenth-century novel *Trilby* by George du Maurier who mesmerized the main character for personal gain. Today "Svengali" means anyone who manipulates, influences or controls others with mind games.

The prosecutor ultimately dropped the case against the boyfriend because even if their Svengali theory were true, it would be hard to prove. The mother was charged with the crime for a brief period of time but the case against her was also dropped. The medical doctor who initially examined the victim refused to back off from his original opinion as to the time the child had sustained the fatal injuries.

The great Svengali lived in Phoenix and maintained an office in San Diego, spending roughly half his time in each city. Also he had contributed a chapter to the Maricopa County Public Defender's training manual entitled "Coercion and Extraction of False Confessions." With Phoenix connections, he seemed to be the perfect one to reinvestigate the Krone case and was hired to do so in June 2000.

Shortly thereafter I received distressed phone calls from both Svengali and James Kemper, Ray's outgoing appellate attorney, each claiming that the other one was, to summarize, "an asshole." Before Kemper could be notified that a new investigator had been retained for Ray's case, Svengali had shown up at Kemper's office unannounced and demanded to pick up the case file, which consisted of several boxes mostly of trial transcripts. Kemper was sure that no significant new evidence was out there to be discovered and had recommended to Ray that he bypass the Rule 32 and go directly to federal habeas corpus. He was peeved that Ray had not taken his advice and had apparently hired a private investigator. Kemper was not about to release the file to some total stranger. Svengali was miffed that he couldn't just walk into Kemper's office, flash his credentials and get his way.

To me it was an obvious clash of two mighty egos. Kemper displayed his by his overconfidence that he would win the appeal and by his resentment of Chris. Annoyed no end that "Plourd was still calling the shots," Kemper insinuated that Chris was being overpaid. He didn't know that Chris had been working pro bono ever since Ray's second conviction.

Svengali's ego was also ever in evidence. He believed he was right about—and had opinions on—anything and everything and he didn't hesitate to express himself. Although there was something a bit bourgeois about Svengali, I was taken in when he boisterously said things like Judge McDougall was a wimp for not overturning Ray's conviction when he had the chance. He was referring to the motion to vacate judgment that had been filed in McDougall's court three months after he sentenced Ray to life in prison. In it the judge was informed that:

> The jury committed prejudicial misconduct by experimenting with and conducting testing with some of the dental evidence after concluding that the trial evidence expert testimony was unpersuasive in violation of constitutional due process of law and the constitutional right of the defendant to be represented by counsel at all stages of the proceedings [and] that newly discovered evidence exists as to blood stains on the victim's underwear that is susceptible to genetic DNA testing. Defendant requests release of the trial exhibit for...DNA specific tests.

Judge McDougall ignored the motion and did not respond to it one way or the other.

Replacing Kemper's ego with Svengali's, I thought, might be just what was needed to reinvigorate Ray's case.

I schmoozed them both and made arrangements for Mike Pain, Ray's previous investigator, who had an office in the same building as Kemper and who had developed a good rapport with Kemper, to pick up the file and hold it for Svengali. After receiving the transcripts, Svengali quickly absorbed them and became quite knowledgeable about Ray's case.

Normally Kemper would first have been replaced with another attorney to do Ray's Rule 32 and then the new attorney would have hired an investigator. But Svengali came aboard first. So Chris asked him if he knew of a good Phoenix attorney who could do the job. Svengali did and recommended Alan Simpson. Simpson had received his bachelor's degree from Arizona State University in 1976 and his law degree from South Texas College of Law in Houston in 1979, passed the Arizona bar in 1980 and began his legal carrier practicing law in Phoenix. He was an experienced, highly qualified, well-respected criminal defense attorney.

Simpson had used Svengali's services on several cases. One was the retrial of Dan Willoughby. I'd become acquainted with Dan through Ray. They first met in 1992 as cellmates in the Maricopa County jail where they both were waiting to be tried for murder. Dan went first in April and Ray followed three months later. In Florence Ray was assigned to a cell in the same sixteen-man Death Row pod as Dan. Dan was a college graduate and easily got a job in the law library. Ray went to the library as often a possible. Dan and Ray became close friends, comparing notes on how each of them had been screwed. Dan advised Ray with his case and helped Ray also get a job in the law library. When Dan heard that I'd taken an interest in Ray's case he wrote to me seeking help. He made a credible case of innocence.

For Christmas 1990, Dan Willoughby gave his family a vacation to Puerto Peñasco, Mexico, a beach resort situated at the northernmost end of the Sea of Cortez. Visitors from Arizona commonly referred to this seaside village surrounded by miles of sand dunes and windy beaches as "Rocky Point." It was a popular tourist destination for Phoenix residents, who could get there in a half-day's drive. Ray had been there with his friends several times.

On February 23, 1991, ten-year-old Thera rushed into the Willoughbys' rented beach house to tell her mother of her excursion into town. Patricia Willoughby had stayed behind to rest while her husband, Dan, had taken their three children to a local museum for the afternoon. Thera found her mother lying in bed in a pool of blood with a dinner knife protruding from her head, barely clinging onto life. Dan rushed to the local Red Cross for help and then led his children in prayer. The police arrived and Patricia was rushed to the hospital, where she died shortly thereafter.

The murder appeared to be part of a robbery. Two of Patricia's valuable rings and four hundred dollars were missing. After a brief investigation by the Mexican police, Dan and his children returned to Phoenix. Patricia's family were griefstricken. One of her brothers took charge of the three children. Her mother, the matriarch of the family, immediately became suspicious of Dan. She took her suspicions to the local authorities, who opened an investigation even though the crime had occurred in a foreign country.

In no time rumors that Dan and his Latin lover, a much younger, attractive Mexican woman named Yesenia Patino, had conspired and committed the crime together, making it look like a burglary. While detectives from Maricopa County were investigating the Rocky Point crime scene, Yesenia disappeared. Her fingerprints were found on a Coke bottle at the murder site and Patricia's two missing rings were found in her abandoned apartment. A warrant was issued for Yesenia's arrest. Nine months later, based upon a tip from a returning tourist, she was arrested in a popular Mazatlan cantina. After a night in a Mexican jail and after learning of the evidence against her, Yesenia confessed, implicating Dan Willoughby as the mastermind. Dan was arrested in Phoenix the next day, December 7, 1991, just three weeks to the day before Kim Ancona would be murdered.

The crime made national news due to an incidental discovery. Eight years before Dan met Yesenia, she had been "Alfredo." Alfredo had had a sex change operation paid for by his boyfriend Jack, who subsequently married the new and improved Alfredo/Yesenia. They divorced six years later and Yesenia soon remarried a man named Able Ramon. In late 1989 Dan picked Yesenia up at a Phoenix bus stop. Though both were married, they began an intense affair. She liked being wined and dined and lavished with gifts, and he liked the newfound excitement.

Dan commanded a six-figure income as an executive for an air freight company. When Ramon was sent to prison for drug trafficking, Yesenia moved into an apartment paid for by Dan and close to Dan's home. To his family he explained Yesenia's presence by telling them that his company was expanding into Mexico and she was his interpreter and Spanish teacher.

The deductadickfromme operation had been perfect, for neither Dan nor Able was able to tell any difference. Dan first learned of Yesenia's root after she had vanished and after a detective had traced her social security number to Alfredo. The headline "Phoenix Man and His Transsexual Mexican Lover Arrested for Murder" was quickly picked up by the national wire service and reported in rag mags like *The National Enquirer* and TV's "Hard Copy."

Dan acknowledged the affair—that it had been a major error in judgment. But he claimed that Yesenia had acted alone, that she had followed him and his family to Rocky Point and, finding Patricia alone, had murdered her. Her motive was jealousy. For obvious reasons, Yesenia was unable to have a family of her own and she coveted Dan's family. After testifying against Dan, Yesenia was sentenced in Mexico to thirty-five years in prison for her part in the crime.

Knowing how Ray had been railroaded, I gave Dan the benefit of the doubt. Concentrating my energy on Ray's case, however, I did not look deeper into Dan's story. I was delighted to hear from Alan Simpson that Dan had been given a new trial.

Dan's appeal had failed but he prevailed on a Rule 32 when new evidence and ineffective assistance of counsel were considered. To say his trial attorney was incompetent was an understatement. Dan's defense attorney barely cross-examined the state's witnesses and when the prosecution rested its case so did he. Not one witness was called to testify in Dan's defense nor was Dan allowed to testify, although he told his attorney repeatedly that he wanted to take the stand. Also, Yesenia had recanted her story. She claimed that she had been promised a reduced sentence to testify against Dan. She became upset when she was given thirty-five years after having been led to believe that she would get ten to twenty years for her cooperation. After serving five years she made a videotaped confession in which she stated that she alone had murdered Patricia and demonstrated on camera how she had struck the fatal blows.

After being retained by Willoughby, Simpson sent Svengali to the Mexican prison in Hermosillo to interview (that is, to hypnotize the truth out of) Yesenia. Simpson was delighted to have her sworn statement that she was the lone killer and he was extremely confident as the trial date approached.

I decided to check out Ray's new attorney in action and attended Willoughby's second trial.

Dan claimed that he had been framed by Phoenix detectives who kluged up the murder weapon to be a "mace," which Dan allegedly fabricated and took with him to Mexico to do the deed. Yesenia, cooperating with Phoenix police, said that Dan had attached a ten-pound metal ball to a rope and swung it eight to ten times striking his wife repeatedly in the head. The mace was never found and Yesenia was the only one purported to have seen it. Dan claimed it was Maricopa County's way of securing jurisdiction for a crime that occurred in Mexico. Arizona law provides that to have jurisdiction over a crime that occurred outside the state it must be proved that an element of the crime had occurred inside the state. The mace was the necessary element. Dan claimed that Mexican doctors had determined that the murder weapon was "a bar or pipe or some long, narrow object" inconsistent with the phantom mace. Arizona medical examiners and prosecutors referred to the fatal wounds as "egg shell fractures." Dan's incompetent attorney failed to have an expert challenge the state's specter scepter theory. Consequently, the Arizona courts took jurisdiction and Dan was put on trial.

Witness by witness the state built its case against Dan. In July 1990 after a several months whirlwind with Yesenia, Dan lost his job. He was fired because of increased inattentiveness to work due to blatant indiscretions with Yesenia that lead him to pad his expense account with exorbitant entertainment expenditures. Without an income, the high cost of maintaining Yesenia soon became frustrating for Dan, who was now dependent upon his wife for money.

Patricia was in partnership with her mother in an expanding and lucrative herbal supplement business. In 1990 she and her mother grossed $324,000. The estimated valued of their business was at least $2,500,000. Patricia became suspicious and confronted Yesenia, who agreed that she would stop seeing Dan.

But Dan was paying her rent. It was then, the state maintained, that Dan hatched his scheme. Dan and Patricia carried a $150,000 life insurance policy. Another one was taken out on Patricia in the amount of $1,000,000. Dan rented the condo at Rocky Point and he and Yesenia traveled there twice before the family outing, it was argued, to reconnoiter the area.

Yesenia's brother drove her to Rocky Point on the fateful weekend. On the day of the murder, Dan rendezvoused with Yesenia on a secluded beach. After Dan left to pick up his kids at the beach house, Yesenia dropped her brother off at a park and inconspicuously followed Dan in her brother's pickup truck. After loading his three children into the van, Dan went back inside, where Patricia lay napping, "to retrieve his passport." While Dan was inside his oldest daughter attempted to enter but "the door was locked." After approximately five minutes Dan reemerged "tucking in his shirt and adjusting his belt." Dan then drove his children to the local museum.

Unobserved, Yesenia from afar watched Dan's van drive off. She entered through the back door, which had been left open for her and proceeded to make the crime look like a burglary. She took a knife from a kitchen drawer and stabbed the comatose Patricia several times, leaving the knife embedded in her temple. She took two rings from Patricia's fingers and $400 cash from her purse, strewing the rest of its contents about the room. Yesenia returned to the park and picked up her brother. They both hightailed it back to Phoenix. Within days Dan collected on the first insurance policy.

The state's case was compelling. Credible witnesses established the facts. One was Yesenia's ex-husband Jack. He had remained friendly with Yesenia and had become acquainted with Dan. He testified that a few months before the murders he had on two separate occasions dined out with both Dan and Yesenia. He said that a frustrated Dan had revealed his intent to do away with his wife, pondering different methods like drowning her while scuba diving or pushing her off the rim of the Grand Canyon. Rocky Point was eventually selected because "anything can be accomplished in Mexico."

Talking with Dan across the rail that separated spectators from players during one timeout (also known as a "recess"), I was forewarned of Jack's impending court appearance—that he couldn't be trusted. To give his testimony, Jack had been removed from his Oregon prison cell, where he was serving time for a sexual offense, and escorted by sheriff's deputies to the Arizona courtroom. Yet I found Jack's testimony convincing, especially when he emphasized his concern that Yesenia was headed for trouble and advised her, "Don't get involved with this crazy thing." If *I* believed Jack, I could imagine how the jury received his damning testimony, not knowing that he was a disgusting pedophile. For Dan to have a chance, I thought, star witness Yesenia Patino must confess in front of the jury to be the lone perpetrator of the crime.

And she did. Under Simpson's cross-examination, Yesenia told the jury how she was jealous of Patricia, wanted Dan and his family all to herself, was angry that Dan was going on a vacation without her, followed them to Rocky Point, waited for Patricia to be alone and then beat her and stabbed her to death. The only problem was that under direct examination she sang the state's song—that Dan masterminded the murder and for Yesenia's help promised to whisk her off to Mexico a millionaire once he cashed in on his wife's business and the insurance policies. She flip-flopped again under the state's rebuttal. "Now that's not the way in really happened?" asked the prosecutor of her "confession" to Alan Simpson. "No," she affirmed. It was apparent that the institutionalized Yesenia had learned to give the answer the asker wanted.

I thought Simpson had done a great job, considering that his client didn't have much going for him. Dan Willoughby's only hope rested on Yesenia's "confession" being believable. It wasn't. Nevertheless, Alan Simpson gave an impassioned, energetic and impressive closing statement. As soon as it was over and the case was in the jury's hands, the well-dressed black man who was sitting two seats away from me and directly behind Willoughby was the first spectator to his feet. He was about the size of a middleweight. As he grabbed Simpson's hand I overheard his congratulation, "Fantastic!"

Being the next one to shake Simpson's hand, I asked, "Who was that?"

"Rubin Carter."

I caught up with Carter in the hall and told him that I had followed his case since being introduced to it by Dylan's "Hurricane." I was shocked when he had been convicted a second time and I told him that I was elated by his release from prison.

"So was I!" Hurricane Carter responded as we shook hands.

Carter had visited Dan in the Maricopa County jail some months earlier while he was in Phoenix taping a segment for ABC's "Politically Incorrect" and had pledged his support to Dan. I wondered whether Carter would have been so sympathetic toward Dan if he had attended the whole trial.

While I agreed with Dan that he had been framed with the mace, I could not disagree with the jury's swift guilty verdict. I believed, after witnessing all the evidence unfold, that at least this time they had framed the right guy.

π

Once Alan Simpson was retained, Chris called periodic meetings in Simpson's Phoenix office. I attended all of them, silently observing along with Svengali. My old friend Gene Burdick attended some of these meetings. I always enjoyed Gene's company because we shared the same sense of humor. It was fun joking with him before and after these meetings. I learned that Svengali too had a sense of humor, if a bit bizarre. Chris dominated the meetings and, though I thought it a long shot, his main thrust was to get the victim's clothing retested for DNA in the hopes that the true killer left some and could somehow be identified. As we walked out of one meeting, Svengali joked, "And if we can't find the real killer, we'll frame somebody." Everyone including me smiled or laughed at his obvious jest.

Chris and Alan clicked right away. And Simpson did a great job implementing Chris's plan. At the first meeting, Chris emphasized the particular items of clothing most promising for finding telltale DNA. Simpson was instructed to file the necessary motions to get the specific items tested. Chris recommended that Simpson ask the court to have the Phoenix police crime lab do the analysis. Because of our past experience with Piette and the police crime lab, this recommendation surprised me.

After the meeting I asked Chris, "Do you trust them?"

"Not really, but they're free."

Following the conviction, we'd gotten to this point cheaply, incurring only minimal travel expenses. But now it had been necessary to arrange sizable retainers for both Svengali and Simpson. The time was also right to revisit the bra sample and at Chris's direction I'd already sent funds off to Dr. Blake to do so. Chris had wanted this retesting done on the q.t. and Blake had at his disposal, stored in his lab, the unused portion of the sample he'd used for the first round of tests.

Though I had reservations about the Phoenix police crime lab doing the additional court ordered DNA testing, the word "free" appealed to me too and I let it go.

π

Late one afternoon in my office, making travel arrangements to attend Willoughby's trial, I had opened an e-mail from Simpson to find attached Ed Blake's report on the retested bra sample. Excited, I forwarded it on to Ray's parents, Jim and Carolyn Leming. I always kept them abreast of developments in Ray's case. I knew Simpson would have e-mailed Chris also. I printed a copy for myself and hurried home.

After dinner I enthusiastically delved into the report. Blake had identified thirteen genetic markers, up from the six he'd found five years earlier from which he couldn't exclude Ray. I was looking for the marker that Blake found to be different from Ray's. Just one discrepancy was all that it would take to positively exclude Ray.

But I couldn't find any. I searched again and again and finally gave up. I called Chris.

"Blake's report doesn't look good," I said.

"No, it doesn't."

"What's the probability?" I asked.

"About one in ten trillion."

I listened to Chris in stunned silence, wanting to believe that there was some mistake.

My denial didn't last long. "It's got to be his," I interrupted, thinking, Holy Moses, Schanfield was right!

"No doubt," Chris agreed.

"What do we do now?" I asked.

"Bury it!"

Unlike a prosecutor, who could be charged with a felony for withholding exculpatory evidence, there is no such obligation for a defense attorney to disclose incriminating evidence. I now understood why Chris wanted the sample tested on the q.t. Unless the newfound DNA definitely pointed to the true perpetrator, an exclusion would have had little effect, just something to add as an item to the Rule 32. But should it get out that Ray's DNA was without a doubt on Ancona's bra, Ray would be done for good.

"What about Ray or his parents?"

"There's no need for them to know," Chris emphasized.

Immediately after hanging up, I was in my car heading back to my office. I hoped that the Lemings' hadn't picked up the forwarded e-mail. We shared the same Internet service, which had the feature that an e-mail could be canceled so long as the receiving party hadn't yet opened it. Time was on my side, I hoped. I had forwarded Simpson's e-mail after 8 p.m. Eastern Time and with luck the Lemings had retired and not opened it. It was after 11 p.m. when I arrived at my office. To my relief, I found the e-mail resting in the send queue. I cancelled it and headed back home wondering how in the world Ray's DNA could possibly have gotten onto Ancona's bra?

An obvious way was that it got there the Wednesday night of the Christmas Party. Ray had taken Ancona to the party and then driven her back to her car, parked in front of the CBS Lounge. Had Ray made a move that left some of his DNA on Ancona's bra, which then lingered on through the fateful Saturday night? I had to find out.

On a day when Willoughby's trial was in recess I drove to Yuma and visited Ray. We met outside in the fenced visitation yard. It was not all that hot for a summer's day so we strolled along the fence. Under the guise of writing a book, I asked Ray to go over the details of his involvement with Ancona. Ray was a fast talker and he'd told this story many times. Moving along at a good clip, Ray soon got to the Christmas party.

I jumped in when Ray reached the part, "We got there about one in the morning—the party was pretty much dead. We stayed about an hour, then I drove her back to her car and went home."

"Any way your DNA could have gotten onto her bra?" I asked matter-of-factly.

"I don't see how," Ray answered without missing a beat.

Then he abruptly stopped his narrative and looked deeply into my eyes. Ray was too savvy. He knew that Blake was retesting the bra sample. He knew what I was telling him. For the rest of the visit Ray was off in the clouds, no doubt pondering the ramifications of what I had indirectly revealed to him.

"That's Mexico just over there isn't it?" he said at one point, gazing through the fence across desert sands.

"I don't know," I answered, shuddering inside at what Ray might be thinking.

If it weren't Mexico we were looking at, it was close. The state prison was south of Yuma, tucked into the southwest corner of Arizona three miles from the Mexican border. In Ray's shape I knew he could make it on the run without even breaking a sweat if somehow he were able to find himself unnoticed on the other side of the fence. But then he would have to scale a border patrol fence or swim the Colorado River.

I changed the subject and told him some good news. Carrying out Chris's strategy, Simpson had gotten the judge to order the testing of Ancona's tank top and panties and those results would be in by Christmas. It was mid-2001.

I regretted having depressed Ray by unintentionally spilling the beans. I hoped that he wouldn't try anything foolish. But I'd found out what I needed to know. I was convinced that Ray was not the one responsible for his DNA's being on Ancona's bra.

On the way back to Phoenix I pondered another not so obvious but plausible explanation—some of Ray's reference sample had been deliberately put on Ancona's bra before it had been shipped off to Ed Blake's lab for testing. It would have been an easy thing to do. The Romley complex, for all intents and purposes, controlled the evidence, just as they had controlled the mace fabrication in the Willoughby case.

When I got back to my hotel room I called Chris and told him of my visit with Ray. When I suggested my snake-in-the-grass-tampering theory, he listened to my diatribe without disagreeing. I was left with the distinct impression that he too independently shared the notion. In future talks with him, I came to believe that Chris had suspected monkey business ever since Blake's first test on the bra, leading me to wonder if Chris really wanted the bra surreptitiously retested to confirm his suspicion. He was certainly not as surprised as I that Ray's DNA was on Ancona's bra.

Chris reminded me that it had been Levy, not he, who wanted the bra tested. Indeed, Rawson had written a letter to Levy suggesting specific DNA testing to support the conjured-up bloody-tooth-marks-on-the-bra theory. But Levy was the one pulling Rawson's strings. Levy initially had fought tooth and nail not to let the defense test any of Ancona's clothing. It was a good strategy because it was just as likely as not that DNA testing would hurt rather than help his case, so why take the chance? Then why did Levy change his tune and allow one of his puppets to suggest that DNA testing be done on the precise spot that contained Ray's DNA? A coincidence? Hmm...

As I thought more about the fact that Ray's DNA was indeed and without a doubt on Ancona's clothing, I could only marvel at how Chris had minimized its impact at trial. His blood spatter expert convincingly refuted Rawson's bloody-tooth-bite-theory and set up the state's star witness to be turned into a buffoon. He spun Moses Schanfield around to exclude Ray from the sample swabbed from the bitten breast and then maneuvered to have Moses's correct opinion on Ray's DNA's being on the bra stricken from the record.

π

A claim made by a defendant, without convincing proof, that he had been framed would go nowhere. It would be viewed by virtually every crony in a robe as a desperate attempt to explain incriminating evidence.

How could it be proved?

It couldn't.

Ray's DNA on Ancona's bra and the suspicion how it most likely got there were buried together for good.

CHAPTER 25
PHIL BARNES RIDES AGAIN

P hil Barnes fancies himself a sherlock. His perception of the justice game, however, came from fiction. From shows like "Perry Mason," a 'sixties TV series, in which the premise of each weekly episode was the same—the mentally challenged district attorney always brings the wrong person to trial and brilliant defense attorney Perry Mason, in the course of defending his innocent client, solves the crime, dramatically eliciting a confession from the guilty party under cross-examination. What made this show fiction was not that the prosecutor was not smart enough to solve the crime himself, but that he still had the job for the next episode.

In almost every law and order type show, whether a movie or a TV series, the good guys prevail and the bad guys are caught and punished. I'd stopped watching TV regularly long ago, depriving Phil of his fill of nonsense, but one show did catch my eye shortly after Attorney Alan Simpson and Dr. Svengali were retained for Ray's case. It was an episode of "18 Wheels of Justice," which aired for the 2000 and 2001 seasons on TNN. I could make it through only part of one episode because Phil began jumping up and down with unpleasant memories. Although unable to solve the Ancona murder, Tex Brown had apparently been successful in selling his yarns to a TV producer. The show took its name from the title of one of Tex's books. Both Phil and I had learned the hard way that Tex's stories were fiction. The lead character, a studly young truck driver working for the Justice Department and assigned to go undercover and "infiltrate the organization of a deadly and vicious crime boss," was far from the Tex we knew. The villainous crime boss, played by G. Gordon Liddy of Watergate fame, was more like the real Tex.

If entertainment mirrored real life, then about one cop show in ten would depict an innocent person getting screwed. Recently (2006) ABC television has attempted to fill this void with the series "In Justice," which dramatizes "cases of justice run amok, cases in which an innocent person has been wrongly convicted of a crime." This series too is fiction in that each episode makes it look relatively easy for an innocent person convicted of a crime to be exonerated. "In Justice" did not survive for a second season.

Unbeknownst to me, Phil Barnes had been watching when, as a teenager, I read *The Complete Sherlock Holmes*. In each of the four novels and fifty-six short stories, the supersleuth used his powers of deduction to resolve each and every clue and identify the culprit. Phil always tried to solve each case before Holmes. He never did. It took awhile for him to realize that in order to build suspense, Sir Arthur Conan Doyle invariably held back a key clue, known only to Holmes, who would dramatically reveal it only after he'd identified the culprit.

Deduction works in fiction because the author controls the clues and the logical deductions leading to the solution. In real life, however, clues are left by the perpetrator. Police and prosecutors collect and control the evidence. Most of the time clues are interpreted correctly and accurate deduction prevails. The good guys win and the bad guys lose. But every now and then their deduction runs amuck and the wrong man goes down. In Ray's case, the bite mark was misinterpreted by inept inexpert Dr. Piakas from the get-go (Figure 1). Detective Gregory took a look a Ray Krone's uneven front teeth and guessed wrong. Prosecutor Levy went along. And Ray Krone was no sooner locked up than the investigation bearing his name was launched. Within hours of arresting Krone, perfect witness Dale Henson told Gregory that bearded Ray Krone was not the clean-shaven person he'd seen enter and exit the crime scene at the time of the murder. Within days the size of the bloody footprints made by the

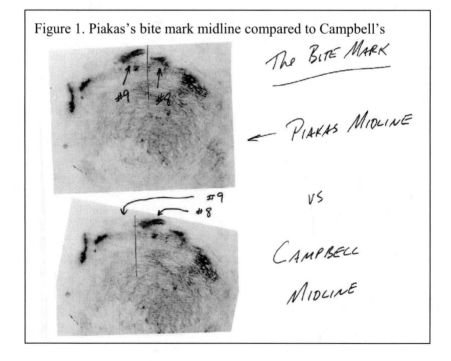

Figure 1. Piakas's bite mark midline compared to Campbell's

The BITE MARK

← PIAKAS MIDLINE

VS

CAMPBELL
MIDLINE

Converse brand tennis shoes worn by the person hovering over Ancona moments after she'd been killed was determined to be one and a half sizes smaller than the size of the MacGregor tennis shoes worn by Ray Krone. To any sane person these clues logically suggest that the wrong man had been arrested.

This way of thinking is known as "reductio ad absurdum" (Latin for "reduction to the absurd") and has been around since antiquity (Aristotle used it) and it remains a valid scientific tool today. Basically it says that your assumption is false if any fact leads to absurdity. Had this principle been applied to either of these two clues, it would have rendered the "Ray Krone Did It" assumption absurd. But instead of letting Ray go and looking for the clean-shaven American Indian who wore size 9½ Converse brand tennis shoes, the Romley complex cinched its blinders up tight and reduced their investigation to looking for a Ouija Board Certified Odontologist who could and would make the bite mark fit and to "fixing" the evidence that didn't.

In no time all the troublesome evidence was covered up. A well-credentialed Las Vegas politician and dentist, Dr. Ray Rawson, was pimped with something like "the boyfriend is in custody and he's all but confessed." So this hoodwinked hired gun joined the team, ordained the case by replacing "reductio ad absurdum" with "eye-brain coordination" and under the guise of science rendered his almighty bite mark guess (Figures 2 and 3).

$$\pi$$

Early on, as I looked at the evidence in relation to cousin Ray, Phil wondered, If not Ray, then who? Oh boy! An actual crime with real clues. Phil couldn't resist approaching the adventure like Sherlock Holmes. Unlike the shoddy, blinkered investigation that led to Ray's indictment, Phil determined not to let a single clue go unexplained.

As he read the police reports, Phil initially suspected that the killing might be drug related.

Beth and Tennessee Mike were the last to leave Kim Ancona alone at the bar. In a pre-trial deposition taken by Ray's first attorney, Geoffrey Jones, Beth remembers Kim's shoeing everybody out at closing time. "It was odd that she didn't want us there to help her close." Indeed Kim and Beth were best friends. They had spent Kim's last afternoon together, parting at 5 p.m., when Kim needed to get ready for work. Beth went to Tennessee's place across the street from Kim's house. Beth and Tennessee showed up together at the CBS Lounge about 8 p.m. and stayed until closing time.

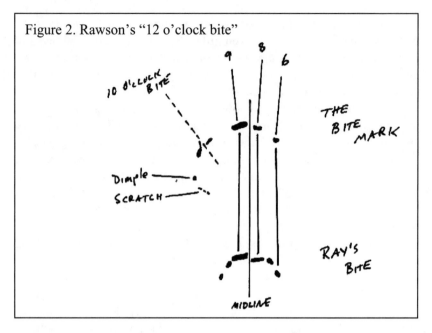

Figure 2. Rawson's "12 o'clock bite"

Phil reasoned, It makes no sense that Kim Ancona would not let her best friend stay behind to keep her company while she cleaned up the bar. Even if Ancona were expecting Ray to show up and help (as prosecutor Levy had "deduced"), would she not have wanted to show off her new boyfriend?

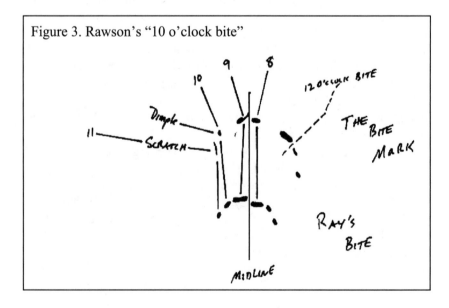

Figure 3. Rawson's "10 o'clock bite"

Phil didn't find Kate Koester's testimony believable. She was the afternoon bartender whom Ancona relieved at 6 p.m. She hung around the bar until about 8 p.m. She had recently had a run-in with Ray at the bar and didn't particularly like him. Absolutely no other witnesses, many much closer to Ancona that evening, corroborated Koester's hearsay testimony that Ancona had told her that "Ray was going to help her close the bar." Did Koester misinterpret Ancona and/or was she unduly influenced to help The Ray Krone Did It investigation? Who knows? In any event, Phil believed that Ancona had neither intention nor expectation of seeing Ray the night she was killed.

So why did Ancona go out of her way to clear out the bar? Well, thought Phil, drug deals don't happen in the open. Indeed, not even best friends are invited. Beth remembers hearing the door lock behind her. The bucket originally prepared with clean, soapy water by cook David Torres was found full of dirty water in the kitchen, indicating that Ancona had finished her chores. Afterwards she must have unlocked the front door expecting someone, because Dale Henson, who was cleaning the sidewalk outside, noted that the person who whisked by him entered the bar quickly. Further evidence that Ancona must have known her assailant was the fact that there was a finished mixed-drink glass sitting at the end of the bar and an opened bottle of Ancona's preferred beverage, Bud Lite, sitting next to her purse, a scene indicating they'd socialized immediately prior to the attack.

Ancona had been twice divorced. Her first marriage, to Mark Miller, had ended thirteen years earlier. He lived in California. They had two sons, Chris, 18, and Daniel, 14. Ancona had a third child, a 10-year-old daughter, Kelly, with her second husband, John Supler. Earlier the year of her death, in February, Kim had lost her house, her job and custody of Daniel and Kelly. Down and out, she accepted Paul Clark's generosity and moved with her older son Chris into Paul's house. Clark kicked Chris out in late summer for being "lazy." From the police report on Supler:

> He [Supler] advised that...they had been divorced approximately three years ago and their divorce was brought about by alcohol and drugs...that Kim was involved in drug dealing and approximately two years back one of her roommates...was killed in the Phoenix area [over drugs].

In an interview with former bar manager Trish's neighbors Dorsey and his girlfriend (also named "Kim"), it was learned from neighbor Kim that Ancona was known to be the one to see for drugs. Trish also confirmed that Ancona dealt drugs and while bartending would excuse herself to the ladies room several times during the evening to snort "crystal crank" (methamphetamine) from a small silver spoon about the size of the head of a match—a spoon designed specifically for that purpose. She kept the crank in a brown vial in her purse. "Head shops," as they were called, were popular and not uncommon in the 'eighties and early 'nineties and openly provided such drug paraphernalia. The autopsy toxicology report confirmed that Ancona tested positive for methamphetamine. She was negative for alcohol and cocaine. In her purse were found more than a gram of "speed" (another name for methamphetamine) and half a gram of marijuana.

Also contributing to Phil's "drug connection" speculation was Ancona's next-door neighbor, Kathy. She testified that she went to the CBS Lounge just before it closed for some "cigarettes" and left her business card with Ancona expecting a call from her as soon as Ancona got home. Phil wondered why she would drive past several convenience stores and go all the way to the CBS Lounge just for some "cigarettes." She *would* have made such a trip, he thought, to place a last-minute drug order.

The drug trade is cash and carry—there's no such thing as credit. Kathy's business card, along with two one-dollar bills, was found in a back pocket of Ancona's jeans. That was the only money found on Ancona or in her purse. No money appeared to have been taken from the cash register or the safe. Phil wondered where Ancona's money was. She had worked the bar alone that night and could be expected to at least have had some tip money other than the overlooked two dollars. Had Ancona's money disappeared along with the drug order money she was holding when she was killed?

"A drug deal gone bad" seemed a plausible scenario to Phil Barnes. But then there was the location, position and condition of the body. It was found in the men's restroom naked (except for socks) on its back, legs spread-eagle, with a bite mark on its breast. OK, a drug deal turned into a rape? But why then did it happen in the men's room—thirty feet across the bar and down a hall from Ancona's unfinished bottle of beer, the place where a rape could reasonably be assumed to have begun? Finding Ancona's body in the men's room would make sense if Ancona had simply been accosted while she was mopping the restroom floor. But it is extremely unlikely that the assailant would have returned the mop and bucket to the kitchen afterwards. If she had excused herself to the restroom and subsequently been accosted there, then her body would have been found in the women's room and not in the men's room farther down the hall. Other evidence also suggested that the attack began at the end of the bar right after Ancona's "friend" had finished a cocktail. From there footprints led into the kitchen to the knife rack and back out to where Ancona was most likely in a stupor from having been hit in the mouth. (The medical examiner determined that the contusion to the inside of Ancona's lip was made by her own teeth consistent with having been slugged in the face.)

Phil surmised that Ancona was then spirited at knifepoint across the room and down the hall to the men's room. The stab wounds to her neck were consistent with having had a knife held to her throat. The same footprints from the kitchen reappeared on the men's room floor, between Ancona's outstretched legs, tying the whole scene together.

These perplexing clues raised Phil's doubts that the crime had been a drug deal or a spontaneous rape. So he turned to "the lesbian connection." In a police report written by Officer Joe Petrosino, two individuals had independently approached Petrosino with "talk on the street":

On 12/30/91 [the Monday after the murder, at 4:35 p.m.] I returned to the CBS Bar at the request of the owner [Hank Arredondo]. He said he heard some information, talk on the street...He told me that if it appeared that Kim [Ancona] had been murdered but not sexually assaulted that there was a possibility that it was a homosexual killing. The talk around the bar was that Trish and Lu...possibly had killed Kim...that Trish, former employee, and her girlfriend Lu, Indian female, former military...had been responsible for Kim's death...Squeakie Valdez came over and spoke to me. Squeakie explained that she had been in the bar the night that Kim was killed...She was somewhat upset and worried about the fact that Kim could have been killed by Trish and Lu. I asked her why she believed that to be the case. She then explained that she was somewhat skeptical of Trish and Lu because of some things they had done recently. [Earlier the same day] she received a call from Lu asking if they could borrow several hundred dollars from her. Squeakie told her that she did not have any money that she could loan at that time. There had been no problem with the refused loan, however Lu and Trish then went "skiing" for a couple of days. They had also asked if they could bring over one of their friends, Gloria, to Squeakie's house. Squeakie told them no.

She said that all of this had made her uncomfortable about Trish and Lu.

This police report was part of the stack of discovery material provided by prosecutor Levy to defense attorney Jones prior to the first trial. As Chris Plourd catalogued this material, he noticed that the computer program used by the Phoenix police department to generate police reports appeared to assign a serial number to each report. Thorough as usual, he verified this fact with the PPD, which indicated that their system assigned a sequential number to each report of a particular case. Chris was concerned because he'd notice that fourteen serial numbered reports were missing. He requested a complete printout. The PPD obliged and assured him that once a report is entered into the system it and its serial number cannot be changed or deleted. Nevertheless, the "complete" printout was still missing two reports that were most likely written by Detective Gregory, because the ones immediately before and after had been written by him. These two erased reports were gone for good.

"Looks like about eighteen minutes worth," Phil joked.

Only after Ray Krone had been arrested, at 4 p.m. on Tuesday, December 31, 1991, did Gregory get down to the necessary paperwork. Each of his twenty-minus-two reports was dated that evening at 8 p.m. But he could not possibly have written or finished writing all of them that evening because he had an appointment to see Dale Henson. "On 12/31/91 at 2150 hours [9:50 p.m.]. I contacted Dale at his residence," began his report of the Henson interview. Henson probably jarred Gregory's train of thought because Henson did not pick Ray out of the photo lineup. In fact, he was adamant that the bearded Ray Krone was not the one he'd seen entering the CBS Lounge at 2:30 the morning of the murder.

Whether Gregory went back to the station and finished his reports that night or came in another day is not known. Most likely he took the rest of the night off to contemplate the ramifications of Henson's damaging eyewitness exclusion of his one and only suspect. Henson's revelation must have raised doubts. But the bite was on—the R-complex was programmed to hold fast—the cerebral cortex went along, dutifully changing the time Henson said he observed the murderer enter the bar from "2:30 a.m." to "6:00 a.m." in his report.

It is clear that Gregory was myopically fixated on Ray's uneven teeth and ignored the possible lesbian connection. Nevertheless, in one report, missing for the first trial but recovered for the second, Gregory made reference to Trish and Lu's possible involvement:

[Steve Hall calls Detective Gregory at the main police station and tells him about being at Trish's Christmas party and seeing Ray with Kim Ancona, then] Steve went on to say that he had heard that Kim was going to move in with Trish. He advised that he believed the Indian girl...appeared to be jealous of this. He believes that Lu possibly was responsible for this murder.

Phil, zooming in on the lesbian connection, noticed discrepancies in Trish and Lu's alibi. Trish had testified at the first trial:

Q. Where were you Friday, December 27th?
A. I had gone to lunch at Hunan's with a bunch of friends, and then we headed up towards Indian Wells late that afternoon.

Q. Where were you Saturday? [the day before the murder took place after midnight]
A. At Indian Wells in Holbrook.

Q. And where were you Sunday?
A. Still in Indian Wells. I came back late Sunday night.

Q. Indian Wells is near Holbrook? [a four-hour drive from Phoenix]
A. Yes.

Q. What time did you arrive back in Phoenix?
A. Somewhere around—I'd say between 8:00 and 10:00.

Q. P.m.?
A. Yes.

Q. Where did you go?
A. Straight home.

Q. Did you ever receive the news with regard to what happened to Kim Ancona?
A. When I left to leave that weekend, I gave my neighbors [Dorsey and Kim] the key to my house, because I wanted them to feed the lizard, and when I got back Sunday, there was a message on my sink, and it said, "Trish, call us as soon as possible, important," and I called. I called Dorsey. When I called him, he told me what had happened, that Kim had been murdered.

Q. That's the first you heard of it?
A. Yes, sir.

Q. And what did you do?

A. I threw a fit, started crying, and threw the phone down. Lu was with me, and she picked the phone up and said, "What's wrong," and I said, "Kim has been killed," and she talked to Dorsey for a few minutes, and that was it.

In another recovered police report, Gregory writes:

On 12/29/91 [murder Sunday] at approximately 1700 hours [5 p.m.], I was contacted by Patricia...who used to work for the CBS Lounge up until the recent past. Patricia goes by the nickname Trish. [Details of Trish's Christmas party follow. Then:] Patricia related she had quit Thursday and had left town and had not got back *until late last night* [emphasis mine]. She was...advised *this afternoon* [ditto] of what had happened at the bar by friends.

Gregory's report clearly contradicts Trish's sworn testimony. "Late last night" was before the murder. "This afternoon" and the time "5 p.m.," when Trish approached Gregory, were well before Trish claimed to have returned to town. Arredondo remembers that it was still daylight when Trish approached him that Sunday afternoon yelling, "If you hadn't fired me this wouldn't have happened."

With a little investigation, Phil confirmed that Trish and Lu were indeed in town Sunday afternoon. And it was confirmed by others too. Trish's neighbors, Dorsey and Kim, were out riding bikes when they were attracted by the yellow tape and commotion outside the CBS Lounge that afternoon. They stopped and learned that Kim Ancona had been murdered. After returning to their apartment, they went over to Trish's place to feed the iguana and left a note for her on the kitchen counter. Trish called that evening, "between seven and eight." They said she broke down crying and they thought nothing of it at the time, thinking Trish's reaction was normal for someone hearing of Ancona's death for the first time. But the next afternoon Kim and Dorsey stopped into the Caravan Lounge, where a group of Ancona's friends had congregated. The talk of course was about the murder. Kim said in an interview:

After somebody had mentioned [that Trish was back in town Sunday afternoon talking to Detective Gregory and shouting at Arredondo], I remember thinking, This is really weird! And the whole thing was weird for her [to go] out of town. I remember thinking, This is strange—just the way it happened. And I have to feed her iguana—like, give me a break.

Kim wondered why she'd been asked to feed Trish's lizard in the first place. Friday morning Trish had called and asked her if she would feed her iguana while she and Lu were out of town. Kim went over for instruction. She observed an apartment in disarray. There were empty booze bottles everywhere. Trish and Lu had obviously stayed up all night after Trish had been fired. At the time, Kim felt that Trish was less interested in having her pet fed than in having Kim "be sure to call Dennis [Trish's ex-husband] and let him know that I'll be out of town this weekend."

Phil learned from Dennis that Trish had given him a photo of herself and Lu taken while they were out of town that weekend and thought it odd. What ex-husband would want a picture of his ex-wife frolicking in the snow with her lesbian lover?

Supposedly, Trish and Lu left town to visit Lu's aunt on the Navajo reservation at Indian Wells, in northeastern Arizona. Instead of making the entire four-hour drive, however, they decided to stop along the way. Trish produced a receipt showing that she had paid cash for a motel room outside Flagstaff. Phil Barnes drove to the motel, whose owner verified that the two did in fact spend Friday night there. As the story goes:

> On 1-2-92 [two days after Ray's arrest] at 1238 hours [12:38 p.m.], I [Detective Gregory] talked to…Lu…She…stated that last Friday morning 12-27-91, both Patricia and herself had gone to Indian Wells in Northern Arizona. On Friday night they had stayed at the Twin Pines Motel and had checked into room number 204 at that location using Trish's name. She said the Twin Pines Motel was approximately fifteen miles south of Flagstaff on I-17. They left there and went to her aunt's house. Her aunt's name was Lucy…, who lives in Indian Wells, Arizona. They returned back from there Sunday 12-29-91.

Gregory didn't get around to checking Trish and Lu's alibi for some time. When he did, he contacted a Navajo tribal policeman, Sergeant Justin Begay, and asked for assistance. Begay replied via fax:

> Detective Chuck Gregory, Homicide detail, requested assistance in obtaining information relating to a homicide that occurred in Phoenix, Arizona at the end of the year.

Detective Gregory provided the name of Minnie..., residing in the community of Indian Wells, Arizona. [Minnie's] daughter, Lu, had told detectives that she was at her parent's residence during the time of the homicide. The information needed was to confirm Lu's story.

On June 9, 1992, at about 2:45 p.m., I contacted [Minnie]. I told [Minnie] the purpose of my contact and she provided the following information.

[Minnie] said, she does recall her daughter [Lu] returning to her residence. However, she does not remember what day she visited her. She did mention that her daughter was with an Anglo female that day. They both stayed the night and left the following day...

The interview was conducted in the Navajo language...

Gregory was obviously not investigating Trish and Lu. Ray's first trial was about to start and, as Begay's report stated, "the information needed was to confirm Lu's story." It was part of The Ray Krone Did It Investigation. Phil Barnes, however, noted the obvious discrepancies: Lu said they left "Friday morning" while Trish testified that they had "lunch at Hunan's with a bunch of friends, and then we headed up towards Indian Wells late that afternoon." And Lu first said they visited "Aunt Lucy," but the alibi was provided by Lu's mother, "Minnie."

The Hunan lunch had in fact occurred the Monday *after* the murder and not the Friday before, when the lesbians claimed they left for the reservation. On Monday, Lu called Squeakie Valdez to borrow several hundred dollars to go "skiing" (in quotes in the police report). Squeakie said that Trish and Lu were with another lesbian friend, Gloria. The Monday lunch bunch was Gloria, Trish, Lu and Lu's cousin, Betsy. After lunch Trish and Lu disappeared. They did not resurface in Phoenix until Wednesday, after Ray Krone had been arrested. Curiously, Trish had not asked Dorsey or Kim to feed her iguana this time.

Hmm, thought Phil, left town in the morning/afternoon...Hunan lunch Friday/Monday...visited Lucy/Minnie...hmm—Mickey Mouse alibi.

Phil had taken it upon himself to investigate the lesbian connection even before Chris Plourd came on board. Afterwards, between duties helping Chris prepare for trial, Phil continued to investigate Trish and Lu. Interviews with those named in the police reports continued. Phil wanted to talk to Trish also and saved her for last.

Dennis and Trish had had one child together. Dennis knew going into the marriage that Trish was bi-sexual. He dealt with it as best he could but lost it when he came home to find Trish and Lu in bed together with their daughter in the next room. Dennis left Trish and got custody of their daughter. Trish and Lu moved in together. While married, Dennis frequently came to the CBS Lounge at closing time to help his wife close. After their split, Lu assumed those duties, amid suspicions that Trish was taking money from the cash register to pay Lu. Dennis and Trish remained friendly after the divorce.

Dennis told Phil that Trish was "angry" about being fired. This description of Trish's reaction was an understatement according to Arredondo, who said that "Trish was in a state of shock," and also according to Ancona's best friend Beth, who used the word "hysterical."

In the early morning hours after being fired, a frantic Trish called all the barmaids she had hired to work at the CBS Lounge and vented her rage against Arredondo, demanding that they quit in protest. All were sympathetic except for Kim Ancona. She wanted Trish's job. According to her boyfriend Paul Clark's rambling deposition:

> Trish got fired on Thursday, which was a couple of days after Christmas. Christmas was on Wednesday, I believe. Thursday was when Kim came home and discussed it with me—that she was going to be taking over Trish's place because Trish had gotten fired. In fact, just before Christmas she had mentioned that she felt that Trish was messing up and maybe she should tell her. She asked my advice. I said no, that's between Trish and [Arredondo] anyway. And then Thursday and [she] got promoted and was going to be working full-time and she was looking forward to that...She had talked about moving in with her girlfriend for a while but once she knew she had a steady job and as soon as she got that promotion, like I was talking about. Christmas Eve was when she was really hyped up because she could get her car fixed and...she had some dental work she needed done and she had some tickets to pay to get her driver's license back and she was excited about that...She could get enough time to get her act together...She could get an apartment, get her stuff out of storage and you know get her life back together, get her kids back.

Ancona had told several others that she was the new bar manager. On her last afternoon she mentioned it to both best friend Beth and next-door neighbor Kathy. It was a bit of wishful thinking on Ancona's part because new bar owner Arredondo said he was in the early stages of evaluating the bar's operation and had yet to decide whom to name as the new manager. Nevertheless Kim believed that she was going to replace Trish. Her excitement most likely did not go unnoticed by Trish, who might have assumed that Ancona had bad-mouthed her to Arredondo. Ergo, Phil deduced, the motive. In his interview with Dennis:

> [Dennis] stated that his ex-wife [Trish] would not be capable of such an act [but] that Lu was capable of doing such a crime and that at one time [Lu] stated to him that she had killed someone in the course of being in the army and that it wasn't hard to do. He said that Lu was a person who frequently lost control and drank too much and that she could become physically violent...He also stated that he was glad someone was looking into the conviction of Mr. Krone, as "my gut feeling is that he didn't do it."

In Phil's interview with Trish's neighbor Kim, Kim added:

> Lu—that Indian girl—was really scary. She always scared me when I first met her. She gave me the creeps. And the whole thing was just so weird. There was something about her that really scared me. I heard that she—at a party—supposedly pulled a knife on somebody and held it to their throat. She was a scary person. She was the first person I thought of because she was scary.

Lu was butch. Several of those interviewed said that when they first met her they thought she was a man. From Ancona's best friend Beth's deposition:

> Q. How would you describe Lu's appearance? What did she look like?
> A. When I first met her I didn't know she was a girl...She's a very masculine looking woman and she's Indian, but never wore make-up, never wore feminine clothing...I was surprised when I found out she was a woman...That's a catty thing to think...is that a girl or a guy?

Trish was rarely seen without Lu close by. In social situations where Trish was in danger of being "hit on" by male or female, Lu was known to hover over her lover. Two sources reported seeing Lu break a beer bottle over the end of the bar and toss a male suitor up against a wall. Another source said that three weeks out of the army she had beaten up a policeman in Oklahoma.

Lu frightened many people. Her name appeared several times in the police reports almost always followed by "former military." Lu bragged that she'd seen combat in Grenada, presumably when US forces invaded that Caribbean Island country to take it back from the Cuban-supported Marxists who had overthrown the government in October 1983. The combat training Lu would have received meant that she knew how to wield a knife. In a US Army manual on combat techniques, Phil found a picture in the knife attack section that showed a right-handed soldier plunging a knife into the right side of the enemy's back. The resulting fatal injury that the manual described was virtually identical to the one Ancona died from except that the knife penetrated the corresponding spot on the left side of her back.

To Phil, Lu fit the bill in so many ways. She doted on Trish and would do anything for her lover. She could easily have been the clean-shaven "man" wearing a green army fatigue jacket that Dale Henson saw at the crime scene at 2:30 in the morning. She helped clean the bar and kitchen and knew where the knives were kept. Ray had confirmed that Lu wore Converse brand tennis shoes. No doubt she'd been issued a green fatigue jacket when she entered the army. Did she still have it and was she left-handed? Phil hoped he would learn the answers when he talked to Trish. But when he showed up at the cocktail lounge at Sky Harbor Airport where Trish worked, he was told that she had "breast cancer" and had left town. No one knew where she was.

There was no doubt that Trish had learned from Dennis and others that there was renewed interest in the Krone case and that someone was focusing on her. Was her disappearance a coincidence? Maybe. In any event, a stifled Phil in frustration turned to Tex.

It didn't take long to figure out that Tex's talk was bull...Phil feared a boondoggle. Mike Pain confirmed it. Tex said he'd located Trish in Bullhead City, but Mike found out that she'd moved east, not west. In Phoenix, Trish worked for the Marriott Corporation, which had the Sky Harbor concession. She had asked to be transferred. Mike located Trish working in the cocktail lounge at the Marriott in Lexington. The Tex tangent behind, Phil flew to Kentucky.

He caught his suspect by surprise. "Are you Trish?" he asked, approaching her in the crowded barroom.

"Yes."

"I came from Phoenix to find you."

"Are you serious?" She acted flattered, as if Phil were another one of many suitors who had the hots for her.

"You remember Ray Krone?" Phil got straight to the point. "There's a possibility that he's going to get a new trial."

Her mouth dropped open and she quickly covered it with her free hand as she took one step backward, nearly spilling the full tray of drinks she was carrying in her other hand.

"Can we talk?" Phil continued.

After checking with her manager, Trish sat down with Phil in a corner booth. She assumed Phil was a detective, which was fine with Phil. It had been more than three years since she'd testified at trial. Phil brought her up to date. He told her that the case had been reopened because of the bite mark and that a highly qualified odontologist from New Mexico recently looked at the evidence and concluded that Ray Krone could not have inflicted it.

"You remember a detective having you bite into Styrofoam?"

"Yes."

"Good—I want you to know that Dr Campbell has excluded you." Phil paused. "But he can't exclude your friend Lu."

"Impossible!" Trish interrupted. "She was with me the entire weekend."

"That's why I'm here."

Phil listened as Trish detailed her alibi. She waffled a bit at first, acknowledging that she went skiing, but when asked to elaborate reversed herself. "I never went skiing."

Though it was a virtual certainty that Trish and Lu had left town twice around the time of the murder, Trish's story eventually merged into one trip: after lunch at Hunan's on Friday, she and Lu dropped Gloria off at her apartment in northwest Phoenix. With Lu's cousin Betsy, they headed north to spend Friday night in Flagstaff. They continued on the next morning to the Indian reservation. They dropped Betsy off at Lu's Aunt Lucy (Betsy's mother's) place in Indian Wells. They went to an Indian bar in Holbrook and shot some pool. They spent Saturday night sleeping in the same bed at Lu's mother Minnie's place. And they returned to Phoenix Sunday evening to find a note on Trish's kitchen counter and learn for the first time of Kim Ancona's death.

Trish seemed quite anxious as she rapidly answered Phil's questions. As the interview progressed, her alibi became more and more consistent but didn't always fit the facts. Phil knew that if Betsy went with Trish and Lu to the reservation, then it had to be on the

Monday after the murder and not the Friday before because the receipt from the Twin Pines Motel indicated only two persons—no sign of Betsy. And it was certain that the three had left town Monday after their Chinese lunch and after dropping Gloria off at her apartment. But Phil didn't bring this up. He listened quietly to Trish's rendition of the "skiing and/or reservation" excursion, knowing that if he pointed out too many known discrepancies she might stop cooperating before he found out what he wanted to know about Lu. Also, Phil wanted to know more about a particular phone call.

"You can see where I'm coming from," Phil continued. "Ray Krone had an alibi but he was convicted by the bite mark. Now an expert says it's not his and that Lu can't be excluded. If this expert comes back and says it's Lu's bite mark—"

"I would say, yeah, it could be Lu," Trish interrupted, "if she hadn't been with me on the reservation."

"Do you know," Phil interjected while shuffling through his notes, "is Lu right-handed?"

"I don't remember."

Phil paused, slowly scribbling her answer onto his notepad.

"No wait—come to think of it, when she shot darts, she shot left-handed."

Phil went on to find out that Lu had indeed kept her green army-issued fatigue jacket and wore it frequently, especially when out to the gay bars. "It still has her name on it."

Too bad, Phil thought, that Henson hadn't been able to read it.

Trish also verified that Lu wore "cheap" tennis shoes but she couldn't remember the brand.

Phil had with him a folder of related material: police reports, notes, depositions, etc. He noticed that Trish would cock her head to try to get a look as he went through them one by one.

"We have information that you telephoned Ancona the morning of the day she was murdered?" Phil said, opening the document he was holding to the page earmarked with a paperclip.

"Don't remember anything about it," Trish answered, trying to get a better look.

Phil set Beth's deposition down at an angle and pushed it toward Trish:

Q. Did you know that she [Trish] had gotten fired on the 26th?
A. Yes, I did.

Q. Did Kim [Ancona] talk to you about that?

A. Yes, she did.

Q. Did Kim indicate to you that Trish was blaming her in part for getting fired?
A. Yes.

Q. Tell me what you remember about what Kim said.
A. Trish was fired. She was given the reason was because of the party. She closed the bar on Christmas and then everyone drank for free...but Kimmie [Ancona] thought that it was really because [of] her relationship with Lu. [It] had pretty much come out of the closet and it was pretty blatant and there was a new owner coming in and he didn't want to establish that as going to be that kind of bar. When Trish was fired she expected the other three bartenders to quit with her and they all basically said, "Yeah, right." You know, "Are you going to pay our rent?" And Kimmie had a little guilt because she cared very much for Trish and they had a—they were good friends. But, you know...that was her job and so she felt, she was torn, she felt like she had been put in a bad situation but she decided that she was going to keep her job and her and Trish did make up Saturday, basically, or talked again. It seemed like they had made up.

Q. In what sense?
A. Just that she [Trish] apologized, she was overreacting the first time. I think at least Kimmie had thought, the first time, when she called Kimmie, she wanted everybody to quit. She was hysterical and upset.

Q. So Saturday the 28th she [Trish] and Kim talked, to your knowledge?
A. Yes. I believe so.

Q. Was she at the bar or what?
A. I think it was a phone call that morning, from what Kim said.

Q. OK. Are you telling me that Kim had let you know at some point that Trish had called her on Saturday the 28th?
A. That's what I remember.

"I have a recollection of it," Trish now said, handing Beth's deposition back to Phil. "But I wouldn't have anything to apologize for anyway..."

Phil agreed that Trish didn't call to apologize. He had his own theory why Trish called Ancona that morning when she supposedly was on the road to or already in Indian Wells. This was 1991, long before cell phones were common and affordable. It would have been costly and inconvenient, to say the least, to interrupt a vacation to make such a seemingly innocuous phone call.

Phil was pretty proud of himself. He had resolved all but one clue. And he didn't have to hide, obscure, manipulate or alter any of them to fit his suspects—the way the sherlocks in the Phoenix police department had.

The unresolved clue was finding the car that Henson saw drive into and leave the parking lot and from which had emerged the person he saw enter and exit the CBS Lounge. Henson described this vehicle as "foreign-made medium green Gremlin type compact sedan." This description didn't match the vehicle Lu drove, a pickup. Nor did it match Trish's car. Also, Phil wondered where Trish and Lu lay low after they doubled back into Phoenix. Perhaps finding the getaway car would reveal their hideout.

π

The drawback to "reductio ad absurdum" is that while it can prove a hypothesis to be false by finding a single contradiction, it can't prove the hypothesis true by finding no contradictions—as Phil had found none to render "the lesbian connection" absurd. Trish had a motive (she was upset with Ancona for taking her job), the means (Lu) and an alibi that didn't hold water. But all Phil really had was circumstantial evidence. Finding the getaway car and the lesbians' lair would also fit into that category. So, for the time being, Phil put these issues on the back burner and concentrated his attention on the other unresolved clue of note, the bite mark. It had been substantial enough to convict Ray Krone. Would it, if properly analyzed, be substantial enough to implicate Lu the left-handed lesbian?

"She [Lu] had a tooth that was turned kinda' funny," Trish had told Phil in Lexington.

Phil remembered Dr. Homer Campbell's explanation of the bite mark evidence. Campbell had traveled at my invitation to Phoenix, gone into the evidence room in the basement of the Maricopa County Courthouse and evaluated the bite mark evidence. Afterwards we sat down together at a corner table in the courthouse cafeteria. Based upon his comparison of Ray's teeth cast with the evidence bite mark photographs, he assured me that Ray was positively excluded.

Also in evidence were six Styrofoam bite impressions of individuals the Romley complex had excluded: bar owner Hank Arredondo, cook David Torres, Ancona's ex-husband John Supler, Ancona's boyfriend Paul Clark, Trish and Lu. What did Campbell think of these other suspects?

Around a photograph of the bite mark, Dr. Campbell spread the six photocopies of the other suspects' teeth patterns and asked me to pick the one that best fit. Phil pointed to Lu's bite mark pattern. Campbell lit up and pushed the other photocopies aside. It was clear that Phil had selected Campbell's own choice. Campbell went on to show and explain the correspondences between Lu's upper teeth and the bite marks in the photo.

The day after Phil returned home from his interview with Trish, he called Dr. Campbell. It was more than six months after Campbell had looked at the bite mark.

"You remember the bite mark in the Krone case? You said there was a mark Rawson had overlooked…"

After a pause, Phil added, hoping to jog Campbell's memory, "…made by tooth nine [the upper left front tooth]."

"Yeah, I remember it. I think it's there."

"What can you say about it?"

"I think it was made by a rotated tooth," he answered without hesitation.

Phil wondered what the difference was between "twisted kinda' funny" and "rotated"?

After talking with Campbell, Phil went to work analyzing the bite mark evidence, taking into account what he'd just learned:

1. Dr. Piakas initially misaligned the bite mark as he took photographs. Instead of setting the midline between the two front teeth (#8 and #9), he set it between the marks made by the upper right central incisor (front tooth #8) and the adjacent lateral incisor (#7). These two teeth (naturally uneven) were matched to Ray's two front teeth (#8 and #9) (Figure 1) and away he went.

2. This boner was subsequently carried through by all bite mark experts except for Dr. Campbell, who placed the midline one mark counterclockwise from Piakas's setting. Because of the distraction caused by Piakas's misalignment, no one but Campbell noticed the faint mark left by the assailant's upper left front tooth (#9). (Figure 1)

3. Consequently, Dr. Rawson had to conjure up a two-bite theory to make Ray's dentition fit. He called one the "twelve o'clock bite" and the other the "ten o'clock bite." In doing so he used a dimple and a scratch to fill in the blanks. (Figures 2 and 3)

4. With the midline adjusted as Campbell suggested and the innocuous tooth #9 put into play, the symmetry of the bite mark jumped out at Phil. He compared it with Lu's teeth pattern and voilà! (Figure 4)

I shared Phil's findings with Chris, imagining that he would call Trish and/or Lu to the stand and pull a Perry Mason—press one of them into dramatically confessing in front of the jury. But that's how the Hollywood justice game is *portrayed*, not how the real justice game is *played*. No court is going to allow witnesses to be harassed, and rightly so. Otherwise every attorney would badger every adversarial witness to death. At Ray's first trial Judge Hotham did not even allow the jury to learn that Trish and Lu were lesbian lovers. In her testimony, Trish stuck to the "facts." Ray was the only one in the courtroom who knew that Trish was exaggerating to the point of lying about Ray and Ancona's "budding" relationship. I would be extremely

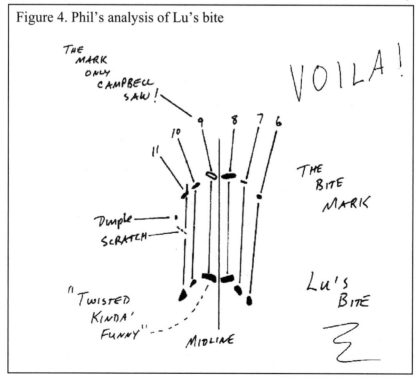

Figure 4. Phil's analysis of Lu's bite

surprised to learn that there has ever been a murder trial outside of Hollywood in which the actual killer confessed on the witness stand. Nevertheless, Phil was disappointed that Chris decided to go with Tennessee Mike as the "other dude" who did it.

At trial, however, Phil was impressed by the way Chris twisted Mike's and especially Beth's testimony to give the impression that they were hiding something. After the bar closed, Mike had taken Beth to his house across the street from where Ancona lived with Paul Clark, both waiting for Ancona to show up. She didn't. Mike got impatient and made a move on Beth. Beth got upset and demanded to be taken home. Mike obliged. On the stand, Mike denied that he returned home via the CBS Lounge. His testimony was followed by witness Teri. She had also been at the CBS Lounge the night Ancona was murdered. But more importantly she testified that in the past she'd been sexually active with Mike and that "he bit [me] on the neck…and breast." It was very effective. Some of the jurors noticeably cringed during Teri's testimony.

Could Tennessee Mike really have been the one who, after being denied sex and after taking Beth home, stopped in to the CBS Lounge, a loaded pistol, and raped and killed Kim Ancona after biting her the same way Teri said Mike had bitten her? Not likely, according to Phil. He took Teri's testimony for what it was. Teri had gotten Chris's name out of *The Arizona Republic* article written by Susan Leonard under the headline "Murder Retrial Focuses on Bite Marks." It detailed the bite injuries to Ancona. Teri called Chris the next day and parroted the details, inserting Mike as the perpetrator. Mike had jilted Teri and this, Phil surmised, was her way of getting even. Not one of Mike's many other conquests came forward to corroborate Teri's biting story.

And what about the bite mark Phil thought he'd correctly analyzed? Well, Chris knew full well that there is no validity to bite mark analysis and having a defense expert come in and realign the bite mark differently from the state's star witness would generate a pissing contest with the experts volleying back and forth between Rawson's scratch and Campbell's faint rotated tooth mark. It would be a crapshoot as to whose "eye-brain coordination" would prevail. Nevertheless, Phil argued that it had to be somebody's bite mark and boasted to me, "Hey! My guess is better than theirs." To soothe Phil, I emphasized that the Latin translation of "bite mark analysis" is "reductio ad bullshit 'em." Three years later Phil would prove this translation to be accurate by snookering the phenomenal Mississippi Ouija Board Certified bite mark expert, Dr. Michael West, into

Figure 5. The West Phenomenon

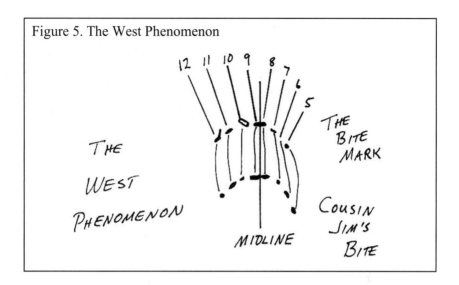

matching my dentition to the bite mark evidence that had twice been used to convict cousin Ray (Figure 5).

As it turned out, Teri's testimony played well in court and that's what the game is all about. It would have been difficult for Chris to start, wage and win a secondary bite mark battle and then break Trish's prosecution-supported "perfect" alibi while she batted her innocent "Who, me?" hazel eyes at the jury.

Chris made the right choice and Phil understood.

π

Attorneys deduce. Their guesswork is called "final argument." This final discourse is where each attorney tells the jury what he thinks the evidence means. There is no requirement that their yarns resolve *all* the clues, the way a Sherlock Holmes story does. In the Simpson case the only evidence of any real importance for the defense was OJ's blood stained leather gloves, which he tossed into the bushes, where they got wet and shrank. At trial, OJ was unable to pull them over the rubber gloves he was required to wear. Forget about the trail of blood dripping from OJ's cut hand and accompanying the footprints of his Bruno Magli shoes leaving the crime scene. For defense attorney Johnnie Cochran, the only deduction needed was captured by his jingle, "If it doesn't fit, you must acquit."

All that was necessary for defense attorney Chris Plourd to resolve the circumstantial evidence was to show that someone else could just as easily have committed the crime. In court, circumstantial evidence is as good as direct evidence, provided that no other reasonable explanation exists. Tennessee Mike was not only a likely candidate, he was an even better candidate than Ray. He was known to have been out and about in the early morning hours of the murder in the vicinity of the CBS Lounge. He was horny. He wore Converse brand tennis shoes. He owned a green army fatigue jacket. He was clean-shaven.

But the jury accepted Dr. Piakas's and Dr. Rawson's dollar-induced dental deductions. They were all that prosecutor Noel Levy needed to make up the story that Ray and Kim had a budding relationship, yet to be consummated, when Ray went to the CBS Lounge to help her close up. He went expecting sex but when he was denied it he went berserk, kidnapped, raped, bit and killed her. While Levy in his final argument paid lip service to "consider *all* the evidence," he emphasized that "if Ray Krone bit her, *he* killed her."

Justice game jingles—"burden of proof," "innocent until proven guilty," "beyond a reasonable doubt"—were bantered about during the whole process and then rolled up into one big jangle at the end of the trial. The jury was instructed that "the defendant is innocent until proven guilty and the state has the burden of proving the defendant guilty beyond a reasonable doubt." But from what Phil and I observed, this justice game jingle jangle was too esoteric for the jury to comprehend and had no real impact. Interviews with several jurors shortly after their verdict indicated that while "reasonable doubt" was briefly mentioned it was barely discussed and none of them seemed to know what it meant. Understanding the concept of the state's having the "burden of proof" also must have eluded the jury. When Levy failed to meet this burden, they simply "discounted all the evidence." Then, unable to accept the notion of "innocent until proven guilty," the jurors put the burden upon themselves to prove Ray guilty beyond their own personal reasonable doubt by independently reanalyzing the bite mark evidence.

π

Here's Phil Barnes's final argument, presented to you who have just heard his evidence:

Eight days before the murder of Kim Ancona, Hank Arredondo purchased the CBS Lounge. Under the previous owner, Trish "had it made" as the bar's manager. It was good money. She ran the operation virtually unsupervised. She had hired all the bartenders, including Kim Ancona. Her constant companion Lu was not on the payroll but helped Trish close the bar each night.

Arredondo (according to Trish) initially led Trish to believe that she would continue on as bar manager with business as usual. He caught her completely off guard when he took her aside, right after she'd completed her Thursday night shift, and fired her. Trish said she "was laid off because I made too much money." While this may have been a factor, Arredondo, not wanting his establishment to turn into a "gay bar," was concerned about Trish's sexual preference. He also suspected that she hosted "after-hours drug parties" in the bar.

Trish returned to her apartment with Lu, furious with Arredondo. Wasting no time in those early morning hours, she called the bartenders she'd hired and urged them to quit in protest. All were sympathetic except for Ancona, who coveted Trish's job and assumed she would get it. Hysterical, Trish let her thoughts get out of hand. Most likely she would have calmed down in time, had it not been for Lu, who would do anything for her lover. Together they stayed up drinking and drugging, eventually plotting to kill Kim Ancona. They selected Saturday night because Trish knew that Ancona would be working and she knew how to get her alone.

To establish their alibi, Trish called neighbor Kim to her apartment, ostensibly to feed her pet iguana, but in reality to serve as an alibi witness. This is the reason why Trish seemed less interested in having her lizard fed than in having neighbor Kim "be sure to call ex-husband Dennis" (another alibi witness) and tell him that she would be out of town for the weekend.

Trish and Lu then left town and drove to Flagstaff, where they spent Friday night. Trish paid cash for a room at the Twin Pines Motel making sure to get and retain the receipt for alibi purposes.

The next day, instead of continuing on to the reservation, Trish and Lu doubled back to Phoenix. From their hideout Trish immediately called Ancona, pretending that all was forgiven and forgotten. But this call was in reality the setup call to get Ancona alone. Trish led Ancona to believe that she had scored a large quantity of drugs, probably cocaine, because one source reported that Trish had a penchant for the drug and even dealt it out of the bar to support her habit. This source also said that in the past Trish had dumped a boyfriend named Jim, an engineer by trade, when the cocaine ran out.

Trish told Ancona that she had planned to unload the score during her shift that night at the bar if she hadn't been fired, but now that Ancona was "the manager" would she help? Trish would make it worth her while and of course Ancona must tell no one her source and must be alone when the drugs were delivered. Ancona agreed and started taking orders from her trusted friends. Neighbor Kathy didn't get her order in before Ancona left for work, which is why she showed up at the bar right before closing time.

Ancona called Trish after performing her closing chores and assured Trish that the coast was clear. She then unlocked the front door and waited. Soon Lu drove up in the "Gremlin type" mystery car and parked in front of Dale Henson, who was power-washing the sidewalk. Henson diverted the hose to let Lu pass and enter the CBS Lounge.

Exactly what transpired inside the CBS Lounge in the early morning hours of December 29, 1991 is anybody's guess. The Hollywood producer/director who films the movie version of *Jingle Jangle* may stage it as luridly and vividly as he wishes. However, the gist of what happened is that Lu, "former military," was on a combat mission to take out her lover's nemesis. She donned her army issue green camouflage jungle jacket for the task. She did not bring a weapon because she knew the terrain and knew where to find one. (Phil: "Did Lu know where the knives were kept?" Trish: "Lu cleaned the bar and knew where everything was.")

Lu's favorite drink was rum and Coke. As soon as Ancona saw Lu enter she mixed one up and placed it on the bar next to the drug money, already laid out for the expected drug deal. Lu wasted no time. She chugalugged her drink and pocketed the drug money. Ancona barely had time to take a sip from the bottle of Bud Lite she'd opened for herself. Lu slugged her squarely in the face. Ancona fell to the floor and sustained the injuries to her right knee, elbow and hand detailed in the medical examiner's report. Ancona on the floor in a stupor, Lu rushed through the swinging door into the kitchen and returned in no time with the boning knife selected for its sharp, relatively thin blade. Lu pulled Ancona to her feet, threw her into a hammerlock and held the knife to her neck with her left hand. She forced Ancona across the bar and down the hall to the men's restroom, inflicting five superficial stab wounds on the way.

The plan was to kill Ancona in the men's room and stage a rape so as to throw investigators off the track that it was a premeditated, cold-blooded killing. The men's room was selected to obscure the fact that the "rape" was done by a woman. The plan was executed to perfection. The only barrier was the door broken off its hinges and propped open with a wooden shim. It was knocked off the shim as Ancona was forced past it.

Once inside the men's room, Lu plunged the knife into Ancona's back, through both her blouse and her tank top, deep into the left lung.

"This is a high shock-producing injury," reads the combat manual; "blood pressure drops precipitously." And so did Ancona drop, so heavily onto the knife protruding from her back that its blade bent. (Prosecutor Levy claimed that the knife bent when Ancona was stabbed, arguing that Ray Krone committed the crime in a particularly heinous and depraved manner.) As Ancona writhed on the floor, Lu went to work staging the rape. She removed Ancona's shoes and wiggled off her jeans and flung them under the urinal.

Then she rolled Ancona over enough to retrieve the knife, which she used to slit the panties up the side. She flung them near the jeans. She cut the tank top and bra up the middle and removed them and the already open blouse, leaving the garments on the floor under the torso. She then spread Ancona's legs and used the broken wooden shim to finish the "rape."

Using paper towels and water from the sink, Lu cleaned the knife of blood and fingerprints, deposited it under the plastic bag in the waste container and dropped the soiled paper towels into the plastic bag.

Then, after wiping her fingerprints off the cocktail glass on her way out, she once again passed Dale Henson, jumped into the mystery car and exited the parking lot heading west on West Camelback Road. Mission accomplished.

Phil would have agreed with Levy that the pubic hairs found on Ancona's abdomen were random hairs picked up from the restroom floor. While the FBI determined that they came from an American Indian, they could not be matched to any particular individual. They could easily have adhered to Ancona as Lu was rolling her about to stage the rape…or when Detective Olson at one point rolled the corpse onto its stomach to examine the fatal injury before the body was taken to the morgue. Not even Phil's active imagination could come up with a scenario in which Lu would have bared herself to leave her own pubic hairs behind. But then Phil doesn't have a clue what lesbians do.

Somewhere along the way Ancona was bitten. Lu could easily have inflicted the injury before she hit Ancona in the mouth by pushing up her tank top and bra.

Some justice game players think that Ancona was bitten through her clothing. But Phil thinks that Lu left her mark while removing Ancona's clothing, as Ancona lay dying on the bathroom floor. It could have been merely a part of staging the rape or something Lu added for her own perverted pleasure. Forensic statistics do support the fact that biting occurs more frequently during homosexual assaults.

Finally, Phil argues that sometime the Sunday evening after the murder reality set in for Trish. Perhaps aware of the "talk on the street," fear kicked in that Phoenix's finest might actually solve the crime and that she would go to prison for a long, long time. This fear explains why Trish decided to get out of Dodge the next day and leave town a second time to go "skiing."

π

In the year 2000, Phil still thought the lesbians did it.

That year, at each of the several meetings with Ray's new Phoenix attorney, Alan Simpson, Chris Plourd emphasized that "We must find out who did it." Chris's strategy was simple—have Ancona's clothing retested for DNA, have the results plugged into the nationwide DNA database known as CODIS (the Combined DNA Index System) and hope that the perpetrator popped up. The FBI had launched CODIS in 1998. Arizona's Department of Public Health was busy gathering and entering DNA profiles of prison inmates (sex offenders first) into the system when Ray's appeal ended and Svengali and Simpson came on board to assist Chris in doing the next phase of Ray's case, a new evidence discovery Rule 32.

While it was a good idea to pursue all avenues, Phil didn't think much of this strategy. After all, Lu was still walking the streets. Phil always wanted to resolve the last piece of his lesbian puzzle and find the getaway car. Something Trish had said in the Lexington interview gave him the clue where to look. He'd wanted to pursue the lead right after we'd returned from that road trip but it was just before Ray's second trial was about to start and it would have required another road trip. Chris had decided to go with Tennessee Mike as the other "dude" who did it, so no matter what Phil might discover, it would have been of no practical use. Helping Chris prepare for trial thwarted sherlock Phil's work on the final piece of his puzzle. Now that Ray's Rule 32 was cranking up, Phil was back in the saddle.

A detailed search at the Department of Motor Vehicles located the suspected vehicle in a junkyard in Parker. So, while Chris and company were putzing around with DNA, I mounted up and rode along with Phil to check out the car firsthand and see if by chance it fit Henson's description.

Along the way I couldn't help but notice on the map that Parker was, like Bullhead City, a border town on the Arizona side of the Colorado River and they weren't all that far apart. Bullhead City was where Tex last said the crime could be solved. I wondered whether Tex might really have been on to something and maybe I had cut him loose too soon. It would be disconcerting if I were to learn that the vehicle's owner went by the nickname of "Sugar" or "Hot Lips." I put that flash from the past out of my mind and consoled myself that if the six-hour round trip from Phoenix to Parker turned into another Tex type boondoggle, at least we wouldn't be out ten grand this time. Riding along with Phil was cheap.

The car's last-recorded owner worked at the Indian casino in Parker, where Phil found her to be on her break. He relayed through a manager the message that he would like to talk with her about the Krone case. The manager returned and said that she had just become sick and gone home. The manager didn't know if she went by a nickname or not.

At the junkyard, Phil located the Volkswagen Jetta. It fit the bill, being in the "Gremlin type" class of vehicles popular back when...It was blue, so under the amber lights it would have appeared green to Henson the night he saw it drive up and park in front of the CBS Lounge.

The final piece of the puzzle was in place. Phil decided to wait until after the DNA fizzled out to triumphantly reveal his latest discovery.

But Phil was in for a little surprise.

CHAPTER 26
A LONE SOLDIER

"**T**hat's the guy who did it!" said Chris Plourd with marked enthusiasm.

It was late in the afternoon in mid-March 2002. I was on a conference call with Chris and Alan Simpson, Ray's Phoenix attorney. Simpson had finally received the DNA report from the Phoenix police crime lab and had faxed in on to Chris and me. We'd been expecting it since December. Phil was chomping at the bit, thinking it wouldn't amount to anything and he could reveal the identity of the lesbian owner of the getaway car. The report put Phil and his lesbian theory into a tail spin.

In January the previous year Simpson had filed a petition with the superior court for DNA testing in Ray's case: "DNA testing technology has advanced considerably since the examinations performed in this case...[which] allow the forensic scientist to identify DNA genotypes from multiple contributors in mixed evidence samples." The petition cited the Arizona law passed the year before that allowed post conviction DNA testing provided that a reasonable probability exists that the petitioner would not have been prosecuted or convicted if exculpatory results had been obtained, the DNA evidence still exists, and the evidence was not previously subjected to the requested testing whose results might resolve an unanswered question (like who actually committed the crime).

County Attorney Rick Romley, through a deputy attorney, naturally and routinely opposed the petition. "The evidence produced at trial does not suggest 'real doubt of guilt.'" That evidence was the bite mark and Rawson's testimony that Ray's teeth matched the bite wound, "none of [which] has been impugned or questioned." The County Attorney's Office's statement ignored defense experts Sperber's, Vale's and Campbell's contrary opinions. It went on to say, "None of the scientific methods used to analyze the evidence in this case has been found invalid or unreliable." Obviously Romley's gang was not aware of the West sting, in which these same "scientific methods" were also used to match the bite mark on Kim Ancona's breast with the teeth of "the shady Mr. Rix."

Nonetheless, the Honorable Alfred Fenzel ordered the Phoenix police crime lab to do the requested DNA testing.

Criminologist Kelcey Means, who replaced Scott Piette, performed the new tests. In the report she submitted on February 20, 2002, she noted,

> The mixed DNA profile from at least three sources was obtained from the bloodstained lady's tank top with a cut on the backside and ripped or cut up the front and found on the floor under the victim in the men's bathroom. The major component of this mixture is from an unidentified source. This profile will be searched against the profiles in CODIS and any matches will be reported.

In August 2000, Arizona had received a $201,250 grant from the National Institute of Justice to analyze DNA samples obtained from convicted criminals and load the results into CODIS, the FBI's Combined DNA Index System. "We must do all we can," said Attorney General Janet Reno, "to help our state and local partners employ 21st Century technology in their efforts to make communities safer. Increasing law enforcement's ability to use DNA evidence in the fight against crime makes sense and, ultimately, gets violent offenders off our streets."

This grant helped Arizona's Department of Public Safety erase its backlog of four thousand unanalyzed samples and continue its program of DNA-profiling the state's entire prison population. Because it was a huge project, sex offenders were the first in line. There were twenty-two thousand Arizona inmate profiles in the computer when the DNA results from the tank top were plugged into CODIS. And, voilà, a convicted sex offender popped out.

When Chris said, "That's the guy who did it!" he was thumbing through the material Simpson had faxed. Attached to Kelcey Means's report was the dossier of one Kenneth Phillips. Four weeks after the murder of Kim Ancona, Phillips had been arrested for child molestation. He'd pleaded guilty and was sentenced to ten years in prison. He was an American Indian who at the time of the murder lived three hundred yards, within walking distance, of the CBS Lounge. He was currently serving time in Florence and was scheduled to walk in four months.

When Simpson first received the fax he called a contact in the county attorney's office who assured him that the report didn't mean anything because it was "unverified." So Simpson was less than enthusiastic about the DNA report. He remembered a previous one. The wind had left his sail ten months earlier, at the burial ceremony of the report of Ed Blake's that had identified Ray's DNA on Ancona's bra. Ten minutes later, however, the wind was back in Simpson's sail.

Chris explained the protocol to me. Whenever there's a CODIS hit a new sample is taken directly from the suspect, rerun and compared a second time with the evidence sample. This verification process guarantees that no errors or mistakes have been made along the way and that the crime scene DNA donor has absolutely been identified.

"This hit is not of someone in Illinois who had never been to Phoenix," Chris emphasized. "It is of an Indian who was arrested within weeks of the murder for a sex offence and who coincidentally lived around the corner from the crime scene. What are the chances there's an error?"

Excitement erupted in the Krone camp, to say the least.

The hot poker was up the prosecution's ass. What were they going to do with it? They'd been sitting on it for weeks. An informed source revealed that after receiving the report, the Romley complex refused to accept it and someone from the county attorney's office showed up at the crime lab and announced that the report couldn't be correct because Ray Krone had committed the crime, then proceeded to go round and round with the crime lab personnel, pressuring them to fix it. But the crime lab held its ground, ending the confrontation with, "What do you want us to do, change the results?"

That there is merit to this revelation is supported by suspicions that the report did not get into Simpson's hands through normal channels. The crime lab reports to the Phoenix Police Department, which then reports to the county attorney. When the crime lab completes its work on a case, regardless of whether the work was ordered by the court at the request of a defendant, the report is sent to the case agent, a detective in the police department. After it is reviewed it is normally routinely forwarded to the defense council. Crime lab technicians are prohibited from directly contacting the other side without permission from a prosecutor. It is a serious infraction to do so and could cost the offender his job.

Detective Dennis Olson inherited the position from Detective Chuck Gregory for the second trial and remained the case agent. He received a preliminary copy of the report on February 20. The CODIS hit came in on March 8. Ten days later, out of the blue, the report showed up on Simpson's fax machine. But that's not the odd part. The police file on Kenneth Phillips was also attached. At some point, Detective Olson was obliged to turn the DNA report over to the defense. But he had no obligation to turn over Phillips's police record.

Since when does the Phoenix Police Department help the defense when it doesn't have to? Not even Olson is that dumb. While the unknown source of the fax could have been Olson having some sort of cerebral malfunction, it's more likely that the source of the leak was someone inside the police department or its crime lab who was fed up with the Romley complex shenanigans. Be that as it may, the cat was out of the bag.

In a heartbeat the leak was leaked to the press. The defense was doing all the talking, providing reporters with anything and everything they wanted to know about the DNA matching a convicted sex offender who was about to be released from prison. The Romley complex "took the Fifth," saying very little and downplaying the match as insignificant and "unverified." No doubt, behind the scenes it was trying feverishly to come up with some sort of "unindicted coejaculator theory" that would keep Ray Krone in prison.

The next day Chris and I were in Phoenix meeting with Simpson and Svengali to assess the situation. The consensus was that County Attorney Rick Romley was certainly not going to free Ray at least until the DNA match was confirmed, which would take the better part of a month. Suspicion was that someone was telling Romley he should retest *all* the evidence. This scuttlebutt, if true, was of great concern. Finding Ray's DNA on the bra would be just what was needed to support an "unindicted coejaculator theory."

Simpson was enjoying the notoriety. As attorney of record he was the point man for all inquiries and the recipient of the accolades. He seemed content to simply wait for the DNA confirmation. But Chris wanted to keep the hot poker moving.

Chris urged Svengali to "get down to the prison and talk to Phillips before he lawyers up."

Svengali had been silently hanging out on the periphery of our meetings with a puckered brow. He was the only one of us not excited. I couldn't understand this man's lack of exuberance. After three days in Phoenix, I returned home to await further developments. A week later a call from Chris explained Svengali's sour puss.

"You've got to get some money to Svengali," Chris said.

"What for?"

"He's dragging his feet getting down to see Phillips." Chris was noticeably frustrated.

Svengali had been retained two years before to do the necessary investigation for the Rule 32. In the beginning he appeared to be fired up. He obtained the record for both trials and became quite familiar with the case. He also drove down to the prison to see Ray. As time passed, however, I could discern nothing else that he might be contributing to the case. More and more I wondered what he was doing beyond reading the trial transcripts and visiting Ray. He had attended the several meetings in Simpson's office over the two years but said next to nothing. I assumed that his services would be needed should the DNA tests prove to be negative.

But the results were anything but negative. The case appeared to be just about over and Svengali wanted more money. Throughout the game I never second-guessed Chris. He didn't nickel and dime us. Since losing Ray's trial six years ago he remained passionately involved and didn't ask for a single penny for himself. The most I did for him was pick up his airfare to Phoenix whenever there was a meeting. So when Chris said Svengali needed some money I didn't argue and, although I was skeptical of its necessity, I told him I would see what I could do.

I called Svengali and told him I would like to take care of his account. Would he send a statement itemizing the work he'd done so far as provided in his standard fee agreement?

> Consultant *may*, at the request of the Client submit periodic billing statements to Client itemizing amounts charged under the basic hourly rate [$200 per hour] and/or expenses for which Consultant is entitled to reimbursement.

The contract required a $4,000 retainer, which equated to twenty hours work—about the time it would take to read the transcripts and visit Ray. I hadn't notice the word "may" when I signed the original contract, and Svengali now opted to use it. He declined to send an itemized statement. Instead he sent another one of his standard fee agreements as if he were starting over. This time he wanted a $10,000 retainer—whoa!—shades of Tex. All Chris wanted him to do was drive down to Florence for a talk with Kenneth Phillips. To me it was another Tex type gamble. If I were Phillips I would clam up. But Chris thought it was worth a try. He'd made fun of me over Tex. I was prepared to take another gamble and risk a Svengali fiasco in talking to Phillips.

Because Ray qualified as an indigent after his second trial, the State of Arizona paid for his appeal. Over the appeal's four years, fortunately, only minimal expenses needed to be covered. However, cranking up the Rule 32 had required significant funding. When the Rule 32 began in earnest two years earlier I called Ray's parents to discuss money. It was clear from the conversation that they had yet to recover from the devastating second trial and I didn't push it. From the beginning, my brother Dan, who ran the day-to-day operation of our business, agreed that this was a worthy cause and we jointly saw to it that the necessary funding continued. For me, the inconvenience of postponing for a few years some planned home remodeling and landscaping paled in comparison with Ray's suffering. We invested more funds, another twenty thousand dollars, to keep the ball rolling. Svengali and Simpson were retained and Ed Blake was paid to retest the bra sample. Now with a substantial result, the DNA hit, to offer Jim and Carolyn Leming, I called them and explained the Svengali situation. They said they would send five thousand dollars. I called Svengali and told him I would have a check for him when I was back in Phoenix the following week.

Svengali got off the dime but I feared it might not be in time. Three weeks had passed since the DNA hit and Detective Olson had already been to Florence to see Phillips. As was learned latter, it was a short meeting (twenty minutes) in which Phillips agreed with Olson: "You weren't in the CBS Lounge on the night of December 28, 1991, were you?" and "You didn't kill Kim Ancona, did you?" Fortunately Olson failed to emphasize to Phillips that he was a serious murder suspect and it would be to his benefit not to talk to anyone else.

Svengali was in luck. His hour and a half interrogation started slowly with denial after denial. But before it was over, Svengali had Phillips all but singing like a canary:

Q: What happened?
A: She, uh, I can't remember. I know, I don't have memories that...she said, I think she said, you know, "Get out of here. I'm cleaning," you know. I can't remember the rest of what I told her. I think I told her that, "I need to use the restroom," you know. And I walked...I think I walked out and she mumbled something, like in anger. I don't...I remember that...that just, I kinda got upset, because you gotta go. It kinda upset me...

Q: ...so she said something to you and it was, she was very angry and muttered something and you were upset, you were very angry yourself, right?
A: Yeah...

Q: Well, isn't it, isn't it true that what you did was you got a knife and you went back in there to get her out of there so you could use the restroom. A fight started. Isn't that what happened?

A: Might have happened...

Q: Might have?

A: Might have.

Q: Do you remember taking her cloths off of her? This would have been after she was down on the ground.

A: No.

Q: But that's a possibility also?

A: Could be...

Q: But you do have a recollection, based upon what I hear you saying, that there was a time when you woke up one morning and you were wondering where did this come from? And you had blood on your cloths?

A: Yeah...

Q: So you raised up from the sofa in the living room and what's the first thing you look at where you see blood?

A: The first thing I looked at was my hands.

Q: Blood on your hands?

A: Yeah.

The check had already been written when I boarded the plane in Reno. I heard the news of Svengali's trip as soon as I arrived in Phoenix. I was surprised, to say the least, to hear the successful outcome and thought, It's not going to be enough. I hadn't been able to bring myself to write a check for ten grand, or even half that, for what I fully expected would be a boondoggle. It was for a mere three thousand dollars.

"Here's part of it," I said and handed him the check.

He kept smiling and continued to detail how he had extracted the "confession." It wasn't really a confession because Phillips never actually admitted killing Ancona and had trouble recollecting any details. But Phillips's statements were certainly incriminating and were played up in the media as if they *were* a confession. Svengali was so pleased with himself at his triumph that at one point he said to me, "Jim, I could even get you to confess to [doing something obscene with] an elephant!"

Svengali pocketed the check. In terms of time spent he was overpaid but in terms of accomplishment he was underpaid. I didn't broach the subject again, fully expecting to hear from him in the near future. But I never did. He would find another way to get paid.

The "confession" was leaked to the press at the speed of sound. The local TV stations played the "blood on the hands" sound bite over and over.

The hot poker was continuing its journey north but there was still no significant movement from the Romley complex. Then, a week after the "confession," the DNA confirmation of Kenneth Phillips came in. The next day, a Friday, Alan Simpson tweaked the hot poker with a letter to the county attorney emphasizing the indisputable evidence of Phillips's guilt, which equated to the undeniable truth that Ray Krone was innocent and that he, Rick Romley, and Maricopa County would be held liable for damages to his client for continued incarceration.

Romley sat on it over the weekend and then held an early Monday morning press conference. When I saw the reruns, to me the man looked visibly whipped when he acknowledged that new DNA evidence made it clear that Ray Krone was the wrong man. "He deserves an apology from us, that's for sure. A mistake was made here...What do you say to him? An injustice was done and we will try to do better. And we're sorry."

He ordered the immediate release of Ray Krone. Of course he didn't technically order it. Only a judge can do that. But no Arizona judge was going free Ray Krone without specific instructions from "the most powerful man in the state."

π

It was unusually warm that April day at Lake Tahoe. There was still skiing at Heavenly Valley but the snow was slushy. Already thinking of summer, I was readying my boat to launch when I got the call. It was nine in the morning.

"They're letting him out today." Chris Plourd sounded choked up, as if there were tears in his eyes.

He had been on his way to court in San Diego when Alan Simpson called. He immediately phoned the judge and told him he couldn't make it that day, made a right turn onto Interstate 8 and headed for Yuma. For him it was a two-and-a-half-hour drive. It was three hours for Simpson because Yuma is farther from Phoenix than from San Diego. He had gotten a late start because of all the nitty-gritty of Ray's release, and when he realized he couldn't make it in time he turned around and headed back. It was fitting that Chris be the one able to accompany Ray to freedom.

I dropped everything, jumped out of my boat leaving the hatch open to the elements, quickly packed my overnight bag and headed for the Reno airport. There was no way I could make it in time. The first flight I could get would arrive in Yuma by way of Phoenix at sundown. I was waiting to board the flight when Chris arrived in Yuma. He parked just beyond the TV broadcast vans, already set up with satellite dishes pointing in the air. Some thirty yards away from the front gate of Yuma State Prison he walked through the line of reporters, microphones in hand, being held at bay by several police officers. Chris flashed his bar card to announce that he was Ray Krone's attorney and was given a thumb up over the shoulder to pass.

At high noon on April 8, 2002, the inmates in the prison yard watching what was going on outside their barbed wire cage simultaneously let out a yell, "Way to go, Ray!" as he came into view, emerging like the immolated mythological bird reborn from its smoldering ashes. For the first time in ten years, three months and eight days, Ray stepped into sunshine unshackled and unobstructed by walls or fences.

Standing next to Chris before rolling cameras, Ray told the press, "For ten years I felt less than human. This is certainly a strange feeling, and I think it'll take a while for it to set in." While he felt betrayed by the justice system he refused to cast any blame, saying, "Maybe it was a simple mistake?"

Ray spent the afternoon with Chris. Dr. and Mrs. Svengali showed up late in the afternoon. At dusk Chris headed back to San Diego and the Svengalis took the phoenix back to Phoenix.

I waited for him in the bar of a hotel near Simpson's office where I'd taken a room and reserved one for Ray. I wasn't alone. Fifteen or so of his friends also anxiously waited his return. He arrived shortly after 8 p.m., to a standing ovation. I had the honor of buying him his second beer in ten years. Chris had had first beer honors in Yuma.

Ray mingled for a long time with his friends. Then abruptly he came over to where I was sitting and dropped to one knee. I had not expected this. I already knew he was very grateful to me and others who had worked hard for this day. He had given me "The Memphis Belle" model he had fashioned from the meager materials he was able to scavenge while on Death Row. The Mississippi River paddlewheel boat was three stories tall and quite elaborate. The paddlewheel was made from the ends of Styrofoam cups and the smoke stacks from toilet paper spindles.

The look in his face and the sincerity of his watery-eyed "thank you" was clear indication of the monumental burden that had been lifted from his shoulders that day.

It was Ray's choice for dinner. He wanted to go across the street to a Mexican restaurant. There was a dart board in the bar. The first dart he threw in ten years was a bulls-eye. He hadn't lost his touch. He was kind to me, letting my score stay close to his before closing out the game by hitting the double twenty on his first try. After dining, I discerned that it was going to be a late night. Before taking my leave, as the "old man" of the group, I passed onto Ray in cash the remaining two thousand dollars initially earmarked for Svengali that his parents had sent me.

π

Ray was out but not out of the woods. He had been released on his own recognizance pending a hearing to be held exactly three weeks after his release. Until then he was still a convicted murderer.

To alleviate the pressure on the hot poker, the Romley complex had on the surface acknowledged Ray Krone's innocence by conditionally setting him free. Underneath, however, the crime lab was ordered to retest all the evidence employing the new, sophisticated, more definitive DNA technology that had identified Phillips. I wondered why. Phillips's DNA was all over the tank top. Finding more Phillips DNA wasn't going to help them. For what were they looking? And who was suggesting they look?

Chris and I were much concerned because we knew about Ray's DNA on the bra. Phil Barnes had abruptly turned from skeptic to cynic when his lesbian connection theory was shot down. "They're trying to find it," Phil kept whispering into my ear. I kept Phil's suspicions to myself. Simpson seemed content to wait and see. He didn't have Chris's killer instinct. Chris made several attempts to contact William Culbertson, the deputy county prosecutor newly assigned to the case. But Culbertson wouldn't return Chris's calls. He wasn't obligated to do so because Chris was not Ray's attorney of record. I wondered if he'd heard about Chris from Noel Levy, the man who had twice successfully prosecuted Ray. During this time, Levy didn't make a sound in public, nor did he show his egg-covered face there. There was speculation that Levy was "on vacation," but Chris later told me that he got through to Levy one time during this period. Levy made no apologies, was skeptical of the DNA and still believed his whores—I mean experts. A while later, after all the fanfare had subsided, Levy finally acknowledged Ray's innocence to Chris, but only after one of the many previously unidentified latent fingerprints found at the crime scene was matched to Phillips. Bewildered by DNA, Levy was at least able to fathom fingerprints.

Chris was frustrated that Simpson's hand was on the hot poker and not his. Chris wanted to grab onto it and shove, twist and turn it some more. A week after being released, Ray signed the necessary paperwork to put Chris on record as co-council. Now Culbertson had to talk to him. Chris immediately called a meeting with the prosecutor to discuss the status of the case and particularly to educate him on the DNA evidence. I was allowed to attend.

Bill Culbertson and another prosecutor greeted us as we were buzzed into the secured reception area. He greeted Chris and Svengali, whom he already seemed to know, and then looked at me obviously wondering who I was.

Chris introduced us, "This is Ray Krone's cousin, Jim Rix."

"Oh, yes," said Culbertson, shaking my hand.

No one noticed that my shadow a.k.a. Phil Barnes was also present.

Phil, a stickler for explaining *all* the clues, was delighted to attend. Okay: Phillips's DNA was found on the tank top, his fingerprint was found inside the bar, he couldn't be excluded as a source of the mongoloid pubic hairs found on Ancona and he made statements about waking up with blood on his hands. Incriminating, yes, but did the bite mark fit Phillips? Why would Ancona be having a cordial drink with Phillips before he spirited her off at knife point? How did the knife get into Phillips's hand anyway? Was Phillips left-handed? Did he own a green army fatigue jacket? Did he drive his own or someone else's "green Gremlin type vehicle" to the bar the night of the murder Etc.?

Phil knew that Chris had some of the answers because in the courthouse cafeteria he'd previously overheard a portion of Chris's pre-meeting planning session with Svengali in which, for example, their theory was that Phillips wrestled the knife away from Ancona after she realized she was in trouble and in self defense had fetched it from the kitchen.

Chris first empahsized to Culbertson that Dr. Moses Schanfield's trial testimony in which he concluded that Ray was eliminated from the saliva on the breast. If it were Ray's DQα type-[3,3] saliva mixed with Ancona's [3,4] blood then the 3 marker would have been brighter than the 4. But the opposite was true, the 4 marker was brighter, hence Ray was excluded and the actual killer was most likely DQα [4,4]. Chris then pointed out that Schanfield had also excluded both Ray and

Ancona as the source of the blood spot found on Ancona's pants. At the first trial the primitive Lewis test determined that the saliva was from a type-O secretor. Both Ray and Ancona were type O but only Ray was a secretor. Chris ended his DNA presentation by spinning the hot poker with, "The saliva and blood on Ancona's body and pants genetically match Kenneth Phillips. Phillips is a blood type-O secretor with DQα type [4.1,4.1]." And he noted that the DNA on the tank top matched Phillips to a probability of 1.2 trillion (1,200,000,000,000) to 1, a number substantially larger than the number of human beings who have ever lived, or about 8 billion (8,000,000,000).

Culbertson and friend asked few questions. They seemed overwhelmed by the DNA evidence. No other clues were discussed. Phil left the meeting disappointed. The CODIS hit had gone off like a flash bulb in their faces, blinding them to any other clues. Indeed they were too preoccupied trying to find a loophole in the DNA evidence to school themselves on any of the other elements of the crime.

π

Detective Olson had had Phillips bite into Styrofoam during his brief visit. The bite impressions were passed on to Dr. John Piakas, now a full-fledged board certified bite mark expert. There was concern that he might exclude Phillips. However—perhaps influenced by the DNA hit and the "confession" dominating the news—the man who six year earlier had opined that there was a "high probability" that Ray Krone inflicted the bite mark now indicated that Phillips's bite mark was a better fit than Ray's.

Having engineered "the West sting" and fancying himself somewhat of a bite mark expert, Phil was delighted to get his hands on photographs of Phillips's Styrofoam bite mark. He was having trouble letting go of his lesbian connection theory. But he could see immediately the similarities between Lu the left-handed lesbian's bite pattern and Phillips's. Though not as pronounced, Phillips too had a rotated front tooth. (Figure 6) Phil wouldn't go as far as Piakas, but he had to acknowledge that Phillips could not be excluded. With this revelation, Phil accepted that his lesbian theory was dead in the water. He threw in the towel, not bothering to go hunting for Phillips's getaway car.

π

After hearing that Ray was being released, Jim and Carolyn Leming were on the road in no time, heading west to pick up their son and take him home to Pennsylvania. It was too late for them to turn back when they heard that Ray couldn't leave the state for three weeks. In

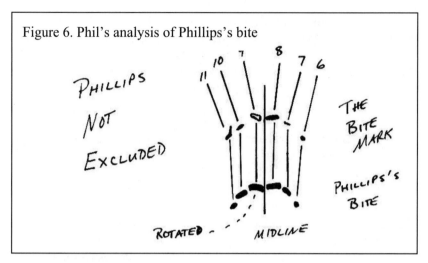

Figure 6. Phil's analysis of Phillips's bite

hindsight, they should have delayed their trip until Ray's final day in court. Despite the positive media attention, the wait in Phoenix was stressful for them—and the extended lodging expensive. They could ill afford to take off a single week from work, let alone the four it would eventually take them to retrieve Ray.

The weekend before the hearing, however, Ray was allowed to leave the state. With the help of Ray's attorney Alan Simpson, who secured permission from the court, I treated Ray and four of his friends (Bob Lewis, Robert Cooper, Nick Meyer, Steve Junkin) to a long weekend at Lake Tahoe. The warm whether had turned. A late winter storm blanketed the area with snow the day before everybody arrived. At lake level it melted quickly in the next day's sunshine, and my visitors helped me finish the job of launching the boat. With all the commotion, I hadn't paid attention to the recent freeze in the engine compartment, which I'd left open to the storm. The boat trip lasted only about a hundred yards into the lake before the engine's overheat light came on, accompanied by a loud buzzer. We were forced to idle back to the dock. Fortunately it was only the water pump that was frozen and broken. By car we took a trip to Emerald Bay, formed by a volcanic spur off the main volcano whose eruption eons ago had formed the lake's basin.

Everyone thoroughly enjoyed the scenery and Ray enjoyed hiking up to Eagle Falls with his buddies. The next day I suggested we all go skiing. Ray was the only taker. The fluke storm had deposited more than a foot of powder on the higher slopes, which had been groomed to my liking. The temperature above eight thousand feet remained cold enough to preserve the perfect ski conditions. It was the last great day of the season and Ray and I had the mountain virtually to ourselves. I marveled how Ray took to the slopes after his long hiatus. He was a natural. I had trouble keeping up with him on Canyon Run.

π

Worries over the telltale bra were for naught. The court hearing went without a hitch. On Monday, April 29th, Ray officially became a free man. All charges against him were dropped with prejudice, the legal term meaning that no matter what, Ray could never again be held accountable for the murder of Kim Ancona.

"Anything else?" asked the judge.

"Yes, your honor," said Chris, rising to his feet attempting to hide a grin. "Who do we send the bill to for solving the crime?"

The judge looked over at Culbertson. The prosecutor had nothing to say. The judge looked back at Chris with an expression that could only be interpreted as, "Good luck collecting." As his gavel fell to end the ceremony, the Honorable Alfred Fenzel broke into a smile recognizing Chris's japery for what it was—sticking it to the Romley complex one last time.

Outside, the press was set up once again and it recorded the exodus from the courthouse. Chris, Ray and his parents stood beaming before the cameras. Bill Culbertson's back was against a wall as he answered the reporters' questions. With the press on the far side and cameras in front, Jim Leming sidled up next to the prosecutor, pinning him in. Jim wouldn't budge until he heard what he wanted to hear. Culbertson had nowhere to go but offer a public apology to Ray Krone. And he did.

The two mothers were also caught on camera. Patricia Gasman and Carolyn Leming consoled each other—one for the loss of a daughter and the other for the ten-year loss of a son.

Ray was in the driver's seat as he and his parents left for Pennsylvania.

Chris and I went back to Sky Harbor Airport, where we had parted many times before over the past eight years. It seemed odd to be heading home at the beginning of a week, not on a Friday evening.

π

A few weeks later I attended a reunion/Christmas/birthday party for Ray in his hometown of Dover. A hundred or so friends and family members attended. It was a fun time. Ray beat everyone at horseshoes. It had been fifty-two years since I had visited and I enjoyed seeing Mom's side of the family once again. Hazel, spry for being in her nineties, was there. She remembered me. I remembered her too but mostly from hearing Mom talk over the years of her older sister. It was great reminiscing.

Before I left town, Ray and I met with Richard Willing in the lobby of my hotel. Willing was and still is a reporter for *USA Today* and covers exonerations of convicted felons, particularly those on Death Row. He'd come to town to interview Ray for an article. I was surprised how much he knew about Ray's case. In one article he even revealed a Phil Barnes caper. It was an article on how "Police dupe suspects into giving up DNA."

Secretly collecting and analyzing DNA arguably violates one's constitutional right to privacy. "Ruses rummaging cops have used to get DNA samples," wrote Willing, "have withstood court challenges." If cops could do it so could Phil. At one time Phil wanted to have Lu's DNA surreptitiously tested and he put the word out among Ray's friends that if they ever saw Lu drinking in a bar to grab her glass. Bob Lewis rose to the occasion. On evening after work he was in his usual watering hole when he spotted Lu having a drink. Bob immediately fetched a paper bag from his car outside and then patiently watched and waited. Soon Lu headed for the restroom, and before her empty glass could be picked up Bob moved to the barstool next to it and distracted the bartender by ordering a beer for himself. With the bartender's back turned, Bob quickly grabbed a bar napkin so as not to contaminate the evidence and stealthily dropped the glass into the paper bag. Mission accomplished. The DNA on the glass was tested. Phil had kept the negative results quiet, but Willing reported the episode, noting that the other side too uses ruses to collect DNA: "In Phoenix in 2000, defense investigators [that would be Phil Barnes and his irregular company] seeking to exonerate Ray Krone from a murder conviction followed other potential suspects into bars, seeking to lift DNA from their drinking glasses. The samples did not match any DNA left at the crime scene. But Krone was released after a neighbor's DNA was matched to the crime."

Phil knew that only Chris and I were privy to Phil's capers and he wondered which one of us had leaked it.

Chris met Richard Willing in Washington not long after Ray had been convicted the second time. To stay on the cutting edge of forensic technology, Chris had become a member of the President's Commission on DNA and Willing was *USA Today*'s correspondent assigned to report on the Commission's progress. Chris introduced Willing to the Krone case at their first meeting. Indeed, I had observed

Chris at several AAFS meetings bending anyone and everyone's ear who would listen about the Krone case. He had fought hard and long for Ray and had lost almost every battle. Losing the trial was particularly devastating. A close friend and colleague of Chris, Sheldon Ostroff, confided in me that he had feared for his friend's well-being afterwards. But Chris pulled himself together and got back into the swing of things even though he carried a thorn in his side. On the surface he was keeping abreast of forensic science. Underneath he was always thinking of ways to get Ray out.

Chris introduced respected Arizona Superior Court Judge Ron Reinstein to the Krone Case. Reinstein was also a member of the President's Commission on DNA. Though Chris was in the technical section and Reinstein in the jurisprudence section, they became good friends. Reinstein was on the committee that drafted the recommended language for the legislation to get DNA testing accepted and he was instrumental in seeing to it that Arizona became the second state (behind Illinois) to plug into the CODIS database. Chris's friendship with Judge Reinstein no doubt helped grease those wheels.

But then Chris had to wait until a significant number of DNA profiles from Arizona inmates were entered into CODIS. Plugging the tank top DNA results into a sparsely populated database had little chance of bearing fruit. Chris had a contact inside the Federal Bureau of Investigation. "How many are there now?" Chris would periodically ask. Chris had had Simpson hold off filing the Rule 32 petition. When Chris heard from his FBI informant that more than twenty thousand Arizona names had been entered into the system he gave Simpson the go ahead.

His strategy worked.

At the time of Ray's welcome home birthday/Christmas party, Richard Willing came into town [Dover, PA] from Washington to interview Ray about the dismal compensation states offer exonerees. At the interview Willing took time to talk about Ray's case. Covering the President's commission and reporting on DNA cases, Willing had over the years become an expert on the inner workings of DNA exonerations. He told Ray and me that he was surprised how things worked in Ray's case. He'd never seen anything like it before. Usually police and prosecutors use the CODIS database to solve unsolved crimes. As far as the Romley complex was concerned, the Ancona murder was solved. Ray Krone did it. The Romley complex wouldn't approve inmate DNA testing that might come back and bite them in the ass by proving they had prosecuted and convicted an innocent man. It was a mystery to Willing how the exculpatory DNA got run through the database in the first place. I would later confirm that it was a mystery by searching through the court papers filed by Simpson. I would find no evidence that he had requested the tank top DNA to be run through CODIS, nor would I find a court order to do so. Nevertheless, Willing attributed the success to "excellent lawyering."

On the flight home from Dover, I reflected upon my involvement in Ray's case. Though I had flailed about at times listening to Phil Barnes, the luckiest thing that happened for Ray was that I crossed paths with Chris Plourd. After losing battle after battle Chris pulled himself up time and again to fight on until he found a way to win. Playing a justice game stacked against him with unlimited treasury, dishonest and dumb cops, reptilian prosecutors, forensic whores, cowardly judges and salted juries, he and he alone came up with the strategy that prevailed. On his own he fashioned the hot poker sharpened with the truth that in the end he shoved where the Maricopa County sun doesn't shine, twisting and turning it until smoke came pouring out through which he was able to walk his client to freedom completely vindicated.

> *There's a lone soldier on the cross, smoke pourin' out of a boxcar door,*
> *You didn't know it, you didn't think it could be done, in the final end he won the war*
> *After losin' every battle.*
>
> – Bob Dylan

CHAPTER 27
SVENGALI

Ray Krone was front page news. "EXONERATED PRISONERS ARE RARELY PAID FOR LOST TIME" was the headline above Ray's picture in *USA Today*'s June 18, 2002 edition. Ray's case was featured in the cover story on the country's policies for compensating people freed from prison. Despite the fact that DNA has caused an increase in exonerations, it isn't easy for exonerees to receive restitution. Richard Willing detailed the "daunting obstacles" facing the wrongly convicted:

> Fifteen states, the District of Columbia and the US Government have laws that offer compensation. But these laws rarely are used because they typically demand that anyone seeking compensation must first receive an official pardon or that a court declares them innocent. That means a DNA test that exonerates an inmate by showing "reasonable doubt" that he committed a crime often isn't enough by itself to qualify him for compensation.

It would be a miracle for a politician like the governor of Arizona to pardon even the most obviously innocent person. It's bad for votes. Knowing this option to be impossible, Chris Plourd asked Judge Fenzel at the exoneration ceremony to make "a factual finding of innocence." Face-saving apologies from the county attorney's office weren't enough to give the court the go-ahead and it stopped short of making this ruling, thereby making more difficult the job of getting compensation for Ray's ten lost years. Willing's article continued:

> In every state court and in the US system, prosecutors and law enforcement officers usually are immune from lawsuits. Such immunities date back several centuries, when they were put in place to protect prosecutors in England and to keep governments from being bankrupted by officials' errors. Today most states have immunity laws, which have been upheld by the US Supreme Court. Law professor Adele Bernard of Pace University in White Plains, NY says "[these laws] never contemplated the exposure of wrongful convictions and the explosion in exonerations we're experiencing [due to to DNA]."

Under Arizona law, police, expert witnesses and the prosecutor who charged Ray are virtually immune from lawsuits and are not liable for any mistakes they make as long as they can show they acted in good faith.

Faith played a big role against Ray. The detective arrested Ray, taking on faith the hometown dentist's initial match of Ray's dentition to the bite mark. On faith, Ray accepted a court-appointed defense attorney. On faith, the Las Vegas bite mark expert accepted the implication that the "boyfriend has confessed" and consequently fingered Ray before a jury predominately of the same religious faith. Ray was presented to the jury as one without faith (or underwear). Despite misgivings, the judge faithfully accepted the jury's verdict and sentenced Ray to death in prison. And the prosecutor had faith in everyone: I didn't arrest him, the police did; I didn't identify him as the victim's boyfriend, the witness did; I didn't say he bit her, the expert did; I didn't convict him, the jury did; I didn't sentence him to death, the judge did; and (if it had happened) I didn't execute him, the warden did. Then, after Ray's innocence was proved beyond a shadow of a doubt, the prosecutor was able to hide behind his immunity by claiming something like, "I had faith in my expert," failing to mention that he pimped him to the tune of fifty thousand dollars.

> Lawyers for those seeking compensation [Willing's article continued] have begun to shift tactics. In Illinois, where 13 men have been released from Death Row since 1987, lawyers no longer seek to file in federal court, where dismissals have become common. Instead they file in state court and allege official misconduct. Police and prosecutors are not immune from misconduct such as coerced confessions and fabricated evidence.
>
> The law leaves Plourd little to work with in trying to get compensation for Krone. Plourd, of San Diego, says he is examining whether Krone could claim rights violations that aren't covered by immunity laws such as willful misconduct.
>
> For Krone winning money could be tougher than winning his freedom.

When Ray Krone walked out of Arizona State Prison he was handed a check for $50. Chris gave Ray two twenties and a ten in exchange for the check. He framed the check and hung it on the wall in front of his desk as a reminder of the final task in front of him.

There were strong suspicions that Ray's DNA was deliberately placed on Ancona's bra before it was sent off to Dr. Ed Blake's lab for analysis. Such tampering with evidence, if true, goes way beyond implied immunity. But how could it be proved? It couldn't. And bringing up such a speculation without proof might cast doubt upon Ray's innocence in the minds of the adjudicators of his civil suit. Not good. Richard Willing noted in his article how an appellate court shot down the lawsuit of a freed Death Row inmate who was released on the technicality that the police and prosecutor withheld important exculpatory evidence. The appellate court judged that there was ample other evidence of guilt.

Chris did, however, have an ace in the hole. He'd noticed in the videotape of the autopsy that the cast of Ray's teeth was pressed into the bite injury. Also there was a photograph taken at the same time showing someone clamping onto Ancona's breast with Ray's upper and lower teeth casts. Afterwards Dr. Piakas made a plaster cast of the breast. Dr. Rawson told the jury that Ray's lower teeth matched the indentations in the mold of the breast and several jurors had fiddled with the cast of Ray's teeth and the plaster mold before coming to the same conclusion as Rawson.

Chris felt that this procedure resulted in the fabrication of evidence. He had already consulted with several odontologists, who agreed. Manufacturing evidence, whether through incompetence or by design, could win big in a civil case.

Ray was out of prison and could have managed the civil case on his own, but he deferred—as he had in prison—to me. Chris suggested that his friend and colleague Sheldon Ostroff do the civil case. Chris and I met with Sheldon in Sheldon's office building, which took up half a square block of prime downtown San Diego real estate. I was already duly impressed with some of the cases Sheldon had won. The award for one case alone was twenty million dollars. After listening to the two attorneys discuss strategy I was even more impressed. When I learned that Sheldon owned his office building outright and that he lived in a multi-million dollar mansion in La Jolla overlooking the Pacific Ocean, the deal was done as far as I was concerned. This civil litigator was an obvious winner. I reported back to Ray.

Throughout the selection process I kept getting phone calls from Svengali wanting to know what was going on. Chris was getting them too. It was obvious that Svengali wanted to participate in Ray's civil case. I was already tuned into Svengali's love of money. Before I handed over the three thousand dollar check to him in Phoenix after his success with Phillips, I talked with him casually about his private investigation practice. Just before he jovially bragged that he could get me to confess to doing the wild thing with Dumbo he confided, "What can I say? I like money!"

I talked with Chris about Svengali's obvious lobbying for a piece of Ray's pie. Chris said that Svengali could be used for any necessary investigation but that the civil case would demand high-powered lawyering and, if no settlement was forthcoming, a lengthy trial would require skilled litigating. To me Sheldon Ostroff was the right man.

Svengali was also in Ray's ear about attorney selection, although it was clear to me that Svengali's criterion was which law firm would offer him the largest finder's fee. I explained to Ray that the law prohibited non-attorneys from receiving a percentage of a court settlement. If Ray wanted to he could take care of Svengali out of his pocket after the settlement came in. While no one can argue with the success of Svengali's only discernable contribution in extracting incriminating statements from Phillips, it didn't seem to me to warrant a percentage of Ray's pie. I suggested to Ray that when his ship came in he give Svengali whatever he thought Svengali was worth. I hoped Ray would see through Svengali—a cop turned private investigator with an exaggerated opinion of himself, materially motivated but bringing little to the table for the upcoming civil litigation.

Svengali was persistent and I had to endure a conference call with him and Ray regarding attorney selection. Svengali pressed hard for his preference, a Los Angeles attorney. I told Ray I would check out Svengali's guy. Svengali continued to push. Ray finally had to tell him, "Look, after what Jim's done for me I'm not going to go against what he decides."

While Svengali's guy seemed okay, he didn't impress me as much as Ostroff. Besides, he was way up in Los Angeles and I thought it important that Ray's civil attorney be nearby and willing to work with Chris because Chris knew the case inside out.

Chris had hired Sheldon Ostroff fresh out of law school. At the time, Chris was lead public defender for Imperial County. During the initial interview Chris asked him, "What's first degree burglary?"

"One degree."

Chris hired Sheldon on the spot. He was just the type of guy Chris wanted on his team—a smart aleck not afraid to get in a district attorney's face. Sheldon learned quickly and ripped off a string of six "not guilty" verdicts. Though close, not even Chris matched this record. After two years as a public defender, Sheldon went to work for a civil law firm, taking to trial and winning several big cases. He soon opened his own law firm. His success was phenomenal. Not only did he own substantial property in San Diego County, he also owned a home in Israel, where he and his wife vacationed. Sheldon was the one who told me of Chris's despondency over losing Ray's trial. They were good friends and mutually respected each other's talents.

Most civil suits are handled on a contingency basis, which means that the attorney receives a percentage of the award. If there's no settlement or the case is lost in court, the attorney is out his time and expenses. The usual attorney's fee is one-third. Ostroff wanted forty percent. This percentage seemed high to Ray so I negotiated it down to thirty-eight percent. Ray had no money for expenses. When Ostroff earmarked more than a hundred thousand dollars of his personal funds to get the ball rolling, I knew he was committed. With Chris intending to partner up with Ostroff to provide his invaluable intimate knowledge of the case, I thought it was a good deal.

"Look," I said to Ray, "you're going to want to take care of Chris after all he's done for you. The additional five percent will do that. It's a sweet deal!"

Svengali was on the phone to me as soon as he learned that the Law Offices of Sheldon Ostroff had been selected. "I don't know who this guy is," he said.

"Why do you need to know?" I said, not finishing my thought, which was, You're just an investigator.

Svengali was miffed. He got the message that I wasn't impressed with his puffed-up ego, which fancied and promoted him to be the guru of everything. And he was no doubt frustrated that I wasn't susceptible to his self-serving mind games. Svengali never did make the attempt to get me to confess to poking a pachyderm. It was the last time we talked, although we would see each other one more time.

In the same week that Ostroff was retained, I received a fax bearing both Ray's and Svengali's signatures. It was another one of Svengali's famous "fee agreements"—only, this one was prefaced with the word "contingency." Svengali wasn't about to be cut out of Ray's pie. For "five percent of any sums recovered" Svengali would among other things "determine the parties responsible for damages suffered and provide strategy in the preparation and prosecution of any legal action." He was going to have Ray pay *him* for what the attorneys would do. This simple-minded but crafty private investigator had somehow manipulated his way into becoming Ray's private counsel. I wondered how Ostroff would receive Svengali's trying to tell him how to litigate the case.

A meeting was scheduled at Ostroff's office.

"Ray, can you be in San Diego tomorrow? Tickets are waiting for you at the airport." I'd waited until the last minute to tell Ray, hoping that Svengali would be off doing something else and miss the meeting. But Ray showed up with Svengali attached. Chris and I were also at the meeting. Chris had already spent hours with Ostroff bringing him up to speed. Svengali sat close to Ray, ostensibly taking notes and every now and then grunting "Good" and "I like that" for the benefit of his host. I sat across the table and watched. Svengali contributed nothing of substance. Neither he nor I said one word to each other the entire time. Our eyes met only once and, as I would learn at dinner, we were at that moment on the same wavelength, thinking the exact same thing about each other. Unlike me, Chris stayed friendly with Svengali and continued to talk to him. Chris told me that evening over dinner that Svengali thought I was a "flaming asshole."

The meeting ended with Ray giving the go-ahead and expressing his desire that "everyone work together."

I felt sorry for Ray. He wanted to please everybody. But he was caught in the middle between those of us who truly wanted to kick some serious Maricopa County ass and the parasite in his ear. I took Ray aside. I don't remember exactly how I phrased it but I told him that I'd been around Svengali enough to know that he didn't work well with others. He was a maverick who wants to be in charge. I emphasized to Ray that at some point in time he might have to make the decision who he wants to run the show, a high-powered attorney or a run-of-the-mill private investigator. I praised Svengali for the job he did on Phillips, saying "it was the icing on the cake," but I emphasized that "Chris baked the cake" and now is the time for a skilled civil litigator. I stopped short of relaying my additional perception of Svengali as a moneygrubber whose usefulness had ended. I hoped that Ray would get my drift and soon see through Svengali's obvious cupidity.

Within a month after the meeting, Ostroff initiated the process by serving notice on Maricopa County and the City of Phoenix that Ray was going to sue them if they didn't substantially reward him for time served. Before an individual can file suit against a government entity, he must first notify them of his intent to do so. The government then has ninety days to pony up before a lawsuit can be filed with the court. Of course, the government never does.

Svengali was no fool and he used those ninety days to his advantage. He correctly recognized that he was neither needed nor wanted by Ray's San Diego team. From day one he caused problems. I began receiving phone calls from Ray expressing worries about the civil case that I strongly suspected Svengali had induced. I'm not one to cast aspersions on others, so I kept my suspicions to myself and took the time to answer rationally all of Ray's concerns. As Ray's stress level rose so did my suspicions. In one call he questioned Ostroff's qualifications. I again went over Ostroff's many successes and the outward signs of his prosperity. I hoped Ray would associate the picture I drew of Ostroff's office building and Pacific Coast home with Svengali's digs, which he had seen at a party Svengali hosted for him him before he was allowed to leave the state. While it was an okay rancher in an upscale north Phoenix neighborhood, it did not compare to Sheldon's palatial home. "Sheldon wouldn't have taken your case unless he was confident he could win big," I emphasized.

Another call began, "Is [Ostroff] doing anything? Shouldn't he be doing [this, that and the other thing]?" It was clear that "this, that and the other thing" was coming from Svengali. Again I calmed Ray down and explained that Ostroff and his staff were working diligently on the civil suit but couldn't file it until the ninety-day period had elapsed.

The kicker call came when Ray bypassed his usual "hello" and went straight to a distressed, "You know he lost the trial!"

Through my head like lightning went the thought, That bastard has stooped to an all-time low. Now he's badmouthing Chris.

"Where did you get this?" I asked, constraining myself from answering my own question.

"Svengali says..." This armchair quarterback had taken plays out of the propaganda playbook—attack your adversary and provoke anxiety. I sensed that Svengali had twisted the fact that Chris had lost the trial into a fear in Ray that Chris and his colleague would likely lose again and Ray get nothing.

Again I tried to calm him down. "Hey, Ray, you were there, Svengali wasn't. You saw what happened. What did Chris do wrong? You know you were railroaded."

I alluded to his DNA on the bra, which Ray now knew about.

"Yeah, he lost the trial," I continued. "But no one could have won with the cards stacked against him. You know what he's done for you. He didn't give up. And ultimately he found the way to get you out."

After calming Ray down I observed, "You know, you don't have to talk to him. You don't have to take his calls."

"I can't," said Ray. "They're friends of the family."

"They...?"

Ray told me that after his homecoming party Mrs. Svengali and his mother had been e-mailing one another. It would be an understatement to say I had second thoughts about treating the Svengalis to plane tickets to Pennsylvania for the party. Since then, while Dr. Svengali was working Ray, Mrs. Svengali was working his mother.

I sensed trouble and I was right.

Around this time, *People* Magazine was doing a story on Ray. It wanted a picture of Ray and me together, so I flew to Pennsylvania for the photo op. Jim and Carolyn showed up as the photographer was setting up his equipment to use the cornfield adjacent to their backyard as a backdrop. Jim sauntered up to me and initiated the conversation. I hadn't talked to Ray any more about Svengali, but when Jim asked I unloaded. Jim listened with keen interest. It seemed to me that he too questioned Svengali's sincerity. As I described my dealings with Svengali, Carolyn circled around us with arms folded. At one point, Jim beckoned to her. "Come over here and listen to this." With a quick shake of her head she declined and widened her circle.

Carolyn was particularly vulnerable. Her ten-year ordeal paralleled Ray's. It began while she was going through a bad divorce, with the news that her son had been arrested for murder. She was understandably unable to help financially at that time. Listening to Ray's "Don't worry about me; I'll be all right," she didn't attend the first trial. For the second, she and her new husband scraped together every last penny they could and mortgaged the farm, and she took valuable time off to attend. She had also visited Ray in prison as much as she could. After the second trail, both her anxiety over her son's welfare and the financial stress continued. There is little doubt that she had misgivings about Chris after the second trial and was upset that her hard-earned money had disappeared for naught. She didn't deal with Chris on a day-to-day basis as I did and after the lost trial she expressed reservations about his performance. At one point, for example, she openly questioned his decision not to call Florida bite mark expert Dr. Richard Souviron.

It would have been easy for the Svengalis to gain her trust. Endear yourselves to her by listening to her qualms and then offer support coated with subtle suggestions that Chris had done nothing and wasted her money.

Mrs. Svengali sold real estate. In sales as with propaganda, the fear of loss is a far more powerful motivating force than the expectation of gain. Exploiting the fact that Chris lost the second trial with subtle reminders that "you don't want that to happen again" would go a long way toward subverting Chris's efforts on the civil case.

Svengali not only had a master's degree, he was also "Dr. Svengali," with a PhD in Human Behavior. His doctoral thesis was on hypnotism. It was clear to me that this master hypnotist had twisted my "don't talk to him" a hundred and eighty degrees. Carolyn didn't want to hear anything negative about her newfound friends.

I didn't talk to Ray about the civil case during the photo session. I'd already said enough over the phone and I hoped that Jim Leming, who seemed to understand the situation, might have some influence. However, I left Pennsylvania feeling uneasy.

Sure enough, Svengali's twist also got to Ray. He stopped calling me. Jim Leming and I didn't talk again and I assumed that either he, like me, had to bite his tongue or in time he also fell under Svengali's spell. In any event, a month or two later I received official word by telephone from Chris. "Ray has changed attorneys."

By then I was more disappointed than surprised. But Ray was a big boy. If he wanted Svengali to run the show that was his decision. But I continued to feel sorry for him. He had endured ten long, hard years in prison, was financially stressed and now had to endure Svengali's *argumentum ad nauseam.*

$$\pi$$

After Ray's release, I hosted two parties a year for him and his friends at Lake Tahoe. The first summer party was over the Fourth of July weekend. It was a non-stop beach bash featuring wave runners on the lake, rum runners at the Beacon Bar and Grill, a live band on the beach and fireworks over the lake. The winter party initially happened over Martin Luther King, Jr.'s birthday weekend. I shared King's birthday and turned sixty at the first party. Ray gave me a great telescope, which I use to view the moon and stars from a rooftop deck. I'm still learning how to track the planets. Ray's birthday is four days later than mine so there was a party for him too. Skiing and snowmobiling replaced wave running. A whole day was spent motoring on snow between Hope Valley and Blue Lakes. After two birthday-oriented parties, the festivities migrated to Super Bowl weekend to avoid tourists. The parties continued unabated after Svengali's coup d'état.

Now out of the loop, I would occasionally ask Ray how things were going with the civil case, wanting to know particularly what Svengali was doing for him. Invariably his consigliere would have come up with some new gossip on Detective Gregory. One such "discovery" was that Gregory in his patrol officer days had gotten caught and reprimanded for having sex with his female partner while on a stakeout. Gregory was the point man for Ray's troubles, the one with whom Ray had had the most contact before his arrest and the one who arrested him. Ray naturally didn't like Gregory. It seemed to me that Svengali was feeding Ray what he wanted to hear, stroking him with newfound dirt on the detective to make Ray think he was doing something meaningful. Going after Gregory could only have been for Ray's benefit. As Chris pointed out, "Cops are immune from actions arising out of stupidity." I paid little attention to the alleged tryst and didn't care to know if it were true or not because it would go nowhere in Ray's civil case. Wasting time digging up dirt on Gregory reminded me of something Chris had observed about Sheldon. "He knows where to find the money." Sheldon would not have spun his wheels chasing useless scuttlebutt but would have devoted his energy to unearthing pay dirt.

With each party, the distance between Ray and me grew. I talked less and less about his case as the skepticism in his expression grew more pronounced. The Doctor of Hypnotism was clearly in control. I could only imagine what propaganda he was feeding Ray.

> *The magician is quicker and his game*
> *Is much thicker than blood and blacker than ink*
> *And there's no time to think.*
>
> -Bob Dylan

π

The "complaint for damages" was filed in July 2003. Plaintiffs Ray Krone and his mother Carolyn Leming named Maricopa County and the City of Phoenix as defendants. Individually named were prosecutor Levy, Doctors Piakas and Rawson, detectives Gregory and Olson, and lab tech Piette. "Accurately considered a decision maker," County Attorney Rick Romley was at the top of the list.

The voluminous complaint covered all the bases: prosecutorial misconduct; altering and manufacturing evidence; concealment and destruction of evidence; expert-shopping; refusal to adequately investigate the crime and the real killer; perjured documents and statements; unfair, prejudicial inflammation of public opinion; and conspiracy.

Chris's contention that the bite mark evidence was altered to fit Ray made it into the complaint:

In the process of performing his analysis, Defendant Piakas either deliberately and maliciously, or with such reckless disregard and neglect for proper scientific procedure and analysis as to constitute malice, altered the bite mark impressions made on victim Ancona's left breast by jamming and/or twisting the plaster case of plaintiff Krone into the decedent's breast tissue.

Phil Barnes was surprised to see that another possibility was raised as to how Ray's phone number got into Ancona's address book:

Plaintiff Krone['s name] was one of many male names and phone numbers found in the decedent's address book by the time of trial. However, the handwriting in the address book did not appear to be either the victim's handwriting or Plaintiff Krone's handwriting.

Phil too had noticed the handwriting discrepancy in Ancona's address book and wondered how it might compare with that of the defendant detectives.

Also in the complaint was the suggestion of a dingle dangle conspiracy:

[Svengali,] through contacts of his, discovered that the prosecutor's office was attempting to [get] Phillips [to agree] that if Phillips would give testimony that Plaintiff Krone conspired with, or assisted him, in murdering Ancona, the County would not seek the death penalty against Phillips.

Reading in the complaint about Noel Levy's appearance on TV reminded me of Mike Pain's story of happening to meet Levy while waiting in line at a bank one day. Levy remembered Mike as someone from the court but couldn't quite place him. It had been seven years since the trial. After awhile Levy asked Mike where they'd met.

"I did some investigation on the Krone case...I see he got out about a year ago."

A little later Mike casually alluded to the civil case.

"I made a mistake there," Levy said.

"What mistake was that?"

"I went on TV."

There's no implied immunity when performing on a nationally televised documentary. The complaint continued:

"Arrest and Trial" was a sensational exposé of the killing of Kim Ancona. Defendants Levy, Gregory and Olson proudly stand by and exhibit blood-soaked sheets, and falsely claim that the sheets were soaked in victim Ancona's blood and that the sheets were found in Krone's car.

Blood-soaked sheets never existed.

Defendants assisted in portraying Krone as a molester, rapist and killer of women while Krone was in prison and subject to being killed by other inmates who might see and become incensed and outraged by their outrageous, scurrilous and untrue portrayal. Krone received death threats immediately after the airing of the show.

Lastly, the complaint weighed in on the proposition that "the color of justice is green":

The financial resources of Plaintiff Krone and his family were exhausted. Well over $100,000 had been expended by Krone's mother and her husband trying to save her son's life by opposing the two state agencies, Defendant County and Defendant City, who were determined to execute her son if they could.

Krone's second defense attorney, Chris Plourd had long since been funding the case, appeals and technical experts out of his own pocket and with donations from another family relative, Jim Rix, who had been viciously and publicly attacked by Levy for "interfering." Actually Rix's only "interference" was that he had donated a considerable sum of his personal money for the defense of Plaintiff Krone in an attempt to obtain justice before, during and after the second trial.

This family funding was necessary because Defendant City and Defendant County had and/or have an unconstitutional policy, custom and practice of hiring defense lawyers for complex capital cases, and then deliberately underfunding the[ir] legal fees, investigatory fees and expert-witness fees. The County funded a paltry $1,500 for defense experts while funding prosecution experts in excess of $75,000.

The complaint concluded by asking for compensatory damages in the amount of $100,000,000.

π

When Chris was at the helm I was privy to all the nitty-gritty going on with Ray's case. But with Svengali in command I would get only bits and pieces. I did, however, hear about major developments. About six months after filing the complaint for damages, Svengali's guy bailed out. The "official" story I was given was that this attorney and his staff were having trouble meeting deadlines and were using as their excuse that Ray was having psychiatric tests. This excuse didn't wash. From past conversations with Ray I knew he wasn't receptive to the idea of feigning dementia. Anyway, at the time Ray was supposed to be in psychoanalysis he showed up in Arizona and gave a well-received speech. I guess it embarrassed Svengali's guy into quitting.

At the next Tahoe party I learned the real reason. By then Ray and I had stopped talking about his civil case, but my friend Heather learned from Ray that Svengali's "qualified" guy was having internal strife. Apparently he was "too busy" to actually do the work on the civil case himself and turned it over to two other attorneys. These attorneys realized that after having to share the pot with Svengali and his guy their portion wasn't going to be enough to warrant further efforts so they quit—but not before sending Ray a sizable bill for the work they had already done.

I wondered whether Ray and his parents would now discern what was obvious to me—that Svengali was essentially deadwood. But they didn't and in no time another Svengali-selected attorney stepped in. I wasn't told his name and didn't bother to find out.

π

Three years later, as my tale was nearing its end, I would learn more about the Svengali phenomenon. On a trip to visit Mom in my home town of Tulare, a small farming community in the heart of California's fertile San Joaquin Valley, I left an early draft of my manuscript with my old high school teacher and good friend, Morris Knudsen. Of all my teachers, I remember Mr. Knudsen as the best. He went way beyond teaching Latin, French, and English. He always started class by making his students think about some current event. For me languages weren't as easy as science. I thank Mr. Knudsen for planting seeds that sprouted many years later, when this story needed to be told.

Not long after this trip, I heard from another good friend (and high school classmate) also named Morris. Morris Dean was also a student and friend of Mr. Knudsen, and on a visit with Mr. Knudsen asked to read the manuscript.

I did well in math and science but Morris did well in everything. He went east to Yale and we didn't stay in close touch over the ensuing years, seeing each other only occasionally—at a high school reunion or at Mr. Knudsen's. Anyway, Morris read the manuscript on the airplane home to Chapel Hill, North Carolina and volunteered (with an enthusiasm that hasn't let up) to edit it. As a result, our friendship has been rekindled, and the fact that you have made it this far into *Jingle Jangle* is a testament to his expertise.

Morris also volunteered to do some research for me. Until he got in touch with Ray and his parents my suspicions had yet to be verified that they had been hoodwinked. What Morris learned didn't surprise me.

Carolyn indicated that she was impressed that Svengali was a "doctor" who billed himself to be an "international" investigator. Of course, I knew that "international" meant only that the investigator had had a caper or two in Mexico.

To Morris she revealed the bombshell, "You know, they're the ones who found Phillips's DNA. They are my heros!" "They" were Svengali and Alan Simpson. Svengali had taken credit for Chris's achievement as if it were *he* rather than Chris who had told Simpson what to do. In order to become the "hero" it was obviously necessary to diminish Chris's roll. All Carolyn would say about Chris was, "He had good intentions, but..."

Once she had accepted Svengali's propaganda, it was easy for "Doctor Hero" to divert his true intention from her by also creating great concern as to what had happened to all their hard-earned money. I say this with some authority and will share the evidence with you a little later—an e-mail from Ray.

π

Ray's civil suit was destined to be settled out of court. But there was one minor roadblock on the way there. Before Maricopa County would make an offer, it was necessary for Ray to drop all claims against defendant Dr. Ray Rawson. I was told it was because he was merely acting in good faith and that there was no viable case against him. I wondered why the same didn't apply to the other bite mark expert, Dr. John Piakas, who was also paid by the county although not nearly as much as Rawson received. Phil Barnes wondered whether those magic underwear really work.

Hearing about the settlement, I asked Chris, "How much?" and wondered how close it would be to his prediction.

Chris was great at forecasting outcomes. In the OJ Simpsin case he'd foretold the verdict. In the civil case he did for me he accurately predicted the outcome to the penny. In Ray's case, he had guessed the county would settle for $2.8 million. Not even he could foresee how bad it was going to be.

"Cut it in half," he said. "One point four million."

Such a measly amount, I thought, considering all that Ray had been through.

And it got worse. Before Ray could collect his portion of the $1.4 million, he had to pay two claims against him. Under Svengali's rein, Ray had changed horses in midstream not once but twice. Sheldon Ostroff naturally wanted to be paid for the work he'd done prior to being cut loose. And so did Svengali's guy before he gave up. The total amounted to approximately $200,000, the lion's share going to Svengali's guy. Ray was visibly upset about it at the Fourth of July party while the settlement was pending. He didn't see it the same way I did, and I didn't volunteer what was on my mind: that this slice was the snooker portion of the pie, the amount it cost Ray for being snookered by Svengali.

At the snowmobile party after the settlement Ray handed me two checks of equal amounts, one made out to Chris and the other to me.

"Is that all?" asked my brother Dan, a bit perturbed when he saw the amount, $10,000.

I assured him that there would be more after Ray settled with the City of Phoenix.

Dan and I worked together running a computer-based business that processed insurance claims electronically. We would collect claim information from medical and dental offices. Then, with software I'd written, we would reformat the data and send it on to insurance companies who would adjudicate each claim and send payments off to our clients. We'd been in business several years before the Internet came into being and initially transferred the data over phone lines using telephone modems. It's a labor-intensive business requiring significant phone support. When I was away from the office, Dan's workload doubled. I kept him abreast of the progress with Ray's case and he didn't complain. Nor did he protest when I contributed company money to the funding of the project. He simply wanted to be assured that, should Ray be freed and receive restitution, our contribution would be repaid.

"Do you have a contract with him?" he asked one time.

"No. But I have a good feeling about Ray. Should the time come, he'll do the right thing," I insisted.

But I hadn't counted on the Svengali factor.

Ray settled with the City of Phoenix for $3 million. The Fourth of July party came and went. It became evident that Ray wasn't going to volunteer any more.

"Well?" asked Dan.

I was now in the uncomfortable position of having to ask. I called Ray and chatted about the situation. Ray sent five thousand dollars and said he would have another five for me at the next party. With each successive Super Bowl party the number of participants snowballed to include not only Ray and his friends but also nearly one hundred local Tahoe friends. The next party was a great time notwithstanding that my team the Seattle Seahawks were beaten by Ray's team the Pittsburgh Steelers. Ray left a check for one thousand dollars.

When someone says one thing and does another, the writing is on the wall.

I asked Chris's advice. He was philosophical, saying that Ray had been "squeezed" and, "It is what it is."

How many times had I heard him say this? Chris is one of the most remarkable individuals I've ever met. Before getting to know him my perception of lawyers had been pretty much the punch line of the joke: The attorney tells his client, "I discovered some important new evidence." "What's that?" asks the client. "You're out of money!"

Chris didn't fit this stereotype. Don't get me wrong. He would welcome a big payday same as anyone else. But unlike Doctor Hero, it's not what trips his trigger. When he informed me of Ray's settlement with the county he didn't dwell on the paltry amount. He said instead, "There goes a dream of mine."

"What's that?"

"To face Levy, Gregory, Olson, Piakas and Rawson at the defendant's table."

Having to use a few more words than "It is what it is," I attempted to explain Ray's metamorphosis to my brother.

"So what?" said Dan with heat when I suggested that Ray had been brainwashed by a low-life leech. "If you don't do something about it, I will!"

At my insistence, Dan showed his e-mail to Ray to me first. He didn't mince words. To get Ray's attention, Dan started with "Ray, you slime ball…" Then, after a few pointed paragraphs too harsh for me to quote, he said (and I paraphrase), "Before taking care of yourself, you should have paid your parents back and then taken care of those who went to bat for you." Dan ended by saying, "I used to take personal pride in your situation and ultimate release from jail...Now if I had a choice I'd let your sorry ass rot in jail for the rest of your life."

I felt compelled to intervene and spare Ray Dan's wrath. I talked Dan out of sending his e-mail and was once again in the unpleasant position of having to appeal to Ray. I didn't want this process to go on forever so I thought it best to give Ray a number to shoot for. I decided on an amount substantially less than half of what we had expended but which was enough to placate Dan.

In good conscience I couldn't overlook Chris although he'd told me emphatically, "Leave me out!" I'd already sent him half of the additional six thousand dollars Ray had doled out at the parties. So I asked for an equal amount for Chris. In total, my e-mail requested less than two percent of Ray's total settlement.

Ray replied immediately with an e-mail of his own:

No Problem, Jim, since all this money wasn't expended all at one time, I will pay you and Chris $5,000 each per year for 7 years and first payment will be [one year from now]. Hope that keeps your brother off your back. I'm not going to tell [my parents] about it, though, because they kept thorough records of their expenses and get real angry when I tell them what you and Chris claim to have spent and wonder just where all the money they sent you went. They warned me about people wanting money right away but fortunately it's only happened once. I appreciate all your help and Chris's too; tell me, though, would you rather have spent those 10 years in prison for $2 million instead!

The writing was now indelibly tattooed on the wall and I might have taken it personally had I not known that is was really Svengali talking to me through Ray.

Morris later confirmed my deduction that Svengali hypnotized Ray and his parents. Carolyn told him that Svengali was "shocked" to learn that she and her husband had contributed anything at all, the implication being that I was taking the full financial credit for Ray's release. Phil Barnes believes that Svengali pulled the old switcheroo by convincing Ray and his parents that I, not Svengali, was the one coveting a piece of Ray's pie.

π

My brother was less concerned about the money than the principle of the thing. But Dan wasn't sympathetic to Ray's subjugation to Svengali so I didn't share Ray's response right away. He was a busy man. I'd calmed him down sufficiently by telling him that I'd sent Ray an e-mail and he'd gone about his business temporarily forgetting about it. I bided my time and waited for the inevitable. Some weeks later out of the blue it came.

"Hey! Whatever happened with Ray?"

"We shouldn't expect any more from him," I answered bluntly, offering as few details as possible. Then I stood there for the better part of an hour shaking my head up and down listening to Dan's tirade. Afterwards I took it upon myself to accommodate him for his loss. After all it was my boondoggle, not his. I don't know whether Dan ever sent Ray his blistering e-mail.

Dan and I had different perspectives. For me the real villain was Svengali. Whenever I listen to "Idiot Wind," where Dylan sings, "You'll find out when you reach the top, you're on the bottom," I'm reminded of this bottom feeder who feasted at Ray's expense.

When Morris related Carolyn Leming's disgust that "[the settlement arrangements] cost Ray more than fifty percent" and her blaming it not on her "hero" but on "those attorneys," I wondered what the percentage would have been without Svengali's "help"?

"About thirty-eight percent," answered Phil Barnes, who is perpetually attuned to my thoughts. "And the settlement might have been for a good deal more," he added.

π

Early on I'd asked Chris what he thought he and Sheldon could get for Ray. He didn't bat an eyelid. "Twenty million dollars." Even if he were only half right Ray would have received twice as much he did. Of course, it was Ray's prerogative to accept the first offer of settlement. But it's hard to imagine that Ray would have done worse by staying the course with Chris and Sheldon. And no snooker or parasite portion would have been skimmed off the top.

For better or for worse, Ray chose Svengali. "It is what it is." Nevertheless, I continue to ponder what might have been. Whenever I wonder whether Ray and his family will ever figure out that Svengali played them like a fiddle, turning the truth upside down and in all likelihood costing Ray hundreds of thousands if not millions of dollars, Phil Barnes pipes up, "They're too far gone. You'll have to write them a book!"

CHAPTER 28
LIFE GOES ON

When Ray Krone walked out of prison he became the one hundredth Death Row inmate to be exonerated since 1973, when the Supreme Court reinstated the death penalty. He immediately became the anti-death penalty "poster boy."

It couldn't have happened to a better person. Ray was not some expediently railroaded career criminal. Before going to jail he had been a fine, upstanding citizen and he continued to be one after he got out. If he harbored any animosity toward the individuals responsible for his incarceration, he kept it to himself. Outwardly he blamed no one. He realized that if it hadn't been those particular individuals it would have been others. He'd learned much about the justice game—that it was he who had the burden to prove he was innocent beyond *all* doubt.

Ray proved to be an articulate speaker and, with his positive outlook, was soon in heavy demand to tell his story. He's already logged more miles traveling to speaking engagements than I can count, all over the United States and in Europe.

Court TV's "Forensic Files" and German Television made documentaries about his case and he has appeared on numerous TV talk shows, including "Larry King Live" hosted by Nancy Grace. He was even selected for ABC's "Extreme Makeover." Chris Plourd appeared on the show and "sentenced" Ray to eight weeks of cosmetic surgery. His snaggletooth and uneven jaw were finally fixed.

Days before Ray was to arrive for one of my Tahoe parties, he broke an ankle sliding into second base. But he wasn't about to miss the party. Against doctor's orders he showed up on crutches—only a day late. That same weekend his favorite rock 'n roll band was performing in Reno. His entire Phoenix support group, Bob Lewis and Selena Black, Steve Junkin, Nick and Bonnie Meyer, Guy and Carolyn Keller and Jim Ballard, trucked him to the amphitheater, where in a wheelchair he had a front row center seat to see the show. At the next Tahoe party he showed up sporting a brand new accoutrement, a tattoo of the title of his favorite Lynyrd Skynyrd song, "Free Bird," alongside his favorite date "4-8-02."

Despite all, Ray's portion of the settlement afforded him the means to purchase a twenty-five or so acre farm not far from his parents' place. He leases out the farmland and lives in a comfortable old house in a corner of the property. Wise investments ensure that he should live comfortably for the rest of his life—a well-deserved sequel to his ten-year ordeal.

And he has found a profound calling in opposing the death penalty and fighting for prison reform. He has worked with Sister Helen Prejean on a number of projects, participated in a United Nations event in Geneva calling for a moratorium on judicial executions and served on a couple of state commissions (so far).

π

In February 2006, members of the Arizona State Senate publicly apologized to Ray. One was John Huppenthal, the chairman of the Judiciary Committee. He said he had been shocked when he learned that none of the evidence pointed to Ray as a suspect, much less as a murderer. On the floor of the senate, Huppenthal said, "In a way, it's a lesson for us all that this can happen in a modern society. When we think we have foolproof systems where this could never happen, it *has* happened. And we need to be aware that it truly could happen again and *is likely happening again.*" Despite this revelation, the senator stopped short of endorsing the abolition of the death penalty. Rather, he suggested that there should be "guidelines." "If you have a case like [Ray Krone's, where there's no record of violence or sexual misconduct], it's not a death penalty case."

Ray was overwhelmed by this official apology. But he offered a reason other than his own odyssey through the justice system for putting an end to the death penalty:

> If we kill somebody to teach them a lesson that killing is wrong, we don't show the sanctity of life. The God-given gift of life is important. If we as a nation have the right to take your life to solve our problems, then we're not different from that murderer on the street.

π

All that Jim and Carolyn Leming were able to salvage of Ray's assets was his 1970 Corvette. It was rolled out when Ray returned home to Pennsylvania. In time, the Lemings recovered from the financial obligations they incurred fighting for Ray's freedom. Their planned retirement was delayed a bit, but nevertheless Carolyn was able to retire two years after Ray's release. Jim still works part time in construction—because he enjoys it. They live quietly and comfortably in Dover, Pennsylvania.

π

Dear Carolyn, my good friend Gene Burdick's wife, died of cancer in October 1997. I remember with affection their hospitality in opening their home to me on many, many occasions during my trips to Phoenix. Gene retired from law practice the year before Ray's release. He remarried in 2002. On several occasions Gene and Mary have been welcome visitors to my campfire, a pit in my back yard, from which we've watched the sun set behind Mount Talac.

Gene is now a grandfather, thanks to son Alex, a photographer in Phoenix. Son Chris is a policeman in Sierra Vista, a small town in southeastern Arizona, and son Adam is in neurosurgery resident at the University of Florida.

π

It was Mike Pain who introduced me to Phil Barnes, on my first trip to Phoenix. Gene told me this private investigator, a good friend of his, could find anybody. Hearing of Ray's plight and my interest in the case, Mike volunteered his services.

Mike's office was on the ground floor of the Luhrs Building, conveniently located across the street from the courthouse. I met with him often in the early days and sometimes used his office as a place to relax. One time I overheard a phone call.

"Phil Barnes here," said Mike. "Are you...?...Do you know...? I'm trying to locate him."

Mike had sources in the phone company. But even if he couldn't get the number of the person he wanted he would almost always get the number of a friend or a relative.

"I'm with...We sent him a refund awhile ago but it came back with no forwarding address and we'd like to get the check out to him...Oh, he's moved...Thanks for the new address."

People go into hiding for various reasons, most commonly to avoid creditors. Phil helped Mike find them. One time Mike's client wanted to know how much someone—an author—had received in royalties. Posing as the author's accountant, Phil called the publisher and got through to the accounting department.

"I can't read this fax he sent me and I can't get in touch with him because he's on vacation. Can you help?"

Phil soon had a list of every royalty payment the author had received.

Mike's staff had instructions to take a detailed message whenever someone called for Phil Barnes.

This ruse worked until caller ID became popular. Phil could no longer use Mike's phone, so he'd go into a drugstore and ask to use their phone to make a local call. Phil would pose as a clerk from the camera department and say he had some prints that had been there for a long time. He just wanted to get them out of there. He'd mail them for nothing if he knew where to send them. Otherwise he'd have to toss them out. Mike said it worked every time.

Many of Phil's appearances in this story were in reality Mike Pain, like the Trish interview in Lexington. When I decided to test for bite mark bias, I borrowed Phil and used what I had learned from Mike. For example, Phil called Dr. West from a Phoenix hotel room. I was in town attending the Willoughby trial. Phil was there "on another case." After that, Phil became the sherlock in my head, not infrequently confusing me with facts.

Mike continues to investigate in the Phoenix area. His Phil won't tell my Phil his latest ruse.

π

Maricopa County Attorney Richard "Rick" Romley chose not to run for reelection. During his sixteen-year tenure, the longest for any Maricopa County prosecutor, the county grew from fourth to third largest in the nation. There was speculation that he might run for governor but the run never materialized, perhaps because incumbent Governor Janet Napolitano was considered to be unbeatable. He spent a few months in Washington, DC as a special deputy to the head of the Veterans Administration. Then, in Pinal County (where Ray did much of his time behind The Walls in Florence, the county seat), he served as special prosecutor on a public corruption case against the county manager. He is now a consultant in the Phoenix area.

π

A year and a half after Ray's release, Noel J. R. Levy received the Arizona Prosecuting Attorneys' Advisory Council's Lifetime Achievement Award. The Krone case wasn't among the six cases cited as Levy achievements. He continues to prosecute people in Maricopa County.

π

After Ray accepted the settlement from the City of Phoenix he was told that two persons wanted to talk to him. Detectives Charles "Chuck" Gregory and Dennis Olson both apologized and said thay were sorry for what happened. But Gregory added, "You shouldn't have lied to us."

π

Criminologist Scott Piette left the Phoenix crime lab to attend medical school and is now an osteopath somewhere in Iowa.

π

Judge Jeffrey Hotham continues to sit on a bench of the Maricopa County Superior Court.

π

In August 2000, Judge James McDougall retired early. After being rotated into Family Court he was apparently unable to keep up with the caseload. In numerous cases he failed to render a decision within the sixty days mandated by law. "JUDGE NOT," read the headline in the *Phoenix New Times*:

> By letting cases languish, a veteran Family Court judge and his assistant created havoc in the lives of parents and children...[The assistant allegedly] backdated official court documents to make it appear her boss was ruling on cases in a timely manner.

The scandal ended with the assistant's being fired and McDougall's retiring.

When Ray Krone was exonerated a year and a half later Judge McDougall told the Associated Press: "I'm still very shaken about the whole thing. I keep going over it in my mind, and it still bothers me...It's not easy to tell a jury you think they're wrong."

π

Perfect witness Dale Henson was killed in an automobile accident on October 17, 2000.

π

Dr. John Piakas is Arizona's only board-certified odontologist. He continues to practice dentistry in Phoenix and shows up regularly at forensic meetings.

π

Dr. Ray Rawson retired from forensic odontology, resigned his $187,000 salary as director of dental programs at the Community College of Southern Nevada and in 2004 lost his bid for re-election to the Nevada State Senate. The next year, after being inducted into the Senate Hall of Fame, Dr. Rawson was appointed to the Nevada Gaming Commission.

π

In 2006, the American Board of Forensic Odontology once again charged Dr. Michael West with ethics violations. West signed his e-mail of resignation "with great disdain." This ethics complaint seems to have had more of an effect than the one filed thirteen years earlier that resulted in only a one-year suspension. His rambling resignation puffed up his credentials, defended his "phenomenon" (trick photography) and chastised his "accuser."

I could not disagree with one of his points:

> The Board has been reworking the 'ABFO Bitemark Guidelines.' Well, you would have spent your time better by rearranging the deck chairs on the Titanic...The Board's stated goal is to advance the science, but for the last several years I [have] seen and heard nothing of the kind.

He referred to the lack of scientific advance as the "elephant in the room."

However, I do disagree with Dr. West if he thinks that what he is does is science. He wrote, "I'm told that if the *opinion* [italics mine] of an odontologist is contrary to DNA, then the odontologist has not made an error but the *science* of bitemark analysis must instead be in error—I disagree."

True science always comes up with the correct answer. Phil Barnes proved that Dr. West's work falls short of this criterion. The West sting was part of the second ethics complaint. "[My accuser]," West wrote, "cites a 'sting' (his words) conducted by a family member of Ray Krone. *Infra dignitatem.*"

Dr. West peppered his resignation with numerous Latin idioms, perhaps to impress himself and others with his knowledge of this ancient language—waning in liturgy but alive in science and law. My recollection of Latin is a bit rusty since I last studied it as a sophomore in high school. Nevertheless, I wonder what part of Dr. West's anatomy turned "infra[red?]"? After all, it must have been quite embarrassing to learn that his "dignitatem" had been exposed.

Before coming to his "ultimum vale," Dr. West wrote, "This action, these latest 'ethics' complaints, in my opinion, is [sic] only a ruse to affect the upcoming retrial of Kennedy Brewer in Mississippi, nothing more, nothing less."

"*Non compos mentis!*" says Phil Barnes.

π

Poor Kennedy Brewer. After spending six years on Death Row, he learned that DNA proved that he did not rape three-year-old Christine Jackson. But another six years later and he is still in prison.

At Brewer's 1995 trial, Dr. West said that five of the nineteen marks found on the child's body matched Brewer's teeth pattern. Dr. Richard Souviron, the expert for the defense, told the jury that the marks weren't even human bite marks—they were insect bites! After deliberating a mere forty-five minutes, the jury convicted Brewer of rape and murder. The next day he was sentenced to death.

DNA tests done in 2001 showed that the child was raped by two men and neither one was Kennedy Brewer. Noxubee County District Attorney Forrest Allgood said the right thing: "Nobody wants to execute the wrong guy." But when the Mississippi Supreme Court overturned Brewer's conviction, he decided to prosecute him again anyway.

"Forrest Allgood!" ejaculated Phil Barnes, "How could a Southerner born with a name like that not grow up to become a prosecutor?" Indeed, "Forrest" may well have come from the great Confederate general. When the Civil War broke out, Nathan Bedford Forrest was a wealthy slave owner in Tennessee. He enlisted as a private in the Confederate Army and, despite having no military training, quickly rose to the rank of lieutenant general. He became a brilliant cavalry commander and his tactics in guerilla warfare are still studied today. In battle he had his horse shot out from under him thirty times and was credited with having killed thirty-one Yankees. "I was a horse ahead in the end," quipped "the Wizard of the Saddle."

Because of his notoriety, Forrest was elected the first Imperial Wizard of the Ku Klux Klan, which began as a social organization for Confederate veterans. Four years later, Forrest resigned from the Klan in disgust, urging it to disband because it was "being perverted from its original honorable and patriotic purposes, becoming injurious instead of subservient to the public peace." While the KKK continued on to become the hate organization it is today, Forrest went in the opposite direction. In 1875 he became the first white person to speak before the Independent Order of Pole-Bearers Association, a civil rights group of former slaves that later became the NAACP. Forrest encouraged the audience to elevate its role in the election process, emphasizing that they had the right to vote for the candidates of their choice.

Today Nathan Bedford Forrest, although sometimes mistakenly credited with having founded the Ku Klux Klan, remains a genuine American hero. If I had made up the names of the characters in this book, I would have been hard-pressed to think up one more ironic for a prosecutor than "Forrest Allgood."

What evidence will be used against Kennedy Brewer at his second trial? Dr. West's bite mark analysis? "Absolutely," says Prosecutor Allgood—that is, if he gets his way. Lawyers for Brewer have filed a motion "to exclude testimony of Michael West, DDS." The motion details problems with bite mark analysis in general and Dr. West in particular. For example, "None of the nineteen wounds Dr. West considered 'bite marks' even arguably show evidence of impression by lower teeth." That's right, Dr. West, defying common sense, says that only Brewer's upper teeth made marks. The mere physics of a bite demands that the force from the lower teeth equal that from the upper teeth. Yet West says that it is not unusual for only upper teeth to mark.

"Da mihi locum intermissum!" shouts Phil Barnes, wondering whence emanated this *merda turi*. *"Ex culo?"*

Dr. West is chomping at the bit to testify at Brewer's second trial, scheduled for September 2007. "I don't know who killed this girl, but Kennedy Brewer's teeth were on her body. It's not rocket science."

No it's not. It's junk science.

A lone wolf now that he has been forced out of three professional organizations, Dr. West seems deluded that a second conviction of Kennedy Brewer would be vindication that West is right and his numerous critics are wrong. *Si iudices merdam tauri meam credunt, non sum igitur magnus culus!*

And it could happen if the motion is denied. Prosecutor Forrest Allgood has acknowledged that the DNA results have changed the case. His new *totum bonum* theory might very well be that while the defendant was inflicting nineteen bites using only his upper teeth, two unindicted co-ejaculators were doing the raping. Also, I have heard talk that Dr. West will not be the only witness for the prosecution. There may be a jailhouse snitch waiting in the wings ready to sing like a canary.

Jingle, jangle—dingle, dangle—*vita perseverat.*

π

After the Honorable Thomas Thode ordered Death Row inmate Bobby Tankersley re-sentenced after the discovery of exculpatory DNA on the piece of rubber tubing used as a murder weapon, the Arizona Supreme Court wanted to know why Judge Thode didn't go all the way and vacate Tankersley's conviction. They sent the matter back to the Yuma County Superior Court for clarification.

Judge Thode declined to come out of retirement to explain his rational. The Honorable Richard Donato, a former deputy sheriff and Yuma County prosecutor, was assigned to the case. In his decision

Donato wrote, "The undersigned undertook a complete and painstaking review of the files, orders, published opinions and full transcripts of all proceedings in this case, utilizing every spare moment from court duties and ten days of Christmas vacation," then ordered that Thode's order for re-sentencing be vacated. Bobby Tankersley was once again sentenced to death.

There seems to be a caveat to Ray Krone's observation that in Arizona those convicted of a capital crime who are subsequently proven innocence are rewarded for it by being given life in prison. The caveat is that, if in the process of proving yourself innocent you disturb a judge's vacation, then it's back to Death Row for you.

It seemed to me that Judge Donato snubbed the supreme court. Instead of clarifying Thode's decision as he was instructed, he told the high court, "The undersigned cannot agree with his predecessor's decision...the evidence supports both verdict and sentence..."

Donato's bizarre decision also made references to the Krone case. Of Dr. Ray Rawson, who was also Tankersley's bite mark nemesis, Donato wrote, "That Mr. Krone was apparently wrongly convicted (or at least the trial judge so found) is a tragedy worthy of the greatest ancient Greek playwright. It does not, however, follow that since one mistake [Rawson's boner in the Krone case] (or even another ninety-nine mistakes) happened, that one occurred in Mr. Tankersley's case." Not only does Donato seem unconvinced of Ray's innocence, he apparently believes that even if an expert is wrong ninety-nine percent of the time, it's no reason to think he might be wrong in the instant case. I hope that the Mississippi judge considering Kennedy Brewer's motion has a more rational mindset.

It's amazing to me the inane roadblocks that pop up when new evidence points to innocence. Fortunately for Bobby, Donato's sideways decision was vacated by the high court. However, more DNA testing has been ordered—apparently to see if Bobby is really innocent. His case remains in limbo.

π

In February 2007, the American Academy of Forensic Sciences once again held its annual meeting in San Antonio. Attending this meeting completed a full circle for me, for in San Antonio thirteen years earlier I had sat down with Dr. Homer Campbell, listened to his interpretation of the bite mark left on Kim Ancona's left breast, became convinced of cousin Ray's innocence and began my enlightening spectatorship of the justice game.

The 2007 meeting had two highlights for me. One was Workshop #8, "Anatomy of a Wrongful Conviction: A Multidisciplinary Examination of the Ray Krone Case." It opened with a talk by Chris Plourd, who began by noting that it was right there in San Antonio that Dr. Campbell had introduced him to me and I introduced him to the Krone case. Ray ended the workshop with a moving description of his ten-year ordeal. He presented to a crowd that had grown by day's end (as word spread) to "standing room only."

The second highlight was a button. A month before the meeting an article entitled "The Good, the Bad & the Ugly: A Critical Look at the Forensic Value of Bite Mark Analysis" appeared in *Forensic Odontology News*. It was written by Dr. David Senn, an ABFO Diplomate concerned about the growing list of individuals convicted by seriously disputed bite mark evidence. Dr. Senn listed eleven "ugly" cases, one of which was Ray Krone's. Of these krones, nine had been released from prison through having their charges dropped, being acquitted at trial, having their conviction vacated or receiving a directed verdict of innocence. The appeals of the other two were denied. One might have gone free had the actual murderer who confessed to the crime not had all of his teeth removed before doing so. The other one was Fredrik Torgersen who was convicted in Oslo, Norway in 1958, of the murder a sixteen-year-old girl, a case suggesting that flawed bite mark analysis dates back half a century. Torgersen served a life sentence. In the justice game, fortunately for Torgersen, "life" doesn't always mean "life." He was paroled after seventeen years in prison. To this day, at age 73, he steadfastly maintains his innocence and is still trying to prove it. In 2001, Dr. Senn and three other odontologists presented evidence that excluded him. But, the Commission for Review of Criminal Cases denied Torgersen's appeal..

Senn noted the big ("bad") problem that persists in bite mark analysis:

> [Iain] Petty and [David] Sweet's 2001 words still ring true in 2006…"Despite the continued acceptance of bite mark evidence in European, Oceanic and North American Courts, the fundamental scientific basis for bite mark analysis has never been established."

Senn prefaced the "good" by saying, "The art and science of bite mark analysis…is showing signs of approaching maturity." His offer of proof: "the ABFO #2 scale" [a ruler]; "standard-setting organizations...are beginning to realize, although much too slowly, that...they must...seriously and actively enforce standards and ethics" [they can have my dad's belt]; "seeking second opinions...is routinely practiced by some" [why not all?]; and "many forensic odontologists have recognized the problem of 'observer effects' that may induce expectation bias" [I know an individual or two who would gladly volunteer to whack off a few pendulums].

His referring to bite mark analysis as "art" caught my eye. From what I've seen, bite mark analysis is all art. And to me, letting art into the courtroom under the guise of science is ludicrous. Let the attorneys artfully present their case but why not require forensic testimony to be all science. After all, art, like beauty, is in the eye of the beholder. When Doctor Artist is commissioned, he is expected to paint a picture the way his benefactor wants.

Many ABFO members are no doubt responsible, ethical artisans. But they must be in the minority; otherwise bite mark analysis after fifty years would be well beyond "approaching maturity."

Learning that he was going to San Antonio, Phil Barnes got the bright idea to produce a campaign button that would point out the perpetual infancy of bite mark analysis. It was captioned "Ouija Board of Forensic Odontology" and pictured a hand holding a pendulum above a Ouija board with "Your guess is as good as mine" written on it.

Phil had fun with the button. He stuck a bunch of them on bulletin boards in the registration area and then watched them disappear. Many smiled and laughed. Others did not. He deduced that the buttons left alongside the place settings at the Odontology Executive Committee luncheon were not well-received because after lunch he was accosted by the sergeant at arms while dropping more buttons on a table outside their general business meeting.

This guy introduced himself as a "Dr. Somebody" and Phil used his "Jim Rix" alias. The man then politely suggested that it was neither the time nor the place to criticize odontology and wanted to know why Phil was doing it. Phil mentioned Dr. Senn's article.

"I know Dr. Senn," said the sergeant, perking up and indicating that Dr. Senn was his mentor.

"What do you think of his article?" asked Phil, whipping out a copy of "The Good, the Bad & the Ugly."

"It's very good."

"I thought so too," said Phil. "What do you think of all these guys who were convicted by bite marks who were in fact innocent?"

Phil pointed to the list.

"Is that a lot?" was the bright-eyed response.

Phil almost lost it but restrained himself and listened on.

"Industry makes mistakes all the time. Why are you chastising us for a few of our mistakes while ignoring our successes?"

Phil tried to keep his cool. "In industry mistakes usually don't cost innocent people their lives or their freedom. If they do make mistakes, they fix the problem real fast if they want to stay in business."

Phil wanted to use the Apollo Space Program as an example. After three astronauts lost their lives in a tragic fire during a launch pad test, NASA accepted its failure, redesigned the command module and successfully landed three Americans on the moon on schedule. Phil refrained from stating the obvious, that bite mark analysis has had enough time to fix itself. Instead he politely asked, "What successes?"

Phil knew of only one bite mark "success" story—Dr. Richard Souviron matched bite marks on a buttock to a notorious serial killer. But, unlike the numerous failures where the only evidence was bite marks, there was an abundance of other evidence against Ted Bundy.

The sergeant couldn't think of any success stories, so he changed the subject and claimed that there is validity to bite mark analysis.

"Are you referring to Workshop #4?" Phil asked.

"Yes, that's the one!" He seemed delighted to have hit upon something positive.

"As you know, then, it was a dismal failure."

Realizing that he was about to lose it and that he was banging his head against a wall, Phil turned around and walked away. The jingle jangling sound of buttons being cleared from the table reminded him of the Mexican bandito's line in John Huston's classic film "The Treasure of the Sierra Madre": "Badges? Badges! We don't need no stinking badges!"

π

All of Ray Krone's bite mark experts were in San Antonio. Due to failing health, Dr. Homer Campbell has all but retired from odontology and for the past several years has attended the AAFS meetings in a wheel chair. Dr. Norman "Skip" Sperber and Dr. Richard Souviron remain active in odontology. Dr. Gerald Vale revealed that he is close to retirement. Vale opened his speech in San Antonio by saying, "On a personal note, I'd like to say that having now reached my eightieth birthday, I fully expect that this will be my last and final presentation to the Adacemy."

And it was a good one. It was on the survival of bite mark analysis:

> The reality is that...we've had a series of disastrous cases in recent years in which innocent people have been sent to jail on the basis of bite mark evidence...[Vale praised the work being done] to establish bite mark evidence solidly on a scientific basis[, which is projected to take three to five years, but added]...My concern is that the patient may die during this process.

For the remainder of his talk, Vale urged that bite mark analysis be subornated to DNA. He gave an example of a case where he stated in his report that his conclusions were "preliminary" and should be "substantiated or rebutted by DNA evidence."

I knew what Phil Barnes was thinking: Dr. Vale sees the writing on the wall. Why fiddle with bite marks when there's DNA?

Ray's four experts plus a handful of others comprise the upper echelon of bite mark analysis. If this group were the whole of odontology and would insist upon peer reivew, I firmly believe there would be few if any bite marked krones. I commend this group for their outspoken concerns and their sincere efforts to clean up bite mark analysis and I apologize to any of them who may have been unhappy with the button. And, as I continue to reflect, perhaps I've been a bit harsh toward their organization, because the whores within its ranks were spawned by an outside force—supply and demand. *It's the justice game's demand for whores that creates the supply.*

The buzz phrases "innocent until proven guilty," "burden of proof" and "beyond a reasonable doubt" create the illusion that our justice system seeks truth. The reality is that it is by and large about winning at all costs. This means it's also about green, which equates to power. The one with the most green is more often the one in the driver's seat. In OJ's case, was it the truth or the juice that prevailed? While district attorneys have budgets to manage, they get to spend other people's money. The indigent "bad dude," regardless of innocence or guilt, is hard-pressed to compete on the relative pittance doled out. In Ray's first trial, for example, it was just enough to create another illusion—that the scales of justice are balanced.

I do not mean to point fingers only at prosecutors. Defense attorneys too have their stable of whores ready to ride into court—if their clients can afford them. When they can, murder trials like OJ Simpson's and Phil Specter's become much more entertaining to watch.

It's common sense that so long as there's the demand for whores there'll be a supply. Bite mark analysis is particularly venal because its accuracy depends upon competence and integrity rather than scientific validity. However, whores skilled at spinning evidence are scattered to some extent throughout all forensic sciences.

Until the justice game is able to change its focus from winning at all costs to discovering the truth (a tall order) it will be business as usual in which "truth is relative."

π

The unfortunate popularity of a 2005 book by former prosecutor turned TV commentator, Nancy Grace, probably only added to the false impression that all's fine with our criminal justice system. Here's an example of the fantasy views to be found in *Objection!: How High-priced Defense Attorneys, Celebrity Defendants, and a 24/7 Media Have Hijacked Our Criminal Justice System*:

> Believe me, if the U.S. justice system were so ineffective and unfair, I'd be the first to join in with the death-penalty protest. But this is simply not the case. Our justice system is the soundest in the world, with defects rare and rules of evidence that are typically all too favorable to the prisoner...Our system is so stacked in favor of the defendant that countless guilty people are deemed not guilty. Factor that into the 7 percent [of cases remanded for retrial on guilt-innocence issues that ultimately end in acquittal] and find this conclusion: The incredibly low levels of acquittal on retrial bear out that the system works. The unvarnished truth is a far cry from the claim that we convict and execute the innocent. We don't. [pp. 266-7]

It's amazing that Ms. Grace makes this statement. She interviewed Ray Krone on "Larry King Live" and knew that "we" not only convicted an innocent person, "we" convicted him twice. And Ray is not alone. The latest (May 11, 2007) Death Row exoneree was also twice convicted. After twenty-one years in prison Curtis Edward McCarty walked free after the Innocence Project was able to break Black Magic's spell. Crime scene DNA that Oklahoma City criminologist Joyce Gilchrist (Black Magic) testified came from McCarty didn't. Judge Twyla Mason Gray wanted to know, "Where is Joyce Gilchrist and why isn't she in prison?" Prosecutor Robery H. Macy was cited for misconduct. The Macy-Gilchrist team sent seventy-three persons to Death Row—twenty have been executed. Macy "believes executing an innocent person is a sacrifice worth making in order to keep the death penalty in the United States."

Another twice-convicted krone that comes to mind is Rubin "Hurricane" Carter. He was convicted solely on the testimony of two eye-witnesses whose recantations after the first trial resulted in a second trial at which the recanters recanted their recantations.

These cases suggest that the rate of multiple convictions is not a very good indicator that "the system works." It appears that Ms. Grace uses statistics as a drunken man uses a lamppost—for support rather than illumination. It's well known that statistics can be used to prove anything—even the truth. According to the Death Penalty Information Center, forty-four of the one hundred twenty-three individuals released from Death Row since 1973 were acquitted at retrial. That's 35%.

Pro-death penalty advocates seem to me to latch onto a few exaggerated or pseudo statistics like the one noted by Ms. Grace to promote their "system works" mentality and ignore the abundance of bona fide statistical evidence to the contrary. I will mention two more.

The one statistic that really jumps out is the reliability of eyewitness testimony. Of the 200 plus individuals exonerated through the efforts of *The Innocence Project,* eyewitness misidentification played a role 75% of the time. It has been known since 1932, when Edwin Borchard studied sixty-five wrongful convictions and published *Convicting the Innocent*, that eyewitness misidentification is the leading cause of wrongful convictions. Barring recantation, which is all too often ignored by the courts when it does happen, eyewitness testimony by itself is irrefutable. Considering all this, it would be difficult for the cerebral cortex not to conclude that at least some individuals who were sent to the gallows convicted by eyewitness testimony alone were in reality innocent.

The other staggering statistic is that since Ray walked away from prison a free man, one Death Row inmate has followed his footsteps on the average of every two months (through February 2006). Four of these lucky individuals were pardoned in 2003 by Illinois Governor George Ryan two days before he left office because "It was the right thing to do." Defending his decision, Governor Ryan added:

"Three years ago, I was faced with startling information. We [Illinois] had exonerated not one, not two, but thirteen men from Death Row. They were found innocent. Innocent of the charges for which they were sentenced to die. Can you imagine? We nearly killed innocent people. We nearly injected them with a cocktail of deadly poisons so that they could die in front of witnesses on a gurney in the state's death chamber. That's a pretty gruesome picture...[Since 1977] we had released more innocent men from Death Row than the [twelve] hopefully guilty people we had executed...It is a shameful scorecard. Truly shameful...How do you let innocent people march to Death Row without somebody saying, 'Stop the show'?...

"If we haven't got a system that works then we shouldn't have a system."

π

Christopher Plourd continues to practice criminal law in San Diego, California.

In our last hurrah, he and I met in Phoenix on August 18, 2006, as we had done so many times over the preceding ten years, for the sentencing of Kenneth Phillips. There was little fanfare. There would likely have been no press coverage at all if Chris hadn't alerted a contact in the press. I recall only one other person in the spectator's gallery besides myself, Chris and the lone reporter. No one from the victim's family was present. Kim Ancona's mother, Patricia Gasman, had died the previous year. Ancona's son, Daniel Miller, could not be located and her daughter, Kelly Supler, who was ten years old at the time of her mother's death, was unable to attend.

Seven weeks earlier, Phillips had avoided the death penalty by pleading guilty to one count of first-degree murder and to one count of sexual assault. From the pre-sentence report:

[Phillips] last drank alcohol on the day of his arrest in January 1992, and acknowledged drinking a case of beer. On weekends, he usually drank a case [24 cans] of beer daily and sometimes during the week also. He is an alcoholic who has abused alcohol since he was a teenager. Alcoholism runs in his family...The defendant admitted walking inside the bar that night, but could not clearly recall what happened. However the next morning, when he learned of the murder and saw the blood on his hands, he wondered if he was involved.

The judge wanted to know why the state was willing to drop the death penalty. Prosecutor Catherine Hughes told the court:

[T]he extensive mitigation materials...[were] sufficient to call for dropping the death penalty...[E]ven if he were released on the murder charge after 25 years, he would still have an additional twenty-eight years to go [on the sexual assault charge]...[which] effectively keeps him in prison for the rest of his life.

The mitigation materials included Phillips's notebook, which was not made public. One of Phillips's attorneys, Elizabeth Todd, told the court:

I have to say, of all the clients that I've worked with, he has been by far the most grateful client that I have ever worked with. He was genuinely a pleasure to work with...He asked only that we save his life...and that he would do anything that was necessary in order to accomplish that...I know that Mr. Phillips doesn't look good on paper, but I've come to know him, and he has a genuinely good heart. He's a good man.

Phillips's other attorney, Maria Schaffer, added:

The crimes in the case were horrendous and I know there's nothing I can say to justify what happened to Ms. Ancona in this case, but I can tell you that Mr. Phillips is worthy of a life sentence...[I]t's been rather therapeutic for him in that he realizes how he got to this point, how he could have committed such a horrible crime. He's come to terms with his alcoholism. He's come to terms with some of the dysfunction that's in his family...and he is one hundred percent completely at terms and at peace with the fact that he is going to die in prison...[H]e realizes he needs to pay for what he did...and he takes full responsibility for what he did...

The Honorable Linda Akers sentenced Kenneth Phillips to "life with the possibility of release after twenty-five years" for murder and to twenty-eight additional years for sexual assault.

When the proceedings concluded, Phillips went over to the clerk's desk and signed the necessary paperwork. Then he looked toward us and asked who we were. His attorney whispered something in his ear.

He said, "Oh," then turned and preceded the bailiff out of the courtroom.

π

Mom passed away on October 27, 2004 at the age of ninety-five. The saddest thing for me to watch as she moved on in years had been the deterioration of her great mind. She was the first person I called after hearing of Ray's impending release.

"I have news. You remember your sister Hazel's daughter Carolyn and her son Ray Krone?" (I'd gotten in the habit of making clear whom I was talking about.)

"Oh?" she said.

"You remember. He was sent to prison some time ago…" I gave her time to try to recollect. Then I briefly related some recent events, ending with, "Well, they're letting him out today. He's free!"

I knew that she understood because she didn't end the conversation with her usual "I love you," but with "Thank God!"

CHAPTER 29
JANGLE JINGLE

What looks large from a distance,
Close up ain't never that big.
– Bob Dylan

hil Barnes was stunned by the revelation that DNA found on Kim Ancona's tank top belonged to a convicted sex offender.

Not too many months earlier, Phil and I had returned from Parker, Arizona with the final piece of the puzzle fitting beautifully into the hypothesis that Ancona had been murdered by two lesbians.

The getaway car, which perfect witness Dale Henson had described in detail, was baffling from the beginning. The Phoenix Police Department made no attempt to find it, especially after Henson failed to pick *their* suspect out of the photo line up. The defense team made an effort but abandoned the search after roaming the streets of Phoenix for only two days.

The clue where to look came from Phil's suspect during the Lexington interview. "Ask Gloria," Trish had urged him when he questioned her alibi.

The bi-sexual Trish was a very good-looking woman, attractive to both sexes. Gloria was another lesbian hung up on her. After breaking up with Lu, Trish dated Gloria until leaving Phoenix. Although it had been awhile since Trish moved to Kentucky, Gloria stayed in touch and remained infatuated with her.

"She has to learn to let go," Trish confided to Phil.

Gloria's name appeared briefly in the police reports. She was with Trish and Lu on the day they left town to go "skiing" but she hadn't been investigated. On the trip home from Lexington, Phil wondered what automobile Gloria was driving at the time of the murder. A straightforward inquiry of the Department of Motor Vehicles records revealed that in 1991 Gloria owned a 1984 Harley Davidson motorcycle and a 1983 Volkswagen Jetta. Whoa! A "Gremlin type" vehicle, as Henson had said. Phil got excited. Was it the same color Henson had noted?

Now, eight years later, it was resting in a junkyard on the Colorado River Indian Reservation. The reservation was established in 1864 to accommodate American Indians indigenous to the Colorado

River area north of Yuma. These tribes were the Chemehuevi and Mohave. In the 1940s members of the Hopi and Navajo tribes were relocated there. These four tribes consolidated and in 1995 opened the Bluewater Resort and Casino on the banks of the Colorado River just outside of Parker, an incorporated town on Indian lands. With her true love gone to Kentucky, Gloria had no reason to stay in Phoenix. She returned to the reservation and took a job at the new casino. Sometime later she junked her Jetta.

I flew to Phoenix and rode along with Phil to Parker. Our first stop was the junkyard. The car lay trashed in the back of the lot. I took pictures of it. Sure enough it was blue, which would have appeared "green" to Henson under the yellowish amber lights illuminating the parking lot in front of the CBS Lounge. Phil pulled up the driver's side floor board carpet on the outside chance that Lu's Converse tennis shoes picked up some of Ancona's blood after the murder and deposited traces of it on the floor mat as Lu drove back to Gloria's place. It was an extremely long shot and subsequent DNA tests on the floor mat did indeed draw a blank.

Our next stop was the Bluewater Casino, where we hoped to catch Gloria off guard and have a chat with her about her lesbian lover's alibi. Phil had already verified that Gloria was working that day. He didn't know what she looked like and didn't see anyone who fit the bill after walking the casino floor. He went up to a pit boss.

"I'm looking for Gloria," Phil told him. "I understand she works here."

The pit boss looked around and said, "She must be on break. What's this about?"

"I've come from Phoenix and would like to talk with her...A friend of hers—Trish—said I could find her here."

"I'll go get her for you," he volunteered and disappeared into a back room. He returned shortly. Gloria wanted more specifics.

"I'm investigating a murder that happened awhile back in Phoenix. Her friend Trish said she might have some information about it. I only need about ten minutes of her time." Phil hoped that mentioning Trish's name a second time would have some effect.

The pit boss again disappeared and didn't come back for a while this time. "I'm sorry. She's gone home sick."

Sherlock Barnes, a stickler for resolving all the clues, was nevertheless satisfied. Not only had he found the getaway car, he was convinced he had also identified Trish and Lu's hideout the night of the murder. Gloria lived in northwest Phoenix, seven miles from the

CBS lounge and a mile east of Interstate 17, the freeway to Flagstaff. Phil surmised that instead of continuing on to visit Lu's aunt in Indian Wells, the duo doubled back to Phoenix, arriving at Gloria's place sometime before noon the day of the murder. That's where he believed that Trish, with a little help from her friends, staged operation "Get Kim." The first order of business would have been to call and set up the phony drug deal. Trish knew that Ancona could not resist the opportunity to take over Trish's drug turf. The ruse worked. Ancona agreed to keep the drug rendezvous quiet and to be waiting alone in the bar after closing.

Gloria's abode was the ideal spot to lie low and await the appointed hour. It was located in the outskirts of Phoenix far enough away from the bar scene and Trish's turf that Lu's pickup would go unnoticed. Using Gloria's automobile was perfect. Gloria never went to the CBS Lounge. She preferred to hang out in the area's gay bars habitually decked out in leather. Unless it was raining she would ride her Harley. It was unlikely that anyone who frequented the CBS Lounge would recognize Gloria's VW Jetta.

When Ancona called and said she was alone waiting, it would have been just a ten-minute drive down the freeway for Lu's combat mission.

Dressed in her camouflage green army fatigues and wearing her Converse tennis shoes, Lu arrived on schedule that rainy night. She didn't have to carry a murder weapon because she knew where she could find one.

Ancona would have had Lu's favorite beverage mixed and waiting at the end of the bar when Lu walked in after passing Dale Henson as he power washed the sidewalk. Lu must have chugalugged the rum and Coke because Ancona seemed to have had time to take only a sip of her Bud Lite before Lu attacked. After disabling Ancona, Lu would have rushed into the kitchen and retrieved the Chicago Cutlery boning knife from the rack next to the stove. Phil pictured Lu holding the knife point to Ancona's neck as she spirited her down the hall and into the men's room. There he saw Lu plunge the blade through the backside of Ancona's blouse and tank top deep into the left lung. Ancona dropped to the floor falling onto the protruding knife handle causing the blade to bend. Lu rolled Ancona over just enough to extract the murder weapon and then proceeded to stage a rape by ripping and cutting off the victim's clothing and spreading her legs apart. Along the way Lu brutally bit Ancona on the left breast. She cleaned the murder weapon with paper towels, deposited the debris in the trashcan after dropping the knife under the plastic liner. Perhaps she was wearing gloves. If not she wiped the crime scene clean of her fingerprints. Unwittingly she left her footprints behind. She exited the bar and once again passed Henson, this time from behind, jumped into the Jetta and jetted back to the lesbian lair. It would have been a clean getaway had in not been for Henson's astute observations.

Phil didn't miss a thing, noting that Henson had observed "the car exit the parking lot and head west on Camelback," which, as Phil pointed out, was in the direction of I-17 and Gloria's place and in the opposite direction from both Ray's house and Trish's apartment.

For Phil Barnes the case was closed. He was biding his time waiting for an opportune moment to reveal his latest discovery when the DNA hit. At first skeptical, Phil inconspicuously watched the case against Kenneth Phillips unfold, becoming more and more withdrawn as more and more incriminating evidence came in. Phillips lived in the neighborhood. He could easily have been the American Indian whose pubic hairs were found on Ancona's abdomen and the one who was seen loitering in the alley behind the CBS Lounge in the early morning hours. His teeth pattern was consistent with Dr. Campbell's interpretation of the bite mark. His fingerprints were identified among the numerous prints lifted from the crime scene. His DQα genetic marker was the same type as was determined to be present in the mixture of saliva and Ancona's blood swabbed from the bite mark. And he remembered waking up the morning after with blood on his hands.

Phil inconspicuously backed away from his lesbian theory and waited to see how the rest of the evidence and clues fit Phillips. The bottom line, however, was that Ray was officially exonerated and out of prison. It was time for me to return home and I did so, encouraging Phil to forget about his theories.

He remained quiet for a while...until I resumed writing this book. I'd begun the project right after Ray's second conviction and had progressed through most of Part Two, hoping without much hope that such a book could somehow rescue Ray from spending the rest of his life in prison. But analyzing the justice game had made me more and more pessimistic. After Ray's release, I took a hiatus to collect my thoughts. Two years later I had regained my bearings and was back on track. Phil began to stir as soon as I began to revisit the facts of the case.

I was reading the transcription of the interview of Kenneth Phillips by Detective Olson conducted after CODIS identified Phillips as the source of the DNA found on Ancona's tank top:

> *Olson*: Today is March 22, 2002, the time is about 1345 hours. Hi, I'm Dennis Olson, Phoenix PD...I want to talk to you about some things. Back in December 1991, before you were arrested...some things came up...You're not really a suspect or anything, but your name did come up in [another] case and that's what I want to talk to you about. Okay?
>
> *Phillips*: What is it?
>
> *Olson*: A homicide.
>
> *Phillips*: Homicide?
>
> *Olson*: Yeah. You're not a suspect, okay? It's just that your name came up. We just need to clarify. I'm sure there's an explanation why your name came up and that's why I want to talk to you. But because you're here...in custody, I have to read you your rights.

Phillips waived his rights and agreed to talk. Olson established Phillips's residence at the time of the murder and Phillips acknowledged he knew where the CBS Lounge was located but he denied ever having been inside, not even to use the restroom. He stated that he passed by the lounge frequently to go to and from Fry's Supermarket. Phillips said he had no recollection of a murder occurring there.

> *Olson*: What kind of car were you driving back then? Did you have a car?
>
> *Phillips*: No...[I was] on foot.
>
> *Olson*: ...Did you have access to a car back then? Like your mom's car?...Did you drive your mom's car?
>
> *Phillips*: My mom and I don't drive.

π

Rip van Barnes wakes up with a bang, "It doesn't fit!"

"What doesn't fit?"

"The evidence—it doesn't fit Phillips."

"What do you mean?"

"The car—Phillips could not have been the one Henson saw drive up and go into the bar. He didn't know how to drive!"

Indeed this fact is corroborated by other documents. His driver's license number is always left blank or the word "unknown" is inserted in police reports and court records. Though twenty-five years old, Phillips has never obtained a driver's license. No one in his immediately family knew how to drive either, except his father, but he was killed in an auto accident when Phillips was five years old. His dad's death affected Phillips deeply. Court-ordered psychological reports all mention how much he missed his dad. He wasn't very close to his mother and said that he had no one to talk to. His mother could not afford a vehicle. She subsisted and took care of her family on a meager tribal allowance. Phillips lived with his mother, sister and two nieces in a small two-bedroom apartment not far north of the CBS Lounge. He slept on the sofa in the living room. Being poor and with no one to teach him, Phillips never learned to drive. There's absolutely no evidence available that Phillips was ever behind the wheel of a car.

"Perhaps someone drove him to the bar?" I volunteer as devil's advocate.

"Not possible," Phil corrects me. "Henson said he saw the individual exit the driver's side."

"Okay. But his fingerprints were found inside the bar. One on the front door," I remind him, "and one on the condom machine on the wall above a urinal."

"What does that mean?" Phil demands. "There were thirty other fingerprints in the men's room that were never identified. All it means is that he was in the bar at some point in time leaning up against the condom machine taking a leak. It doesn't mean he was the one who killed her."

"Okay. But his saliva was on the bite mark."

"Not necessarily. It was only one genetic marker, the DQα, which matched the saliva. You know the statistics. Four in ten American Indians are [4,4] and Phillips is an Indian. It could easily be a chance match."

I don't bother to confront Phil with the pubic hairs found on Ancona. They were less definitive than the DQα. None of them had its follicles intact. All the FBI could say was that they were mongoloid in type, "consistent" with having come from an American Indian.

"Ancona was most likely stabbed by a left-handed person," Phil continues, "and, as you know, Phillips is right-handed. You were at his sentencing and watched him sign the plea agreement."

"What about the bite mark?"

"Give me a break!" Phil shouts. "You can easily find some forensic doctor dimwit who will, for the right price, say it matches. What did Dr. Piakas say? First he said that it fit Ray. Then, after the

DNA hit, he said Phillips was a 'better' match. Ridiculous! Why, even some Ouija board certified kook said you were the one who bit Ancona!"

I'm sorry I'd mentioned the bite mark. While Phil calms down I continue to read Olson's interview of Phillips:

> *Olson*: She was stabbed and sexually assaulted…We have what could be your DNA on her blouse…I don't think it's blood or semen…but like saliva, perspiration…That's why I was asking you if you've ever went into the bar to use the bathroom for any reason at all, or were you inside there and had a couple of drinks?…I'm trying to explain why your DNA would be on her blouse…Do you have any explanation for that?
>
> *Phillips*: No, I don't.

Then Phillips claims he was in prison at the time of the murder, sending Olson scurrying off to the records office to check it out. Phillips and the Romley complex would be off the hook if it turned out to be true. Olson returns an hour later with printout in hand showing without a doubt that Phillips was not in custody at the time of the murder.

> *Olson*: I'm going to flat-out ask you. Did you kill Kim Ancona…the bartender?
>
> *Phillips*: No.
>
> *Olson*: Okay.

Olson doesn't press the issue. Phillips doesn't know that Olson is really his friend, out trying to find an explanation other than his being the murderer why his DNA was at the crime scene.

It certainly appears as if Phillips is hiding something. He says he was in prison at the time of the murder, when he wasn't. He maintains that he has never been to the CBS Lounge, when his fingerprints were found inside. And he claims he has never had a blood sample taken, yet his profile was in the CODIS database.

Transcribed spoken words can only reveal so much. He could easily be shuckin' and jivin', knowing that they have the goods on him. But I remember the incriminating TV sound bite that came from Phillips's own lips, something about finding blood on his hands the next morning and hearing of the murder on TV and wondering, "Did I do that or what?"

I remind Phil of this.

"False confessions are not uncommon," Phil responds. "Twenty-five percent of those released from Death Row…"

"Now you give me a break!" I interrupt. "You could quote statistics until the cows come home. But staggering as it might be that one in four of those exonerated by DNA had falsely confessed, Phillips did say he woke up the next morning with blood on his hands. What'd he do—make it up?"

"You heard the tape. Did Phillips say anything that wasn't first suggested to him? He admitted to nothing. See for yourself. Listen to it again."

True, I have listened to the "confession" only once. It was during the commotion preceding Ray's release. I now remember only the sound bites.

I locate a cassette copy in one of my numerous boxes of Krone stuff, dust it off and insert it into the tape player.

The interrogation occurred five days after Olson's visit. I turn on the tape player and this time focus on what is said to Phillips as opposed to what Phillips says. I also pay attention to the tone of Phillips's voice.

The interrogator first tells Phillips he's being questioned because he "lived in the general area" where this "thing" happened. Phillips confirms that he lived with his mother, sister and two nieces in a small two-bedroom apartment near 15th and Colter, which was within walking distance of Fry's Supermarket just beyond the CBS Lounge. Phillips is assured that this "thing" has nothing to do with the charges that landed him in prison. Phillips already knows that the "thing" is "murder."

In the dialogue that follows, ellipses (…) *indicate that extraneous, redundant or inconsequential words have been omitted, and* brackets [ ] *enclose short summaries of wordier material.*

> *Interrogator*: The incident happened at a lounge way back when and we talked to some other folks that frequented this place…and your name came up…You seem to be squared away right now, but way back then, I think you were probably drinking a lot, which may have had something to do with [why you're in prison].
> *Phillips*: Yes.
> *Interrogator*: Is that a pretty accurate assessment?
> *Phillips*: Well, I did drink a lot but, uh…
> *Interrogator*: Was it alcohol…you think…that got you here?
> *Phillips*: Yeah, alcohol…probably.

Phillips then names a bar he frequented, "next to a Circle K." It wasn't the crime scene but he knows where the CBS Lounge was located and maintains that he was never inside it.

The interrogator then asks him a series of questions related to the crime:

Interrogator: It looks like you might have a broken tooth...[it has a] kind of a gap...[have you gone] to a dentist while [in prison]?

Phillips: Oh no. I don't mess with dentists...they pull 'em [before they fix 'em].

Interrogator: Describe...your favorite jacket...that you would have worn around January, about the time you were taken into custody.

Phillips: Mostly like I wear a regular shirt.

Interrogator: ...in the middle of the night...it's cold. Wouldn't you wear a jacket or something?

Phillips: If it's cold, I just wear like a flannel shirt.

Interrogator: Okay. Somebody said that they thought that you had like a field jacket.

Phillips: Like a jacket?

Interrogator: Like a green field jacket or something like that.

Phillips: Green? I wore flannel [shirts].

Interrogator: What kind of shoes?

Phillips: I think like tennis shoes...like Nike.

Interrogator: Could they have been Converse?

Phillips: Nike, I'm pretty sure.

Interrogator: What's your favorite brew?

Phillips: Budweiser, Bud Lite...Miller or even draft Miller.

Interrogator: Why Budweiser *or* Bud Lite? Usually guys drink one or the other...Trying to control your weight?

Phillips: No [laughing].

Interrogator: Liked the taste of it?

Phillips: Yeah.

Interrogator: You know the alley that's behind the CBS Lounge?...You ever been back there...to drink a beer?

Phillips: No.

Interrogator: Did you ever have times when you're drinking and all of a sudden you find yourself doing something that

you didn't think you were gonna do? Or you find yourself
someplace else and you're surprised that you're there? You
don't remember how you got there—in other words, you had
like a blackout?

Phillips: Like a blackout?

Interrogator: Yeah.

Phillips: No, no, not really.

Interrogator: That's never happened?

Phillips: No.

Interrogator: Did you ever hear the name Kim...a girl?

Phillips: No.

Interrogator: Did you ever hear about anything bad happening
at the CBS Lounge?

Phillips: As I recall, no.

Phillips is cooperative and subdued. His answers are timely and
straightforward. While the interrogator is fishing for facts that fit the
crime, Phillips gives no indication that he has any recollection of the
murder or that he's making up answers that are favorable to him. He
mentions "Nike" before the interrogator mentions "Converse." The
only detail consistent with the evidence that Phillips offers is that "Bud
Lite" was one of several brands of beers he drank. However, no one
disagrees that it was victim Ancona who was drinking the Bud Lite
and not the assailant. To me, Phillips seems simply curious about
what's going on.

Interrogator: Has anybody ever come in here and talked to
you about the CBS Lounge?

Phillips: Yeah, the PD.

Interrogator: What'd they ask you?

Phillips: Just asked me questions like you asked me.

Interrogator: How long did he spend talking to you?

Phillips: Let's see, I'd say about not more than twenty
minutes.

Interrogator: Did he advise you of your rights?

Phillips: Yeah.

Interrogator: Did he tell you that you were a suspect of
anything?

Phillips: Yeah.

Interrogator: What did he tell you that you were a suspect of?

Phillips: [Hems and haws]...It had something...some lady was murdered.
Interrogator: Well, then it was murder?
Phillips: Yeah.

Interrogator: Did he tell you about fingerprints?
Phillips: Fingerprints? No, he didn't say anything about fingerprints.
Interrogator: Did he tell you about DNA?
Phillips: He said something about DNA.

Interrogator: Well, let me ask you this...a "what if?"...I'm not suggesting that this is the actual case. This is a "what if?" If you did something, say ten years ago, and you knew you had done it and the wrong guy got convicted and sent to prison, how would you feel about that?
Phillips: I'd feel bad.
Interrogator: It would work on you?
Phillips: Yeah.
Interrogator: You'd want to maybe get that off your chest and talk about it...that sort of thing?
Phillips: Yes.
Interrogator: Okay. I'm not the police. Do you understand that?...I'm an investigator.
Phillips: Yes.

Convicts are naturally suspicious of the police, especially when they've been read their rights. The interrogator is soft spoken. He emphasizes that he isn't the police but an investigator simply trying to sort things out. Phillips has to be concerned that a policeman has told him his DNA was found on a murder victim. Not trusting the police, Phillips may be unconsciously putting his faith in the "investigator."

Throughout the session, the interrogator repeatedly plays the "blackout" theme.

Interrogator: Is there a possibility that you could have been involved in something like this ten years ago and just put it out of your mind?
Phillips: Ten years ago? No, I can't recall it. No.
Interrogator: Is there a possibility...well, let me put it this way: Has there been a time when you know you've done something, but you can't exactly remember specifically how it happened? But you've had a bad feeling? In other words,

if the circumstance were, you don't have all of the facts…but there's something you want to talk about…

Phillips: If I would've done something like, a year ago, or ten years ago, whatever, or longer, I would remember it.

Interrogator: This was actually three weeks before you were arrested. This happened December 29th, 1991 at the CBS Lounge, which is just walking distance from where you were living.

Phillips: Yes.

Interrogator: Yeah. There's a bottle on the bar…alongside a glass, and the bottle is Bud Lite…the fingerprints that are on this bottle haven't been compared, as yet, but the fingerprints weren't compared because there was no one to compare them to…Is there a possibility, even if you were in there earlier, and had nothing to do with this, that those could be your fingerprints on that beer bottle?

Phillips: No.

Interrogator: Okay. If they turn out to be your fingerprints on the beer bottle…how do we explain this?

Phillips: …How are you going to explain it?…

Interrogator: Well, you'd be the one that would have to explain it…

Phillips: You would have to re-do it. I don't know.

Interrogator: … I don't want to put you into a situation where you're not telling the truth. I don't want to stuff words in your mouth. I don't want to…make false accusations, anything like that. I am not the police. It's not my job to make a case against you. I'm simply trying to get to the bottom of what happened.

Phillips: Yes.

Interrogator: Because it appears, based upon the evidence, that the wrong guy is doing time for this…That's what it looks like and that guy [Olson] that came in and talked to you is saying that your DNA was in the bathroom where this woman was found. And I'm simply adding to the mix the fact that…there are fingerprints on the bottle [of Bud Lite]. We don't know who they compare to as yet. But if they come back to you, then that would mean that your fingerprints are in the bar, and it would mean that your DNA is in the bathroom…on this woman. So my concern is how do you explain this? When they compare [the DNA] to millions of different people it's weird that unless there's a mistake in the system, which they don't make mistakes like this, that it comes back to you who lives out of all the millions of people checked...just a couple of minutes away from the CBS Lounge.

Phillips: Yes. All I know is I've never been in that bar...

Interrogator: You know, I read in one of your probation reports that you're upset that your dad passed away when you were five years old and that you wished you had a father to talk to. Do you remember that?

Phillips: Yes.

Interrogator: And you wished you had people you could talk to. Okay. This is a situation like that right now. I'm not the police. I'm not trying to make a case against you. I'm trying to get to the truth of whether this other guy still oughta be in prison. And it doesn't look like it. But if you're involved...I think you'd feel better about yourself if you just said, "Yeah, maybe I could have been involved. I just don't know."...I'd hate to see you carrying a burden around like that.

Phillips: Yes.

Interrogator: ...The bottom line is this, Ken...this isn't just some kind of opinion...This is a hard physical piece of evidence...You've heard about DNA?

Phillips: Yes.

Interrogator: It's positive confirmation. Right now they're double-checking it...If you wanted to talk to someone about this, I'm not the police...this is a good chance to do that. Is there a possibility you could've been in the lounge and done this thing?

Phillips: No. Nope.

Interrogator: Is there a possibility that someone stole your DNA and planted it?

Phillips: I don't know. I just know that I ain't been in there. You know, never been in there.

Interrogator: Is there a chance now, thinking about what I'm talking about, that you could've done something like this and you just don't have a clear memory of it?

Phillips: If I did something I would remember.

At this point the interrogator asks Phillips to recall things that happened in his past. Phillips remembers well the 1988 incident in which he entered a neighbor lady's apartment brandishing a cap gun and assaulted the woman. When the lady saw that it was a toy gun she herself tossed Phillips out before calling the police. Because Phillips had not used a real gun and seemed harmless, he received probation. But he can't remember the sexual assault on the seven-year-old girl for which he pleaded guilty and is now serving time. The interrogator reminds him that he was out drinking with the girl's father, came back to the father's house to sleep it off, woke up in the early morning hours, went into the girl's room and fondled her inappropriately.

The interrogator then suggests possible scenarios at the CBS Lounge.

> *Interrogator*: There are times when people get involved in situations. They get involved in a fight, or an assault, or some kind of a confrontation with someone and things happen. It gets out of hand, you know, it goes beyond what they intended. Maybe if it's a woman, maybe they just wanted to talk to her a little bit and one thing leads to another and she gets scared. Maybe she does something that provokes an incident and all of a sudden, it picks up speed and somebody winds up getting very seriously hurt or killed. And that isn't to suggest that the person that did it went in there intending to hurt somebody, it's just something that got out of hand. Is that what happened here?
>
> *Phillips*: No.
>
> *Interrogator*: ...Let's assume you say to yourself, "Yeah, that's my DNA in there," okay? You got two poles. One is you think about her. You've seen her before. You've watched her. So you premeditate what you're gonna do. You think about how you're gonna do this. You're gonna wait until everybody leaves the bar and then you're gonna go in there when she's all by herself. You're gonna make your way back into the kitchen and you're gonna pick up a knife. And then you're gonna get her in a situation where she can't defend herself—she can't run. You're gonna kill her. You're gonna stick her with that knife, cut her throat, and take all of her clothes off of her and pick up a little piece of wood, stick it up inside of her. And you're going to get all bloody doing this. That's one possibility. Another possibility is you simply go in there and try talking to her. For some reason, she feels aggressive. She gets, uh, resistive. She gets even violent with you and you react to that. And one thing leads to another and

a tragedy takes place. And it shouldn't have happened, but it did. But it's not as bad as the first incident that I described to you. Is there a possibility of either one of those circumstances being the reason that your DNA is in that bathroom?

Phillips: No.

Interrogator: If you put twelve people into a courtroom and you say, "If you people believe the experts [who say] that the DNA belongs to Kenneth Phillips, then you have to convict him of murder." How are you going to describe the fact that your DNA is in there, Ken? You can't just say, "Do it again because it really isn't mine," because the bottom line is, it is yours. I am not the police. I am not trying to make a case against you. In fact, I'm not even sure at this point that anything you would tell us is even admissible against you. So based upon that sort of thing, do you want to tell me what happened at the CBS Lounge?

Phillips: I was never at the CBS Lounge.

Interrogator: Do you remember going behind the lounge and maybe having a bottle of beer leaning against an open door back there? Remember that?

Phillips: No.

Interrogator: Because there was a gentleman [in the] apartment building right behind the alley [who] says he saw you. Is there a possibility that you were just walking past and stopped, or that maybe you even went in and bought a bottle of beer and went back outside?

Phillips: Nope.

Interrogator: [The interrogator takes some time to elaborate on DNA technology]...It's like fingerprints...only really specific...They weren't looking at you [but] the computer spits out your name [and] it's awfully peculiar that you look like you're behind the bottle...I read your reports and...damn, in 1991 you had a real rough year. You were on intensive probation...You had a lot of curfew violations. Even though they wanted you not to drink, that wasn't working...There's a lot of people that really drink too much. You don't remember, you blackout, you just don't remember, and you do things that you normally don't do...I think that's the explanation of why we have your DNA there...

[Tape ends and continues on side two.]

Ken, first of all, we've got the DNA, which they are saying came back to you. Secondly, we have three hair fibers that [the FBI] says are American Indian. You are an American Indian. Next, of all places in the entire world that were queried concerning whose DNA this is, it comes back to you, who lives 600 yards away. Next, we've got a sexual assault in addition to the murder carried out against her, and you've got a record for such things. So you see the volume of information that's coming back aimed directly at you. We need an explanation of this. Like I say, I think what happened here is that something got out of hand in the bar. It just picks up momentum, it takes on a life of it's own...But you're the one that has to confirm that, if that's what happened...It looks spontaneous, it looks like something that just happened, you know, very quickly, and so my invitation to you is, if that's accurate, let's deal with it.

Phillips: [pause] No.

Interrogator: Well, you're gonna have to deal with it eventually, Ken...[What are you going to tell the prosecutor?]..."I've never been in the CBS Lounge. I don't have any reason for my DNA and blood to be in the men's restroom...on her. I don't have any explanation as to how three hair fibers come back to...an American Indian, [and] winds up on her as well"...I can see the prosecutor licking his chops because a more difficult thing for a prosecutor to explain is for you to say, "Yeah I've been in the bar before, I might have been in the bathroom and I'm always cutting myself on this or that and that could explain my blood."...But when you say, "I've never been in there ever," that makes his job a lot easier because he can prove you were there. You've got to think about this. As I told you, I'm not even sure what you're telling us would be admissible in court against you. That's the prosecutor's responsibility. My main concern is the wrong guy is in prison for this...You've been a real gentleman to talk to and I don't want to antagonize or upset you, but the fact is you did it...

Phillips: I ain't been in there.

Interrogator: [Have] you ever been told that you did something that you really didn't believe you had done and later found out that you had done it? Sometimes that happens with people who drink a lot...You don't remember having any contact with that seven year old girl but yet that's what happened...You pleaded guilty to that...but you really don't remember it happening...You had a blackout. You don't remember blacking out...If there's an explanation for this stuff it could be...[you] got into a fight with this gal. She was arguing...she's gonna grab a knife. She was cleaning up the place, "Get outta here, get outta here," and then a fight takes place, the fight escalates. The next thing you know you're in the bathroom...

Phillips: Yes. I know, I don't know but I know I drank...drank a lot.

Interrogator: ...You could probably drink a lot back in those days.

Phillips: Yeah.

Interrogator: ...Eighteen cans of beer was like in one report.

Phillips: Yep. Yeah. I know. I drank a lot. I had a problem with drinking. I missed my dad.

At this point Phillips appears to grasp the ramifications of what he's been told. The evidence laid out against him (proximity to the crime scene, fingerprints, pubic hairs, DNA), coupled with the fear of what the prosecutor will do to him, seems to have had an affect. But he doesn't act like a person who is knowingly guilty by claming up or making up a story. Rather he seems to accept "the fact is you did it" and to believe the "blackout" explanation. From this point on he comes across as if he wants to help the interrogator and is almost apologetic that he can't remember doing the "thing."

The interrogator continues to submit possible scenarios, to reiterate the incriminating evidence and to push the drinking/blackout problem. Phillips no longer makes denials and eventually parrots some of the interrogator's suggestions.

Interrogator: ...could it have happened that the woman left the door opened unlocked?...You want another beer...she wants you outta there...she picks up a knife...she's fighting and arguing with you...it gets outta hand...There's really gotta be a reason why [the DNA] is there...

Phillips: Probably, probably, something like that...I can't hardly remember.

Interrogator: How about the next day...Did you wake up...like...something fucked up...you had a cut or blood on you or something like that?...Then you heard about what happened in the CBS Bar...It was big news back then...

Phillips: I don't know, but I can't remember. You know, I heard about it, you know.

Interrogator: ...You wake up, you realize, "Maybe I fucked up. Maybe it was me 'cause I got blood on my clothes. I don't remember how that blood got there," something like that...

Phillips: Maybe, yeah.

Interrogator: ...Where was the blood?

Phillips: I can't recall, I can't remember.

Interrogator: But you do remember having the feeling about there was some blood and you wondered how'd this get here?

Phillips: Yeah, you know.

Interrogator: Okay. Well, was it on your pants, or shirt or shoes?

Phillips: I can't remember, 'cause I was drinking a lot that day.

Interrogator: ...It's easy to drink eighteen beers, no big deal...You get blotto...based upon what I hear you say that there was a time when you woke up one morning...wondering where did this come from? And you had blood on your clothes?

Phillips: Yeah.

Interrogator: You recall when you were arrested on the charges that you're in here now for, January of 1992, do you remember that?

Phillips: Yeah.

Interrogator: Okay. How much before that was it you saw the blood?

Phillips: I think, I can't recall, I think the next day. I'm not too sure.

Interrogator: ...The next day, from hearing the radio reports and the TV reports about what happened at the CBS Lounge, that made you worry?

Phillips: Yeah, and 'cause you're thinking I was seeing something.

Interrogator: Right.

Phillips: I seen the blood and...

Interrogator: Wondering about it.

Phillips: ...wondering...you know?

Interrogator: You're trying to make sense out of it?

Phillips: Yeah.

Interrogator: Right. So you hear things on the radio, you know…

Phillips: I hear things…not on the radio but TV then…just thinking to myself and then all of a sudden, "Naw, it can't be," you know.

Interrogator: Right. That makes sense…he could have been drunk…these people cleaning up bars leave the door open…letting out the smoke…He could walk in…she could have grabbed the knife…got into a…wanted him out…that's a possibility that that could have happened?

Phillips: Yeah, it could've happened, but you know…

Interrogator: …You don't remember it?…You were drinking too much, right…But the next day, though, you were worried about the blood on you…

Phillips: Yeah.

Interrogator: …That you couldn't explain?

Phillips: Yes.

Interrogator: …The next day you have a feeling…after hearing this television and you're looking at this blood. There must've been enough for you to notice…if there's a little spot you wouldn't have seen it. So, is your best recollection that there was a lot of blood you saw?

Phillips: Um.

Interrogator: I mean more than a little tiny spot?

Phillips: Not a lot, I don't think.

Interrogator: Okay. Do you remember where it was, like on your pants, or maybe on your shoes?

Phillips: I can't remember.

Interrogator: …You're at your mom's place and where did you normally sleep, on the sofa?

Phillips: I used to sleep on the sofa in the living room.

Interrogator: You're on the sofa in the living room with your clothes on, right?

Phillips: Yeah, I had them on.

Interrogator: So you rose up from the sofa in the living room and what's the first thing you looked at where you see blood?

Phillips: The first thing I looked as was my hands.

Interrogator: Blood on your hands?

Phillips: Yeah.

Interrogator: Was it on the insides, or was it on the backs of you hands?

Phillips: I can't recall, I think it was, I can't recall. I think it was inside or something.

Interrogator: You think you see blood on the inside of your hands?

Phillips: Palms, palms.

Interrogator: ...You hear the TV reports...you can't explain why you got some blood on your hands...Let me ask you about feeling bad the next day...Can you describe how you felt?

Phillips: Well, I felt like the next day when I heard it on TV and I was sitting there, you know, thinking like, like and thinking the only thing that came through my mind was, "Naw, it can't be." I was sitting there, you know, thinking, you know, you know, saying over and over in my mind, "It can't be, it can't be. Did I do that or what?" You know, I'm just saying to myself and I tried to, you know, block it off.

Interrogator: So you had been in the bar the day before?

Phillips: ...That day.

Interrogator: The day she was killed?

Phillips: Yeah.

Interrogator: ...Do you remember...a voice coming to you out of the darkness that says, "Ken," or "Hey, you go home!"—of something like that?

Phillips: Might have, I'm not sure.

Interrogator: Do you remember...someone...trying to push you outside?

Phillips: Wrestling?

Interrogator: Fighting. Okay...tell me about going into the men's room. We both know what happens when you drink a lot of beer, you've got to go to the men's room.

Phillips: Yes.

Interrogator: ...Do you remember Kim being in there when you tried to use the restroom—the bar maid?...Cleaning up?

Phillips: Might have.

Interrogator: Do you recall her arguing with you, yelling at you, being upset...[you] being mad or angry at her because she wasn't being nice to you? She was being mean.

Phillips: Yeah...I think...yeah...sure.

Interrogator: What happened?

Phillips: She, uh, I can't remember. I know, I don't have memories that…she said, I think she said, you know, "Get out of here. I'm cleaning," you know. I can't remember the rest of what I told her. I think I told her that, "I need to use the restroom," you know. And I walked…I think I walked out and she mumbled something, like in anger. I don't…I remember that that just, I kinda got upset, because you gotta go. It kinda upset me…

The interrogation ends shortly thereafter.

Phil Barnes has a point. Phillips volunteered nothing that wasn't first suggested to him.

"But," I point out, "when he accepted the plea bargain he bowed his head to the court and said, 'I'm sorry for what I've done.' For all intents and purposes he confessed to the crime."

"Yes, but what else could he do?" Phil counters. "His DNA on the tank top was a slam dunk. If he went to trial he would certainly be convicted and sent to Death Row. He opted for life."

Phil reminds me how the "blackout" explanation occurs frequently in "confessions" that have proved to be false. It's a known technique to convince an unsuspecting drunk, drug addict or otherwise compliant individual that the evidence against him is overwhelming and the reason he doesn't remember doing the crime is that he "blacked out." Once a malleable suspect is hypnotized he plays along, succumbing to the power of suggestion. Phil argues that that may very well be what happened to Phillips.

At his sentencing hearing, Phillips appeared to me to believe he committed the crime. But at his request it was stipulated that he was not required to talk about or give any details of the crime even though nothing more could be done to him.

In any event, the "confession" by itself meant little and it's tough to argue with Phil that like Ray, Phillips was up against only one piece of substantial evidence. For Ray it was the bite mark bullshit. But Phillips was up against solid DNA evidence.

Phil resumes his fixation on the lesbian connection and surmises that Phillips's DNA got onto Ancona's tank top the same way it was suspected that Ray's DNA got onto her bra.

"What? You think someone put it there to krone him?"

Phil nods. "It's possible. Except for Phillips's DNA, the clues fit the lesbians. But all that evidence was circumstantial and no match for the Romley complex's hang-up on Ray. You know what Sherlock said, 'Circumstantial evidence is a very tricky thing. It may seem to point straight to one thing, but if you shift your own point of view a little, you can make it point to something entirely different.'

"Don't you see? The only way to get them off Ray was to overwhelm them with something like DNA."

Phil speculates how it might have been accomplished. He reminds me of the *USA Today* article that reported that the police and "others" have been known to go fishing for DNA and then on the q.t. have it compared to DNA left at crime scenes.

"Cops stick together," he continues. "All it would take is for some police type to approach a prison guard with, 'There's a sex offender inside who's about to get out and we think he did another rape. If we could get his DNA we could prove it. Would you help by getting him to spit into a Dixie cup and put it into a plastic bag for me? Be careful not to contaminate it.'"

How it got onto Ancona's tank top is another matter. Phil wonders if there could have been a Watergate type break-in at the Phoenix police crime lab, where the tank top was stored. The lab is no longer in the basement under the police station. It has moved into a separate building some blocks away. Even so, I think this conjecture a bit farfetched because unless the burglar was able to case the joint beforehand he'd be hard-pressed once inside to locate Ancona's tank top among the thousands of items of evidence.

Phil suggests the possibility of an inside job. "After all, they didn't like him."

We've heard that many conscientious crime lab technicians despised Noel Levy for the heavy-handed pressure he exerted on them to spin their forensic findings to fit his agenda. This tidbit was no surprise to us because when we sat in on a meeting between Levy and a defense expert, we saw that the prosecutor wasn't one to be confused with facts. We also observed criminologist Scott Piette's fear of the man and watched Piette out and out lie under oath that the serology implicated Ray. Finding a disgruntled insider miffed with Levy couldn't have been all that difficult.

Phil's mind is racing with copious conspiracy theories. I'm envisioning the headline, "SCHIZOPHRENIC CLAIMS 'CONFESSED KILLER INNOCENT—LESBIANS DID IT!'"

Before he ventures too far into outer space I interrupt with a less radical suggestion. "Perhaps there was some DNA-exchanging event between Ancona and Phillips that didn't include murder."

Phil scoffs. "Like what?"

"Suppose Phillips was out that night and had those eighteen beers before heading home. He's passing the CBS Lounge when nature kicks in. He finds the door unlocked and goes inside to use the facilities."

"Well, that would explain his fingerprint on the front door. Then what?"

"He stumbles into the men's room and surprises Ancona mopping the floor? She tells him, 'Get out of here—the bar's closed.' But to no avail. So she backs out and lets Phillips relieve his bladder."

"Ah, the fingerprint on the condom machine. Continue."

"She goes and opens the back door at the end of the hall. To make it easier to hustle him out. She returns and he's on his knees praying to the urinal. About to go down for the count."

"So," Phil interrupts with the logical next step, "she calls the police to come and get him."

"No, no—she can't do that. She's expecting a drug deal."

"Ah, yes—the lesbian connection!" Phil's getting into this now. "Then—"

"She wrestles him to his feet and, in the process, he slobbers all over her."

"Excellent, Watson, excellent! Kelcey Means." Phil won't let me forget our conversation with the lab technician who replaced Scott Piette and found Phillips's DNA on the tank top. She told us that this case was unusual because typically she is only able to find minute traces of an assailant's DNA on crime scene evidence. But there was so much on Ancona's tank top that she said, "Phillips must have slobbered all over her."

I continue, "Then Ancona throws him out the back door and locks it behind him. He falls to his hands and knees and cuts himself on broken glass before passing out next to the dumpster. He comes to around four in the morning and that guy, Frederickson, peering out his bathroom window sees him drag himself to his feet and stagger down the alley. Phillips gets home before sunup and crashes on his sofa. At about noon he's woken up by the TV reporting last night's murder at the CBS Lounge. He sees blood on the palms of his hands and briefly experiences déjà vu. Four weeks later all is forgotten. He's arrested and charged with sexual assault and soon afterwards shipped off to prison."

Phil's impressed. I've covered all the bases. The lesbian connection's intact and I've even lent credence to the "confession."

He claps me on the back. "Very good! You've just described the perfect crime."

I'm taken aback. "How so? The wrong man's doing time."

"Yes, Watson, but the lesbian got away with murder. It doesn't get more perfect than that. And she was no brilliant Professor Moriarty. She and her lover left many telltale clues. They got away with it because of blinkered police ineptitude, a pimping prosecutor, a puppet crime lab technician, Ouija science, job-fearing pussy judges, faithful jurors, an ambitious administrator and complacent voters brainwashed into thinking the system works."

Of course, I've heard all of this before.

"How many times have I told you, Watson, when you've eliminated the impossible, whatever remains, however improbable, must be the truth?"

Ah yes, truth...

And justice? True justice is when the relative truth and the absolute truth are one and the same. I've seen the relative truth pass from Ray Krone on to Kenneth Phillips. I've listened to sherlock Barnes's deductions about Sugar and Hot Lips. But what is the absolute truth? Most likely I will never know for sure and continue to be haunted by mordant thoughts along the lines of Dylan's jangle jingle...

> *To see him obviously framed*
> *Couldn't help but make me feel ashamed*
> *To live in a land where justice is a game.*

GLOSSARY

absolute truth – reality.

art – one man's opinion; relative truth.

asshole – that part of the human anatomy where the sun doesn't shine; a place to warm the reptilian-complex; a person with a warm reptilian-complex.

assholiness – the state of being an asshole.

bad dude – scapegoat ripe for kroning.

bite mark analysis – Ouija science; guesswork.

blind test – a scientific prodedure in which the source of the data is hidden.

bullshit – the cerebral cortex's rationalization for the connivance of a warm reptilian-complex, such as the eye-brain coordination or unindicted co-ejaculator theory.

burden of proof – a justice game jingle that sounds good to the defendant until he realizes that he's the one with the burden.

catch-22 – a contradictory rule, such as "You are innocent until proven guilty provided that you can prove yourself innocent"; a jangle jingle.

cerebral cortex – that part of the human brain where thinking occurs. When dominant over its counterpart, the reptilian-complex, truth prevails. When dominated, bullshit prevails.

cop in lab coat – a forensic whore employed in a police crime lab.

denial – a delusion of the reptilian-complex whose major symptom is bullshit, such as "The system works" and "We don't convict and execute innocent people."

Department of Corrections – misnomer for Department of Punishment.

doctor – a person who has earned the highest academic degree conferred by a university; an expert licensed to render opinions.

dingle dangle – false testimony induced by favors such as motion to ejaculate.

discovery – the sharing of evidence between prosecution and defense.

discovery violation – the withholding of evidence (most commonly exculpatory) from the defense.

DNA – deoxyribonucleic acid, the molecule of life, virtually unique in all human beings except for identical twins.

dry labbing (also dry benching) – reporting scientific results without having done the science; having sex in one's mind.

exculpatory evidence – evidence favorable to the defendant.

expert – anyone whom others think knows something.

eye-brain coordination – the ability to see things that do not exist.

fiery darts of Satan – temptation.

forensic whore – a venal forensic scientist or technician.

forensics (also forensic science) – science as it applies to law.

garment – see *magic underwear*.

green – the color of justice.

"guilty until proven innocent" – justice game jangle.

harmless error – an error made by one court determined to be inconsequential by a higher court.

hired gun – a forensic whore.

His Assholiness – the top asshole in any hierarchal organization.

horse sense – antonym of horseshit; welcome relief when seen in the justice game.

horseshit – see bullshit.

"in my opinion…" – an ejaculation commonly preceding bullshit.

"innocent until proven guilty" – justice game jingle.

jangle – a harsh sound.

jingle – a harmonious sound; a catchy repetitious verse.

jingle jangle – the sound made by a tambourine; a catchy-22 novel about the harsh realities of the justice system.

john – one buying a whore's wares; a juror.

junk science – pseudo science; voodoo; witchcraft; opinion science.

jury selection – critical part of the justice game where the team captains alternately select individuals most likely to believe their bullshit; a crapshoot.

justice – when relative truth and absolute truth are one and the same.

justice system – a game played on an uneven field where the team with the most green plays downhill with the wind at its back.

krone [noun] – an innocent person convicted of a crime; e.g., Ray Krone.

krone [verb] – to convict an innocent person.

magic underwear – protective clothing covering areas subject to temptation believed by some cults to actually work; protection from the firey darts of Satan.

mental masturbation – see bullshit.

Miranda room – a place where interrogations take place; a place to extract a confession.

money – pendulum grease.

motion to ejaculate – having sex on a prosecutor's desk.

motion to vacate judgment – asking a court to set aside a previous court judgment.

Nifong disbarment – a very good start.

nifonged – kroned in the State of North Carolina.

no harm, no foul – all's fair so long as the bad dude is convicted.

opinion – a hired gun's bullet.

opinion science – oxymoron.

Ouija board – canvas of bite mark analysis and other forensic arts.

Ouija Board of Forensic Odontology – American Board of Forensic Odontology.

Ouija science – junk science reeking of bias.

pendulum – a hired gun's gun.

pernicious prick – a term used in an early draft of this book to describe a justice game player but deleted on advice of counsel.

pimp – one who procures whores; an attorney.

pink – the color of underwear in Sheriff Joe Arpaio's jail.

polygamy – moral justification for a large libido.

"Prove it!" – mantra of those in denial.

puppet master – one who orchestrates a kroning.

pussy – someone afraid to stand up and shout "bullshit" when he sees and/or hears bullshit; an asskisser.

reasonable doubt – to the cerebral cortex signifies the real possibility that the defendant is not guilty; incomprehensible to the reptilian-complex.

relative truth – blind faith; reptilian perception of reality; a jury's verdict.

reptilian-complex – that part of the human brain in common with snakes and programmed primarily for survival which when stuck where the sun doesn't shine dominates the cerebral cortex.

Romley complex – a county or district attorney's office and its stable of asskissers: courts, sheriffs, deputies, detectives, policemen, cops in lab coats, hired guns, etc.

science – the objective pursuit of truth.

sherlock – one who fancies himself a supersleuth; e.g., Phil Barnes.

unemployed public servant – a government worker who turns out not to be a pussy.

unindicted co-ejaculator theory – bullshit concocted to offset evidence of innocence.

venal – capable of being bought.

venal envy – coveting your mentor's pocketbook.

Watergate mentality – loyalty supersedes integrity.

walk on water – an ability many experts believe they have.

whore – a venal person.

whorehouse – a place where whores ply their wares; a courtroom.

APPENDICES

APPENDIX TO CHAPTER 20

CALIFORNIA V. BUTLER

In the early morning hours of January 6, 1988, police officer Jerry Hartless was shot dead by a gang member he and his partner had been chasing through Lincoln Park in southeastern San Diego. Fellow SDPD officers responded to the partner's frantic call for help. "Get the guy in the green jacket!" They soon found Willie Goudine in a green jacket at the nearby "La Paz house," a hangout for black neighborhood youths. It turned out that Goudine was the half-brother of veteran SDPD police detective Jim Kelly. A fellow officer called Kelly, woke him up and explained the situation, at which point Goudine was spirited off to his momma's house. Detective Kelly went there too and after listening to Willie's tale checked in with his supervisors.

Meanwhile, back at the La Paz house, a green New York Jets sweatshirt, not a jacket, was found in Stacy Butler's room. Butler obligingly donned his sweatshirt and paraded in front of the late Hartless's partner, who said that he didn't think Butler was the killer because the sweatshirt had "too much white on it" and Butler "had too much meat on him."

At dawn, Sergeant Tom Payne searched the La Paz house and surrounding yard with his K-9 unit. A police dog, trained to find smoking guns, found no such weapon in the house or in the back yard, which was dominated by a large, lone lemon tree. Sometime after the search, detective Kelly again called his supervisors from momma's house and told them that brother Willie said the murder weapon could be found under the lemon tree. Sergeant Payne and his dog searched the ground around the lemon tree a second time. Again nothing.

An hour later detective Kelly and his half-brother arrived at the La Paz house. Kelly went immediately into the back yard, knelt down under the lemon tree and stood up holding what would later be confirmed to be the murder weapon. Is he good or what? It was a .22-caliber revolver. No fingerprints were found on the gun but its owner was soon identified to be Darin Palmer, whose name was printed on the drug prescription bottle containing .22-caliber bullets that was later found at the crime scene.

Kelly related brother Willie's story one more time for his supervisors: Shortly before the police arrived at the La Paz house Butler had shown up with the gun in hand and given it to Willie to hide. Willie took the weapon outside and threw it under the lemon tree. He said that a friend of his, Lisa Johnson, who was also at the La Paz house when Butler arrived, would corroborate his story. But Johnson said she neither saw any guns that night nor heard any discussion about hiding guns. When asked by his supervisors why he hadn't mentioned that the murder weapon during his initial phone call, Kelly said it had slipped his mind.

Stacy Butler was arrested.

Sergeant Payne heard how Kelly had effortlessly found the murder weapon in the tall grass under the lemon tree. He told Deputy District Attorney Keith Burt and Burt's investigator, Eddie Cervantes, "You've got problems with your evidence." To prove it, Payne replayed his K-9 search with a test gun hidden under the lemon tree. The dog found it within thirty seconds. Instead of accepting the strong possibility that detective Kelly planted the murder weapon to protect his half-brother, Burt pulled out and played one of his magic marbles. He sent investigator Eddie to see Darin Palmer. Unless he fingered Butler, Eddie told Palmer, he would likely be charged with the murder because he owned the murder weapon and his loaded pill bottle was found at the crime scene. Palmer cooperated and became prosecutor Burt's star witness. Fall guy Butler was subsequently charged with and tried for the first-degree murder of Officer Hartless. Burt sought the death penalty. But the jury deadlocked six-six. A retired Marine Corps major and member of the jury told the press that he was convinced that the district attorney and the SDPD were trying to frame Butler.

Prosecutor Burt was undaunted. Some time after the mistrial Palmer was arrested for armed robbery and faced a "third strike" violation, which is very serious in California. Even the most minor third infraction carries a hefty sentence—a minimum of twenty-five years. The prosecutor could now play the second of his three special marbles. He continued with marble one to threaten to pin the Hartless murder on Palmer. He then secretly struck a deal whereby Palmer would be given time served for the armed robbery in exchange for newly fabricated testimony against Butler. Marbles one and two amounted to the carrot and the stick. Marble three would be much more fun than a carrot.

Burt had a new plan. He would try not only Butler but also some of his fellow gang members for felony murder. This strategy relieved Burt of the burden of proving who actually pulled the trigger. Palmer would provide the details as dictated by Burt. To keep stool pigeon Palmer happy and cooperative during the lengthy process, Burt played his third and final special marble and granted Plamer his motion to ejaculate. He saw to it that his snitch had plenty of snatch. In addition to a very comfortable cell, unlimited phone calls and an abundance of fast food, Palmer was frequently taken from his jail cell and treated to conjugal visits with his wife and trysts with other women. About fifty of these sexual encounters occurred in the district attorney's own private office.

Even though detective Kelly told the second jury that he had lied about some of his actions the night of Hartless's death, the jury convicted Butler and four of his fellow gang members of felony murder. Burt's new strategy paid off. With the help of his well-coached star witness he convinced the jury that Palmer's fellow gang members were conspiring to kill a rival gang member when Officer Hartless intruded and was shot and killed. The defendants were convicted and sentenced to long prison terms. Darin Palmer was released from jail. The San Diego District Attorney's Office gave Keith Burt their annual prosecutor of the year award in recognition of his winning albeit marbled strategy.

Several years passed and Palmer found himself in jail again, this time on a narcotics charge. For the second time he faced a third-strike violation. But he too had a couple of marbles. He hadn't trusted prosecutor Burt (imagine that!) and had his wife smuggle a camera into the prosecutor's office. She knew how to play marbles too. The wife accosted Burt and Eddie in the halls of justice after Palmer's bail hearing and flashed a "get-out-of-jail-free" card. It was a photograph of her frolicking naked, playing marbles with her husband on the prosecutor's desk. Unless her husband was released this photo and others like it would end up in the press. Succumbing to blackmail, Burt again let Palmer, coincidentally a black male, go free. He told the police department that the case was too difficult to prosecute. The PD complained and the case was transferred to the attorney general's office. The AG eventually obtained a life sentence for Darin Palmer and in March 1997 the San Diego Union-Tribune spilled the marbles.

Butler and friends subsequently filed petitions for habeas corpus. Superior Court Judge William Kennedy, who presided at both the first-degree murder trail and the felony murder trial, heard their petitions. Kennedy conducted a three-month investigation, listening to fifty-two witnesses and viewing more than three hundred exhibits. He concluded that the case was wrought with "a pervasive history of misconduct." The convictions were overturned and when Judge Kennedy was selected to preside over yet a third trial, he disqualified prosecutor Burt and the entire San Diego District Attorney's Office from participating. Before going to trial the defendants accepted the plea bargain offered by the California Attorney General's Office. They pleaded guilty to voluntary manslaughter in exchange for a sentence of time served and were immediately released.

A civil suit was filed against Burt and investigator Eddie Cervantes that they had violated Butler and his gang's civil rights by not disclosing the special treatment that Palmer had received. Apparently it's not a foul in the justice game to dangle dingle in front of a witness's pendulum so long as everybody gets to see the pictures.

Burt and Eddie claimed that they had "absolute immunity." The case made it to the United States Ninth Circuit Court of Appeals, where, after a plethora of legal mumbo jumbo, the court sided with these two pimps. Vindicated in the courts, they still had to face the tabloid scandal. Investigator Cervantes was fired and, according to the *San Diego Union-Tribune*, "prosecutor Keith Burt was voluntarily transferred to a less prestigious job." Perhaps it's prosecutor jive talk for "promotion"? Burt continues to prosecute to this day.

Framed by a dingle dangled snitch and then saved when his dangled dingle was exposed, Stacy Butler and his friends had nothing to show for their lost decade.

But they were lucky, compared to David Wayne Spence.

THE LAKE WACO MURDERS: TEXAS V. DAVID WAYNE SPENCE

Late in the afternoon of July 14, 1982, two fishermen stumbled upon the bodies of three teenagers in a wooded area of Speegleville Park, a recreation area near the banks of Lake Waco outside Waco, Texas. Kenneth Franks, eighteen, Jill Montgomery, seventeen, and Raylene Rice, seventeen, had last been seen the previous evening at Koehne Park on the other side of the lake. They had driven together in Rice's orange Pinto to a local teenage hangout. The car was found abandoned there.

Listening to police scanners, the media descended upon the crime scene as fast as did the police. It was a horrible crime that would occupy local media for many weeks to come.

I can attest to the brutality of the murders, having seen the crime scene photos of the Lake Wako murders in the office of Dr. Homer Campbell during my visit with him in Albuquerque. Franks was fully clothed, still wearing his sunglasses. The two girls were nude. They appeared to have been raped. All were gagged and their hands bound behind their backs. Each teenager died from multiple stab wounds to the chest and throat, forty-eight wounds altogether among them. It was a savage attack.

Given the sensational nature of the case, fueled by media blitz, every wacko in Waco wanted to help. The police were inundated with phone calls, as many as fifty per hour. The phone volume must have overwhelmed the Waco police department, making it difficult to ferret out the calls that had merit. Several such calls came in from witnesses who reported that Terry Lee Harper had bragged about killing three people at the lake. Harper had a history of wielding a knife in committing mayhem. He'd been arrested for assault no fewer than twenty-five times, including assault with intent to murder. Other witnesses from Keohne Park saw the victims talking to a person in a van that matched the description of the one Harper drove. When he was briefly taken in for questioning, he refused to cooperate any more than provide an alibi. He was subsequently released. The inundated detectives failed to determine that Harper was doing his bragging well before the bodies were found and before the story broke. No one bothered to check out the alibi. This likely candidate simply slipped through the cracks.

In less than three months the investigating detectives essentially gave up. By September the case had been declared inactive. Enter cocky narcotics Officer Truman Simons. He boasted that he could solve the crime within a week and asked police chief Larry Scott to be assigned to the case. Though Scott had misgivings because Simons frequently formulated theories and then ignored any evidence that didn't fit, he reluctantly let the enthusiastic officer give it a try.

True to form, Simons identified a suspect in short order. Muneer Mohammed Deeb, a Jordanian who owned a convenience store, neither had a criminal record nor had ever been suspected of a crime. Simons arrested Deeb, claiming that his suspect was responsible for the murders, mainly because Deeb and Franks did not like each other. Franks routinely taunted the foreigner every time he went into Debb's convenience store to see his friend, Gayle Kelley, an employee. Deeb admitted to having a crush on Kelley. When the suspect passed a three-hour lie detector test, police chief Scott ordered his release. Fellow officers ridiculed Simons, poking fun at his far fetched murder theory. A laughing stock, Simons resigned the police department a week later in humiliation. He soon became a night-shift deputy sheriff assigned to guarding prisoners at the county jail. There, with unsupervised access to the county's jailbird population, he applied dingle dangle and continued undaunted his investigation into the Lake Waco murders.

Shortly after Simons became jailer, David Wayne Spence and Gilbert Melendez were brought in for assault. Though neither was ever mentioned as a murder suspect nor his vehicle ever sighted at the crime scene, Simons believed that they fit the profile of the Lake Waco murderers. Not giving up on Deeb, the ace detective concocted an elaborate murder scenario to fit his suspects. He found out that Deeb had an insurance policy on Kelley and claimed that Deeb had paid five thousand dollars to Spence, Melendez and Melendez's brother Tony to kill Kelley in order to collect the twenty-thousand-dollar insurance benefit. Somehow Spence then mistook Montgomery for Kelley and the conspirators raped and killed the three teenagers instead.

Simons rehearsed his rogue's gallery of jailbirds, teaching them to sing like canaries. It was made clear that those willing to parrot Simons's tune would receive special favors, including sexual trysts. What jailbird's pendulum was not going to swing in that direction? Seven did. Soon Simons had his hands full of trained stool pigeons who all claimed to have overheard David Spence and Gilbert Melendez talking about how they and Gilbert's brother Tony had tortured and killed three teens in Koehne Park.

Simons then elicited confessions from the Melendez brothers. To get Gilbert's cooperation, Simons told him that Spence and Deeb had confessed and implicated him in the murders. It took some time for Simons to straighten out Gilbert's pendulum. Over the next two years, Gilbert provided five contradictory written statements. Each one fixed errors in the previous one. Simons's hypothesis was that the murders occurred in Koehne Park and the bodies were later dumped in Speegleville Park. At first Gilbert said that the bodies had been transported in Spence's station wagon. But Spence didn't buy the station wagon until weeks after the murders. Then Gilbert said they must have used Spence's gold Malibu. After the FBI dismantled the vehicle and found no trace of the victims, Gilbert "remembered" that the bodies had really moved in his own pickup truck.

When visiting the crime scene, Gilbert, left to his own bewilderment, had trouble locating where the victims had abandoned the orange Pinto and been murdered and where their bodies had been dumped. No problem for supersleuth Simons. He grabbed firmly onto Gilbert's pendulum and didn't let go until it pointed out where these events had occurred.

Before trial Gilbert Melendez recanted his confusion and refused to testify. However, his highly implausible, convoluted version of the crime was used at trial—a murder-for-hire scheme that went awry because of mistaken identity.

Though the evidence was exceptionally flimsy, prosecutor Ned Butler took Spence to trial anyway. Relying solely upon the half dozen jailhouse snitches, however well-snatched, was risky. More "evidence" was needed. While preparing for the case, the prosecutor noticed some marks on Jill Montgomery's body that the forensic pathologist had classified as "bruising." Could they possibly be bite marks? He wondered. He sent photos of the injury to a fledgling forensic odontologist and voilà!—not only were they bite marks, they matched Spence's dentition! Dingle dangle coupled with jingle jangle did Spence in. He was easily convicted and sentenced to death for the murder of Jill Montgomery.

David Spence was then tried again, this time for the murder of Kenneth Franks. Simons made it clear to Gilbert Melendez that unless he changed the angle of his dangle he and his pendulum would hang along with Spence. To sweeten the deal, and with the blessing of newly elected District Attorney Vic Feazell, Simons also dangled immunity from prosecution in front of Gilbert. Succumbing to the dingle dangle, Gilbert recanted his recantation. Brother Tony, also fearful that he would follow Spence and be railroaded onto the lethal injection gurney and believing that he would be granted immunity from prosecution along with his brother, joined in and confessed. Both Gilbert and Tony's testes lied against Spence at a second trial. They detailed the trio's trumped-up involvement in Simons's pimped-up murder-for-hire scheme. Spence was convicted for the murder of Kenneth Franks and sentenced to death a second time.

The alleged mastermind of the murder-for-hire conspiracy, Muneer Deeb, was also charged with capital murder. Expecting to collect on the promises of leniency, Gilbert testified against Deeb. A jailhouse snitch testified to overhearing Deeb's co-conspirators describe their nefarious adventure. Deeb too was easily convicted and sentenced to death.

Six years later, acting as his own attorney, Deeb convinced the Texas court of appeals that the dingle dangle was hearsay. The Melendez brothers refused to testify against Deeb at his second trial because District Attorney Feazell and company had welshed on their promises of leniency. Both were given life sentences. Deprived of dingle dangle, the state was seriously hampered. Deeb was acquitted.

Deeb's exculpation produced a legal conundrum. The state's theory for the motive of the Lake Waco murders was murder for hire. The Texas justice system had determined that no murder for hire had taken place because the alleged hirer had been exonerated. But the one ostensibly hired to do the deed was on Death Row. So, technically, Spence was condemned to die for a crime that Texas law had determined had not occurred. Was Spence released from Death Row or at least given a new trial? No. In the justice game innocence is merely a technicality.

Ten years after Spence's conviction, Raoul Shonemann, a staff attorney for the federally funded Texas Resource Center, a now defunct organization that assisted Death Row inmates, took on Spence's case. In no time he discovered a rat's nest of disturbing facts surrounding the Lake Waco murders:

The Waco police department: Lieutenant Marvin Horton, supervisor of the murder investigations, said, "I do not think David Spence committed the offense"; police chief Larry Scott said, "I have really never been convinced [of David Spence's guilt]"; homicide detective Ramon Salinas said, "My opinion is that David Spence is innocent."

The murder-for-hire theory: Deeb had taken out policies on all of his employees; they were cheaper than workman's compensation and paid only for accidental death or injury; they specifically did not pay for murder or suicide. Not one of his employees had ever been hurt or injured on the job.

The mistaken-identity theory: Though Montgomery and Kelley looked alike, Spence knew Kelley well because his girlfriend worked with Kelley at Deeb's convenience store.

The screaming victims theory: In his confession Gilbert Melendez said that the victim's screamed wildly during the attack. There were twenty or so witnesses at Koehne Park. None of them heard any screaming. To explain the gags found on the victims, Gilbert said that they had been gagged *after* they were killed.

The pickup-transport theory: Gilbert Melendez's mechanic stated that Gilbert's truck, which was supposedly used to transport the bodies between murder site and dump site, was in the repair shop at the time of the murders sitting on blocks with a broken ignition and three flat tires.

The ace in the hole: No one was ever charged with or tried for the murder of Raylene Rice. Truman Simons admitted that her murder was left open as an "insurance policy" against possible recantations by Gilbert and Tony Melendez.

The recantations: Screwed by deputy sheriff Simons and District Attorney Feazell with life sentences and parole rejections, both Melendez brothers recanted their confessions, notwithstanding that the murder of Raylene Rice was being held over their heads. "I didn't commit these crimes and anything I said about anybody else [is] just a lie," said Gilbert Melendez. "I would give a statement [and] the cops would say it couldn't have happened that way, so I would change it." He died in prison in 1996. Tony Melendez said, "I did not murder Jill Montgomery, Kenneth Franks or Raylene Rice. I do not know who killed them...I was not present during the crimes. The statements and testimony that I gave in the past that implicated me, David Spence and Gilbert were not true." Tony remains in prison serving a life term.

Tony Melendez's alibi: It was proved conclusively that Tony was one hundred miles away in the town of College Station working as a painter at the time of the murders. Yet he confessed! Ahhh...the power of dingle dangle.

> *I must be guilty of something,*
> *You just whisper it into my ear.*
>
> – Bob Dylan

Terry Lee Harper: Not one of the Koehne Park witnesses said that they saw Spence or the Melendez brothers in the park the night of the murder. But about half of them said they saw Harper with the victims that night. Seven other witnesses said that Harper had told them about murdering three teens at Lake Waco. Three of these witnesses confirmed that Harper had bragged about the killings before their bodies were found and the crime publicized—an extremely significant fact, I would think. When asked why Harper was not pursued as a suspect, police investigators said that he had an alibi. Yet no alibi was mentioned anywhere in the police reports. When deposed by Shonemann, Harper claimed to be at home watching *Dynasty* on TV. But the show didn't air on the night of the murders. In 1994 Harper shot himself to death as the police stormed the home of the elderly couple he had just assaulted. The husband subsequently died from stab wounds similar to those found on the Lake Waco victims.

The hard-on evidence: Most of the jailhouse snitches took back their stories, claiming that they had been coached by Simons in exchange for special favors and promises of leniency. One of them, Robert Snelson, said, "We all fabricated our accounts of Spence confessing in order to try to get a break from the state in our cases." Another stool pigeon, Jesse Ivy, signed an affidavit that stated, "You can say that Truman Simons and [prosecutor] Ned Butler put the facts of the case in my mouth, and I put them into the mouths of the other guys in the jail [in return for sexual favors]." A handwritten note discovered on the prosecutor's official stationary read, "He [Gilbert Melendez] did not know anything [about the triple homicide] but was going to make up a story to get off of the sexual abuse case [for which he had originally been arrested]." The recanting stool pigeons confirmed that they were given special food, cigarettes, phone calls and sex sessions in exchange for their pimped up testimony.

The Simon says theory: Truman Simons's hypothesis that the murders occurred in one park and the bodies were dumped in another was proved absolutely false. Blood spatter analysis was in its infancy at the time of the murders. Fifteen years after the Lake Waco murders, Tom Bevil had become one of the foremost experts in blood spatter analysis, having studied the science at Scotland Yard. Bevil concluded that the victims were killed on the spot of ground exactly where they were found. "There were no changes of blood flow patterns visible in any of the photographs. Had the bodies been thrown into the back of a pickup, driven around the lake, pulled out and then dumped, you would expect to see some changes in the direction the blood traveled on the bodies." Also, if the bodies had been piled on top of one another, blood from one victim would have been found on another. However, the blood found on each victim belonged to only that victim.

A white, foamy secretion is emitted from the mouth when a lung is punctured. Called a "blood froth cap," it occurs very near the time of death. "A blood froth cap can be seen in one of the crime photos lying next to the head of Raylene Rice," said Bevil. "They are very fragile, so it is highly unlikely that it would be present if she were killed somewhere else."

The hard evidence: Strands of hair and pubic hairs were found on the victims' bodies. When sent to the FBI crime lab for analysis they were determined not to belong to the victims. It is reasonable to believe that the source of the hairs, particularly the pubic hairs, was the rapist/murderer. It was conclusively determined that none of the hairs came from Spence or the Melendez brothers. Unfortunately, Shonemann could locate no DNA from Terry Lee Harper for comparison.

The bite mark evidence: The supposed bite marks surfaced only after Ned Butler became the prosecutor of the Spence case. They were the only ostensibly hard physical evidence presented at trial. Butler had used forensic odontology in a previous case and knew what it took to get an odontologist's pendulum swinging. He was the first to suspect bite marks. Then his hunting buddy, a dentist and neophyte bite mark expert, matched them to Spence. Shonemann soundly refuted Butler's bite mark expert. He commissioned a noted board-certified forensic odontologist, Dr. Thomas Krauss, who taught at the FBI National Academy, to evaluate the evidence. He did so the way bite mark analysis should be done. He set up a *blind* test whereby five experts were asked to evaluate the bite mark material without knowing any of the details of the crime. They were given five teeth molds, one of them Spence's, to compare with the life-size photos of the injuries. Not one of the experts found conclusive evidence that the injuries on Jill Montgomery's body were in fact bite marks. Two experts came close to matching the mold of one of Dr. Krauss's patients with one of the injuries. Spence's dentition was absolutely excluded by all five experts. One expert concluded that the bite mark testimony bordered on the "unbelievable." Dr. Krauss concluded that the methodology used to convict David Spence "was well outside the thinking in mainstream forensic odontology." Shonemann also discovered that Ned Butler's expert had erred in a most basic odontology task, the comparison of dental x-rays with skeletal remains. The body identified by Butler's expert as Melody Cutlip had been buried shortly before the real Melody was discovered to be alive and well in Florida, much to the relief of her family.

Prosecutorial misconduct: The state did not disclose that its seven jailhouse snitches were dingled and dangled with threats of punishment, promised leniency and given special favors in exchange for their testimony. The state withheld from the defense the exculpatory evidence that there were other viable suspects, including Terry Lee Harper. Rumors that victim Kenneth Franks was in debt over drugs or was a drug associate of Harper were not disclosed. Nor was the information that frequently, when a high-profile crime occurred, local young people would call the police station and implicate Harper.

Raoul Shonemann vigorously presented these newly discovered facts to the courts. David Wayne Spence's appeal worked its way up to and eventually ended in the United States Fifth Circuit Court of Appeals.

As I read this appellate court's decision, I couldn't help but think about the hapless Oklahoma judge who was busted for masturbating while court was in session. To save this man from further embarrassment I will refer to him simply as "Judge Jack Hoff." During a murder trial, Judge Hoff surreptitiously attached a penis pump and, not so quietly, pumped himself—according to two ear witnesses who were court employees. The telltale penis pump, which the judge claimed had been given to him as a joke, was found under his bench. It and his robe were tested for DNA and came back positively pointing to the judge. Hoff resigned and was subsequently convicted of indecent exposure and sentenced to 4 years in prison. Ray's case and other capital cases like *California v. Butler* and *Texas v. Spence* suggest to me that perhaps Judge Jack Hoff is way ahead of his time. He may have discovered that it is better to literally jack off before rendering an important decision than to figuratively do so with legal jargon and effectively screw an innocent defendant.

It took the Fifth Circuit Court of Appeals more that forty ejaculations to reject Shonemann's monumental effort to save David Wayne Spence. The court jerked off fifteen times opining that the dingle dangle was *immaterial.* Another fifteen or so orgasms were variations on the theme that the dingle dangle, *if proved, would not have affected the jury's verdict.* Three big comes came when the court chose to believe the lying cop over his pimped-up jailhouse snitches— *the state did not knowingly* dingle dangle. These judicial ejaculations, made under the cloak of *harmless error*, were necessary to justify the questionable decisions made by fellow club members from the lower courts.

Only judges are able to use this ridiculous logic in real life. Can you imagine telling a traffic cop as he or she writes you a ticket, "Sure, I was speeding but it was a 'harmless error.'" Yeah...that's going to work every time. Or try taking it into court. Not only is the judge going to fine you big time, the judge's going to say something like, "Throw that jerk-off outta my court!"

Exhausted in the courts, Shonemann took the facts of Spence's case to the governor of Texas. "The governor had a lot more information available to him than the jury," said Schonemann, "and there is no way a rational person looking at it would believe Spence was guilty beyond a reasonable doubt. The standard for a governor should not be less than for a jury. If there's significant doubt, he should commute. We're not asking that he let him go home."

But in the justice game, "innocent until proven guilty beyond a reasonable doubt" is too often merely a buzz phrase. The gangbang of David Spence ended in the governor's office.

> *The foreplay:* "In reviewing requests for reprieve, the governor examines whether the applicant has had full access to the courts and whether there exists any credible new evidence indicating that the applicant is innocent."

> *The ejaculation:* "Spence's application failed to meet these standards of review and thus his application is denied."

The dingle dangle in the Spence case apparently passed muster for the Texas goobernor, who, after less than thirty minutes consideration, drove the final screw into Spence's coffin by signing the death warrant.

David Wayne Spence was executed on April 4, 1997.

APPENDIX TO CHAPTER 22

THE TEMPLE MURDERS

On August 10th, 1991, the worst mass murder in Arizona history had occurred on the far west side of Phoenix, at the Wat Promkunaram Buddest Temple. The bodies of six monks, two temple acolytes and a nun were found cloistered together in what appeared to be an execution style hit. The nine unfortunates had been sprayed with several shotgun blasts and then, as they lay on the floor, shot in the back of the head one to three times with a .22-caliber rifle.

Rumors that the murders were related to drug trafficking carried out by Asian gangsters were initially investigated by the sheriff's department. Detectives were sent to Thailand's Golden Triangle to explore the possible connection between the temple murders and the heroin trade. Most of the world's heroin production is in Asia's Golden Triangle, an area shared by Myanmar (formerly Burma), Laos and Thailand.

Although no drugs were found at the temple, two drug sniffing dogs independently reacted to the same two areas there—a filing cabinet in the abbot's room and a long platform covered with a blue cloth in the sanctuary. A piece of paper bearing the temple's letterhead was found on a table next to the bodies. On it, written in Thai, were directions from the temple to a specific pay phone in a school parking lot in Placentia, a small town in Orange County, California, with instructions to dial a local phone number and ask for "Phet." Presumably that number had caller ID to verify that the call came from the parking lot phone. At the bottom of the "Phet note," as it came to be known, was the statement translated as "It now weighs 1,083 pounds."

Seven weeks earlier, in Hayward, a town on the east side of San Francisco Bay south of Berkeley, the largest heroin bust in US history had gone down. Agents confiscated 1,080 pounds of pure China white heroin worth as much as $2.5 billion on the street. The heroin had originated in Thailand. Was the three-pound discrepancy a rounding error or perhaps someone's commission—or was the similarity between "1,080" and "1,083" just a coincidence? Agents rejecting the coincidence hypothesis believed that the assassins had left the Phet note as a sort of calling card. A recently constructed secret compartment was discovered beneath a trap door hidden from view behind the temple's alter. Was this secret chamber to be have been the distribution center for the Hayward cache?

There were other troubling coincidences. Earlier that year two men had been arrested in Hong Kong for attempting to smuggle heroin in statues of Buddha. In April, just before the beginning of "Buddhist Lent"—when many Buddhists traveled to US temples to hand these religious figurines out as gifts—the temple's chief priest, Pairuch Kanthong, had traveled to Thailand and returned with several cases of Buddha statues. Drug enforcement officials confirmed that smugglers exploited Buddhist Lent as a cover. Several empty statues were found at the temple along with the nine bodies—one of which was that of chief priest Kanthong.

Also returning from Thailand with the chief priest was a peculiar twenty-one-year-old Thai, Chirasak Chirapong, who became known around the temple compound simply as "Boy." Boy was a misfit among the ascetic monks, a bit wild, embracing Western culture, sporting long black hair, wearing stylish clothes. He was known to flash large rolls of cash. Investigators suspected that Boy was dealing drugs out of the temple. He had no religious duties at the temple and was the only one of the murder victims not wearing the traditional orange garb.

Investigators also discovered that six of the executed monks had been in Thailand less than a month before the massacre. Three of them were from Chiang Mai, a city in the heart of the Golden Triangle where many families are raised in the drug culture, with children working alongside their parents in the poppy fields. The father of one of these monks had been arrested in Thailand some years earlier for smuggling heroin.

Five phone calls had been made from the temple to a private residence in Placentia, two the week before the murders. Other calls had been made to Florida, Las Vegas, South America and Southeast Asia. An FBI agent testified in court that these phone numbers were those of known drug dealers. One call had been made to the Thai Tepparod restaurant in Hollywood nine days before the massacre. Its owner, Bruranasombat Chow, would later become a fugitive from the FBI in connection with a contract hit of a police informant. He was also suspected of being involved in the heroin trade between Las Vegas and Florida.

"Because of the sensitivity of it, we just left [the investigation] completely up to the county attorney's office," said a DEA agent without explanation, handing the case to the Maricopa County law enforcement complex.

Apparently there were too many coincidences for an R-complex to bite into. The Romley complex immediately dropped the Thai heroin connection theory and soon announced that the motive for the mass murders was "a hate crime."

The Phet note needed to be explained. It was shrugged off as referring to aluminum can recycling with the explanation that the price for aluminum in California was higher than in Arizona. While the temple did recycle, a half-ton of aluminum cans would require a container twelve feet wide and seventeen feet long piled twelve feet high. No one could identify the vehicle the monks intended to use to carry such a load nor was there such a pile of cans lying around the temple compound at the time of the murders. Also the difference in price was only pennies per pound, making the venture a losing proposition considering the cost of the gas it would take to transport the cargo 350 miles. More significantly, the note was incoming to the temple informing its recipient(s) that something on the outside weighed 1,083 pounds, not vice versa. Also, why would such elaborate drug deal type instructions as contained in the Phet note be necessary simply to deliver a load of cans?

News of the temple murders was received with horror in Thailand. The murder of a Buddhist monk—let alone six—is one of the worst crimes imaginable. The country observed a national day of mourning. The Thai ambassador to the United States was sent to Phoenix to get to the bottom of the tragedy. A month after the murders, wealthy fifty-three-year-old Smith Thongkam hosted a dinner party at his restaurant, The Spicy Thai, for the ambassador and Phoenix's finest: sheriff Tom Agnos, Arizona Attorney General Grant Woods and Maricopa County Attorney Rick Romley. In the wake of the massacre, Thongkam had become spokesman for the Thai community. He had been one of the founders of the temple and helped select its location. Throughout the evening, as the luminaries dined, word spread that the case had been solved. In Tucson a young man was arrested in a psychiatric hospital who Maricopa County Sheriff officials said had information about the crime. Soon three of his friends were arrested and all were subsequently indicted. They became known as "the Tucson four."

The publicity of the event undid Smith Thongkam. He'd been recognized, and the following month DEA agents from Los Angeles arrived in Phoenix to arrest him. It seems that Thongkam was one and the same Lamthong Sudthisaard who thirteen years earlier had been convicted in absentia from Los Angeles for trafficking in heroin after failing to show up on the fourth day of his trial and forfeiting a

$75,000 bail bond. He had not vanished to Thailand as the DEA agents had surmised but had moved 350 miles east to set up operations in Phoenix.

The revelation that he, Rick Romley, had been a guest of honor of a drug lord associated with the crime scene didn't phase the county attorney or alter the investigation. He continued to ignore the Thai connection/temple murders street talk, just as the lesbian connection street talk was being ignored in the Kim Ancona murder investigation at roughly the same time.

In no time after being subjected to the interrogation procedures of the Romley complex, each of the Tucson four made incriminating statements linking himself and the other three to the temple murders. But shortly after being released from "the Miranda room," all four recanted.

The *Miranda v. Arizona* decision had done little to slow down Maricopa County inquisitors. Indeed, false confessions are not uncommon in the justice game. Of those individuals who have been exonerated by DNA analysis nationally, false confessions played a roll in more than twenty percent of the cases.

Why would someone confess to a crime he didn't commit? According to the Capital Post Conviction Project, false confessions occur when the suspect is vulnerable and the interrogator employs psychological coercion. Youths are particularly vulnerable. Juvenile exonerees had confessed forty-four percent of the time. Mental disability accounts for sixty-nine percent of all bogus confessions.

Coercing a false confession begins with the interrogator's engaging the suspect in small talk about the crime, seeming to seek his help. Then the interrogator demonstrates his willingness and ability to punish the suspect if he doesn't cooperate. Rewards like food, sleep, and medical care are withheld for hours on end while the interrogator feeds the suspect details of the crime interspersed with suggestions of how the suspect might be implicated in them.

Securing "confessions" from the Tucson four was straightforward: youth and mental disability. But the Maricopa County Sheriff's Department had too hastily selected the Tucson four. Tucson is a hundred eighty miles south of Phoenix. Employers for two of the four produced time cards showing that they had punched in and out on the day of the murders, rendering the logistics of the confessed crime virtually impossible. The suspected murder weapon, a rifle belonging to a brother of one of the four, could not be tied to the crime. It failed ballistic tests.

In two months, the case against the Tucson four unraveled so completely and publicly that the Romley complex was forced to let go and put its bite on the taxpayers' wallets instead. The four youths were awarded $8 million in damages.

Enter Rolando Caratachea, Alex Garcia and Jonathon Doody. Ten days after the temple murders, Caratachea, with Doody a passenger in his car, was stopped by a security officer on Luke Air Force Base. In the back seat of his '72 Nova was the .22-caliber rifle his mother had bought for him as a birthday present. The officer made a note of the rifle and had Caratachea put the gun in his trunk. Guns are popular in Arizona and .22's are common. Because the monks had been murdered with a .22, the officer reported it to the sheriff's investigating task force.

Three weeks later a task force detective confronted Caratachea at the restaurant where he worked. The youth voluntarily agreed to turn over his rifle for testing and accompanied the officer to the apartment he shared with Doody to retrieve it. The officer spoke with Doody and a friend of his who by chance was also there—sixteen-year-old Alex Garcia. Because the Tucson four had "confessed" and were the hot suspects at the time, the rifle wasn't immediately tested but got mixed in with 75 or so other weapons that had been collected in connection with the crime.

After the Tucson four fiasco, Garcia and Doody became the prospective krones and were spirited off to the Miranda room. Doody, a seventeen-year-old Thai with a marginal understanding of English, made incriminating statements and after fourteen hours of non-stop interrogation Garcia "confessed":

> ...[I]n June of 1991, Jonathan Doody and I got together and planned to rob and burglarize the Thai Buddhist Temple. Part of our plan was to leave no witnesses. On the evening of August 19, 1991, we started to put our plan in action. Jonathan and I drove to the temple. I was armed with a 20-gauge pump shotgun. Jonathan was armed with a .22-caliber semiautomatic rifle...Before leaving the temple, Jonathan told me, "No witnesses." I told him, "Robbery is one thing, but murder is another." Jonathan repeated to me that there could be no witnesses. He then stepped to my right and, while armed with the .22-caliber rifle, began shooting the nine occupants while they were lying on the floor. I began firing my 20-gauge shotgun, but fired not to kill anyone. I fired four rounds from my shotgun toward the nine people lying on the floor.

A signature of coerced false confessions is that they do not add new details and they contain information contrary to the facts. Such was the case with Garcia's "confession." The medical examiner reported that the victims were standing when they were shotgunned.

Once outside the Miranda room, both Garcia and Doody quickly recanted—but to no avail. Based upon their "confessions," the Romley complex now promoted a new motive. The murders were a "robbery gone bad" and the murder weapon was the rifle Doody "borrowed" from Caratachea to do the deed.

Garcia and Doody were duly tried and convicted of the temple murders and sentenced to life in prison.

Doody was a bright teenager—135 IQ. Wouldn't he dispose of an $80 murder weapon, especially when it was seen after the fact in the back seat of the car in which he was riding? He was familiar with the temple from having driven his younger brother to and fro when he was studying there. If robbery were the motive why would he have left untouched three collection boxes stuffed with money and a donation money tree with leaves of one- and five-dollar bills—all of which were in plain sight? Nearly $500 in the dead monks' wallets had not been touched. Doody's mother had on occasion invited the temple monks over for dinner. How could a normal, studious teenager with no prior indication of hostility cold bloodily kill nine persons he knew?

The Arizona Department of Public Safety did ballistic tests on the rifles collected by the sheriff's task force. It reported that "item 10092, a Marlin Model 60 rifle, serial #11319753," was the murder weapon. But according to the Bureau of Alcohol, Tobacco and Firearms's transaction record, the rifle Mrs. Caratachea purchased for her son had a different serial number. That number had been scratched out on the BATF form, and handwritten suspiciously above it was the number the ADPS said belonged to the murder weapon.

George Schuester, who was also bailiff for the temple murders trial, personally expressed to me his skepticism that Doody had committed the crime.

Were Doody and Garcia kroned? That's what the The Grapevine, an underground newspaper distributed by Phoenix's homeless, openly contended: "This [serial number discrepancy] can be nothing less than a frame-up. The Grapevine will continue these exposés until Jonathan Doody and Alex Garcia are set free."

While the The Grapevine may have been nothing more than a conspiracy theory rag, its opinions were protected by the First Amendment. But freedom of the press raises havoc with Gila Monster mentality and *The Grapevine* must have struck a cord. Its final headline before going out of business read, "County Prosecutor Destroys *The Grapevine* Newspaper."

The state's leading newspaper, *The Arizona Republic*, made little of the Thai connection to the temple murders. Instead it reported the version of events promoted by politician Rick Romley, an Arizona Republican in good standing.

MANDATORY SENTENCING

It's typically reptilian for those who enforce the law to consider themselves to be above it. Even when they do by chance get caught breaking the law, nothing really happens to them. The police officers who had the misfortune of being videotaped as they brutally beat the defenseless, subdued African-American Rodney King had to endure the minor inconvenience of going to trial only to be acquitted.

The acquittal spawned the worst civil disturbance in America since Civil War draft riots took place in New York City in 1863, in which the five-day mayhem included the lynching of eleven black men and the burning of an orphanage that housed 233 black children who fortunately escaped. Upon hearing the appalling verdict, the public that had viewed the videotaped beating of Rodney King over and over on TV erupted into the streets. Within hours, Los Angeles was in chaos. The burning, looting and mayhem lasted for five days. When the rioting finally stopped and the smoke cleared, more than one billion dollars in property had been destroyed, hundreds were injured, seven thousand had been arrested and fifty-four lay dead. Responding to the public's outcry, the feds tried the four policemen a second time. Two were acquitted. The two who were convicted served two and a half years, some of the time in a half-way house from which they were periodically allowed to leave to visit their families. No one should praise or condone the mob's lawless response, but isn't it sad that rioting was required for justice, however feeble, to be served on the two public servants who crossed the line?

Another example is the DuPage Seven. Four sheriff's detectives and three prosecutors from DuPage County, Illinois were indicted on forty-seven counts of perjury, obstruction of justice, misconduct and conspiracy after a judge determined that Rolando Cruz, then having spent twelve years on Death Row, had been framed for the murder and rape of a ten-year-old girl. They too were punished by having to stand trial and be acquitted.

Occasionally the people don't have to revolt in order for some low ranking official to spend a short time in jail while their boss skates. The few loyal lieutenants who burglarized the Watergate Hotel and then took the fall for their boss come to mind. The boss who opened the floodgate remained high and dry—at least, until he resigned in disgrace.

For any infraction, realistically it takes a miracle for a hometown player to be caught in the first place *and* for the cover-up to fail *and* for the offender to be prosecuted *and* finally convicted. Even so, the offender can expect only a cliquish tap-on-the-hand punishment. So what's to prevent the hometown team from playing down and dirty?

What's frightening is *not* that law enforcement organizations seem dominated by reptilian mentality. The purpose of the Bill of Rights is to put checks and balances upon those whose reptilian brain runs roughshod over their cerebral cortex. What *is* frightening is the power that such organizations are able to wield to circumvent the checks and balances.

More than sixty years ago, Robert H. Jackson, the United States Attorney General who later became a justice of the US Supreme Court observed:

> The prosecutor has more control over life, liberty and reputation than any other person in America. His discretion is tremendous. He can have citizens investigated and, if he is that kind of person, he can have this done to the tune of public statements and veiled or unveiled intimidations. Or the prosecutor may choose a more subtle course and simply have a citizen's friends interviewed. The prosecutor can order arrests, present cases to the grand jury, in secret session, and on the basis of his one-sided presentation of the facts, can cause the citizen to be indicted and held for trial. He may dismiss the case before trial, in which case the defense never has a chance to be heard. Or he may go on with a public trial. If he obtains a conviction, the prosecutor can still make recommendations as to sentence, as to whether the prisoner should get probation or a suspended sentence, and after he is put away, as to whether he is a fit subject for parole. While a prosecutor at his best is one of the most beneficent forces in our society, when he acts from malice, shameless ambition or other base motives, he is one of the worst.

"Today," wrote Gary Lowenthal in *Down and Dirty Justice* after his one-year stint inside the Romley complex, "prosecutors are far more powerful than in Jackson's day," and he called his boss Rick Romley "the most powerful man in the state."

About 1980 the Arizona state legislature enacted several laws requiring mandatory sentencing. Until that time judges had wide latitude in dishing out punishment to felony offenders and could consider each case individually and separately on its own merits. This discretionary power afforded to judges was perceived by the public to be inequitable, especially to minorities, to be unfair to the victims of crime and to be too soft on the perpetrators of crime. The legislature stepped in and stripped this power from the courts by passing laws requiring uniformly severe punishment for all felons.

But this well-intentioned reform unwittingly opened another can of worms—or should I say snakes? Historically the absolute discretionary power of prosecutors to charge citizens with crimes was offset by the judge's discretionary power to impose sentences within a wide range. Mandatory sentencing changed all that and effectively transferred the power to punish from the cerebral cortex to the reptilian-complex. Writes Rudy Gerber in *Cruel and Usual*:

> The prosecutor decides not only which offenses to charge but also whether to seek sentence enhancement and aggravation, whether to offer a plea, what the plea agreement will be and whether there will be a stipulated sentence. These are the most significant decisions shaping a criminal case and the option of trial, and there is no judicial or legislative control over them. The decisions of prosecutors, typically recent law graduates, are discretionary, hidden from public scrutiny and judicially unreviewable. Ironically, the visible courtroom rulings of the more experienced judiciary are reviewable, but these rulings have less penal impact than the hidden, discretionary decisions of prosecutors.

As with most district attorneys in this country, Rick Romley has wide authority to charge or not charge citizens with crimes. This power coupled with mandatory sentencing gives him the muscle to also determine the punishment, which in turn puts him in the driver's seat when plea bargaining. Nine of every ten cases end with a plea bargain. If they didn't, the justice machine, which moves at a snail's pace anyway, would grind to a halt. Before mandatory sentencing, however, defendants had some real clout when plea bargaining. Now the prosecutor not infrequently over-charges the accused and then offers a reduced charge with a substantially reduced sentence as an incentive to accept the plea bargain. Armed robbery becomes robbery. Aggravated assault becomes assault. Twenty years in prison becomes five. Even the occasional innocent person accused of a serious crime is hard pressed not to seriously consider taking ten years if facing mandatory life in prison when up against Boss Romley and his complex, where "innocence isn't always the best defense" and the chances of winning at trial are a crap shoot with Romley's boys supplying the dice.

If truth were the name of the game it would be played differently.

In Ray's case, it's reasonable to believe that the true identity of the killer was hidden in the bite mark swab just waiting to be discovered. But after the home team was through playing with the cotton swab it had become a bare, useless stick. The information that could unequivocally have solved the crime had been destroyed. A spokesman for the Romley complex explained that it had been used up during *their* testing and the results of *their* testing were "inconclusive." Defense Attorney Plourd.", however, ferreted the opposite conclusion from the prosecutor's own DNA expert, eliciting that the test results in fact "excluded" the defendant. I guess that for the Romley complex "excluded" means "inconclusive."

ASSHOLES AND THE DEATH PENALTY

Now I'm not a player in the game—merely a spectator. I wondered how many other Romley type complexes are out there? I took a look and didn't have to go beyond the statistics surrounding the death penalty. I'm not an advocate for or against the execution of cold blooded murderers. I have no objection to serial killers like John Wayne Gacy, Eileen Wuornos and Ted Bundy's being put to death. However, death penalty statistics raise an eyebrow.

In 1972 the United States Supreme Court suspended the death penalty, ruling that it violated the Fourteenth Amendment's protection against "cruel and unusual" punishment. The court held that the death penalty statutes at the time resulted in "arbitrary and capricious" sentencing. It's a historical fact that blacks have been executed at a disproportionately higher rate than whites. Since the Supreme Court reinstated the death penalty in 1976, through September 18, 2005, nine hundred ninety-six individuals have been executed. Nationally, forty-two percent of those executed were non-white, while they comprise only twenty percent of the population. Only twelve whites have been executed for murdering blacks while one hundred ninety-eight blacks have been executed for murdering whites. "Arbitrary and capricious"—what's changed?

Texas is considered to be the death penalty capital of the world, having executed more that one third of the total—three hundred fifty-two individuals. It does not, however, hold the per capital record. That title goes to its neighbor to the north, Oklahoma, which executed one individual for every forty-five thousand people of its 3.5 million population. I am reminded of "Black Magic," the nickname given to Oklahoma City's chief cop in lab coat for many years. Joyce Gilchrist was fired when it was discovered that there was more Ouija than science in her forensic methods. At least twelve Oklahoma executions were tainted with her voodoo.

Texas, the second most populous state at 22.5 million, executed one for every sixty-four thousand of its citizens. The most populous state, California, at 35.9 million, executed a paltry eleven persons—one per 3.25 million. The fourth largest state, New York, has not executed anyone since 1976. Twelve states and the District of Columbia do not have the death penalty. Thirty-eight states, the federal government and the US military do.

If Houston and surrounding Harris County were a state it would rank third in the number of executions behind the rest of Texas and Virginia. One forth of Texas executions originate in Harris County. In 1985, a Houston woman was raped, by "a white male," she said. Kevin Byrd, a black man, was subsequently arrested, tried, convicted and sent to prison for the assault.

Rape is one crime where the perpetrator routinely leaves some of himself behind, such as pubic hairs, skin found under the victim's fingernails, bodily fluids from inside the victim and on her clothing. A rape kit contains these items, which are routinely collected later at a hospital. DNA was not allowed into Texas courts before 1989 and the law allowed Harris County officials to destroy rape kits after a convicted rapist's state appeal had been decided.

Somehow, by chance, the rape kit in the Byrd case slipped though the cracks. After serving twelve years in prison, Byrd's defense attorney was able to locate and get the rape kit tested. The results absolutely exonerated Kevin Byrd. The governor initially did not pardon Byrd, suggesting (through a spokesman) that it was a matter for the courts because the victim still believed that Byrd was white— that is, that he was the one who raped her. Pressured by the national press, the governor capitulated. Kevin Byrd became the first black man to be pardoned by this Texas governor.

Could there be other innocent individuals serving time for rapes in Houston? Well, some Harris County officials may have thought so because they quickly took action, destroying fifty rape kits stored in the county courthouse and earmarking many more for the dumpster. What cerebral cortex would not suspect that this willful destruction of evidence—possibly exculpatory evidence—is not the act of a reptilian mind covering its ass?

"Asses assume," Mom taught me. Nevertheless, I confess to having made an ass out of my own self on several occasions during my lifetime, mostly when under the influence while under the influence of high levels of testosterone. One such incident, however, involved neither. Unable to locate my wallet, I looked everywhere I thought it could possibly be. I knew when I had it last and retraced my steps over and over again looking for it. Frustrated and defeated, I jumped to the conclusion suggested by my R-complex, that my daughter's friend, who had been playing with Aisha at the time, had stolen it. When the girl left I took Aisha aside, explained and told her that her friend was no longer welcome in the house.

Then, lo and behold, a week or so later I happened across my wallet—exactly where I'd left it. Was I the big ass or what? I had made two assumptions that turned out to be false—that I'd looked everywhere possible for the wallet and that my daughter's friend was a thief. There seemed to be two possible courses of action. I'd already cancelled my charge cards and had them and my driver's license replaced. I could easily have covered my ass by simply removing the cash and tossing the "stolen" wallet into a dumpster. No one would be the wiser. Or I could confess to being a fool and apologize to my daughter. If I took the easier, first course I would cross the line from being a simple ass to becoming that part of the anatomy where the sun doesn't shine. Having learned the lessons of Dad's belt in Mom's hand and having observed her knee in action against the newspaper subscriber who tried to welsh $1.50 from her son determined my course of action.

Assholes are not uncommon. Their verbalized rationalizations were known as "horseshit" in Mom's day. Today, perhaps out of respect for the horse, they're more commonly known as "bullshit." A scientific explanation might be that assholes are human beings whose reptilian-complex controls their cerebral cortex. Bullshit is the cerebral cortex's attempt to explain the self-serving decisions and actions of the R-complex.

In my life I have observed that politics, which spawns like-minded bureaucracies, tends to attract this type of individual—the colder blooded ones rising to the top. Being involved firsthand with cousin Ray's case, I have been surprised by just how many such there are in the justice game and by just how low they can slither:

a lead detective who assumes that the man he arrested is guilty and four hours later learns from a key witness that the man doesn't fit the description of the person he saw entering and exiting the crime scene at the time of the murder...then obscures this information;

another detective, blindly following orders, who lifts footprints from the crime scene and when told that they don't fit the arrested man...obediently fixes the "error";

a neophyte bite mark expert who assumes that the bite mark fits the arrested man and when told by his mentor that it doesn't...finds a new mentor;

a lab technician who assumes that the arrested man left the serologic evidence and says so in court...without having tested it;

a prosecutor who assumes that his team's assumptions are correct despite their inability to produce any real evidence, then sends one of them to Las Vegas to...find a ringer who can manufacture some;

a hired gun who assumes that the right man has been identified...then interprets the bite mark to fit;

a judge afraid of his boss who...goes compliantly along with the boss's program to not allow the defendant to proceed with new evidence discovery;

and the boss more worried about his ass than about the facts of the case who...lets his team play to win at all costs.

Pardon my digression.

The real statistic that leaps out is that while nine hundred ninety-six people were being executed, *one hundred twenty-two* others on Death Row were being exonerated. To put it another way, for every eight persons to reach the gallows one walks away completely vindicated. Or another way—more than ten percent of those convicted of murder and sentenced to death in this country have subsequently been shone to be innocent.

And this reality may be the tip of a very large iceberg when this statistic is compared with those of the Innocence Project, run by Barry Scheck and Peter Neufeld. The project takes on cases where DNA is available to determine post conviction innocence. It does not limit itself to death penalty cases. Since 1992 it has achieved the exoneration of more than one hundred sixty-three people, who had been wrongly convicted by:

Serology inclusion (57% of the time)
Police misconduct (44%)
Prosecutor misconduct (48%)
Ouija science (37%)
Bad lawyering (33%)
Microscopic hair comparison matches (30%)
False witness testimony (24%)
Informants/snitches (23%)
False confessions (21%).

But the statistic that stands out is mistaken eyewitness identification. It happens in 88% of all false convictions. How can the victim, as in the Byrd case, initially state that her assailant was "white" and then get away with telling a jury that she was raped by a black man? To some extent this type of misidentification may be due to calculated police suggestion, if not to outright coercion. In any event, false identification happens quite often.

Ray had been lucky to have a beard and the actual killer didn't. If he hadn't I wonder whether Dale Henson would have been strong enough to withstand the five intimidating polygraph sessions administered by the Phoenix police department immediately prior to his testimony. Ray lucked out. Although haggard, Henson stuck to his guns and told the jury that Ray was not the one who entered and exited the bar around the time Kim Ancona was murdered. Ray was unlucky, however, that the jury chose to ignore Henson's testimony.

The Innocence Project's statistics are mind-boggling. I don't believe there's an actuary anywhere who would not be able to extrapolate this data to conclude and testify that a significant number of those who have been executed in this country were in all probability innocent—perhaps as many as ten percent. If true, then one hundred or so of the nearly one thousand individuals put to death since 1976 were innocent.

"Prove it!" you say? Okay, let's see what happens when someone tries. Joseph Roger O'Dell maintained his innocence vigorously, denying that he murdered, raped and sodomized Helen Schartner. Representing himself, he claimed that the blood evidence was copped in a lab coat and the jailhouse snitch was dingle-dangled. His pleas made it all the way to the United States Supreme Court, where justice Harry Blackmun, in the minority, found "serious questions as to whether O'Dell committed the crime." In 1997, twelve years after his conviction, O'Dell made a simple last minute request of the Virginia courts—to have the rape kit retested using some highly sophisticated DNA technology that had recently become available. The court, apparently not wanting to be confused with facts, said no and the state promptly executed O'Dell in July that year. The question of O'Dell's guilt persisted in the minds of many. The Richmond Diocese of the Roman Catholic Church subsequently petitioned the custodian of the evidence, the circuit court of Virginia Beach, to release the rape kit for independent testing, assuring the court that the church would bear all expenses. The court denied the request and went one step further. It burned the evidence.

Identifying by name an executed innocent would deliver a serious blow to death penalty proponents. Including O'Dell, Virginia has put ninety-four individuals to death—second only to Texas. Considering that the people of Virginia allow its courts to destroy evidence that may unequivocally hold the truth, it is not surprising that Virginia has released only one innocent man from its Death Row, the fewest of any death penalty state.

Statistics vary from state to state. Florida releases one person from Death Row for every three it executes. If this ratio holds true for the four hundred individuals waiting on Death Row for *their* ride on "Old Sparky" (Florida's electric chair), approximately one hundred are innocent. Texas on the other hand frees only one innocent person for every forty-four it executes. Is Texas doing a better job at determining guilt than Florida? Probably not. This apparent anomaly more likely suggests that some state courts are more reptilian than others, Texas and Virginia most of all.

Consider *Texas v. Roy Criner*. Four years after the body of Deanna Ogg was found near an old logging road in Montgomery County, Criner was convicted for her rape and murder. Years later DNA testing positively excluded Criner as the source of the spermatozoa left inside the victim. Was this revelation enough to set this innocent man free? No. To counter the cerebral finding, The Texas court of appeals came up with "the innocent bystander ejaculator" theory. Without any evidence to support its theory the court reasoned (if it can be called that) that the sperm *could* have been left by someone else during consensual sex prior to the murder and that Criner *could* have worn a condom or *could* have failed to ejaculate. Criner stayed in prison.

Luckily a discarded Marlboro cigarette was found next to Ogg's body. This butt saved Criner's butt. The Innocence Project, his defense team, managed to get it tested. It proved to be a mixture from a least three individuals. One was the victim. None of the others was Criner. This finding was still no big deal for the Texas sized R-complex until it was discovered that one of the smokers of the telltale butt was also the contributor of the aforementioned spermatozoa. No amount of R-complex bullshit could explain this coincidence. The press jumped in. The prosecutor and the sheriff released their bite. The Texas board of pardons and paroles unanimously approved. The courts sat out. And the governor pardoned Criner.

Governors do not like to pardon convicted felons. It's bad for re-election. This Texas governor was no exception. Even after the evidence of Kevin Byrd's innocence came in, the governor initially rejected his application for clemency, suggesting that the matter had already been decided in the courts. He capitulated only when the press got involved and exposed the "Byrd Follies"—that an innocent man was headed toward execution.

Posing as a "compassionate conservative" while running for higher office, this Texas governor said, "The worst nightmare of a death penalty supporter and of anyone who believes in our criminal justice system is to execute an innocent man." Yet this governor's office would spend only about half an hour on applications for clemency—hardly enough time to consider factual innocence. Obviously the governor's only consideration was voter impact, preferring whenever possible to pass the buck back to the courts. Unless the press gets involved and is able to convince the voters that an innocent man is on Death Row, clemency is denied. So long as the condemned has had full access to the courts, rationalized this governor, justice is served.

That the courts just might be a big part of the problem was of little concern. Here are a few cases that have had full access to Texas courts and received a gubernatorial death warrant:

> No direct evidence linked David Castillo to the stabbing death of a liquor store clerk. Pedro Garcia pointed the finger at his roommate after hiding his own bloody T-shirt and two money bags in Castillo's closet. Castillo was executed on September 23, 1998.

> No physical evidence linked James Bethard to the murder of Gene Hathorn, Jr.'s family. He was convicted solely on the testimony of Hathorn. On Death Row himself, Hathorn later recanted his testimony, claiming to have been solely

responsible for the murder of his family in the hope of claiming Gene Hathorn, Sr.'s estate. Bethard was executed on December 9, 1999.

A juvenile at the time of the murder of Bobby Lambert, Gary Graham was convicted solely on the testimony of an eyewitness who picked Graham out of a lineup after the police showed the eyewitness a photograph of Graham. Graham was executed on June 22, 2000.

The tiny spot of Odell Barnes's blood found on his coveralls that matched murder victim Helen Bass, his longtime friend and lover, was, according to an FBI forensic chemist, either accidentally dropped or planted on the coveralls. Federal and state courts refused to allow Barnes to present this new evidence. Barnes was executed on March 1, 2000.

After Troy Dale Farris was convicted of killing a deputy sheriff, the court of appeals teased him with the finding that "the circumstantial and forensic evidence offered at trial not only failed to connect [him with the murder, but it] also failed in nearly all material respects to confirm the testimony [of the two key witnesses]" before ejaculating that the jury would have convicted him anyway. Farris was executed on January 13, 1999.

David Wayne Spence, executed on April 4, 1997 for the Lake Waco murders. His case was summarized earlier.

This Texas governor learned from his father how to win elections. In 1988, dad was running for president against the governor of Massachusetts. During most of the Massachusetts governor's term, the state had experimented with a controversial prison furlough rehabilitation program for convicted felons. It gave convicts showing promise a taste of freedom by releasing them into society unsupervised for a forty-eight-hour period. Felons who responded favorably could expect an early parole. Willie Horton was furloughed in June 1986. Twelve years earlier twenty-two-year-old Horton had participated with two others in robbing a gas station. The attendant was stabbed nineteen times and bled to death. Horton was serving a life sentence for murder when he was granted a weekend pass. He never returned. Ten months later, in Oxon Hill, Maryland, he assaulted Clifford Barnes, raped his fiancée and stole his car. Maryland sentenced Horton to two consecutive life terms plus eighty-five years.

The Massachusetts governor's opponent produced a TV ad showing Willie Horton exiting revolving prison doors. Although the governor did away with the prison furlough program before the presidential election, the ad did him in. He lost the election by three hundred and fifteen electoral votes.

Four years later, dad lost his reelection bid (by two hundred and two electoral votes) because he hadn't left it at Horton the first time but asked the electorate to "read my lips—no new taxes" and then forgot what his lips had said and signed into law one of the largest tax increases in history. The son got the message—watch your lips, only cut taxes and be tough on crime if you want to win. Not even substantial proof of innocence like that mounted by David Wayne Spence's defense team was able to penetrate the Texas governor's reptilian survival mentality.

That the Texas governor preferred to lay the responsibility for controversial decisions onto the courts was confirmed in the year 2000 when he appealed to the United States Supreme Court and was awarded the presidency of the United States by one judge's vote.

π

There are many cerebral reasons to do away with the death penalty other than the strong statistical implication that a significant number of innocent individuals have already been executed and will be executed in the future. To name three, capital punishment does little to deter crime, is extremely costly to implement (much more so than providing life in prison) and does not undo an executed killer's killing.

Objectively, the death penalty is a dismal failure—moreso by far than the prison furlough program was. Of the 8,802 prisoners furloughed in the United States between 1969 and 1974, a mere 39 failed to return on time and of those only ten were subsequently arrested and/or suspected of being involved in a crime while furloughed—a failure rate of less than half of one percent (.44%). Yet between 1976 and 2007, while 1,072 individuals were executed, 11.5% of that number, 123 individuals, were freed from Death Row. Extrapolating from these statistics and studying cases like that of David Wayne Spence, I believe a conservative estimate would be that at least one in twenty (5%) of those executed in this country are in fact innocent. (This estimate goes beyond the death penalty, suggesting that at least 5% of those convicted of lesser felonies are also innocent.)

No one should turn the other cheek and let transgressors skate, but should eye-for-an-eye, tooth-for-a-tooth mentality be allowed to impose the ultimate penalty when its only benefit seems to be to satisfy the reptilian need for revenge, retribution, retaliation and re-election?

The Death Penalty Information Center reports that about fifty percent of Americans favor the use of "life in prison without the possibility of parole" over the death penalty. But giving a killer "life blah blah blah" doesn't sit well with the other half. Maybe if we called this punishment "death in prison" both sides would be placated without our having to actually kill someone and risk the very real possibility that that someone is innocent.

SKELETONS IN THE BITE MARK ANALYSIS CLOSET

The Spence case was of particular interest to me because the only incriminating forensic evidence was the testimony of a bite mark expert—as in Ray's case. I had seen the gruesome crime scene photos in Dr. Campbell's office. I could imagine how an expert who had seen these photos would very much want to help bring the perpetrator to justice. And if he also learned from his buddy who was prosecuting the case that the suspect was a bad dude who had bragged to a half-dozen fellow inmates that he'd committed the crime, might this expert not tend to see the evidence in a Ouija way? The expert couldn't know that in reality the snitches had been lying about Spence's "bragging" in exchange for snatch. Because of this pimping and the fact that a blind test done by Spence's attorney, Raoul Shonemann, conclusively showed that David Wayne Spence did not inflict the bite mark, I suspected that prosecutor Ned Butler's bite mark expert buddy's pendulum had most certainly gone wacko in the Lake Waco murders case.

I was disconcerted, to say the least, when I learned that this pendulum belonged to none other than Dr. Homer Campbell, the one who got the ball rolling by disputing the bite mark evidence in the case of Ray Krone.

I had been very impressed by Dr. Campbell in San Antonio and later in Albuquerque, where I'd been introduced to the Lake Waco murders. Because Campbell was the expert for the prosecution, I'd assumed that Spence was guilty until I took a closer look at the case. Dr. Campbell seemed conscientious and objective in evaluating the bite mark evidence I provided. His analysis appeared to be right on the mark. He even pointed out an indistinct bruising or abrasion he felt was made by a rotated left front tooth. The supposed out of whack tooth did not break the skin as the other teeth had done. The bruise mark was very faint and not obvious even when pointed out to me. But it was definitely there and didn't take eye-brain coordination to see it. It was visible in almost every bite mark photograph. Had "rotated left front tooth" been added to "clean-shaven American Indian who wore 9½ Converse brand tennis shoes," the description of the murderer, Levy's team might have actually solved the crime.

Because the bite mark had been annotated incorrectly from the get go to accommodate the suspect, this obscure mark did not figure in the bogus analysis. Consequently it went unnoticed by all except Campbell. To this day, no other forensic expert, to my knowledge, has noticed this mark. Perhaps it will help if the actual murderer is identified.

While I still believe that Campbell analyzed the Krone evidence correctly, I am equally convinced, based upon the results of Shonemann's blind test and the dingle-dangled testimony elicited from the jailhouse snitches, that he erred in the Spence case.

Chris seemed to me to have assembled for Ray's case the top bite mark experts in the business. Besides Campbell, there was Norman "Skip" Sperber from San Diego, Jerry Vale from Los Angeles and Richard Souviron from Coral Gables.

Dr. Souviron is one of the best. He had thoroughly analyzed the bite mark evidence in preparation for the trial and excluded Ray as the source of the bite. He did not testify, however, mainly because the defense funds were exhausted—there was not enough to pay even his travel expenses, let alone his required fee.

But Dr. Souviron is not infallible either. He'd made a mistake in a case back home in Florida. Nine-year-old Sharra Ferger's partially clothed body was found in a field near her home. She was stabbed thirty times, sexually assaulted and bitten. A neighbor, Dale Morris, Jr., was arrested two weeks later based upon Dr. Sourvion's and another dentist's bite mark identification. After four months in jail, Morris was released, completely cleared by DNA testing. "What can I say? I was wrong," Souviron acknowledged to me personally.

Dale Morris was lucky that it was 1997, a time when DNA technology had improved dramatically and was being accepted more and more by the courts. Had it been ten years earlier, Morris most likely would have been given a final ride on Old Sparky.

I learned that Doctors Sperber and Vale are not perfect either. In the case *California v. Elias* Sperber was contacted by defense attorney Kerry Steigerwalt to see if he could exclude the victim as the one who left the bite mark on the shoulder of the accused assailant during the attack. Sperber could not. But when he was contacted by the prosecutor, he did a closer analysis and opined, with "reasonable medical certainty," that the bite mark *had* been made by the victim. Sperber was all set to testify for the prosecution when Stiegerwalt informed the court that Sperber had looked at the evidence for the defense and was therefore off-limits to the prosecution. Sperber then approached Vale and showed him his bite mark presentation, already prepared and ready to go. Using Sperber's visual aids, Vale testified for the prosecution.

But then Stiegerwalt dramatically produced several photographs of the defendant in a bathing suit taken years earlier and showing the same mark on his shoulder. It was a birthmark. The suspect was subsequently acquitted.

Incidentally and coincidentally Dr. Homer Campbell testified for the defense. Vale was embarrassed, to say the least, and admitted that he was wrong. Sperber skated somewhat because he was not the one testifying. But he too acknowledged his error.

Sperber was also involved in the Bobby Tankersley case. He was the one who initially took the teeth cast from Bobby in San Diego and rendered the opinion that caused Bobby to be extradited to Yuma to be tried for the murder of Thelma Younkin. Sperber testified at trial that it was "highly probable" that Bobby had bitten Younkin. Rawson also testified against Bobby, using as he did in the Krone case a slickly prepared videotape. He rendered the same opinion Sperber did, but to a "reasonable medical certainty." This jingle-jangled bite mark jargon spelled doom for Bobby.

At a post conviction relief hearing for Bobby, Dr. Souviron discredited the bite mark findings of Sperber and Rawson and definitive testing was presented that conclusively established that it was not Bobby's DNA on the murder weapon but someone else's. The pussy trial judge who looked at the new evidence merely ordered that Bobby be re-sentenced. The Arizona Supreme Court sent the decision back to the judge for "clarification," perhaps wondering why Bobby at the very least wasn't given a new trial. There yet appears to be hope for Bobby that some cerebral cortex will be able to overcome the reptilian resistance to the obvious.

REFERENCES

"Arizona Receives Grant to Eliminate DNA Sample Backlog." *National Institute of Justice,"* 08/21/2000.

"Rawson, Neal in Hall of Fame." *Las Vegas SUN,* 04/24/2005.

Adler, Stephen J. *The Jury—Disorder in the Court.* New York: Doubleday, 1994.

Bailey, F. Lee. *The Defense Never Rests.* New York: Signet, 1971.

Bowers, DDS, JD, DABFO, C. Michael and Gary L. Bell, DDS, DABFO. *Manual Forensic Odontology—3rd Edition.* ASFO.

Boyer, Peter J. "DNA on Trial." *The New Yorker,* 01/17/2000.

Brown, Ray "Tex" and R. Angus. *18 Wheels of Justice.* New York: Pinnacle, 1997.

Brown, Ray "Tex" and R. Angus. *a.k.a. Narc.* New York: Pocket Books, 1991.

Cooper, Scott. "Judge Releases McCarty; Rips Former Chemist." *OCK News,* 05/11/2007.

Decker, Ed and C. Matrisciana. *The God Makers II.* Eugene: Harvest House, 1993.

Decker, Ed and Dave Hunt. *The God Makers.* Eugene: Harvest House, 1984.

DeFalco, Beth. "DNA Frees Arizona Man after 10 Years in Prison." *Arizona Republic,* 04/09/2002.

"Deputy County Attorney Noel J.R. Levy" [Arizona Prosecutor Lifetime Achievement Award Winner]. *The Prosecutor,* 09/2003.

Ditzen, L. Stuart et al. "Philadelphia DA Candidate's Tips on Jury Selection." *Philadelphia Inquirer,* 04/01/1997.

Dodd, Scott. "Sheriff Is Wildest Thing in West." *York Daily Record,* 02/26/1996.

Doyle, Sir Arthur Conan. *The Complete Sherlock Holmes.* New York: Garden City, 1955.

Eidenberg, Eugene. "A Look at the State's Furlough Program." *Illinois Issues,* July 1975.

Epstein, Edward. "Thirty Days on the Grand Jury." *edwardjayepstein.com,* 03/14/2004.

"Facts about the Death Penalty" [Death Penalty Information Center]. 05/01/2007.

Field, Kenneth S. *History of the American Academy of Forensic Sciences.* West Conshohocken: *American Society for Testing and Materials,* 1998.

Fischer, Howard. "Wrongfully Convicted Man Gets Apology after Two Years on Death Row." *Arizona Daily Sun,* 02/20/2006.

Frondorf, Shirley. *Death of a "Jewish American Princess."* New York: Villard Books, 1988.

Gerber, Rudolph J. *Cruel and Usual: Our Criminal Injustice System.* Westport: Praeger, 1999.

Grace, Nancy with Diane Clehane. *Objection!: How High-priced Defense Attorneys, Celebrity Defendants, and a 24/7 Media Have Hijacked Our Criminal Justice System.* New York: Hyperion, 2005.

Heller, Joseph. *Catch-22.* New York: Dell, 1974.

Hetzel, Dennis. "Old Fashioned Newspapering." *York Daily Record,* 05/28/1995.

Kahanna, Roma and Steve McVicker. "7 More Cases to have DNA Tested Again." *Houston Chronicle,* 03/15/2003.

Kaushik, Sandeep. "Innocence Lost: DNA Tests Expose Justice System's Flaws." *AlterNet,* 11/06/2001.

King, Jack. "Grand Jury Reform Urged to Counter Prosecutorial Excesses." *NACDL,* 04/02/1998.

King, Rachel. *Capital Consequences: Families of the Condemned Tell Their Stories.* New Brunswick: Rutgers University Press, 2005.

Kurtis, Bill. *The Death Penalty on Trial: Crisis in American Justice.* New York: Public Affairs, 2004.

Lasden, Martin. "Strong Convictions." *California Lawyer,* 06/2000.

Leonard, Susan. "Murder Trial Focuses on Bite." *Arizona Republic,* 09/11/1995.

Locke, Michelle. "DNA Expert Legendary, but not Seen." *Associated Press,* 06/04/1995.

Lowenthal, Gary T. *Down and Dirty Justice: A Chilling Journey into the Dark World of Crime and the Criminal Courts.* Far Hills: Hew Horizon, 2003.

Martin, Philip. "The Thai Connection." *Phoenix New Times,* 01/13/1993.

McRoberts, Flynn. "Bite-mark Verdict Faces New Scrutiny." *Chicago Tribune,* 11/29/2004.

Mills, Steve. "Top Lab Repeatedly Botched DNA Tests." *Chicago Tribune,* 05/08/2005.

Moreno, Sylvia. "Problems in Houston Lead Call for Moratorium on Executions." *Washington Post,* 10/02/2004.

Murr, Andrew. "A Dentist Takes the Stand." *Newsweek,* 08/20/2001.

Nelson, Robert. "About Face" *Phoenix New Times,* 04/21/2004.

Neufeld, Peter and Barry Scheck. *The Innocents.* New York: Umbrage, 2003.

Newell, Linda K. and Valeen T. Avery. *Mormon Enigma—Emma Hale Smith.* Chicago: University of Illinois Press, 1994.

Pimentel, O. Ricardo. "Pay Ray Krone His $100 Million." *Arizona Republic,* 05/04/2003.

Possley, Maurice and Steve Mills. "Crimes Go Unsolved as DNA Tool Ignored." *Chicago Tribune,* 10/26/2003.

Potter, Jerry A. and Fred Bost. *Fatal Justice: Reinvestigating the Macdonald Murders.* New York: W.W. Norton, 1995.

Quig, Brian D. and A. Scintilla. "Temple Murders News Blackout Ends." *The Grapevine,* 03/08/1996.

Radelet, Michael L., H. A. Bedau and C. E. Putnam. *In Spite of Innocence: Erroneous Convictions in Capital Cases. Boston: Northern University* Press, 1992.

Rix, Jim. [Various issues.] *The Ray Krone Story,* 05/10/1995–07/01/1996.

Rubin, Paul. "Balls in the Air." *Phoenix New Times,* 12/16/2004.

_____. "Judge Not." *Phoenix New Times,* 08/31/2000.

Sagan, Carl. *The Dragon of Eden: Speculations on the Evolution of Human Intelligence.* New York: Ballantine, 1977.

Saks, Michael J. and Jonathan J. Koehler. "The Coming Paradigm Shift in Forensic Identification Science." *Science,* 08/05/2005.

Scheck, Barry, P. Neufeld and J. Dwyer. *Actual Innocence: Five Days to Execution, and Other Dispatches from the Wrongly Convicted.* New York: Doubleday, 2000.

Smith, Joseph. *The Book of Mormon.* New York, way back when.

Spear, Robert K. *Survival on the Battlefield.* Burbank: Unique Publications, 1987.

Starrs, James E. "The Insolence of Judicial Office." *Scientific Sleuthing Review,* Winter 2004.

Stowers, Carlton. *Careless Whispers—The Lake Waco Murders.* New York: Pocket Books, 1987.

Tulsky, Fredric N. "Last Chance, Little Help." *San Jose Mercury News,* 01/27/2006.

Twain, Mark. *Roughing It.* Hartford: American Publishing Company, 1872

Van Biema, David. "Kingdom Come." *Time* Magazine, 08/04/1997.

Waite, C.V. *The Mormon Prophet and His Harem; or, An authentic history of Brigham Young, his numerous wives and children.* Michigan Historical Reprint Series, 12/20/2005 (first published 1868).

Wells, Ida B. "Lynch Law in America*." The Arena,* 01/1900.

Westervelt, Saundra D. and John A. Humphrey. *Wrongly Convicted: Perspectives on Failed Justice.* New Brunswick: Rutgers University Press, 2002.

White, Stephen. *Higher Authority.* New York: Signet, 1994.

Willing, Richard. "Exonerated Prisoners Are Rarely Paid for Lost Time." *USA Today,* 06/18/2002.

_____. "Many DNA Matches Aren't Acted On." *USA Today,* 11/21/2006.

_____. "Police Dupe Suspects into Giving Up DNA." *USA Today*Yardley, Jim. "Oklahoma Jury Focuses on Scientist Used by Prosecutors." *New York Times,* 04/01/2001.

INDEX

ACKNOWLEDGMENT

To Ray Krone—may his ten-year odyssey enlighten and lead us to a world where justice is truth.

ABOUT THE AUTHOR

Jim Rix was graduated from San Jose State University in 1964 with a bachelor's degree in mathematics, chemistry and physics. He is a computer programmer by trade and spent twelve years working in the aerospace industry in Silicon Valley and for the Oceanography Department at the University of Washington. In 1981, Mr. Rix founded SoftRix Corporation, a medical/dental software billing applications firm. He learned in 1992 that his cousin Ray Krone was on Arizona's Death Row. His decade-long involvement in his cousin's case gave him the extraordinary opportunity to peer into our justice system. *Jingle Jangle* is his chronicle of what he saw and learned. It is his first book.

Ah, but I was so much older then,
I'm younger than that now.

– Bob Dylan